GREENER DATA

Volume Two

Greener Data - Volume Two © 2024 Jaymie Scotto & Associates (JSA)

All Rights Reserved. Apart from any fair dealing for the purposes of research or private study, or criticism or review, as permitted under the Copyright, Designs and Patents Act 1988, this publication may only be reproduced, stored or transmitted, in any form or by any means, with the prior permission in writing of the copyright owner, or in the case of the reprographic reproduction in accordance with the terms of licenses issued by the Copyright Licensing Agency. Enquiries concerning reproduction outside those terms should be sent to the publisher.

ISBN: 9798322532804

Contents

Introduction ix
Jaymie Scotto Cutaia, JSA

Foreword xv
David Miller, Managing Director of the C40 Centre for Urban Climate Policy and Economy

Part I
The Power of Aligning Measurements

1. MEASURE TO MANAGE: SUSTAINABILITY METRICS AND REPORTING IN DATA CENTER NETWORKS 3
   Lead Analyst: Mary Allen, InsightaaS
   Report Contributors: Susanna Kass, InfraPrime; Dean Nelson, Infrastructure Masons; Vicki Worden, Green Building Initiative; Shawn Novak, nZero; Patricia Leyva, Equinix

2. HOW GLOBAL ENVIRONMENTAL OBJECTIVES TRANSLATE TO FACILITY-LEVEL EVALUATION AND GREEN BUILDING CERTIFICATION 25
   Vicki Worden, Green Building Initiative

3. SUSTAINABLE SIMPLICITY: OVERLOOKED ESSENTIALS FOR EFFICIENT DATA CENTER OPERATIONS 39
   Robert Painter, Ascent

4. A ROADMAP TO NET- ZERO DATA CENTERS: IT'S THE JOURNEY, NOT JUST THE DESTINATION 51
   Ed Ansett, i3 Solutions Group

5. MAKING YOUR ICT VALUE CHAIN NET ZERO 67
   Alexander Campbell, TDC NET

6. ACCELERATING DATA CENTER
SUSTAINABILITY JOURNEYS WITH
EKKOSENSE 81
Dean Boyle, EkkoSense

7. REVIVING ADAPTIVE REUSE AS A
SUSTAINABILITY STRATEGY: GAMIFYING
CIRCULARITY WITH CARBON ACCOUNTING
CREDITS 94
Sean Farney, JLL

Part II

Renewable & Clean Energy Solutions to Cut Carbon in the Data Center

8. LOW CARBON SOLUTIONS: PATHWAYS TO
ENERGY MATURITY IN THE DATA CENTER 111
Lead Analyst: Mary Allen, InsightaaS
Report Contributors: Jeffrey Barber, Bloom Energy; Michael Donohue, Cumulus Data; Brian Jabeck, Enchanted Rock; Ehsan Nasr, Microsoft; Anand Ramesh, EdgeConneX; Sindhu Sharma, Nxtra by Airtel

9. THE FUTURE OF DATA CENTERS – ABSOLUTE
ZERO 135
Susanna Kass, InfraPrime

10. ZERO-CARBON FUTURE: HOW DATA
CENTERS ARE LEADING INNOVATION 157
Raj Chudgar, EdgeConneX

11. HOW MASTERPLANNING DATA CENTERS
MEETS THE NEEDS OF HYPERSCALERS,
LOCAL COMMUNITIES AND UTILITIES 168
Bill Thomas, CleanArc

12. DUAL RULES: MICROGRID FLEXIBILITY
POWERS GRID, DATA CENTER AND THE
COMMUNITY 180
Brian Jabeck, Enchanted Rock

13. SOLID OXIDE FUEL CELLS: HISTORIC
INNOVATION TO FUTURE CLEAN ENERGY
SOLUTION 191
Jeffrey Barber, Bloom Energy

14. GREEN DATA CENTERS: NURTURING
SUSTAINABILITY IN THE DIGITAL AGE 202
Sindhu Sharma, Nxtra by Airtel

15. SUBSEA CABLE SUSTAINABILITY 216
Erick Contag & Nicole Starosielski, PhD, SubOptic

16. SUSTAINABILITY IS COMPLICATED 229
Loren Long, 3TAG

Part III
Power & Cooling Innovations to Shrink the Carbon Footprint of Your Network Infrastructure

17. GREEN FIRE: INNOVATION IN DATA CENTER POWER AND COOLING 245
Lead Analyst: Mary Allen, InsightaaS

Report Contributors: Jon Summers, RISE; Maikel Bouricius, Asperitas; Maxie Reynolds, Subsea Cloud; Bill Kleyman, Apolo; Tate Cantrell, Verne; Bill Severn, 1623 Farnam; Melissa Reali-Elliott, DC BLOX; Benjamin Crawford, Kohler Energy

18. SUSTAINABLE DATA CENTERS: CHARTING A COURSE THROUGH THE AI REVOLUTION 264
Kim Gunnelius, Verne

19. UNLOCKING A SUSTAINABLE, DIGITAL FUTURE THROUGH POWER AND COOLING INNOVATION 275
Robert Bunger & Marc Garner, Schneider Electric

20. THE DYNAMIC DOMINO EFFECT OF ENERGY-EFFICIENT DIRECT LIQUID COOLING 291
Ken Kremer, Involta

21. WHEN THE CHIPS ARE DOWN: COOLING WITHOUT CARBON 304
Maxie Reynolds, Subsea Cloud

22. ALL EYES ON EFFICIENCY: ENGINEERING DC BLOX'S COURSE TO A GREENER DIGITAL FUTURE 317
M. Reali-Elliott, DC BLOX

23. NAVIGATING THE PATH TO CARBON REDUCTION: STRATEGIES FOR EFFECTIVE BACKUP POWER GENERATION 329
Nicole Dierksheide, Kohler Energy: Power Systems

24. ACHIEVING ENERGY EFFICIENCIES AT CELL TOWERS 339
John Celentano, Inside Towers

25. BEING GREEN TO MAKE SOME GREEN: THE MANY BUSINESS OPPORTUNITIES PRESENTED BY IMMERSION COOLING   353
S. Jay Lawrence, Equus Compute Solutions

26. A YEAR OF NON-STOP INNOVATION: WHAT I LEARNED, AND WHY WE WERE ALL CAUGHT OFF GUARD   362
Bill Kleyman, Apolo

27. THE GHOSTS IN THE TAMARIND TREE: OVERCOMING RESISTANCE TO DISRUPTIVE IDEAS IN A RISK-AVERSE INDUSTRY   376
Karim Shaikh, Cato Digital

28. INNOVATIONS IN POWER AND COOLING: SHAPING THE FUTURE OF DATA CENTER TECHNOLOGY WITH FLEXENTIAL   385
Chris Downie, Flexential

29. SUSTAINABLE INNOVATION IN DATA CENTERS, A CRITICAL MISSION BY SCALA DATA CENTERS   399
Agostinho Villela & Christiana Weisshuhn, Scala Data Centers

30. THE MAGIC TRIO: INDUSTRY INNOVATION, CUSTOMERS, AND CONSUMERS WILL FUEL GREENER DATA   414
Fredrik Jansson, atNorth

Part IV
Building the Business Case: The Financial & Social Benefits of Going Green

31. RECONSTRUCTING THE BUSINESS CASE FOR DATA CENTER SUSTAINABILITY   431
Lead Analyst: Mary Allen, InsightaaS
Report Contributors: Peter Panfil, Vertiv; François Sterin, Data4; Michael Borron, Cushman & Wakefield; Peter Nisbet, Edenseven; Dean Boyle, EkkoSense

32. THE OPEN DATA CENTER: SUSTAINABILITY PROVES THE CASE FOR NEXT GENERATION BUILD   448
François Sterin, Data4 — Mary Allen, InsightaaS

33. RESPONSIBLE AND SUSTAINABLE GROWTH OF DIGITAL INFRASTRUCTURE   463
Dean Nelson, Infrastructure Masons

34. BYOP: THE PATH TO UTILITY
    INDEPENDENCE   477
    Peter A. Panfil, Vertiv

35. CROSS POLLINATION: PEOPLE, BUSINESS &
    BIODIVERSITY WORKING TOGETHER   490
    Garry Connolly, Host in Ireland

36. EMBRACING NET ZERO ECONOMICS AS THE
    PATH TO SUSTAINABILITY   500
    David Craig, Iceotope

37. HOW TO 'PAINT' A SUCCESSFUL
    SUSTAINABLE BUSINESS CASE   509
    Pete Nisbet, Edenseven

38. EVERY WATT COUNTS – HOW INCREMENTAL
    CHANGES CAN DELIVER MAJOR
    SUSTAINABILITY GAINS   520
    Samuel Rabinowitz, LANTANA LED

39. THE INTERCONNECTED DOMAINS OF
    FINANCE, SUSTAINABILITY AND INNOVATION   535
    Scott Willis, DartPoints

40. USING GREEN MICRO DATA CENTERS TO
    SOLVE UN SDG 6 AND 7   548
    R. Scott Salandy-Defour, Liquidstar

    About JSA Publishing   567

Introduction

Jaymie Scotto Cutaia, JSA

Our daughter Ava Capri is now 3 ½ years old.

Recently, her toddler waddle has turned into a dexterous run. Her questions have evolved from just 'why' to 'why is the grass green' and her imagination has turned our family room rug into hot lava as she skips across pillows to safety.

Ava to me is everything promising about our future: the way she looks at the sunrise in awe, pointing, naming all the colors. She lets me see the world around us with a sense of newness, wonder and deep appreciation.

The word 'Ava' means life - a celebration of not just us as humans but of the spirit and lifeblood that connects us all and to our future.

There it is again… 'connects us all'… connections. I've spent so much time in my career defining 'interconnectivity' for our industry, but it's only recently, as a mom, that I have felt the true weight and power of connections. My ancestors humming inside my veins. The strength of my mother's mothers who helped me through Ava's delivery during the pandemic. The strength of my father's fathers who emigrated to America in the fight for more opportunity. I remember how my parents looked at me, and how in turn, I now look at Ava, and I think: this is my watch. What can I do to give Ava a better future?

And as a mom of a toddler, I know one thing: I don't have answers.

But what I've discovered about strong connections is that if we pull one string, the entire system moves, changes, and potentially shifts its trajectory. There is so much power in that one string, and so much power in that flexible system that can alter itself in response to its participants.

One of my favorite scenes from the movie 'Avatar' is when the Na'vi are all connected and aglow as they are praying around their tree of life, their home. This glow runs through the veins of all, from plant to animal alike, and indeed throughout and within Pandora (their Earth) itself. I imagine Pandora as a living, evolving, connected spiritual and physical entity, humming in unity and purpose. And there's a shared reverence for all within Pandora, and for Pandora itself.

My wish is that we as Earth's inhabitants can unite together with the same reverence for one another and therefore connect to the power within us all. When we are guided by a clear and true mission, we can then move in a collective manner, shift mountains and indeed change the very trajectory of our future. Each of us the string. Together we are the system.

So yes, I don't know the perfect name of the color of the sunrise or why the grass is green, but I have hope, a mission to keep this planet sustainable for future generations, and gratefully I have connections to incredible people who are creating potential answers for us daily.

I am blessed to witness it daily, as a listener to my JSA clients and community members from around the world, as they define their next steps to get carbon neutral. I hear innovative cooling solutions and alternative power plans, I witness in action powerful new technologies that can cut into our greenhouse gas emissions, and I see how clarifying which measurements matter, can help us get there faster together. I am hopeful.

Introduction

I am hopeful that if we share these plans, technologies and breakthroughs, that collectively we can solve this climate crisis. We can solve this. We, as in the world's innovators and technologists of our century, and it will take all of us, partnering together, united by heart and mind, to carve a new destiny for this earth.

It is with this hope that I opened up my LinkedIn one November night 2021, in the midst of the pandemic, and sent out a request to the brightest minds I knew, asking if they could share their latest steps forward to getting greener. Within four months, their yeses became chapters which became an Amazon best selling book, *Greener Data - Volume One*, launched Earth Day 2022 with 24 contributing authors.

It was during this time that the world began to open again, awakening after our pandemic pause. Conferences started springing back to life, and event organizers asked for our Greener Data authors to speak at their events, join in roundtable discussions and even keynote. Journalists asked for chapter excerpts to quote and our industry communities took to social media to share, download and push the Greener Data mission forward.

It became clear that one book wasn't enough; we needed to keep up a tempo of education and collaboration. In response, we crafted GreenerData.net to continually publish our authors and community members' relevant white papers, articles and recorded roundtables.

We received calls from companies wanting to use *Greener Data - Volume One* as required summer reading for their entire sales and operations teams. I pinched myself.

Kicking off 2023, we had a wave of technologists approaching JSA, asking for ways to share their new software, hardware or latest tools to help get our data greener and faster. I wasn't sure how to test the validity of their solutions, but also didn't want to be a wall impeding progress and- you guessed it- connectivity- so we at JSA quickly developed and released a Greener Data Directory, on GreenerData.net, for any relevant company to upload their profile, include their product or solution description, and similar to Yelp, our community can search for them, reach out and if desired, even rate them.

Introduction

That brings us to 2024, where words like 'pandemic' have vanished from our headlines, and instead "generative AI" dominates our news cycles. There's an immediate and necessary need to figure out sustainable solutions as bandwidth and energy demands have never been greater. I rang out to my friends and industry thought leaders again, asking for another 3000 words, another chapter contribution, or even just a quote or two, as we compile the most aggressive, current publication on top sustainable practices for our industry: *Greener Data - Volume Two*. Over 50 authors responded.

I have to admit, I didn't think my little tug on a string would result in a book, never mind a second book, and now a movement. But little Ava, you keep teaching me to believe.

So my friends and readers, welcome to Greener Data. It's a continuous pulse, a purposeful conversation with multiple, diverse perspectives from around the world - including not just different locations and climates, but different access to resources, regulations, politics and more. Not one answer, but many, as we each move towards reduced emissions in our part of the world. Individuals yes, but united in purpose and passion.

This book includes over 50 authors (if I repeat it, I will eventually believe it!), unique voices that span 12 countries and share what they are doing within their respective companies and organizations to reduce greenhouse gas emissions and overall energy consumption.

But this book is not just of, for and by our digital infrastructure industry. It is a forming blueprint - a multitude of blueprints- that business leaders around the world can use to inform, adapt and/or apply to their own systems and procedures. It's not just for data centers, or global network operators, but for all businesses who require digital transformation and AI to remain competitive in the years to come.

With this shared education and reach across businesses and lives, we can collectively get to net zero emissions faster, making a much needed impact together.

Introduction

Additionally, Greener Data also serves as a collection of timely answers for those who ask what we as an industry are doing to address this climate crisis. It's our united voice stating that we are here on this watch together, sharing, encouraging and inspiring change.

So remember my sweet Ava that we are never alone. There is a glow inside each of us. Together we can connect, motivate and excel. Together we can make our Pandora hum with longevity, for you and all our children to come. It is possible, together.

About the Author

JAYMIE SCOTTO CUTAIA

As one of the most influential women in marketing for the digital infrastructure industry globally, Jaymie Scotto Cutaia founded Jaymie Scotto & Associates (JSA), an award-winning, industry-focused public relations, marketing and event planning firm, in 2005. Throughout this time, JSA has represented hundreds of brands in thousands of meaningful campaigns and headlines, impacting change and connectivity.

As part of her work at JSA, Jaymie has created and deployed multiple news and networking channels for the telecom, data center and enterprise industries, including: *Greener Data*, the multi-author, Amazon best-selling book series, company directory and movement to educate and promote more sustainable industry and business innovation, collaboration and best practices; JSA TV, a live streaming YouTube channel with over 1.3 Million views and growing, reporting on the top breaking news from key players in our industry; the Women's Speaking Initiative (WSI), to encourage more diverse voices in the industry's conference panels and keynotes; executive portals for direct, industry-specific social networking and 24/7 one-on-one meeting management; educational events and virtual roundtables for decision makers to collaborate on trending topics and opportunities in our industry; an industry blog attracting over 250K+ readers; newsletter and end of week email subscriptions totaling 28K+; and JSA Podcasts to encourage additional coverage by leveraging popular channels such as iHeartRadio, iTunes, Spotify and more.

In addition to JSA and her daughter Ava Capri, Jaymie cites her husband Rory and their marriage and courtship of over two decades as one of her top blessings. Rory J. Cutaia is the founder of Telx and the inventor of interconnection for our industry.

Foreword

David Miller, Managing Director of the C40 Centre for Urban Climate Policy and Economy

Last year my country (Canada) was on fire. Literally. While wildfires have always burned, 2023 was unprecedented in the severity, complexity, and sheer number of fires we faced. The smoke was so bad in eastern Canada and the United States – and the consequences for public health and public safety so serious – that the Mayors of Philadelphia, New York, Boston, Montreal, and Toronto issued an unprecedented joint statement addressing both the public health crisis, and its cause – climate change. They explained:

> *Climate change is making many regions hotter and drier, causing longer and more intense wildfires like the ones we are witnessing today. These are not only endangering lives and displacing communities, but are also significantly affecting the health of residents, especially those at higher risk, including children, the elderly, and those with existing health concerns.*

The Mayors are also clear about everything they are doing today in transportation, urban planning, buildings, waste management, clean energy and more to address the climate crisis and its cause.

They recognize that climate change is, unfortunately, not just an existential future threat to the way of life of human beings and the planet we rely on, it is happening today. If we don't immediately minimize the use of fossil fuels, we face serious consequences indeed. The latest Intergovernmental Panel on Climate Change (IPCC) report, representing the consensus of nearly all of the world's climate scientists, clearly states that our climate system is in crisis now, that it is caused by human activity (the burning of fossil fuels), and that we need to do everything in our power to cut these emissions more or less in half by 2030. At COP28, held in Dubai last November, national governments themselves finally agreed to what scientists, advocates, and those engaged in the development of climate solutions have been arguing for years: that the world needs to rapidly transition away from fossil fuels.

From my perspective, this climate emergency makes *Greener Data - Volume Two* both an important and inspiring initiative. It is an important work, because while IT can be part of the solution to climate change – a simple example is the reduction in transportation emissions connected to the increase in working from home made possible by Skype, Zoom, Teams and the like – it is also part of the problem, due to the exponential growth in our use of data, and the data centres where it is stored and analyzed. That sheer volume of data has the potential to turn IT itself from an opportunity to address emissions (and other environmental challenges) to a risk, and one that demands serious attention today.

Greener Data is both a technical guide,
and the inspiration to do more, sooner.

It is a guide for obvious reasons; each chapter is a compendium of best practices, designed to help accelerate the practice of sustainability in the construction and operation of data centres. In fact, I found the detailed analysis in each chapter so fascinating I couldn't put it down, flipping to different chapters to answer different questions I had. This was not what I expected when asked to review a 500+ page technical book!

The book's editors have organized these chapters so that they answer a whole range of questions. How measurement can help us translate global goals to local actions; how we can incorporate the best global practices in clean energy use into data centres; how operators can use power and cooling innovation most effectively and economically to reduce carbon; and how data centers can build a business case for sustainability that connects to broad societal goals and local community needs, including the need to support biodiversity, resource management, and other environmental goals, as enshrined in the SDG's.

The breadth of technical knowledge in the book is impressive, and raises critical questions like, if AI is going to result in a quintupling of the need for data storage in the next 3-5 years, and if electricity grids even in advanced countries like Canada and United States are unlikely to be able to accommodate, at least in the short term, any huge increased demand for power, where will the power come from? Chapters 6 and 7 show important paths forward for data centres to green the grid through power purchase agreements, to self-generate ("Bring your own power"), and to chart a path to net zero.

There is much more in the book, of course. Beyond the compelling chapter content, it helps us to think about the fundamental question: if we are going to do everything in our power to save the planet from the worst of climate breakdown, how do we ensure that the data centres that support our growing appetite for IT actually help us reduce our overall impact?

This isn't just a technical exercise. The business and government structures around us sometimes unintentionally hinder progress by requiring every positive technical step to justify itself on the bottom line. Thus, for example, we see efforts to build data centres on low-cost land and to cool data centres economically, whereas a different approach might be to locate data centres in places where the excess heat can actually be reused – several chapters speak to the collaboration needed to learn from, and implement the district heating approach used successfully in Scandinavia for decades.

And that to me is the inspiration to take from this important and timely second edition of Greener Data. The chapters themselves are a critical guide to what can be done to lower emissions now, but more importantly, taken together, they start to chart a path forward to what is possible soon, if the industry as a whole begins to prioritize planetary health over short term financial pressures – to become a sector that not only is zero emission, but which can harness innovation to absorb carbon from elsewhere. To me, that's an inspiring conclusion, and I hope the reader too will be similarly inspired: not just to believe, but to act. Today.

About the Author

DAVID MILLER

David Miller is the Managing Director of the C40 Centre for City Climate Policy and Economy. He is the author of "Solved: how the great cities of the world are fixing the climate crisis" (University of Toronto Press).

Mr. Miller was Mayor of Toronto from 2003 to 2010 and served as Chair of C40 Cities from 2008 until 2010. Under his leadership, Toronto became widely admired internationally for its environmental leadership, economic strength and social integration. He is a leading advocate for the creation of sustainable urban economies.

Mr. Miller has held a variety of public and private positions and served as Future of Cities Global Fellow at Polytechnic Institute of New York University from 2011 to 2014. He has an Honorary Doctorate from the University of Waterloo in Environmental Studies, an Honorary Doctor of Laws from York University and is currently Executive in Residence at the University of Victoria.

David Miller is a Harvard trained economist and professionally is a lawyer. He and his wife, lawyer Jill Arthur, are the parents of two children.

Part I

THE POWER OF ALIGNING MEASUREMENTS

ONE

Measure to Manage: Sustainability Metrics and Reporting in Data Center Networks

LEAD ANALYST: MARY ALLEN, INSIGHTAAS

Report Contributors: Susanna Kass, InfraPrime; Dean Nelson, Infrastructure Masons; Vicki Worden, Green Building Initiative; Shawn Novak, nZero; Patricia Leyva, Equinix

As our world plummets closer to climate catastrophe, the data center industry is stepping up with disruptive technologies and inspirational approaches to reduce the sector's growing environmental footprint. But what is the sound of one hand clapping? And how can we motivate the collective action needed to address the sector's carbon impact? Increasingly, industry innovators are working hard to establish the measurement and reporting techniques that can drive the needle on sustainability for individual data center operators, and that demonstrate progress on sustainability goals to the broader community.

Newfound focus on marking environmental progress is a response to mounting social consensus on the need for all industries, including the data center sector, to do their bit to address climate change. The reporting mechanisms designed to support this work, are also rooted in cooperative engagement. Building on input from millions of stakeholders at the Rio +20 conference, in 2015 the UN established 17 universal Sustainable Development Goals (SDGs) designed to meet the urgent environmental, political, and economic challenges of the day. In that same year, the Conference of Parties process was finally able to deliver targets that would ensure a climate neutral world by 2050. At COP21, 197 countries adopted the Paris Agreement, which bound signatories to reduce GHG emissions to the level needed to limit global warming increases to 1.5 degrees Celsius, compared to pre-industrial levels. While these goals and targets operate at the country level, together they provide a framework that many organizations, including data center networks, tie back to as they define sustainability strategies. By aligning environmental action with SDGs on sustainable industrialization (9), sustainable consumption and production (12), action to combat climate change (13), protecting terrestrial systems (15), or by declaring carbon reduction targets based on the science outlined in the Paris Agreement, data centers become part of a global movement, playing their part in the protection of planetary health.

Growing commitment to reporting responsible environmental behaviour is drawing strength from a number of trends, not the least of which is climate urgency. Today, there is considerable debate on the overall contribution of ICT to global GHG emissions, with estimates ranging from 1% of the total[1] to 2.8%,[2] and dire predictions for the future due to explosive use of ICT devices and services[3]. But of that total, data centers and networks account for a relatively small share, while efficiency improvements to computing (Koomey's Law) and facilities infrastructure have translated to relative stability in energy consumption for the sector, despite growth in data service delivery demand.[4] The result is a reduction of approximately 20% in the energy intensity of data centers since 2010.[5] Despite impressive efforts to decarbonize by many leaders within the sector, 1% of global emissions remains significant. And there are elephant(s) in the closet – new technologies such as AI, IoT, blockchain and bitcoin mining, and data rich media such as video streaming, VR and AR, that are likely to drive exponential consumption of data center resources, reinforcing the potential for "rebound effect," where increased efficiencies lead to increased demand.[6] Today, the frame of reference has shifted in response to climate emergency and forecast growth in the sector. Many leading data center operators have articulated ambitious goals – to reach net zero carbon emissions in advance of the Paris Agreement deadline of 2050. There is much to be done, and to be seen to do, through use of reliable sustainability measurement and reporting mechanisms.

Driving Greater Adoption – Who's at the Wheel?

The primary intent of measurement is to establish a solid baseline on resource consumption that draws an environmental/emissions profile of the data center site, which operators then use to mark progress towards achievement of sustainability goals, or to benchmark performance against peers. But there are a number of additional factors driving increased focus on monitoring, measurement, and reporting, and a growing number of stakeholders who are now demanding transparency on environmental claims. The enterprise data center will provide one set of data inputs to broader ESG goals that the corporation has committed to: for example, the financial services firm would include data center reporting in its wide-angle view on the carbon impact of real estate, transportation, and other systems and equipment, and may in fact set specific targets for the data facility. Shareholders and investors are another stakeholder category that is looking for more information on sustainability performance as a form of risk mitigation. Private and institutional investors now ask that companies publish disclosures on ESG, and align these with industry-specific frameworks such as GRESB, CDP, SaSB, ISSB/IFRS, the Global Reporting Initiative, or the Dow Jones Sustainability Index.[7] Data center businesses are becoming an increasingly attractive investment option for this group. In the service provider context, customers and partners are also requesting reporting; as they build out their own environmental profiles, cloud and colocation clients – or partners that deliver out of these facilities – require data on the provider's operations, or on the energy/carbon emissions associated with processing and storing their data. For the hyperscale and large tech companies, transparency on the achievement of ambitious sustainable goals makes good business sense; it establishes Corporate Social Responsibility and promotes good PR.

A final stakeholder is the regulator. Across the globe, there is considerable variation in regulatory regime. With the Corporate Sustainability Reporting Directive (CSRD), the EU requires ESG reporting, while the EU Code of Conduct for Data Centers, the European Energy Efficiency Directive, and EN500 regulations mandate that organizations report resource consumption and emissions (including floor area, installed power, energy consumption, PUE, temperature set points, waste heat utilization, use of water and renewable energy), develop energy reduction plans and implement measures to achieve sustainability goals. Jurisdictions in the Asia-Pacific region, such as Australia, ASEAN, and Hong Kong, lead on ESG disclosures. In the US, there is currently no regulation requiring that data centers report on sustainability. But as sustainability performance comes to deliver an increasingly important competitive advantage, and at President Biden's urging (executive order) for "*assessment, disclosure, and mitigation of climate pollution and climate-related risks in every sector of our economy,*" the reporting imperative looms closer. In 2022, for example, the SEC introduced a proposal for a climate disclosure rule aimed at improving the consistency, quality and comparability of company-reported ESG data; in the spring of 2024, it adopted this proposal, requiring that Scopes 1 and 2 emissions data be included in annual reports and audited financial statements.[8] This financially-driven requirement may be more genial than government mandates that enforce compliance; however, it highlights a trend across many jurisdictions away from an ad hoc, voluntary efforts on reporting to mandatory disclosure.

Fast Tracking the 'E' in ESG – Data Center Metrics

To mark, measure, and report their role in the global movement towards climate responsibility, many organizations have aligned with an array of ESG reporting frameworks, standards, and requirements, of which the most prominent are the GRI, SASB, CDP, CDSB, and the IIRC. Within this broad context, the data center occupies a unique position; facilities are high energy intensity, they consume more power and water than do other commercial real estate properties, they have specialized equipment, and they are experiencing rapid growth due to the ongoing digitization of government, business, and social life. To address these characteristics, a set of specific metrics focused on environmental performance – the 'E' in ESG – have developed over time to capture the impact of data center energy use (both facilities and IT infrastructure), water use, carbon emissions, and waste destined for landfill. Advanced data centers may also capture and report data on land usage and impact on biodiversity.

Typically, these metrics are mapped to recognized frameworks and standards, which offer guidance on how the organization can validate execution of its environmental strategy. A recently published Guide to Environmental Sustainability Metrics for Data Centers has identified 17 frameworks/standards that apply to setting targets, reporting, and certification, as well as 23 key metrics that are used by data centers at the beginning their sustainability journey, by advanced sites, or by leaders in environmental management practices. The list presented in the table below is not exhaustive, and new metrics to tackle new management issues continue to emerge. The table does illustrate, however, something of the complexity involved in measuring, monitoring, and reporting environmental indicators in a data center context, as well as the utility in identifying those activities that can, with the least friction and shorter time frames, help the organization achieve sustainability targets. For example, when energy efficiency improvements offer diminishing returns to a facility with a PUE of 1.06, purchase of renewable certificates, measured as a REF factor, may help the data center more quickly transition towards their net zero emissions goals.

Metric categories	Key metrics	Units	Beginning (6)	Advanced (18)	Leading (28)
Energy (6)	Total energy consumption	kWh	✓	✓	✓
	Power usage effectiveness (PUE)	Ratio	✓	✓	✓
	Total renewable energy consumption	kWh		✓	✓
	Renewable energy factor (REF)	Ratio			✓
	Energy Reuse Factor (ERF)	Ratio			✓
	Server utilization (ITEU$_{sv}$)	%		✓	✓
GHG emissions (7)	Scope 1				
	o GHG emissions	mtCO$_2$e	✓	✓	✓
	Scope 2				
	o Location-based GHG emissions	mtCO$_2$e	✓	✓	✓
	o Market-based GHG emissions	mtCO$_2$e	✓	✓	✓
	Scope 3				
	o GHG emissions	mtCO$_2$e			✓
	Carbon usage effectiveness (CUE)	kg CO$_2$e/kWh		✓	✓
	Total carbon offsets	mtCO$_2$e		✓	✓
	Hourly renewable supply & consumption matching	%			✓
Water (5)	Total site water usage	m^3	✓	✓	✓
	Total source energy water usage	m^3			✓
	Water usage effectiveness (WUE)	m^3/MWh		✓	✓
	Water replenishment	m^3			✓
	Total water use in supply chain	m^3			✓
Waste (6)	Waste generated				
	o Total waste	Metric ton			✓
	o E-waste	Metric ton		✓	✓
	o Battery	Metric ton		✓	✓
	Waste diversion rate				
	o Total waste	Ratio			✓
	o E-waste	Ratio		✓	✓
	o Battery	Ratio		✓	✓
Local ecosystem (4)	Land				
	o Total land use	m^2		✓	✓
	o Land-use intensity	kW/m^2		✓	✓
	Outdoor noise	dB(A)		✓	✓
	Mean species abundance (MSA)	MSA/km^2			✓

mtCO$_2$e = Metric ton of carbon dioxide equivalent

Source: Schneider Electric - Energy Management Research Center

What's in Scope?

Data centers use a lot of water, they produce a lot of waste, and they use a good share of global energy. The metrics used to measure impact in these areas will be familiar to most data center operators: WUE for water, tons for waste and waste diverted, CUE to measure carbon impact of IT infrastructure, PUE to measure energy used by facilities, supported ideally by consumption data provided by the local utility, or even REF to assess the opportunity for carbon reduction inherent in the integration of renewable energy resources. In a climate change context, a key goal for data center operators will be carbon emissions reduction – or even carbon neutrality – however, effective use of these metrics may be less obvious. In the chart above, the primary metrics used to measure, manage, and report different types of GHG emissions are Scopes 1, 2, and 3, categories introduced as part of the Greenhouse Gas Protocol Corporate Standard in 1998. Created to account for all of an organization's direct and indirect GHG emissions, the three Scopes apply in a data center environment as follows.

Scope 1 are *direct* emissions from the organization's owned or controlled sources, and they include:

1. Stationary emissions from industrial manufacturing processes that produce chemical or physical changes.
2. Mobile emissions produced by driving or use of the company's fleet vehicles.
3. GHGs emitted to keep company buildings and facilities in operation.
4. Fugitive emissions from a leakage, such as refrigerants, or escaped GHG gas from appliances, storage tanks, or pipelines.

Scope 2 are *indirect* emissions produced from energy generation that the facility consumes from off-site sources, such as the local utility supplier, and may include energy purchases of electricity, steam, or heat.

Scope 3 are *indirect* emissions from both upstream and downstream in the company's supply chain, and include emissions not captured in an organization's Scope 1 and 2 reporting. Upstream emissions refer to emissions created by products and transportation that are inputs to the organization's build and operations; downstream emissions are produced by the organization's output, as it processes and transports goods to an outside customer.

In the data center, the major source of Scope 1 emissions is that associated with keeping the facility operational (3 + 4), and may include GHG from fuel combustion in backup gensets, gas leakage from switchgear, or HFCs released by cooling systems. Electricity purchases from the utility typically account for most of Scope 2 emissions, which may be offset via purchase of renewable credits or mitigated through Power Purchase Agreements (PPAs) for electricity generated from clean fuel sources. In carbon accounting, Scopes 1 and 2 are often combined, and divided by the total energy consumed to achieve a measure of carbon intensity for the data center. Scope 3 accounts for the majority of emissions. A recent WEF study has estimated that, depending on the industry, emissions from an organization's supply chain may account for up to 95% of total emissions impact;[9] a prominent player in the global colocation space has noted that Scope 3 accounts for approximately 50% of the organization's GHG impact.

Scope Creep and Other Challenges

Double Counting

The separation of emissions impact into three scopes was originally designed to ensure that two or more connected organizations did not each count the same emissions – the so-called 'double counting' that can render sectoral tallies problematic. In practice, circumventing this issue has proved challenging for individual organizations: as the US Environmental Protection Agency explained, "Scope 3 emissions for one organization are the Scope 1 and 2 emissions of another organization." In the data center world, this issue is especially acute in colocation environments. With full control of their own operations – facilities, IT equipment, and the building shell – wholly-owned, enterprise level data centers can count onsite emissions generation as well as GHG from outside energy supply (Scopes 1 and 2) relatively easily. While Scope 3 counting depends to a large extent on the reliability of supplier data, many data centers have begun to establish requirements in their own value chains – codes of conduct or rules for the disclosure of carbon impact information that align with recognized standards to drive consistency and accuracy in their own reporting.

In cloud provider facilities, much the same holds true for

Chapter One

assigning responsibility for emissions in carbon accounting. With full financial and operational control over facilities management and IT infrastructure, as per the GHG Protocol Corporate Reporting Standard, the cloud provider assumes responsibility for reporting Scopes 1 and 2 emissions, while the customer functions as part of the value chain, and is assigned responsibility for remaining Scope 3 impact.

In colocation (colo) environments, this process is complicated by the 'tenant-landlord' nature of the operator's relationship with clients, by 'power structures', and the ensuing uncertainty around the assignment of emissions associated with electricity usage. In colo businesses, the operator has responsibility for, and purchases power on behalf of clients, who in turn pay 'rent' based on power usage. However, while the colo operator retains responsibility for facilities operation, the colo tenant retains control over is own IT infrastructure, and so would likely take on responsibility for emissions associated with power use in servers and other owned equipment (as Scope 2). These ideal GHG Protocol scope assignments are outlined in the chart presented here, developed recently by the Uptime Institute.

	Emissions accounting Scope	
	IT-related emissions	Facility infrastructure-related emissions
IT operator owns data center	2	2
IT operator at a colocation facility		
IT operator	2	3
Colocation operator	3	2
IT operator on a public cloud		
IT operator (cloud customer)	3	3
Cloud operator	2	2
Public cloud in a colocation facility		
IT operator (cloud customer)	3	3
Colocation operator	3	2
Cloud operator	2	3

UPTIME INTELLIGENCE 2023

uptime

Source: Emissions Scope assignments for IT operations in different data center types. Uptime Intelligence.

One approach to this issue is for IT operators (customers) to report emissions from energy use associated with their IT operations via Scopes 2 in colos and Scope 3 in cloud operations. For service provider businesses operating in green locations – where local electricity generation is based on clean, renewable power – assuming responsibility for a client's energy emissions may serve as a competitive differentiator. But in the search for carbon neutrality, and with potential spend for energy attribution certificates (EACs) including renewable energy certificates (RECs), PPAs or other green energy investments used to mitigate Scope 2 impact,[10] other colocation providers may wish to assign emissions associated with IT operations to their tenants. An example of this approach is demonstrated by a key global colocation provider that counts emissions associated with purchases of electricity for clients as Scope 3 emissions – or as part of the supply chain, allowing customers to take credit for their own efficiency improvements.[11] In this client-focused scenario, the colo provider benefits from EAC investments, while the customer is credited with efficiency improvements made to IT operations.

As recognition of the need to report on all three scopes on the part of providers and consumers of data center services develops, this kind of confusion around reporting responsibility is likely to grow apace. Better definition of reporting roles and responsibilities, and more targeted guidance for the data center industry would help address potential friction; in the absence of this, providers and their customers will benefit from clarification of emissions assignments in contractual agreements, such as a service-level agreement (SLA).

Data Accuracy

A related, but broader challenge to progress on environmental reporting is data inaccuracy. Some imprecision in data collection in data center environments may reside in the use of different methodologies. PUE, for example, a widely used metric for reporting energy consumption in facilities, has been criticized for producing varying results, depending on factors such as the time of year data was collected (in different climates), or the data center's occupancy rate. The greatest potential for inaccuracy, however, resides in Scope 3 accounting, which relies on data provided by suppliers, who may measure different emissions inputs in different ways. In general, there are low disclosure rates for Scope 3 emissions across businesses, and those who do report, may do so based on data that is missing, collected from a secondary source, be best guess, or gathered via different methodologies year-over-year.[12]

Scale may also be a factor. Data center portfolios can be quite large, and collecting multiple data points across the entire footprint for Scope 1, 2, and 3 (15 categories with 600 different sources) emissions is a complex task. Manual compilation of the results can lead to reporting errors at Scopes 1 and 2 as well as 3 – human error is a key risk factor. In some cases, methodology may be the issue: using data averages for reporting energy consumption, for example, as opposed to near real time data from the utility provider has been estimated to produce an error rate of 30-60% across Scope 2.[13] Understanding time of use of the energy and mapping that to an hourly emissions figure is critical to obtaining accurate actionable data. A significant gap appears between reporting that relies on consumption averages and an approach that factors in the generational mix (impact of fuel used to generate electricity) from the regional utility on an hourly basis and balancing this against overall power consumption. This gap, and the data center's real carbon intensity is outlined in the figure below, in the client scenario developed by carbon management platform provider, nZero. In the hands of sophisticated operators, such as the large cloud providers, this kind of real time data could be used to further reduce emissions impact; by shifting workloads in the cloud to match the utility's delivery of clean electricity, the provider can shrink emissions associated with computation and data storage.

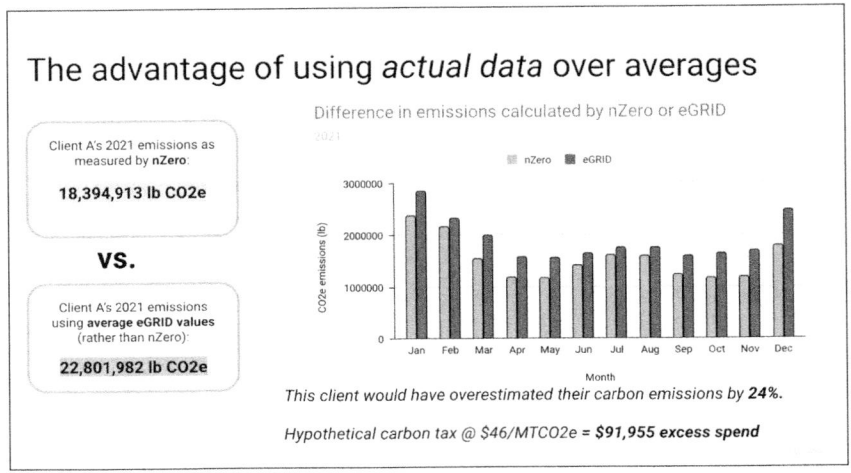

Modelling client emissions savings through use of real time utility data. Source: nZero

Standardization

Frameworks and tools for measuring, monitoring, and reporting environmental impact in the data center are abundant, but agreement on which apply, and which carbon accounting approach is most appropriate is in short supply. As noted above, there are at least 17 frameworks/standards and 23 key metrics that may apply in data center, and potentially more in the extended ecosystem that may be interpreted/applied variously by different suppliers. In carbon assessment on an industry basis, scope emissions tallies do not always add up, suggesting that a lack of standardization continues to hinder carbon measurement and reporting efforts. At the same time, the development of sustainability metrics is an evolving field. Data centers typically feature advanced telemetry, and abundant data from monitoring systems has enabled the creation of new metrics to address ongoing issues, or that help to uncover new opportunities for action. For example, PCE (Power Capacity Effectiveness) measures power capacity that is already built into the data center environment but not utilized, as opposed to energy that is consumed (measured by PUE). The estimate for total unused data center power capacity on a global basis is 36,000 MW, significant capacity that could be utilized through new efficiency approaches – removing buffers in the stack, reducing power oversubscription, and deploying software that can share power across multiple zones or regions.

Ultimately, the goal of applying measurement is to achieve decarbonization as quickly as possible. Metrics can expose the need for action on sustainability, driving behaviour that will help data center operators achieve defined targets. However, not all industry players today are sufficiently aware, educated, or aligned on the definition of a single standard that might be used to compare environmental state across peer organizations. This absence of consensus need not be fatal though. By adopting one of many carbon accounting methodologies that align with broad movements such as the iMasons Climate Accord (iMCA), which pledges members to reduce emissions from building lifecycle, capital goods, and power usage over time, operators can begin to take action. According to the iMCA, in lifecycle assessment fuel consumption accounts for only one third of data center carbon impact. As a result, the organization has developed a labelling scheme that focuses on disclosure of embedded carbon in products and the building shell that can help establish a baseline profile for the data center, or guide procurement through the introduction of sustainability metrics in RFPs. Currently, iMasons boasts a membership of 200 with US$6 trillion in market capitalization – and massive buying power that will insist on carbon labels. By identifying priority systems and linking their metrics to a business discussion on driving maximum usage of data center assets – pushing these requirements out through the supply chain - operators can accelerate the achievement of sustainable outcomes. While complete consensus on a single standard remains elusive, access to this kind of simple, but innovative labelling system and its application across the seven million data centers that exist today, demonstrates the potential of collective action on sustainability.

Transparency

In the data center world, reluctance to share information on environmental profile is endemic, rooted in the operators' historical tendency to privilege uptime over sustainability. Today, some data center businesses continue to provide PUE ratings under NDA to customers only, even though strong PUE performance can serve as a competitive differentiator for advanced facilities. Some contracts even prevent sharing of information on environmental performance. But disclosure of information is vital on several fronts. As operators issue the first report, they receive critical feedback that allows them to fine tune the monitoring and reporting process to build more accurate, and comprehensive measurement techniques that can be applied to the next step on the path to measurement maturity. In addition, reporting on sustainability progress is key to CSR and other outreach to customers who may be looking to source green data center services, it may be required by investors who are looking to include data center businesses in their own sustainable portfolios, or suppliers who need to align their carbon data reporting with that of their clients. Organizations that can get ahead of looming regulatory legislation will emerge as leaders in a growing global drive towards more consistent, and transparent reporting for all three scope emissions.

Verification and certification serve as important mechanisms to validate environmental claims, ensuring auditability in corporate contexts, and helping the organization to avoid greenwashing labels in more public spheres. It may also help downstream if the operator is reporting out through an ESG framework. Third party certifications and validations are often just baked into ESG reporting systems; Green Globes, EcoVadis, LEED and ENERGY STAR certifications, for example, are recognized in GRESB rankings.

A Wholistic View Please!

A typical starting point for most data centers embarking on their sustainability journey is to benchmark energy use – to count Scope 1 and 2 emissions from onsite power generation and purchased elec-

Chapter One

tricity. But Scope 3 accounting is critical as it considers key additional sources of carbon, such as emissions from significant capital purchases including IT and infrastructure equipment, as well as the embedded carbon in the building shell in order to provide a wholistic view, or the actual carbon profile of a data center site. While the average data center takes up approximately 100,000 square feet of space, many are larger – the Range International Information Group, for example, operates the world's largest data center which occupies 6.3 million square feet of space in Langfang China – and can have huge climate impact beyond power usage. To understand the real climate impact of a specific facility, the embodied carbon that is produced throughout the building's entire lifecycle must be taken into account, that produced through material extraction and processing, site construction, maintenance and renovation, and from end-of-life deconstruction and disposal of materials.

While Scope 3 emissions from buildings are not required in all reporting structures, they form part of key rating and certification programs such as the Green Globes that seek to ensure a wholistic view by requiring reporting on the built environment through its lifecycle, in addition to emissions associated with operation of the data center over time. In addition to carbon impact, other inputs to a more comprehensive profile include consideration for use of products with environmental declarations, siting considerations (proximity to public transportation), EV charging stations for vehicles, systems for waste and water management, indoor air quality and ventilation, exposure issues from toxic materials, or sound and lighting that may affect the community outside the data center.

If the scope of this reporting appears daunting, there are tools to help. While the EPA Target Finders and ENERGY STAR Portfolio Manager online services provide baseline numbers for new buildings, and across data center portfolios, other tools focus on products and projects. Building Transparency.org, for example, offers EC3, a calculator for embedded carbon in construction that provides carbon intensity data on a project basis. Tools for products include ENERGY STAR's energy efficiency ratings, or vendor specific labels designed to provide additional information; 95% of Schneider Electrics's products, for example, feature a Product environmental profile, based on an EPD (environmental disclosure) that aligns with the ISO 14001 standard.

Tracking Success for Clean Brand Competition and a Climate Positive World

An evolving field, sustainability measurement and reporting is a foundational input to the data center's ability to address climate change: as W. Edwards Deming suggested, if you can't measure it, you can't manage it. It also represents a source of new business opportunity for data centers to improve resource efficiency and the bottom line, to enhance their positioning as climate responsible organizations, and to drive supply chain environmental performance, motivating collective action to address the industry's impact on global warming. As metrics identify waste – 40-50% of power capacity that is built is never used – they can also stimulate competition between operators. As PUE is now a hallmark of efficient operation, measurement and reporting can serve to generate clean brand competition – and faster action on climate.

Relative to other sectors, the data center industry presents as a capable and comprehensive reporter of environmental impacts, but it's important to look beyond the numbers to their meaning, and to push past current state to the art-of-the-possible. For the individual operator, an important initial task is to understand different climate scenarios, creating a list of risks and opportunities that are relevant to the organization, and that consider what is possible in a particular country – defined, for example, by the Environmental Performance Index. Critical questions emerge in this process that may help the organization define adherence to a particular scenario. For example, the operation using renewable energy in terms of kilowatt per hour consumed or fossil fuels combined with synthetic instruments that act as offsets?

Chapter One

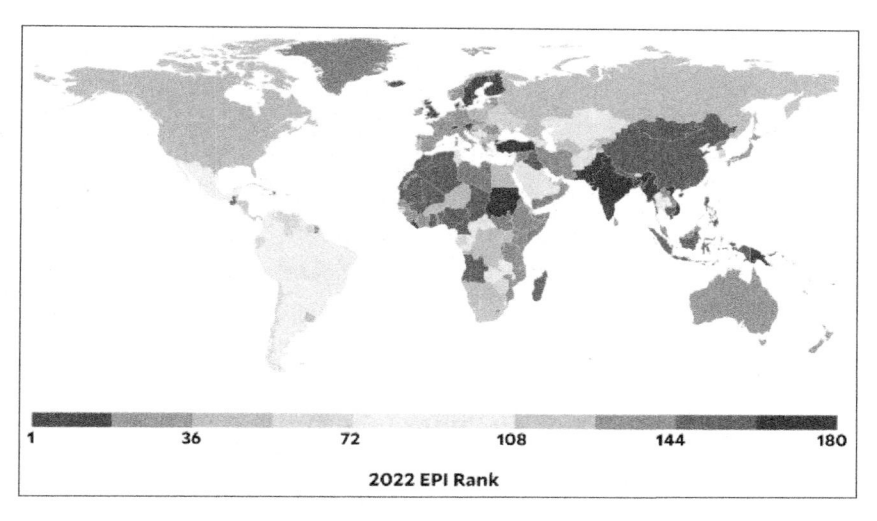

*Environmental Performance Index Ranking for 180 Countries.
Source: EPI*

To support creation of a climate positive scenario, data center siting is key, as various regions offer different opportunities – for use of renewables, for example – as is alignment with an evidence-based framework that incorporates science-based modelling of a hypothetical outcome: global warming limited to 3 degrees, 2 degrees or under 1.5 degrees Celsius. Achievement of climate positive will require new thinking beyond CO_2, a new appreciation for risk inherent in faulty reporting and geopolitical uncertainty, and new metrics and approaches that can quantify the impact of assets and supply chain the organization can control, as well as the social benefits for communities that may be realized outside the data center. These approaches will be critical to realizing the environmental opportunity or harm of the particular climate scenario against which operators choose to measure their data center performance.

Chapter One

Specific Measurement/Reporting Guidance for Operators

- Treat sustainability measurement, reporting and certification as a business opportunity, not a technical problem, aligning metrics with a carbon cost/benefit analysis that can help the data center achieve business objectives, including energy savings and risk management.
- Create a sustainability strategy that establishes short term and longer-term goals, building a roadmap that ties staged activities into reporting frameworks, and that aligns with your optimal climate change scenario.
- Address the issue of green washing by recognizing that the need for transparency on reporting and marketing messaging is intensifying, with an increasingly broad set of stakeholders seeking disclosure on environmental activities and sustainability claims.
- Identify key action areas, and establish specific carbon emissions reduction targets that are defined by metrics specific to the data center context.
- Prioritize various activities, based on ease of implementation and benefit return, establishing timelines for measurement and reporting on quick wins or large impact activities.
- Account for the carbon intensity of your electricity source in counting Scope 2 emissions.
- Avoid double counting through clear agreement with customers and suppliers on carbon assignments.
- Apply a wholistic lens, striving towards reporting maturity by measuring and reporting in a progressively comprehensive way, to ultimately include all scope emissions and activities.
- Know your supply chain. Require disclosure on carbon emissions from suppliers to build accurate Scope 3 reporting, to choose the best suppliers, and to drive more sustainability performance throughout the ecosystem.

- Develop accuracy in measurement and reporting, removing sources of error such as manual data collection in favour of automated platforms that operate in real time.
- Use dedicated resources to manage the complexity in sustainability reporting. If trained staff are not available internally, consider working with an advisor who can establish professional measurement and reporting practices.
- In the absence of a single, ideal standard for data center sustainability, adopt a methodology, individual metrics, and a reporting platform that can support specific environmental goals, and which easily roll up to more broad-based standards and frameworks.
- Consider sustainability measurement and reporting in the data center to be a journey, not a destination. Begin with metrics to manage energy use, and progress through carbon emissions calculations, to capture avoided carbon through the use of renewables or offsets, and apply metrics that can detail reduction in water usage or diversion of waste from landfill. Help the industry define new metrics that can solve efficiency problems in new ways, that can describe impact on land, deforestation or biodiversity, or that assess the benefit of circular activities, such as the reuse of heat from the data center, which will shape positive climate impact on the broader community going forward.

---

1. Lotfi Belkir and Ahmed Elmeligi. Assessing ICT global emissions footprint: Trends to 2040 & recommendations. Journal of Cleaner Production. v. 177, 2018.
2. Charlotte Freitag, et. al. The real climate and transformative impact of ICT: A critique of estimates, trends, and regulations. Patterns. v. 2, 2022.
3. Colin Cunliff. Beyond the Energy Techlash: The Real Climate Impact of Information Technology. Information Technology & Innovation Foundation. July 2020.
4. Jean Malmodin and Dag Lunden. The Energy and Carbon Footprint of the Global ICT and E&M Sectors 2010-2015. Sustainability. August 2018.

Chapter One

5. IEA. Global trends in internet traffic, data center workloads and data center energy use, 2010-2019. Paris 2019.
6. Lancaster University. Emissions from computing and ICT could be worse than previously thought. September 2021.
7. Jane Courtnell. ESG Reporting Frameworks, Standards, and Requirements. Green Business Bureau. July 2022.
8. "SEC Adopts Rules to Enhance and Standardize Climate-Related Disclosures for Investors." U.S. Securities and Exchange Commission. March 6, 2024. https://www.sec.gov/news/press-release/2024-31
9. World Economic Forum (2021). Net-Zero Challenge: The supply chain opportunity. Insight Report. file:///C:/Users/MARYL/AppData/Local/Temp/WEF_Net_Zero_Challenge_The_Supply_Chain_Opportunity_2021.pdf
10. GHG Emission Accounting, Renewable Energy Purchases, and Zero-Carbon Reporting: Issues and Considerations for the Colocation Data Center Industry. BSR. August 2017.
11. To ensure accurate accounting of energy attribute credits, Equinix does not share certificates that are retired on our behalf to ensure there is no opportunity for double counting. Instead we provide customers with their own customized Green Power Reports that cover the power usage, renewable energy coverage, location, and market-based emissions of their deployments within Equinix. Customers can use these reports as part of their own reporting as all of our environmental metrics are 3rd party verified each year to ISO 14064-3 limited assurance standards. See GRI 305: Emissions. Disclosure No. 3. Equinix Sustainability Report. FY 2021.
12. Scope 3 Inventory Guidance. EPA.
13. Cited by Shawn Novak, based on findings from Carbon Management Platform nZero.

About the Authors

Mary Allen is CCO at InsightaaS and Sustainability Lead for JSA. As journalist, analyst, and content strategist, she has covered the range of IT subjects for her own properties, and on behalf of clients. Mary created the GreenerIT, and Sustainability Platform websites, capping this with a stint as sustainability columnist for Bloomberg BNA, to promote the environmental agenda in IT. She continues this work in partnership with JSA on the Greener Data initiative.

Susanna Kass is Co-founder and BOD at InfraPrime, and currently, she is an Operating Partner, Digital Gravity Infrastructure Partners. She is also data center advisor to the UN on SDGs, an inventor with clean energy patents, educator at Stanford, a researcher at CE4A and Climate 50 member. Susanna was COO for eBay International, held global data center operation and innovation roles at HP, Sun, NextEra Energy, and Baselayer. She has led over 3.8 GW of renewable power data center project contracts with clients including Google, Meta Facebook, Microsoft, Equinix, and Walmart that use Net Zero design for site selection, and 24/7 zero carbon energy in their lifecycle. Her passion is Carbon Neutrality.

Dean Nelson is the CEO of Cato Digital and Founder & Chairman of Infrastructure Masons. He is a recognized innovator and experienced technologist. His 32-year career spans leadership positions at Sun Microsystems, Allegro Networks, eBay/PayPal, and Uber. Under Dean's leadership, iMasons has signed a global membership representing over $150 billion in infrastructure projects spanning 130 countries since founding in 2016, and has signed 200 members to the iMasons Climate Accord.

Shawn Novak is CSO at nZero, and has developed data center industry knowledge in senior roles with Switch, CBRE, Uptime Institute / 451 Advisors and EYP Mission Critical / HP Critical Facilities. With nZero, he's looking to help clients achieve the next level with leadership in sustainability reporting by providing the most accurate actionable 24/7 data.

Patricia Leyva is Senior Manager Sustainability Engagement at Equinix. She is an evangelist and storyteller that is elevating ESG value across the business, and the author of high value sustainability reports that have received recognition and several awards from global organizations. She comes to sustainability reporting through marketing roles with a range of IT leaders.

Vicki Worden is President & CEO at the Green Building Initiative. A passionate advocate for stewardship and sustainability, Vicki moved from work in association management to consulting on sustainability strategies, planning, and consensus standards, and then back to non-profit management, bringing 25 years of expertise in buildings and the building environment to leadership of the GBI in 2015.

TWO

How Global Environmental Objectives Translate to Facility-Level Evaluation and Green Building Certification

Vicki Worden, Green Building Initiative

Demand has never been higher for data center decision makers to include carbon accounting, climate resilience, and transparent reporting in their design, operations, and continuous improvement planning. In responding to this demand, key influencers in the value chain are working to evaluate CEO and CFO-level goals, such as to achieve net zero operations by a target date of 2040, 2045, or 2050, and translate those objectives into implementation strategies that are executable and provable at the facility level.

This chapter explores how global environmental objectives set by the United Nations provide a framework to measure progress, and how facility-level accomplishments are reviewed and reported on to demonstrate implementation success.

Global Environmental Objectives

In late September 2015, the United Nations General Assembly convened in New York to adopt the UN Sustainable Development Goals (SDGs), a series of 17 commitments aimed at ending poverty, protecting the planet, and improving the lives of people around the world. The Goals are a part of the UN's 2030 Agenda for Sustainable Development, which establishes a 15-year plan to achieve them.[1]

This year marks the halfway point of this plan. At the 2023 Assembly, member nations reaffirmed their commitment to the UN SDGs, acknowledging both the progress that has been made and the considerable work that remains. UN leaders also warned of stalled progress, citing international conflict, the aftermath of the pandemic, and global economic turbulence as root causes.[2]

This year's Assembly paid special attention to SDG 13, the assembly's climate-focused goal. Its 2023 political declaration reads as follows:

"We also reaffirm that climate change is one of the greatest challenges of our time. We express profound alarm that emissions of greenhouse gases continue to rise globally, and remain deeply concerned that all countries, particularly developing countries, are vulnerable to the adverse impacts of climate change. We emphasize in this regard that mitigation of and adaptation to climate change represent an immediate and urgent priority." [3]

An Emphasis on Climate Action

The United Nations SDG 13 is to "Take urgent action to combat climate change and its impacts." In its expanded version, it reads as follows:

- 13.1 Strengthen resilience and adaptive capacity to climate-related hazards and natural disasters in all countries
- 13.2 Integrate climate change measures into national policies, strategies and planning
- 13.3 Improve education, awareness-raising and human and institutional capacity on climate change mitigation, adaptation, impact reduction and early warning[4]

The UN also emphasizes SDG 13's synergy with the Paris Climate Agreement, which sets forth long-term goals to help countries reduce global greenhouse gas emissions. The Paris Climate Agreement contains the following commitments:

- To limit the global temperature increase in this century to 2 degrees Celsius while pursuing efforts to limit the increase even further to 1.5 degrees;
- To review countries' commitments every five years;
- To provide financing to developing countries to mitigate climate change, strengthen resilience and enhance abilities to adapt to climate impacts.[5]

The UN General Assembly has observed that the Paris Agreement marks the beginning of the movement towards a net zero emissions world, where net zero is defined as the point at which the total emissions of an entity are offset by its carbon capture activities. Taken together, these two frameworks aim to minimize increases in global temperatures and improve the ability of infrastructure and human systems to withstand and adapt to warming-related changes.

Data Centers and the Role of the Built Environment

Meeting SDG 13 and achieving the targets outlined in the Paris Agreement is a complex objective. The transition to a net zero economy will require a total transformation of the global economy, with critical actions organized across the following areas:

- Rethinking energy production and consumption systems
- Decarbonizing global supply chains and human transportation infrastructure
- Reducing food waste and improving agriculture systems
- Retrofitting existing buildings and improving building practices
- Halting deforestation and investing in carbon capture and sequestration technologies

Both the UN SDGs and the Paris Climate Accord also prioritize human outcomes, observing that to be sustainable, climate actions must also reduce global inequality and improve the quality of life for individuals around the world.

The built environment is one of the largest global contributors of CO2 emissions. As of 2023, it is estimated to account for 42% of annual emissions, with building operations responsible for 27% of global emissions and the embodied carbon of building materials accounting for an additional 15%.[6] Data centers represent a particularly energy-intensive building type. The US Department of Energy reports that data centers consume between 10 and 50 times more energy per square foot than the typical office building and account for 1 – 1.5% of global electricity use[7]. As technology becomes more widely adopted —and increasingly advanced technologies like next-generation artificial intelligence tools require more server power—this number is only expected to increase.[8] Experts anticipate that the use of AI technologies will increase data center energy needs at a CAGR of over 25%.[9]

These statistics can be daunting, but for data center leaders, they can also be a source of motivation. There is substantial room for improvement in data center sustainability, and even small efficiency improvements can lead to significant global energy savings and emissions reductions. In other words, progress made on data center building emissions can be a powerful contribution to progress on UN SDGs and Paris Climate Agreement goals.

The Value of Measurement and the Road to Net Zero

At the midpoint of the UN 2030 Agenda for Sustainable Development, there is a deep sense of urgency around decarbonizing the built environment to achieve global climate targets.

One sign of this momentum is the increasing value that both individual and institutional investors are placing on sustainable investments. According to a Morgan Stanley report, three-quarters of institutional investors are willing to divest from companies with poor sustainability performance,[10] and nearly 80% of individual investors also report that they are either very or somewhat interested in sustainable investing.[11]

At the same time, corporate leaders and state, local, and national governments are increasingly making net zero commitments. Over 90 countries (representing 80% of global emissions)[12] and 66% of Fortune 500 companies currently hold net-zero targets.[13] Data center leaders who are decarbonizing operations can increase investor draw and gain a competitive advantage. Those that haven't started yet risk regulatory action and increased risk exposure to a changing energy future.

While the objective is clear, the pathway to net zero has not been. The market requires a standardized and transparent framework to evaluate progress toward building decarbonization, providing guidance for improvement, and recognizing meaningful achievements in emissions reduction and sustainability performance. Objective measurements are also critical for facilitating comparisons between individual buildings, within portfolios, and among organizations. Adopting a consistent and recognized approach allows building owners to compare performance within a data center portfolio as well as in commercial real estate holdings across industries.

Third-party review and assurance are critical in the ramp up to increase confidence in measures that are being implemented successfully. The Green Building Initiative's (GBI) Green Globes assessment and certification programs offer frameworks for all types of commercial real estate, including complex data centers. GBI's Green Globes Journey to Net Zero program leverages rigorous carbon accounting principles combined with a collaborative process to assess achievements in reducing energy and carbon emissions impacts while encouraging all building owners to participate. The program meets the need for transparent reporting of site-level achievements while also creating a business case for owners and operators that tell their story using Green Globes recognition materials that transparently report on specific percent reductions achieved at the facility level all along the journey toward the net zero end goal.

About GBI

GBI's comprehensive and cost-effective approach to certification has supported leading-edge portfolio owners in using rating systems as roadmaps to improve sustainability performance and Green Globes certification outcomes. These efforts identify efficiencies, provide decision-making mechanisms for each phase of a building's life cycle, and validate resulting sustainability implementation efforts. GBI also offers advisory services that support overall ESG efforts, including providing corporate green specifications review to increase the likelihood of compliance with green building objectives. Through membership, education, credentialing, and an inclusive, global network of green building and ESG experts, GBI supports portfolio owners wherever they are in their ESG, decarbonization, and green building journeys.

Making Measurement Count

Holistic green building certifications break down the environmental impact of commercial real estate buildings into discrete categories and provide data-backed assessments and recommendations across criteria. Third-party certification systems can help data center owners and operators evaluate current and improve future performance.

Energy & Water Performance

Data centers require considerable electricity and water to both power and cool servers running around the clock —and they can benefit from a measurement system that both recognizes their particular use case and provides personalized recommendations for improvement.

Providing options to earn credit incentivizes performance and encourages evaluation by those designing, constructing, and operating buildings. Green Globes offers five industry-recognized pathways for assessing energy performance: improvement over an established baseline, ENERGY STAR® benchmarking, alternative building energy performance, ASHRAE Building EQ, and net zero carbon or energy certification. Assessment areas include power use effectiveness (PUE), lighting selection and strategy, equipment selection, building envelope performance, metering, and the integration of renewable energy sources.

Green Globes' Water Environmental Assessment Area evaluates water conservation performance in total and in terms of improvements over baseline measurements, it awards credit for EPA Water Sense high-efficiency plumbing and equipment, alternate water sources, recycling, metering and submetering, and water-saving irrigation design methods.

For both power and water usage, Green Globes also considers variations in demand based on a building's function—a particularly critical feature for data centers with unique water and power usage needs. In both cases, the certification encourages establishing baseline measurements and identifying opportunities for improvement.

CyrusOne's Chandler, Arizona data center earned Green Globes for Existing Buildings Certification and specific commendation for its energy and water use efficiency. The Chandler data center uses reclaimed water from the city for landscape irrigation, incorporates high-efficiency lighting design throughout the property, and uses ENERGY STAR-rated appliances and HVAC systems with negligible ozone depletion potential related to refrigerants.[14]

In 2023, EdgeCore Digital Infrastructure's Mesa, Arizona campus also earned Green Globes for Existing Buildings certification. The data center uses an air-cooled design that includes a highly efficient closed-loop chilled water system with a benchmark water usage effectiveness (WUE) rating of .01 L/kWh. Jason Evans, Edgecore Vice President of Sustainability and Energy observed that this system benefits both the environment and tenants—by reducing operational costs, it also reduces the tenants' cost of ownership.[15]

Site Selection

Site selection plays a major role in data center sustainability. As with any commercial building, a primary concern for data center new construction is the building's immediate impact on local ecology and human systems. The unique needs of a data center also necessitate specific attention to the following areas:

- Access to renewable energy sources, such as the potential for wind or solar project installation
- The reliability of power supply—particularly as primary power sources to be more efficient than back-up sources
- Climate, which directly affects the energy and water consumed for heating and cooling purposes
- Access to efficient transportation for data center employees[16]

The Green Globes Site Environmental Assessment Area criteria evaluates a building's construction process and how use will affect urban heat islands, soil erosion, light pollution, and stormwater runoff. It also provides site-specific environmental enhancement guidance, such as pervious pavements and other stormwater management strategies, vegetated roofs to combat urban heat island effects, and xeriscape landscape design and graywater irrigation systems to reduce water demand.

Materials Sourcing

The materials used in the built environment are estimated to account for 15% of global emissions, which means that material selection can significantly impact a building's environmental footprint. Life-cycle assessments (LCAs), environmental product declarations (EPDs) and third-party product certifications are used to demonstrate material sustainability.

Green Globes encourages the use of locally sourced materials and use-phase waste reduction. The Green Globes certified Internap Network Services Corporation Atlanta features a building facade created from 100% reused and recycled materials, locally manufactured materials in its structural design, and low-emitting materials. Additional sustainability achievements included the use of energy-efficient lighting fixtures, HVAC systems, and chillers; location within proximity to public transportation, electric vehicle charging stations, and use of an indoor air quality monitoring system.[17]

Indoor Air Quality & Environment

Data centers face specific risks related to indoor air quality (IAQ) and occupant health. Overheated servers can emit contents that pose a risk not only to the health of human occupants but also to the data center cooling systems and even server infrastructure.[18]

Building certifications may provide guidance for creating and monitoring healthy interior spaces through proper ventilation, pollutant source control and measurement, daylighting, and thermal and acoustic comfort. Green Globes evaluates the quality of the indoor air and environment based on pollutant concentrations and conditions that can affect the health, comfort, and performance of occupants such as temperature, relative humidity, light, sound, and other factors. Listed volatile organic compound (VOC) content thresholds to minimize indoor pollution and assurance that ventilation systems and thermal comfort meet standards.

Data Center Spotlight: Aligned Data Centers

As a historically resource-intensive industry, there is substantial room for improvement. Yet, a few data center owners and operators have emerged as leaders, not only among data centers but for all commercial real estate. Those with increasingly efficient portfolios have made public sustainability and decarbonization proclamations and have adopted third-party certification as a means of education, standardization, and demonstrating accountability. Aligned Data Centers is one such leader, with over 23 campuses and 60 data centers under management or in development, Aligned Data Centers is a major player in the data center field. It's also leading the way in data center sustainability by prioritizing sustainable buildings with a higher standard of operation and using the Green

Globes certification to set ambitious sustainability goals, evaluate progress towards, and recognize achievements.

Aligned tracks the material traceability of all utility equipment and building materials in its data center portfolio, making it the first company of its kind to report embodied carbon impact to clients and shareholders. The company uses Life Cycle Assessments (LCAs) to evaluate the environmental impact over the course of a product's life cycle. Aligned also uses a suite of technology that enables performance tracking and provides real-time data that informs an overall understanding of each facility's demand and consumption.

Aligned is also an active member of the iMasons Climate Accord, a coalition united to reduce carbon in digital infrastructure to ultimately achieve carbon neutrality. Climate Accord members measure and report on progress in reducing:

- Embodied carbon in materials used to build data centers,
- Embodied carbon of equipment deployed in data centers, and
- The hourly carbon intensity of source power used to operate data centers.

Measurement and reporting are critical components of the company's sustainability and decarbonization strategies, and Aligned uses GBI's Green Globes certifications to ensure that building owners and operators are executing their commitments and to demonstrate accountability to stakeholders.

"While it is a core part of Aligned's mission to lead the industry in data center sustainability, our Climate Accord membership demonstrates an ongoing commitment to raising the bar," explained Joanna Soucy, Executive Vice President of Brand Strategy at Aligned. "Our customers are also helping us lead the charge, and together, we're making great strides toward achieving ambitious net-zero goals."

Aligned Chicago, a 220,000 square foot, 48MW (expandable to 60MW) data center facility, achieved a Three Green Globes rating (out of Four Green Globes) earning 72% of the total applicable points. The facility prioritizes access to renewable energy options, with 100% of the load matched with renewable energy sources. It also leverages air-cooled chillers that use up to 85% less water and 80% less power than traditional cooling systems.

The Green Globes assessment process also helped uncover additional areas for improvement, including transitioning to refrigerants with lower global warming potential (GWP), which Aligned is working to implement in its facilities moving forward.

"Pursuing green building certification was a natural next step for Aligned. We're proud to lead the industry in power usage effectiveness (PUE) and ESG measurement and reporting, and Green Globes has helped us earn additional recognition for our efforts," said Michael Welch, Aligned Vice President of Design and Procurement.

Aligning Data Center Site Goals with Global Environmental Goals

The 2023 updates from the UN General Assembly demonstrate the need for immediate and comprehensive action on Sustainable Development Goal 13, combating climate change and its impacts. The Assembly reports that global temperatures have already increased by 1.1°C, and 2022 emissions data show a continuing upward trajectory.[19] Data centers remain one of the most energy-intensive commercial building types. Without visionary leadership in the data center industry, emission reduction targets may remain out of reach.

There is, however, significant support available. While advances in technology can increase energy demands, they can also help commercial buildings increase efficiency and reduce emissions. As the data center industry continues to set and pursue ambitious sustainability goals, science-based green building certification systems like GBI's Green Globes, and its newest recognition program for those on the Journey to Net Zero, can help business leaders evaluate, third-party review, and report on environmental performance and improvement measures. This will also allow portfolio owners and investors to draw accurate comparisons between site-specific implementation efforts and how they directly translate and contribute to global environmental objectives and a net-zero future.

---

1. United Nations. 2015. "Transforming our world: the 2030 Agenda for Sustainable Development." September 25, 2015. http://undocs.org/en/A/RES/70/1.
2. United Nations. "The Sustainable Development Agenda." https://www.un.org/sustainabledevelopment/development-agenda/.
3. United Nations. 2023. "Political declaration of the high-level political forum on sustainable development convened under the auspices of the General Assembly." September 15, 2023. https://hlpf.un.org/sites/default/files/2023-09/A%20HLPF%202023%20L1.pdf?_gl=1*1cus92j*_ga*MTI3MTg1NjAx-Ni4xNjk5NzI3NTMx*_ga_TK9BQL5X7Z*MTY5OTcyNzUzMS4xLjAuM-TY5OTcyNzUzMS4wLjAuMA.
4. United Nations. "Climate Action and Synergies." https://sdgs.un.org/topics/climate-actionsynergies#:~:text=against%20climate%20change.-,The%20230%20Agenda%20and,-the%20Sustainable%20Development.
5. United Nations. "The Paris Agreement." https://www.un.org/en/climatechange/paris-agreement.
6. Architecture 2030. "Why the Built Environment?" https://www.architecture2030.org/why-the-built-environment/.
7. IEA. 2023. "Data Centres and Data Transmission Networks." July 11, 2023. https://www.iea.org/energy-system/buildings/data-centres-and-data-transmission-networks.
8. Office of Energy Efficiency & Renewable Energy. "Data Centers and Servers." https://www.energy.gov/eere/buildings/data-centers-and-servers.
9. Cohan, Peter. 2023. "As ChatGPT And Other AI Tools Increase Energy Demand, Here's What Investors Need To Know." November 9, 2023. https://www.forbes.com/sites/petercohan/2023/11/09/equinix-and-vertivstock-prices-could-rise-on-generative-ais-energy-use/.
10. Morgan Stanley Institute for Sustainable Investing. 2021. "Sustainable Signals: Individual Investors and the COVID-19 Pandemic." https://www.morganstanley.com/assets/pdfs/2021-Sustainable_Signals_Individual_Investor.pdf.
11. EY. 2022. "Businesses and investors at odds over sustainability efforts." November 11, 2022. https://www.ey.com/en_gl/news/2022/11/businesses-and-investors-at-odds-over-sustainability-efforts.
12. Kelly Levin, Taryn Fransen, Clea Schumer, Chantal Davis and Sophie Boehm. 2023. "What Does 'Net-Zero Emissions' Mean? 8 Common Questions, Answered." World Resources Institute. March 20, 2023. https://www.wri.org/insights/net-zero-ghg-emissions-questions-answered.
13. Murray, Alan and Nicholas Gordon. 2023. "Not a single Forune Global 500 company made a new net zero commitment last year." Fortune. September 19,

2023. https://fortune.com/2023/09/19/no-new-fortune-global-500-company-made-net-zero-commitment/.
14. CyrusOne. 2022. "Chandler Wins One Green Globe Building Designation." June 23, 2022. https://www.cyrusone.com/resources/blogs/chandler-one-green-globe-building-designation.
15. EdgeCore Digital Infrastructure. 2023. "EdgeCore Digital Infrastructure Announces Expansion of Greater Phoenix Data Center Campus and Receipt of Green Globes® Certification for Adoption of Sustainable Building Best Practices." April 27, 2023. https://www.prnewswire.com/news-releases/edgecore-digital-infrastructure-announces-expansion-of-greater-phoenix-data-center-campus-and-receipt-of-green-globes-certification-for-adoption-of-sustainable-building-best-practices-301808994.html.
16. Tozzi, Christopher. 2023. "How Data Center Location Impacts ESG Success." DataCenter Knowledge. February 14, 2023. https://www.datacenterknowledge.com/sustainability/how-data-center-location-impacts-esg-success#close-modal
17. INAP. 2012. "Internap Newly Expanded Atlanta Data Center Named First in Georgia to Achieve Green Globes Certification." January 9, 2012. https://www.inap.com/press-release/internap-newly-expanded-atlanta-data-center-named-first-in-georgia-to-achieve-green-globes-certification/.
18. Camfil. "Data Center Defense: Reduce Airborne Contaminants to Improve Indoor Air Quality." June 17, 2022. https://cleanair.camfil.us/2022/06/17/data-center-defense-reduce-airborne-contaminants-to-improve-indoor-air-quality/#:~:text=Accurate%20air%20filtration%20-cleans%20the,efficiency%20over%20the%20entire%20system.
19. United Nations. "Take urgent action to combat climate change and its impacts." https://sdgs.un.org/goals/goal13#progress_and_info.

About the Author

VICKI WORDEN

Vicki Worden is a sustainability thought leader and President and CEO of the Green Building Initiative, a nonprofit dedicated to making buildings healthy places to live and work while reducing their impacts on the environment.

Worden has dedicated her career to advancing environmental initiatives across North America. Her leadership has grown GBI into a thriving community supporting sustainability and wellness objectives in some of the world's largest real estate portfolios. She is a sought-after speaker, known trend-spotter and passionate, mission-based leader with special expertise in women's leadership in STEM, leveraging remote work structures and organizational change management.

Worden's chapter will discuss how decarbonization and environmental, social, and governance (ESG) trends are shaping decisions and driving change in data and telecommunications.

Worden holds a BA in Political Science and International Relations from West Chester University of Pennsylvania, an MBA from Loyola University Maryland, and is a graduate of the U.S. Chamber of Commerce's Institute for Organizational Management. She lives in Camden, Maine, where she feeds her soul by hiking and skiing with her husband and dogs.

THREE

Sustainable Simplicity: Overlooked Essentials for Efficient Data Center Operations

Robert Painter, Ascent

From the 1950s to today, from raised floors to liquid cooling, there has been a considerable amount of change in how advancements have impacted data center cooling and airflow management. Considerations around flexibility, energy efficiency, and airflow effectiveness called for new technologies and new approaches to meet the demands of data center cooling and airflow to support ever-increasing compute capabilities. This rich history of major innovation has influenced how the industry views emissions, energy metrics, and measurements but can leave data center leaders pondering what efficiency initiatives are best for implementation. A common conclusion is that attempting to optimize a data center's cooling and airflow configurations requires the expensive implementation of a large new addition or component overhaul — instead of a simple, ongoing process improvement involving current parts, practices, and most importantly, measurements. Attempting to address this disconnect is the aim of this chapter.

In *Greener Data - Volume One*, the chapter *Hidden in Plain Site* explored the energy efficiency that can be gained by addressing low hanging fruit with existing data center systems and why these opportunities are so often overlooked. Building from that foundation, this chapter aims to dive deeper into the easily accessible gains related to cooling and airflow, with an eye toward measurement in particular. By looking at examples and data that demonstrate what a considerable effect small changes can have, we'll explore how existing measurements can be applied to present-day, real-world systems every data center already employs. This will open the door to discussing why more data centers aren't collecting and using these measurements more and more effectively.

Why focus on cooling and airflow? In short, because it's an easy and demonstrative target. Cooling and air conditioning components use somewhere between 40[1] and 50[2] percent of the total energy consumption of a data center and more than 80 percent[3] of non-IT related energy. If a facility's sustainability goals include energy conservation, then increasing the power efficiency of cooling systems through better use of metrics and improvement programs is a huge and important place to start — and an apt proxy for the green data center movement as a whole.

Navigating the ins and outs of cooling and airflow with computer room air conditioning units (CRACs) and energy recovery ventilators (ERVs) can be intimidating and time-consuming, but it doesn't need to be. Every data center can make meaningful advancements with the measurements they are already doing. How? Let's investigate further.

The Prime Culprits

When assessing your systems, what in particular should you be looking at? Ascent analysts consistently find that valuable improvements can be made in three key areas: airflow delivery, airflow floor tiles, and computer room air handler (CRAH) management. Let's take a look at airflow delivery first. What we focus on here is unmanaged supply airflow delivery losses, that is, leaks and inefficiencies in the way cool air is brought to servers. Often, data center floor openings, especially around cable cutouts, have not been properly sealed, meaning conditioned air can escape into unused spaces or the general data hall environment instead of being directed to server racks. Another point of interest is blanking plates. Essentially, blanking plates are panels of varying size, shape, and material that prevent air from passing through open portions of the server cabinet. Along with blanking plates we'll also consider partitions, which are meant for dividing the data center space or creating separate enclosures to prevent air from wrapping around cabinets or passing directly from cold to hot aisles. Plates and partitions do two things. First, they minimize airflow bypass, giving cool air the path of least resistance. Second, they prevent hot spots by sealing off unused rack space and maintaining a uniform airflow pattern.

Floor sealing, blanking panels, and partitions are practical, inexpensive measures that can significantly improve the efficiency of cooling systems simply by ensuring that cool air is directed precisely where it's needed. The problem many data centers face is that because they aren't measuring air temperature or assessing their air flow often enough, these elements are optimized sporadically, if at all.

Let's move on to our next key area: airflow floor tiles. Like blanking panels, floor tiles with adjustable dampers address supply-to-load airflow capacity losses, creating an opportunity for more precise control and optimization of airflow, cabinet by cabinet. It goes without saying that not all server racks require the same amount of cooling and dampers fine-tune that directive airflow, allowing for adjustments within 0.01 inches of water column pressure to a cabinet. The problem is that many data centers' floor tiles don't have dampers, and the ones that do seldomly adjust them. Through careful airflow measurement, and astute response to it, floor tile dampers can be on the move with every change of heat-intensive equipment.

Our last key area is the management of CRAC and CRAH units. Even with CRAH and CRAC units being such high-energy equipment, many data centers don't monitor cooling demands closely enough or respond to them often enough. Proper CRAH and CRAC management starts with reviewing set points to potentially shut down some units, modulate them down to a lower speed, or change which units are acting as the lead (doing most of the work) and which are acting as the lag (waiting for work as a standby). In addition, backdraft dampers should be installed and consistently adjusted to prevent the loss of cool air from the intake of any units that are not in use. For units that are on, data centers should ensure all available and applicable CRAC settings are being employed, such as economizer mode to maximize efficiency or team mode to ensure multiple units are connected and working together.

Ideally, CRAH and CRAC management involves differential pressure control, which refers to the idea that a variable frequency drive (VFD) can respond to pressure changes inside a data center and respond across all airflow panels via underfloor sensors or across containment pods to match airflow demands. Controlling all cooling units at once, VFDs can significantly reduce the fan energy consumption during periods of low data center cooling demands.

Impressive Impact

These areas of focus all seem straightforward and it can be tempting to believe they aren't significant enough to prioritize. However, Ascent has the advantage of assessing these issues across dozens of data centers across the country, monitoring them before, during, and after the improvements. What did we find? Here are five case studies from real data center organizations in the past five years, who have implemented changes in *these three areas only*, and their impacts.

Company 1 is an enterprise with several locations throughout the United States. The project consisted of airflow optimization, perforated tile installation and adjustments, CRAC and CRAH setpoint adjustments, and the activation of CRAC economizer capabilities. Company 2 is a similar enterprise-wide organization with the same actions taken. The only additional measure was adjusting CRAC units to team mode in all locations. Company 3 is a similar organization in a similar situation with identical improvement areas, but with the addition of a utility power provider rebate for an extra financial boost. Company 4 is a single, enterprise-sized data center, where floor tiles were reconfigured and CRAH unit usage was optimized. For Company 5, the Ascent team worked on two separate buildings on the campus, each with multiple data halls. Both projects at Company 5 were directly related to airflow management, with the work consisting of floor tile damper placement, airflow balancing, and CRAC setpoint adjustments—all coupled with a utility provider rebate which helped to further reduce operational expense.

Here are the results of those changes, measured in energy savings, carbon reduction, and project return on investment (the amount of time required for the investment to pay for itself through electricity cost savings):

Airflow and Cooling Recommendation Results

	Energy Savings	Carbon Reduction	Project Return on Invesment
Company 1	2.7 million KwH Per Year	2.3 million lbs of C02e per year	1.5 years
Company 2	2.1 million KwH Per Year	1.8 million lbs of C02e per year	1.9 years
Company 3	1.3 million KwH Per Year	1.1 million lbs of C02e per year	<1 year
Company 4	66,000 KwH Per Year	56,000 lbs of C02e per year	<1 year
Company 5 Building A	1.1 million KwH Per Year	940,000 lbs of C02e per year	1.2 years
Company 5 Building B	405,000 KwH Per Year	347,000 lbs of C02e per year	

In total, these five data centers reduced their annual carbon dioxide equivalent greenhouse gas emissions by 6.6 million pounds, based only on improving the three core areas mentioned above. That's the consumption equivalent of 7,000 barrels of oil or 340,000 gallons of gasoline[4]. If these data centers continue to maximize their emissions over five years and 33 million pounds of CO2e emissions, that's comparable to saving 650,000 trash bags from the landfill and the equivalent to carbon sequestered by 18,000 acres of US forests in a year[5]. What would those numbers look like if we applied these basic practices from five data centers to the over 160 million square feet of data center space in the United States?[6]

And, you don't have to take our word for it. Studies on conditions like overly high airflows, wasted capacity, and blocks of airflow that obstruct cooling have reported similar results for some time[7]. Addressing these areas by implementing simple cooling system efficiency measures exactly like the ones mentioned above has been shown to reduce energy consumption by 9% in one data center.[8] CRAH management alone has produced annual energy savings of over 2.3 million kWh in another,[9] which makes sense as increasing fan speed by a factor of 1.7 (shifting from 60% to 100%) surges power consumption by a factor of around five (from1.7 KW to 8.4 KW).[10] In addition to fan speed, isolating the problem of room layout and compartmentalizing cold air supply has been shown to reduce rack inlet temperature by 15-40%,[11] while properly partitioning aisles can lower the server temperature by five degrees.[12]

Why Data Centers Don't Make Easy Improvements

Now, we can address the elephant in the meet-me-room, which is the thought that any task involving energy efficiency involves budgetary consideration. This is a common refrain among data center leaders who want to do better at sustainable business practices. At Ascent, we choose not to look at fiscal considerations as a constraint but rather as an opportunity. While budget constraints can present challenges, there is still great potential for data centers to optimize energy usage, drive innovation, and to demonstrate fiscal responsibility simultaneously with sustainable practices.

What's called for in order to balance the need to reduce energy consumption with budget limitations is careful planning and strategic decision-making. As we've seen, addressing cooling and airflow issues in areas like floor tiles, blanking panels, and CRAH or CRAC management are great ways to identify the most critical energy-efficiency projects that align with budget constraints and offer the best ecological return on financial investment. These three facets demonstrate a way to focus on high-impact initiatives that can be implemented with limited resources.

There are other pro-sustainability considerations, too. For instance, there are government incentives or vendor partnerships to explore. However, in this chapter, we'll center on measurement: namely, monitoring and control systems in relation to regular maintenance programs.

Why Data Centers Don't Act on Their Existing Metrics

Let's focus first on energy monitoring, that is, using measuring systems to track things like energy usage in order to identify areas for improvement. For many data centers, monitoring involves staff periodically looking at, say, an air handler, recording the fan speed on a chart, then compiling those charts in a binder. Likewise, electricity information is tracked by manually pulling utility bills and entering the numbers into a spreadsheet. These data centers collect data, but possible trends can be easily missed — something like fan speed going up seven percent from last month or power usage going down three percent — and asking questions about what the statistics mean, or more importantly, how to respond to them. For many, the solution to this problem was automated software, leading to a related issue — implementing such software. But is that still the case across the industry?

It used to be that tools like building management systems (BMS), building automation systems (BAS), and data center infrastructure management (DCIM) were available, but not widely adopted. However, that's not exactly the main problem anymore. BMS systems in data centers are common, and a majority of data centers IT managers have reported using a DCIM all the way back in 2016[13]. So what's the problem? In a nutshell, the data is being recorded and presented in a more meaningful and accessible way, but it's still not going through the supplemental process of being interpreted and then turned into actionable insights. Whether the data comes in the form of a graph on a screen or a chart in a binder, the question is the same: are we really, truly paying attention to the information we already have at our fingertips?

With efficiency practices constantly evolving, data center staff should strive to take an active role in their operation, as the alternative is a world of set-it-and-forget-it, full blast inefficiency when it comes to airflow and cooling. Let's imagine an example: a data center welcomes a brand new, high-performance cabinet, and the rough calculations show that there is enough total cooling to support it. Once the new cabinet is up and running, who is looking at how the critical load changes will affect things like fluid dynamics or airflow distribution? Should a new panel be installed? A new wall maybe? Does any opening need to be re-sealed? The environment is never optimized for the change, and inefficiencies increase. This pattern can continue for years until the system is broadly functional from an IT perspective, but entirely out of whack in terms of power and emissions efficiency.

The problem, intrinsically, is a process-based one. Thinking there is a silver bullet harkens back to the problem of shiny new object syndrome and the forever fallacy, as looking for a silver bullet has the tendency to cancel out the idea that there is no program in place to properly manage existing equipment, not to mention new equipment—and the problem compounds. Here's the ultimate problem: data centers can't gauge trends or benchmark their performance because they are pulling information but not acting on it. Information is there, but what are we doing with it? Who is looking at it? Are we aggregating information together, then reporting on it? Even if you have a **BMS** and **DCIM**, is it being implemented and operationalized in the right way? How does the data translate into operational best practice? Let's look at a three-step approach to overcome this hurdle.

Chapter Three

A Three Step Approach to Better Utilize Your Metrics

First, a prime issue is internal communication. Often, data center teams are split into two groups. There's the facilities team, tasked with the physical infrastructure of the data center including aspects like power, HVAC, fire suppression systems, and physical security. Then, there's the IT team, responsible for managing the servers, networking equipment, storage devices, and all other IT infrastructure, including jobs like application deployment, network configuration, and virtualization. In many data centers, these two groups do not work hand in hand. In fact, in many cases they work for different contracting companies and report to different leadership teams. They may have separate ticketing processes, communication platforms, and management systems. In order to successfully implement meaningful change from efficiency data, these teams need to be sharing information constantly and coordinating closely.

Second, once these teams are collaborating effectively, a core aspect of maximizing your existing measurements is training. Many critical environment technicians could benefit from enhanced preparation in order to better understand what information to look for and why, how to evaluate that information, or how to apply it to other related information. Most data center organizations do a great job of surrounding their operations team with safety-related training —which is indeed vital—but the data center green movement also needs to introduce sustainability best practice training initiatives to advance efficiency improvements. Whether through internal education programs or third party courses, both the IT team and facilities teams should thoroughly understand the goals and methods involved in energy and emissions efficiency.

Third, once the teams are knowledgeable, the next goal is to allocate time and budget for regular optimization, along with maintenance and servicing of equipment. Airflow configuration of the data center space does not get as much attention as the equipment it supports does, but that needs to change. Instead of addressing airflow balancing only during a new, large initiative like an expansion or new application (or a problem like overheating), airflow balancing should be a routine task equal in frequency with alterations of the critical load.

Consistent recalibration is worth it. When rack density changes, it figures that airflow would need to change in response, but many think the change isn't notable enough to prioritize or even address at all. These changes require effort, but as we've seen, the savings estimates are worth the time and resources. Inefficiencies are lying under the surface, but they aren't dormant. They are leaching needless kilowatts from data centers every day.

In summary, the journey to a more efficient and sustainable data center doesn't have to wait on groundbreaking innovations or complex solutions. While there is always merit in exploring new metrics and advanced technologies, the fundamental principle of optimizing cooling and airflow systems starts with mastering the basics and refining existing operations. By emphasizing operational best practices, data center leaders can harness the full potential of their current infrastructure. It's all about achieving more with what you already have in place. As you continue to focus on these core elements, you'll not only enhance the overall performance of your data center but also contribute to a greener, more cost-effective, and future-ready IT ecosystem. In this pursuit, remember that the power of incremental improvements and a commitment to operational excellence can lead to significant, positive impact on your data center's efficiency and sustainability.

---

1. Han, Zongwei, Xiaoqing Sun, Haotian Wei, Qiang Ji, and Da Xue. (2021). "Energy Saving Analysis of Evaporative Cooling Composite Air Conditioning System for Data Centers." Applied Thermal Engineering 186 (March): 116506. https://doi.org/10.1016/j.applthermaleng.2020.116506.
2. Gao, H., Yue, Q., Kou, Y., Wan, J., Li, L., & Fu, L. (2023). Performance evaluation and modeling of active tile in raised-floor data centers: An empirical study on the single tile case. Frontiers in Energy Research, 11. https://doi.org/10.3389/fenrg.2023.1073879
3. Jin, C., Bai, X., An, Y., Ni, J., & Shen, J. (2020). Case study regarding the thermal environment and energy efficiency of raised-floor and row-based cooling. Building and Environment, 182, 107110. https://doi.org/10.1016/j.buildenv.2020.107110

4. United States Environmental Protection Agency (EPA). 2023. "Greenhouse Gas Equivalencies Calculator." July 2023. https://www.epa.gov/energy/greenhouse-gas-equivalencies-calculator
5. Ibid
6. Ginsac, Ioana. 2022. "Decade in Review: Top U.S. Data Center Sales & Development." November 7, 2022. https://42floors.com/news/data-center-construction-and-sales-report/
7. Karlsson, J. Fredrik and Bahram Moshfegh. "Investigation of indoor climate and power usage in a data center." Energy and Buildings - Volume 37, Issue 10, October 2005, Pages 1075-1083. https://www.sciencedirect.com/science/article/pii/S0378778805000150
8. Brey, T., Lembke, P., Prisco, J., Abbott, K., Emerson Dominic Cortese, Emerson Kerry Hazelrigg, Disney, J., & Larson, S. (2011). Case study: The ROI of cooling system energy efficiency upgrades. https://www.energystar.gov/sites/default/files/asset/document/CaseStudy_TheROIofCoolingSystemEnergyEfficiencyUpgrades.pdf
9. Energy-Efficient Cooling Control Systems for Data Centers. (n.d.). Energy.gov. https://www.energy.gov/eere/iedo/energy-efficient-cooling-control-systems-data-centers
10. Marwah, M., Sharma, R., Shih, R., Patel, C., Bhatia, V., Mekanapurath, M., Velumani, R., & Velayudhan, S. (2009). Data analysis, visualization and knowledge discovery in sustainable data centers. Proceedings of the 2nd Bangalore Annual Compute Conference on 2nd Bangalore Annual Compute Conference. https://doi.org/10.1145/1517303.1517306
11. Nada, S. A., & Elfeky, K. E. (2016). Experimental investigations of thermal management solutions in data centers buildings for different arrangements of cold aisles containments. Journal of Building Engineering, 5, 41–49. https://doi.org/10.1016/j.jobe.2015.11.001
12. Cho, J., & Kim, B. S. (2011). Evaluation of air management system's thermal performance for superior cooling efficiency in high-density data centers. Energy and Buildings, 43(9), 2145–2155. https://doi.org/10.1016/j.enbuild.2011.04.025
13. Boyle, Bill. 2016. Survey: 75% of data center managers installed DCIM to cut costs. Data Center Dynamics. https://www.datacenterdynamics.com/en/news/survey-75-of-data-center-managers-installed-dcim-to-cut-costs/

About the Author

ROBERT PAINTER

With more than 30 years of experience, an operations-driven leader in data center infrastructure solutions, Bob oversees the delivery and execution of all Ascent solutions that deliver, support and complement critical infrastructure operations across North America.

Bob provides leadership, strategy and management of Ascent and its main service lines: mission-critical operations, critical facility management, IT services, engineering & construction and Navigator Platform professional services.

With comprehensive experience in mission critical infrastructure, he and his team develop solutions tailored to address customers' unique challenges in 24x7 facility and IT staffing services, portfolio-wide operational and capital planning, critical systems maintenance programs and real-time business intelligence reporting.

Under Bob's leadership, Ascent has transformed the Navigator Platform to deliver transparency and insight into infrastructure data across diverse critical sites, design topologies and work management systems.

FOUR

A Roadmap to Net-Zero Data Centers: It's the Journey, Not Just the Destination

Ed Ansett, i3 Solutions Group

The journey to net zero is one we all know we must take, but how to get there, and where "there" is, remains controversial.

The journey is particularly important for data centers and their operators because in our increasingly data-driven world, digital infrastructure has become more important than ever and is deemed to be critical infrastructure for any nation.

As the world decarbonizes, digital infrastructure will continue to play an increasingly important role.

However, the data center sector faces several major problems in its net zero journey: Firstly, even if the entire world switched today to an entirely sustainable fuel, not one material used in data centers would be completely carbon-free. For example, research shows up to 80% of data center embodied carbon emissions come from concrete[1].

There is no escaping the fact that emissions remain a part of the whole data center lifecycle—from design, construction and fitting-out to ongoing operations.

Therefore, data centers must take reasonable steps towards net zero, including reducing greenhouse gas (GHG) emissions quantitively (carbon offsets are just part of the solution), while other technological solutions are found. As part of that journey, the data center sector must consider the full facility lifecycle impact, from construction through operation, evolution, and retirement.

The following outlines a staged route map towards net zero, including:

- Making battery energy storage systems (BESS) available to help solve challenges of grid stability and variability as renewables are brought onto the grid
- Switching to hydrotreated vegetable oils (HVO) small modular reactors (SMR), and other fossil fuel alternatives
- Participating in power generation schemes to help governments achieve national ambitions to meet the Paris Climate Accord agreement.

Data Center Classification

Today, data centers can be roughly classified into three categories: legacy (with old and outdated equipment and systems), mixed estates (with both legacy and modern elements) and fully modern. There are opportunities for emissions reductions and efficiencies within each classification, but older facilities present greater challenges.

In addition to legacy designs and systems, older data centers often lack the kind of instrumentation that enables monitoring and management that would give a true picture of efficiency and effectiveness. These facilities have persisted by being reliable, but are also increasingly costly to operate. They can face internal power constraints, and issues of density, capacity, and cooling[2], making them the most challenging prospects in terms of sustainability.

Mixed estate data centers are those that have evolved through their operational lifetime to contain a mixture of legacy, recent, and modern equipment and systems. For example, as recently as 2021, it was reported more than 70% of Fortune 500 companies still ran business-critical applications on mainframes[3], which might sit alongside modern servers and applications that leverage them, adding to the complexity of underlying enterprise data infrastructure.

According to 2025 forecasts, 85% of infrastructure strategies will integrate on-premises, colocation, cloud, and edge delivery options[4], with up to half of new IT infrastructure being deployed at the edge[5]. Combined analyst estimates suggest by 2025[6] distributed enterprise architecture could comprise 20% core data centers, 30% hybrid cloud and 50% edge computing.

The reality is that the more modern the data center estate, the more easily it can be monitored and managed to achieve significant reductions in GHG emissions. Cloud-based monitoring systems, such as the latest generation of data center infrastructure management (DCIM) applications, offer new capabilities to manage disparate resources, including core, on-premises systems across multi- or hybrid cloud environments, and out to edge computing deployments, for a comprehensive picture of operating efficiency and effectiveness.

With the addition of servers and instrumentation, modern generation DCIM can also be successfully deployed in legacy data centers, leading to improved levels of data gathering. Wherever it's applied, the goal is to allow organizations to gain visibility into energy use, potential efficiency gains, effective optimizations and ideas for necessary modernization to move towards measurable decarbonization.

Impact Calculation Tools

Tools and supports exist to help factor in the lifetime operation of equipment. Product Environmental Profiles (PEP) give the detail necessary to calculate the lifetime impact of a piece of equipment, providing greater accuracy for assessment and forecasting of impact during operations[7]. PEPs are currently limited to electric, electronic, and HVAC-R products. However, for server, network and storage equipment, Life Cycle Assessment (LCA) methodologies supported by ISO standards can produce similarly useful and illustrative data[8].

Once a sufficient level of monitoring and visibility has been achieved, analysis can identify problem areas that can be immediately addressed.

Data, Intelligence and Actions

Data and analysis are key: The more granular and widespread the data gathered, the more informed the derived intelligence will be. For legacy facilities, this could mean actionable insights to commence optimization, showing where reconfiguration is feasible and where modernization is needed. For mixed estates, intelligence could form the basis of an automation program, whereby more modern facility systems could be automatically optimized based on historic and real-time data, operational requirements, and environmental commitments and obligations.

Artificial Intelligence (AI) and Machine Learning (ML) are already being leveraged by vendors and operators in this area, allowing them to employ systems that can adapt to operational needs in the context of policies and regulations.

In fully modern facilities, data centers can operate in potentially autonomic "lights out" mode, with no human intervention. There are even instances where functions such as cloud-bridging and cloud-bursting can allow autonomic control of where a workload runs based on factors such as cost, resource requirements, or workflows[9].

At the opposite end of the spectrum, industrial internet of things (IIoT) technologies can bridge the gap, allowing information that was previously unmonitored to be included in intelligent monitoring systems. Management systems allow operators to input operational, cost, policy, and regulation parameters, which allows the system to configure and self-optimize.

Collectively, these efforts are providing more data than ever before to be gathered, analyzed, and turned into intelligence. However, the benefits of such efficiencies and optimizations—regardless of the maturity of the data center facilities—are not fully effective without useful comparisons with the wider industry. While the common reference of Scope 1-3 emissions is useful for defining what must be measured, common reporting goes further[10].

Metrics and Frameworks

It is only by adopting and reporting on standardized metrics and common frameworks that allows operators to obtain a true picture and verified frame of reference of where they are in terms of emissions and competitiveness. Vendors are working hard to provide metrics and frameworks that can improve benchmarking and progress sustainability within the industry [11]. Combined with the work of standards bodies (European Standards EN 50600, 2019[12]) and industry associations (Sustainable Digital Infrastructure Alliance, 2022[13]), common metrics are allowing operators to choose their reporting frequency. Importantly, they also allow illustrative comparisons for competitors, sectors, and geographies. These resources build on the momentum of voluntary initiatives, such as the European Code of Conduct for Energy Efficiency in Data Centers[14], to prepare data center operators for mandatory reporting such as the European Green Deal's Corporate Sustainability Reporting Directives (EU CSRD), which comes into effect for large corporations in January 2024[15]. Voluntary efforts in this area are also detailed under Scope 4, which covers avoided emissions reported on a voluntary basis[16].

Although a European directive, any organization with EU-based subsidiaries meeting the minimum EU CSRD requirements will have to report under the directive. Much like the European General Data Protection Regulation (GDPR) became a reference framework for other jurisdictions, it is anticipated the EU CSRD will have a similar impact. Data center operators will need to consider how to implement reporting to shine a light on efficiency, utilization, and environmental impacts.

Similarly, the 2023 update to the Energy Efficiency Directive[17] requires operators of all but the smallest facilities to implement data gathering, analysis and reporting for energy performance and sustainability of data centers.

Chapter Four

Energy Implications

Once operators have managed to get a true picture of embodied carbon in their facilities and the operational optimizations that have been achieved, the main issue of energy carbon intensity must be dealt with on the road to net zero.

The stark fact remains that the largest proportion of global GHG emissions comes from energy production. Energy-related global CO_2 emissions grew by 0.9% in 2022, by some 321 megatons, to reach a new high of more than 36.8 gigatons[18].

Fossil fuels account for the majority of energy production, with coal accounting for around a third, followed by natural gas at 20%. Low or no-carbon sources include nuclear at around 10%, and various renewable energy sources (RES), including wind, solar and hydropower, which account for the balance[19]. Increased emissions from coal have more than offset reductions from natural gas[20], reaching an all-time high of almost 15.5 gigatons.

Achieving net-zero emissions for the energy sector by 2050 is a key milestone for restricting global warming to 1.5°C [21], which is the accepted limit for a livable planet this century[22]. Data centers and data transmission networks are estimated to account for 1-1.13% of global energy consumption[23].

This issue includes multiple threats and opportunities for data center owners and operators. Many operators have engaged in power purchase agreements (PPAs) with providers for renewably sourced energy as part of their efforts to decarbonize. Some, including Microsoft, Amazon, and Google, have gone further and partnered to build RES capacity, such as solar and wind farms. Analysts have stated that the data center industry is continuing to drive the corporate renewable energy market[24].

While this is a valid means for operators to effectively decarbonize, there is another aspect to no-carbon energy adoption in which data centers can play a significant part.

Chapter Four

Microgrids and Grid Support

With energy constraints being felt in many hubs such as Dublin, London, and Amsterdam, as well as instances in North America[25], on-site energy generation is coming into sharper focus as an opportunity not just to reduce emissions, but also to assist broader efforts to decarbonize energy grids. In this context, a data center or cluster of data centers operating as a microgrid can have benefits for national grids in terms of demand side management, load and frequency balancing, and also in facilitating the more widespread adoption of RES[26].

As national energy grids prepare to adopt greater levels of RES in their generation mix, particularly from variable renewable sources (VRE), operators must make provisions for load and frequency balancing. When renewable sources, such as wind, are producing peak levels of energy, but demand is low, the grid needs to be able to store or manage the surplus. Data centers operating as microgrids will have the capacity to provide support services to absorb and produce energy, such as providing battery storage and on-site generation.

As microgrids, data centers will have the capacity to be energy self-sufficient for extended periods of time by using existing technologies such as uninterruptible power supplies (UPS), Battery Energy Storage Systems (BESS), and generators powered by biofuels, such as HVO, in conjunction with waste heat reuse. They will be able to store and trade surplus energy with the grid, provide VRE balancing capacity, and support the heating needs of local communities.

Significant advances have been made in long-duration energy storage. While pumped-storage hydroelectricity is perhaps the most widely used storage technology with considerable potential in certain regions, battery technology remains one of the more accessible and scalable solutions. Flow batteries[27] in particular, have been put forward as an ideal solution for national grids and microgrids.

Various estimates have shown that as national grids move towards net zero, they are likely, to vary from 60-75% renewable and variable renewable energy sources, with the balance coming from carbon neutral core generation capabilities[28]. To support the speed of adoption, large energy consumers with critical power infrastructure (particularly those operating as microgrids) can support accelerated RES adoption by providing storage and balancing capacity that would otherwise have to be built out by governments and grid operators.

Notwithstanding the support that can be provided by microgrids in VRE adoption, data centers operating as microgrids face challenges at local scale. To operate independently of wider grids for any extended period, energy self-sufficiency faces the same energy mix questions. While VRE on site play a part, there is still a need for a core generative capability. Carbon neutral biofuels to power generators, gas-fired generators, and hydrogen generation are all options under consideration or already in use[29].

Switching standby generators to HVO is an immediate measure that can be taken to reduce GHG emissions when data centers provide grid-interactive services. With little or no modification, existing diesel generators can utilize HVO with nano-additives to reduce carbon monoxide emissions by 52% and hydrocarbon emissions by 47% compared to the B7 base fuel. This also leads to significant reductions in nitrous oxide (NO_x) and particulates[30].

Nuclear Option

Among the most controversial suggestions for core generative capacity are Small Modular Nuclear Reactors (SMRs), which raise issues of safety, environmental impact and cost.

However, unlike nuclear power in previous generations, SMRs are not designed to produce weapons-grade or pre-weapons-grade materials, assuaging fears around safety and proliferation. Contemporary designs are based on failsafe molten salt[31] or thorium cycles[32], which do not produce the kind of byproducts or waste that have previously proven problematic. New designs are seen as safer and more sustainable due to high levels of waste recycling into new fuel, and less hazardous and toxic byproducts.

SMRs with outputs up to approximately 300MW, have been operated with a good safety record aboard ships and submarines for decades. The knowledge gained is informing a new generation of advanced, compact, modular designs that could fit in a shipping container or be mobile on a seaborn barge[33] for easy deployment. Proposed designs in the 10MW scale could potentially be packaged in even smaller units.

These kinds of SMRs could be deployed close to where energy is needed and act as the core generative capacity for a microgrid or series of microgrids, supplemented by any available VRE. Reference designs for such reactors have already been submitted by a European manufacturer to UK authorities for assessment[34].

This kind of generating capacity would significantly reduce the energy-related emissions of the data center, while also working in conjunction with large capacity battery storage and onsite generation to ensure the available VRE proportion can be properly leveraged and provide similar support to the wider grid. There are also opportunities for operators who may have employed temporary gas-fired on-site generation for carbon capture and storage or other mitigation techniques. These methods could reduce emissions by up to 71%[35].

These technologies offer data center operators an opportunity to decarbonize energy, increase resilience, and support national efforts for decarbonization, while easing energy capacity issues at the same time. Collectively, these measures present significant opportunities to allow data center operators to progress on the journey to net zero.

The increasing digitization of energy grids, which is seen as a key decarbonization enabler[36], will enable the grids to better interact with the growing number of microgrids, providing vital support to broader net zero efforts.

Circular Opportunities

Data center operators who adopt circular practices that recognize the value of reusing, repurposing, re-engineering, and disposing of facilities, infrastructure, and equipment, have significant opportunities.

Expert estimates indicate that renovation and reuse of buildings can typically save between 50% and 75% of the embodied carbon emissions compared to a new build[37]. This is especially true when foundations and structures are preserved, which is where most of the embodied carbon resides. There are also opportunities for low-carbon concrete and construction materials such as low-carbon steel and composites[38].

In the procurement of infrastructure and equipment, choosing products that have been designed with these principles can heavily influence the ease with which they can be reused or recycled. Research has found that 80% of a product's environmental impact is influenced by decisions made at the design stage[39]. Modular designs that are engineered for easy dismantling and re-engineering, reduce waste by keeping valuable materials in the economy, which reduces the need for new extraction.

Savings made in waste and new extraction can go directly to a data center operator's carbon bottom line, reducing the need for mitigation measures. Avoided emissions can be reported under Scope 4 GHG emissions[40].

Carbon offsets have come under much criticism. Investigations into some of the largest providers have revealed they may not be moving the needle in an impactful way. For example, one study shows that more than 90% of rainforest carbon offsets are worthless[41]. Concerns regarding claims of carbon neutrality based primarily on offsetting have led to a strong response, in some cases through legislation, with bans over claims of greenwashing[42].

Steps on the Net Zero Journey

The net zero journey for data centers varies depending on the nature of the facility. However, there are common steps for all. Firstly, visibility and data are key. Each facility must be able to monitor, measure and manage emissions, including embodied carbon and waste, throughout the entire lifecycle.

Secondly, data center operators must be able to introduce or implement existing measures to report publicly on decarbonization with meaningful metrics using accepted, common frameworks.

With an understanding of performance and full environmental impact, operators can make further reductions through decarbonized energy procurement and generation. By participating in public electricity, heating supply and distribution schemes, operators can support broader decarbonization efforts while also reducing their own carbon emissions.

By procuring more products designed for circularity, supported by certified documentation, operators can ensure that when it comes to end-of-life considerations, waste is reduced to an absolute minimum.

In the immediate and short term, PPAs can meaningfully reduce emissions. Similarly, even with legacy equipment and infrastructure, modern instrumentation and monitoring tools can be deployed to begin to get the granularity of data necessary for analysis and optimization.

In the mid-term, BESS deployments can store energy from VRE, while on-site generation options can increase resilience and facilitate demand-side management. Smart UPS, in conjunction with BESS, can also be orchestrated to provide load and frequency balancing to extend the use of VRE.

In the longer term, data centers operating as microgrids with near zero-carbon energy generation, can ultimately become autonomic, ensuring adherence to the most stringent targets. With the digitalization of national energy grids, microgrids can be integrated for mutually beneficial operation, including the provision of zero-carbon energy surplus to the grid.

Where there is a carbon deficit, carefully selected, independently accredited carbon credit and offsetting schemes can mitigate a company's carbon footprint until data center operators can achieve true, scientifically verified, net-zero operation.

Research from the World Economic Forum and Accenture[43] indicates that when scaled up sufficiently, digital technologies could reduce global emissions by 20% by 2050 in the three highest-emitting sectors: energy, materials, and mobility.

The means of achieving this, as described here, scaled out for application to other sectors reliant on digital technologies would contribute significantly to achieving the global goals of peak emissions by 2025, and net zero by 2050.

Data center operators not only have a duty to strive for net zero for themselves, but also have a significant opportunity: to provide digital services to other sectors that could contribute significantly to global goals and in turn do good for the world. The imperative is to start and then accelerate the journey for the benefit of all.

---

1. Gensler. 2023. "How can we leverage concrete to reduce the embodied carbon of data centerfs?" https://www.gensler.com/gri/lower-carbon-concrete-in-data-center-construction
2. Rimol, Meghan. 2021. "Your Data Center is Old. Now What?" Gartner. May 3, 2021. https://www.gartner.com/smarterwithgartner/your-data-center-is-old-now-what
3. Auda, Al, Bagmar, Jai. 2021. "Mainframe modernisation – from legacy to cloud" https://www.accenture.com/au-en/insights/technology/mainframe-modernisation
4. Cappuccio, David, Cecci, Henrique. 2020. "Your Data Center May Not Be Dead, but It's Morphing" https://www.gartner.com/en/documents/3990241
5. McCarthy, David. 2020. "Edge Computing: Not All Edges are Created Equal" https://blogs.idc.com/2020/06/01/edge-computing-not-all-edges-are-created-equal/
6. Willemsen, Bart. 2023. "Top Strategic Technology Trends 2024" https://www.gartner.com/en/information-technology/insights/top-technology-trends;
    Brothers, Robert, Middleton, Susan G. 2022. "Moving from Datacenters to Centers of Data" https://www.delltechnologies.com/asset/en-us/solutions/apex/industry-market/apex-data-storage-services-moving-from-datacenters-to-centers-of-data.pdf
7. BRE. 2020. "Environmental Profiles Methodology" https://tools.bregroup.com/greenguide/page.jsp?id=2106
8. Alissa, Husam, Sinistore, Julie, Lio, Kari. 2022. "Open Compute Project: LCA GUIDELINES FOR CLOUD PROVIDERS" https://www.opencompute.org/documents/lca-sop-in-ocp-document-submission-template-docx-pdf
9. Parashar, Manish, Diaz-Montes, Javier. 2021. "CometCloud: Autonomic Framework for Dynamic Federated Cloud Services" techfinder.rutgers.edu/tech?title=CometCloud%3A_Autonomic_Framework_for_Dynamic_Federated_Cloud_Services

10. Read, Simon, Shine, Ian. 2022. "You've probably heard of Scope 1, 2 and 3 emissions, but what are Scope 4 emissions?" https://www.weforum.org/agenda/2022/09/scope-4-emissions-climate-greenhouse-business/
11. Lin, Paul, Bunger, Robert, Avelar, Victor. 2023. "Guide to Environmental Sustainability Metrics for Data Centers" https://go.schneider-electric.com/WW_202111_WP67-Sustainability-Metrics-EN_MF-LP.html
    Infrastructure Masons. 2023. "iMasons Sustainability Framework" https://imasons.org/wp-content/uploads/2023/04/iMasons_Sustainability_Framework_042023-.pdf
12. European Standards SRO. 2019. "UNE EN 50600-1:2019 Information technology - Data centre facilities and infrastructures" https://www.en-standard.eu/une-en-50600-1-2019-information-technology-data-centre-facilities-and-infrastructures-part-1-general-concepts-endorsed-by-asociacion-espa-ola-de-normalizacion-in-july-of-2019/
13. Sustainable Digital Infrastructure Alliance. 2022. https://sdialliance.org/our-publications/
14. European Commission. 2020. "European Code of Conduct for Energy Efficiency in Data Centres" https://joint-research-centre.ec.europa.eu/scientific-activities-z/energy-efficiency/energy-efficiency-products/code-conduct-ict/european-code-conduct-energy-efficiency-data-centres_en
15. Durand, Pascal, et al. 2023. "Corporate Sustainability Reporting Directive (CSRD)" https://www.europarl.europa.eu/legislative-train/theme-a-european-green-deal/file-review-of-the-non-financial-reporting-directive
16. Read, Simon, Shine, Ian. 2022. "You've probably heard of Scope 1, 2 and 3 emissions, but what are Scope 4 emissions?" https://www.weforum.org/agenda/2022/09/scope-4-emissions-climate-greenhouse-business/
17. European Commission. 2023. "Energy efficiency directive: Revised" https://energy.ec.europa.eu/topics/energy-efficiency/energy-efficiency-targets-directive-and-rules/energy-efficiency-directive_en
18. Chen, Olivia, García Tapia, Víctor, Rogé, Arthur. 2023. "CO_2 Emissions in 2022" https://www.iea.org/reports/co2-emissions-in-2022
19. IEA. 2022. "Energy Systems: Electricity" https://www.iea.org/energy-system/electricity
20. IEA. 2023. "CO_2 Emissions in 2022" https://www.iea.org/reports/co2-emissions-in-2022
21. IEA. 2022. "An updated roadmap to Net Zero Emissions by 2050" https://www.iea.org/reports/world-energy-outlook-2022/an-updated-roadmap-to-net-zero-emissions-by-2050
22. UNFCC. 2015. "What is the Paris Agreement?" https://unfccc.int/process-and-meetings/the-paris-agreement
23. IEA. 2023. "Data Centres and Data Transmission Networks" https://www.iea.org/energy-system/buildings/data-centres-and-data-transmission-networks
24. Willson, Adam. 2020. "Surging Data Center Industry Continues To Fuel Corporate Renewables Market" https://www.spglobal.com/marketintelligence/en/news-insights/research/surging-data-center-industry-continues-to-fuel-corporate-renewables-market
25. CBRE Research. 2023. "Global Data Center Trends 2023" https://www.cbre.com/insights/reports/global-data-center-trends-2023

26. Gartner. 2023. "Gartner Glossary: Microgrids" https://www.gartner.com/en/information-technology/glossary/microgrid
27. Service, Robert F. 2018. "New generation of 'flow batteries' could eventually sustain a grid powered by the sun and wind." https://www.science.org/content/article/new-generation-flow-batteries-could-eventually-sustain-grid-powered-sun-and-wind
28. Kroposki, Benjamin. 2017. "Integrating high levels of variable renewable energy into electric power systems" https://www.nrel.gov/docs/fy18osti/70430.pdf
29. Swinhoe, David. 2021. "Kao Data shifts backup generators at Harlow campus to vegetable oil-based fuel" https://www.datacenterdynamics.com/en/news/kao-data-shifts-backup-generators-at-harlow-campus-to-vegetable-oil-based-fuel/
30. Dobrzyńska, Elżbieta, et al. 2019. "Exhaust emissions from diesel engines fueled by different blends with the addition of nanomodifiers and hydrotreated vegetable oil HVO" https://pubmed.ncbi.nlm.nih.gov/32084698/
31. IAEA. 2023. "Molten salt reactors" https://www.iaea.org/topics/molten-salt-reactors
32. World Nuclear Association. 2020. "Current and Future Generation / Thorium" https://world-nuclear.org/information-library/current-and-future-generation/thorium.aspx
33. World Nuclear News. 2023. "ABS approves Korean SMR power barge design" https://world-nuclear-news.org/Articles/ABS-approves-Korean-SMR-power-barge-design
34. World Nuclear News. 2023. "Copenhagen Atomics puts forward SMR design for UK appraisal" https://world-nuclear-news.org/Articles/Copenhagen-Atomics-puts-forward-SMR-design-for-UK
35. Jordaan, Sarah, et al. 2022. "Global mitigation opportunities for the life cycle of natural gas-fired power" https://www.nature.com/articles/s41558-022-01503-5
36. IEA. 2023. "Decarbonisation Enablers: Digitalisation" https://www.iea.org/energy-system/decarbonisation-enablers/digitalisation
37. Strain, Larry. 2017. "10 steps to reducing embodied carbon" https://materiallybetter.com/wp-content/uploads/2019/03/10-steps-to-reducing-embodied-carbon-AIA.pdf
38. Taylor, Rives, Coleman, Cindy, Plotkin, Jacob. 2023. "How can we leverage concrete to reduce the embodied carbon of data centers?" https://www.gensler.com/gri/lower-carbon-concrete-in-data-center-construction
39. Ellen MacArthur Foundation. 2022. "An introduction to circular design." https://www.ellenmacarthurfoundation.org/news/an-introduction-to-circular-design
40. Read, Simon, Shine, Ian. 2022. "You've probably heard of Scope 1, 2 and 3 emissions, but what are Scope 4 emissions?" https://www.weforum.org/agenda/2022/09/scope-4-emissions-climate-greenhouse-business/
41. Greenfield, Patrick. 2023. "Revealed: more than 90% of rainforest carbon offsets by biggest certifier are worthless, analysis shows." https://www.theguardian.com/environment/2023/jan/18/revealed-forest-carbon-offsets-biggest-provider-worthless-verra-aoe

42. Nguyen, Amy. 2023. "Carbon Neutral Claims Under Investigation In Greenwashing Probe." https://www.forbes.com/sites/amynguyen/2023/06/16/carbon-neutral-claims-under-investigation-in-greenwashing-probe/
43. George, Manju, O'Regan, Karen, Holst, Alexander. 2022. "Digital solutions can reduce global emissions by up to 20%. Here's how" https://www.weforum.org/agenda/2022/05/how-digital-solutions-can-reduce-global-emissions/

About the Author

ED ANSETT

With over 30 years in the data centre industry Ed Ansett, Founder and Chairman of i$_3$ Solutions Group, has advanced MEP mission-critical facility design for the world's largest operators in data centre projects across the world.

As a recognised leading design engineering practitioner and pioneering thought leader, Ed has continually extended the limits of electrical design for maximum efficiency, reliability, and utilisation. His patented solutions for Adaptable Redundant Power, a hardware and software control system that overcomes the inflexibility of common data centre electrical designs, and authorship of technical papers on critical facility design have pushed the barriers of what it is possible to achieve with power system infrastructure.

His launch of the Green House Gas abatement series of papers is recognised across the industry and beyond for tackling the sustainability of DC operations in technical depth.

Ed regularly contributes to events, media, and industry groups to promote best practice and the development of better engineering solutions to industry challenges.

FIVE

Making Your ICT Value Chain Net Zero

Alexander Campbell, TDC NET

For those of you who have worked to reduce CO_2 emissions, you know that value chain emissions are notoriously difficult to address. This is especially the case for organizations working in the Information and Communication Technology (ICT) sector, where value chain emissions typically constitute a sizable portion of the total CO_2 footprint[1]. Value chain emissions (also known as Scope 3) are emitted by your suppliers or customers, but they are attributed to you because of your business relationship. Scope 3 features all the elements that make addressing climate change tricky: it's hard to measure, beyond your direct control, requires a longer time horizon and involves changing the behavior of others. Scope 3 is a beast, but after reading this chapter I hope to show you that it is a beast that can be tamed and put to work for the betterment of your entire value chain, and ultimately the world.

If you are on a path toward decarbonization, just think of how much collective work it took to change the behavior of your organization. Think of all the meetings to make it a management priority, all the business cases, and how you had to convince peers and superiors up to the Board of Directors level. Think of the governance structures that needed to be established, the policies that needed to be adopted, the processes that needed to be deployed, the roles and responsibilities of dozens of people that needed to be defined and how they individually needed to be trained. Think of the headache of measuring the emissions, defining the accounting practices, choosing which IT system to use, and getting the data externally assured by an auditing company. With the numbers in place, you needed to set a target in line with the Paris Climate Agreement and work out your transition pathway by identifying all the reduction levers. Don't forget all the work needed with your communications department to report externally on progress every year. Thousands and thousands of person-hours were needed to get to this crucial point: the point where systematically addressing emission reduction can start.

If an organization genuinely cares about shedding its addiction to fossil fuels, getting everything in place is a monumental task that can take years. Now consider that you may have hundreds or thousands of suppliers. For you to achieve net zero, a sizable portion of your numerous suppliers need to follow the same path. Some may be well on their way already, while others may have not yet begun. Some may be fully on board and willing to change, while others may be hesitant or even refuse to collaborate. To complicate matters, if you try to use hard power by contractually requiring your business partners to change, you might cause severe negative outcomes to your business. This leaves you with the sole option of having to use soft power and *convince* them that it's in their interest. You need to use your influence, guile and leverage to incentivize your business partners to work together to address climate change. The end goal is to get someone in each of those hundreds or thousands of supplier organizations to get the ball rolling on climate change as soon as possible. That same ball that took you years and thousands of person-hours rolling to get you to where you are today, only this time it's thousands of balls and millions of person-hours.

I've been working with the challenge of reducing Scope 3 emissions in the ICT sector for a few years now. In this time, I developed a framework that has proven effective at reducing what are typically the largest sources of emissions: *Purchased Goods and Services* and

Capital Goods[2]. This is the framework that I would like to share with the data center community, I call it the *"Net Zero Framework for Purchased Goods and Services/Capital Goods"* and I hope that after reading this chapter you will be able to use it to tame the Scope 3 beast in your value chain.

From this point on, I am going to assume that you already have a basic Scope 3 inventory, with your *Purchased Goods and Services/Capital Goods modeled* using a spend-based approach (i.e. using an Environmentally Extended Input-Output model [EEIO]). You now more or less know where your emissions come from, and who the biggest emitting suppliers are. The data may not be great, and you know that the only way to reduce emissions when using EEIO is to spend less. You need to start by finding a way to measure CO_2 so that you can spend better - and less - at the same time.

Measuring Emissions

We follow the hierarchy of estimating emissions that telecommunication companies agree on in the *"Scope 3 Guidance for Telecommunication Operators."*[3] It lays out in very clear terms how to measure the emissions from suppliers according to the following hierarchy:

Spend based (EEIO) → Supplier Allocation Method → Product Carbon Footprints

Supplier Allocation means that you take your share of suppliers' emissions according to the following formula:

Your Annual Spend on the Supplier/Supplier's Annual Revenue *
(Supplier Scope 1 + Scope 2 market-based + Scope 3 upstream categories)

For each supplier in your top 80% by emissions, try to find out whether you can move them out of EEIO and into the Supplier Allocation method. Some data platforms can do this for you, for example, the CDP Supply Chain Module[4] or the EcoVadis Carbon

Action Module[5]. Otherwise, you can do some old-fashioned desk work and research the sustainability reports of your top suppliers to see if they publish a full CO_2 inventory and put the data in a spreadsheet, along with a note of whether the data has had external assurance as a proxy for data accuracy.

Product carbon footprints on the other hand are lengthy and often very complicated analyses carried out using life cycle analysis tools. Some suppliers publish these on their websites, and others may have them on hand if you ask them for it. Typically, it will be very mature suppliers who have them and even then, it would only be for their flagship products. More information on this can be found in the Scope 3 Guidance for Telecommunications Operators[1] as well as the standard L.1410 from the International Telecommunication Union (ITU). [6]

Defining a Maturity Model for Suppliers

Now that you have all the data in your model as accurately as possible, the challenge becomes where to apply your efforts for maximum effectiveness. The first place to start is to assess the maturity of your supply base to decarbonize. I created the simplest maturity model I could conceive of, which means that the whole maturity assessment could be done in a few person-weeks by focusing only on suppliers who constitute your top 80% of emissions:

Estimate → Set target → Reduce

If your supplier is not reporting CO_2 data and you must estimate based on EEIO modeling, then they go in the "Estimate CO_2" group. Once they've begun measuring their emissions, the best way to make sure that they improve over time is for them to make a public commitment to address climate change, preferably in the form of a Science Based Targets (SBT), validated by the Science

Chapter Five

Based Target initiative (SBTi). SBT are public, so it is easy to check if they have them.[7] This also implies that they should be publishing their full CO_2 accounts annually, preferably having the data externally assured, and reporting. The logic here is that they are putting their reputation on the line if they commit to something and then don't follow through on it. So if they don't act as much as needed, they won't just be sacrificing a good business relationship with you, they will be on the hook with all of their external stakeholders. The supplier now has the basics in place to reduce emissions over time.

Bringing this all together, you can visually represent your maturity model like this:

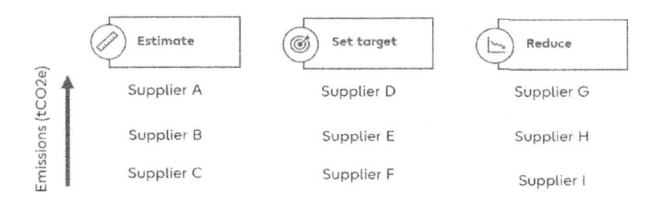

	Estimate	Set target	Reduce
Emissions (tCO2e) ↑	Supplier A	Supplier D	Supplier G
	Supplier B	Supplier E	Supplier H
	Supplier C	Supplier F	Supplier I

You now know who you need to talk to about what, and which suppliers to prioritize. You need to talk to suppliers A, B and C about getting better data; suppliers D, E and F about setting a SBT; and for suppliers G, H and I you can have more in-depth conversations, for example on what kind of integrated circuits they are using and what low carbon products they can offer.

A Roadmap for Supplier Engagement and Category Decarbonization Strategies

You now know where your suppliers are in terms of maturity, so the next step is to determine how you are going to address their emissions through five unique supplier engagement methods: strategic sourcing, supplier relationship management, supplier development, supplier partnerships and industry collaboration.

Strategic Sourcing ⊕ Supplier Relationship Management ⊕ Supplier Development ⊕ Supplier Partnerships ⊕ Industry Collaboration

For each supplier in our top 80% of emissions, we define the internal person responsible for managing the relationship with them. For companies with procurement teams that use a category management structure, it will likely be the category managers. It could also be contract managers, vendor managers or end users depending on the setup. The idea is to agree with them on which method we should use to best engage the supplier based on factors such as where the supplier fits on the Kraljic matrix (is it a strategic, non-critical, bottleneck or leverage supplier?), how long they have until contract renewal, whether they are in scope for an upcoming tender, the complexity of the supply chain, and the leverage you have over the supplier in negotiations. Throughout this process, consider what the relationship looks like now with the supplier and what it will look like in the future.

At this point, you can now build a spreadsheet detailing:

- Supplier name
- Emissions they are responsible for
- Maturity of their CO_2 program
- Responsible person(s) in your organization for that supplier
- Engagement method
- Engagement timeline

When this information is aggregated by procurement category, it forms Category Decarbonization Strategies. When the Category Decarbonization Strategies are aggregated, they form the *Roadmap for Supplier Engagement.*

Strategic Sourcing

This is the tender pipeline; the procurement department knows what contracts are up for renewal, what major requests they will get from the business and where there is potential for financial savings by applying various procurement strategies. It is critical that you tap

Chapter Five

into this process because this is your number one tool to proactively improve emissions from suppliers.

To determine whether climate considerations should be included when tendering, I created a screening tool for the procurement department. By using the EEIO emission factors mapped to our procurement taxonomy, the procurement team simply inputs what they plan on buying in a drop-down menu, as well as the budget for the project, and it will return the estimated emissions in tons. We set a threshold that any purchase with >500 tCO_2 must take climate into account in the Request For Proposal stage, and the bidders must be scored and evaluated according to the maturity of their CO_2 program and the impact on our climate accounts. We've created some internal guidelines that recommend standardized weighting of bids based on impact, so if the purchase will result in >5000 tCO_2, we will weigh climate considerations at 20% of the total tender. We then scale that weight down according to impact down to the 500t threshold that is weighted at 5%.

For the tenders, we use the same maturity framework described previously but break it down into 15 separate questions covering their climate programs. They provide answers and then we have a debrief session with this single slide (as an example):

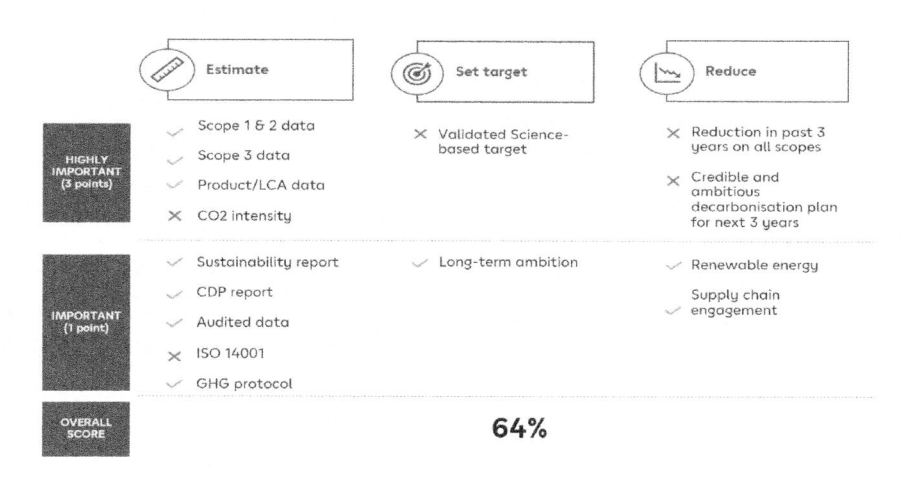

	Estimate	Set target	Reduce
HIGHLY IMPORTANT (3 points)	✓ Scope 1 & 2 data ✓ Scope 3 data ✓ Product/LCA data ✗ CO2 intensity	✗ Validated Science-based target	✗ Reduction in past 3 years on all scopes ✗ Credible and ambitious decarbonisation plan for next 3 years
IMPORTANT (1 point)	✓ Sustainability report ✓ CDP report ✓ Audited data ✗ ISO 14001 ✓ GHG protocol	✓ Long-term ambition	✓ Renewable energy ✓ Supply chain engagement
OVERALL SCORE		**64%**	

If we are buying something that uses electricity (i.e. computer hardware), then we also estimate the impact on our Scope 2. We can then benchmark the impact across bidders and the baseline as-is scenario and allocate some points to the top performers. You could also include the price of electricity for the use phase into the total cost of ownership model if you don't already, and this will have a similar effect.

Even if the winner of the tender doesn't have the most efficient solution or the greatest climate management program, you have at least done your due diligence at this stage. By the time you get to contract signing, you know what they have and what they don't. This is where you can enter contract negotiations and try to get some climate clauses into the contract. Having a comprehensive Supplier Code of Conduct that covers climate is important. we use one that has minimum requirements (*"supplier shall measure scopes 1 & 2..."*) as well as best practices (*"supplier should set a SBT."*) You can also work with your legal team to put your own clauses in the contract, try to get them to commit to publicly disclosing full CO_2 inventory, or to commit to an SBT or provide a minimum guarantee for climate performance. Have the discussion with the supplier and get a feeling for how on-board they are with the climate agenda because this will set the tone for the years to come.

Supplier Relationship Management

It's only occasionally that your organization is likely to go to tender for a specific good or service. However, there is already a supply base of hundreds or thousands of suppliers delivering goods and services that are contributing to your Scope 3. It is important to have regular discussions with them and to show them where they are on the maturity framework, what they agreed to in the Supplier Code of Conduct or the contractual terms, and to make sure they are delivering accordingly. You can also use third party sources of information to benchmark the supplier's performance, for example with CDP or EcoVadis. I run these meetings by asking the key account contact at the supplier to put me in touch with their sustainability department. From there, I have an hour-long meeting where I describe what our commitments are and what our expectations to suppliers are. I give them the floor to discuss the work that they are doing, and then we take time at the end of the meeting to talk about how we will work together going forward. By the end of the meeting, we can have a clear outcome of what needs to be addressed, by whom and when we can expect improvements.

Supplier Development

Whether you've just signed a contract with a supplier who has little to nothing in place to reduce emissions, or you've had your first climate meeting with a current supplier who didn't seem to understand anything you were talking about, supplier development might be the right path forward. At some point, every climate professional and every company with an ambitious target found themselves at this stage. They needed some help, which can come in many forms. However, the most important thing at this stage is recognition from the supplier that change is required as is developing a corresponding willingness to collaborate. Without these, it will be an uphill battle for the entire contract lifetime.

The form that your supplier development takes can be very different from account to account but should be in line with the maturity assessment. The first step is to get suppliers to begin measuring their Scopes 1, 2 and 3 properly. This means that they must either hire a consultant or dedicate an internal resource to do it. If it's an internal resource, you can set up recurring meetings and refer them to external sources (SME Climate Hub[8], Exponential Roadmap[9], the local chapter of your United Nations Global Compact[10], EcoVadis Academy[11], or online training with the Greenhouse Gas Protocol[12]). You can also group suppliers together and hold capacity-building webinars, or a supplier day event focused on climate. What's essential is that you have clear expectations and coherent communication. You will likely find that by spending a few hours with them you will get some real results.

Supplier Partnerships

This involves a shift away from a transactional relationship and more towards a long-term strategic partnership. A prerequisite for success is full alignment between supplier and the ICT company to collaborate on shared emissions reduction initiatives. It often takes a form of profit and risk sharing, for example it could involve an innovation that the supplier would like to bring to market, and the ICT company tests it in a real-world scenario. For it to work well, it is preferable to have a formal setup with a governance structure that includes decision makers from both sides, and a project team or task force that works together towards the decarbonization goal.

Industry Collaboration

The supply chain in every industry looks completely different. However, there are some stark commonalities in what the typical ICT supply chain looks like. There are often a few large suppliers providing equipment or services, and a high number of medium-sized companies buying from them who then provide services to millions of end customers. This market structure is called an oligopoly and is characterized by the buyers having less leverage in negotiations than in a fully competitive market with many alternative choices for supply. This means the individual buying company isn't likely to make a significant change to suppliers' sustainability practices by themselves. One way telecommunication operators have found they can level the playing field is by banding together in industry associations aimed at specific topics. One such association is the Joint Alliance for CSR (JAC)[13], which has 28 telecommunication companies who go *"beyond competition"* to address sustainability in their supply chain. Anti-trust laws prevent JAC from setting any minimum requirements on common suppliers, but it can tell suppliers what 28 individual member companies are doing, the commitments that have been set and what each member asks of their suppliers.

Chapter Five

Net Zero Framework for Purchased Goods and Services/Capital Goods

With the *Roadmap for Supplier Engagement* in place, you now have the structure to build your *Net Zero Framework for Purchased Goods and Services and Capital Goods*. Using the same logic used to reduce Scope 1 and Scope 2 emissions, you need to create a lever catalog of all the possible ways to reduce emissions. You then need to rank these levers by cost and expected decrease in CO_2 emissions to form the marginal abatement curve.

Engage suppliers → Create Lever Catalogue → Marginal abatement curve → Net Zero Transition Pathway

The Lever Catalog

This is a list of all the possible actions you can take to reduce Scope 3 emissions. They are defined by engaging suppliers and finding out what's possible. For example, some suppliers may talk about buying renewable energy at their facility, while others may talk about bundling shipments and using electric trucks to decrease emissions related to their logistics. The type of discussions with suppliers will be related to the data available for CO_2. If they are using the Supplier Allocation Method, you can discuss overall footprints and using renewable energy. If they have product carbon footprints, you can talk about metal alloys and how the integrated circuit boards were made.

You may find that many of the reduction levers are actually in your own control, even if they are occurring at a supplier facility. For example, right-sizing IT hardware to meet and not exceed the needs of your employees can ensure you don't over-buy. Not every employee needs a computer with a high-end graphics card and a wrap-around monitor.

It is important that after every supplier meeting, you record and track the supplier name, reduction levers, estimated cost or effort, estimated reduction in CO_2 from baseline and timeline for reduction.

Marginal Abatement Curve

This is a graphical representation of the data in the lever catalog. By ranking the reduction levers by cost on the y-axis and reduction in CO_2 on the x-axis, you can prioritize which actions will result in the highest CO_2 reduction for the lowest cost. This makes it very easy to communicate to your management where you will be placing your efforts and budget, in what order and when.

Net Zero Transition Pathway

Once you have your total Scope 1, 2 & 3 baseline, your long-term targets (preferably SBTi validated) and the marginal abatement curve, you can project your emissions with some accuracy into the future. By planning on which reduction levers will be applied at what time, you can make a graph showing the expected impact on your scope 3 inventory and how it will contribute to decrease the overall CO_2 footprint of your company and its value chain.

Final Thoughts

And there you have it! By following this framework, you will have a plan that lists all possible ways to reduce CO_2 for Purchased Goods and Services/CAPEX. This won't be built overnight; it will take years to engage all the suppliers and get them to decarbonize. But as long as you follow a clear, structured and logical process that involves all the right internal and external stakeholders, your chances of becoming a net zero company will improve significantly.

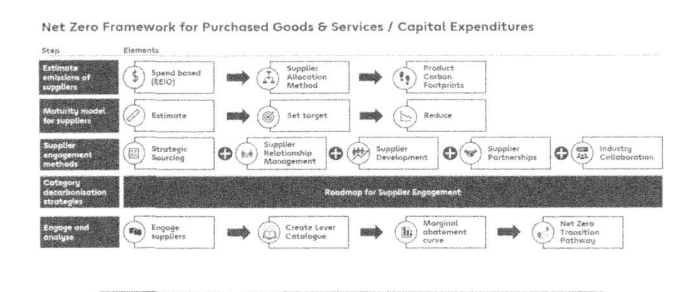

Chapter Five

1. Science Based Targets, "Best Practices in Scope 3 Greenhouse Gas Management", 2018, page 16
2. See footnote 1
3. GSMA. 2023. "Scope 3 Guidance for Telecommunications Operators." June 22, 2023, pages 17 & 18 https://www.gsma.com/betterfuture/resources/scope-3-guidance.
4. CDP. "CDP Supply Chain." https://www.cdp.net/en/supply-chain.
5. EcoVadis. "Decarbonizing at Scale." https://ecovadis.com/solutions/carbon/.
6. International Telecommunication Union. "Methodology for environmental life cycle assessments of information and communication technology goods, networks and services." December 7, 2014. https://www.itu.int/rec/T-REC-L.1410.
7. Science Based Targets. "Target Dashboard." https://sciencebasedtargets.org/target-dashboard.
8. SME Climate Hub. https://smeclimatehub.org/
9. Exponential Roadmap. https://exponentialroadmap.org/
10. United Nations Global Compact. https://unglobalcompact.org/
11. EcoVadis. "EcoVadis Academy." https://ecovadis.com/
12. Greenhouse Gas Protocol. "Online Training." https://ghgprotocol.org/online-training
13. JAC Cooperation. https://jac-initiative.com/

About the Author

ALEXANDER CAMPBELL

Alex is a Senior Sustainability Consultant at TDC NET, Denmark's largest provider of digital infrastructure, where he is in charge of the Scope 3 and sustainable procurement programs. Throughout his 15-year career, he has focused on making infrastructure more sustainable, from low-carbon building materials to humanitarian projects at the United Nations Office for Project Services (UNOPS) and now in digital infrastructure.

He has led numerous sectoral-level working groups to decarbonize the telecommunications industry, including being a lead author and steering group members of the *"Scope 3 Guidance for Telecommunication Operators"* published by GSMA/GeSI/ITU, and co-lead for Supplier Engagement at the Joint Alliance for CSR (JAC) where he was awarded the Climate Change Collaborator Award in 2023. He holds an MSc in Sustainable Development specialized in corporate CO_2 reporting from Uppsala University, Sweden.

SIX

Accelerating Data Center Sustainability Journeys with EkkoSense

Dean Boyle, EkkoSense

Having spent the last 15 years focused on developing innovative, energy-efficient cooling solutions and management software for data center rooms and bringing them to market, it's exciting for me to see data center sustainability, Environmental, Social and Governance (ESG) programs and the whole Greener Data movement begin to have some real force behind it.

Until recently, many corporate ESG initiatives and net-zero commitment programs seemed reluctant to target data centers because of their clearly-acknowledged business-critical role. This was a situation that could never last, as organizations are coming to realize that if they were really serious about their public net-zero commitments, then they need to consider every aspect of their operations. No part of the business can be excluded – especially data centers that continue to be one of the highest organizational consumers of energy.

While the International Energy Agency has reported that data centers and data transmission networks are responsible for nearly 1% of energy-related GHG emissions[1], many think the actual figure is much higher – particularly in popular global data center hubs such as Dublin. The Central Statistics Office in Dublin reports that data centers consumed 18% of metered electricity in 2022[2], with Eirgrid suggesting that data center energy use will double by 2031. It's the same story in other major data center hubs. According to the Financial Times last year, 300 data centers in Virginia now consume 20% of all electricity demand in the state[3].

Access to power and an escalating land grab is attracting attention and placing an increased focus on the sustainability of data center operations – both within organizations and externally. Data centers have become more efficient – but increased workloads mean that overall energy usage is still increasing. Following the introduction of the Power Usage Effectiveness (PUE) metric in 2007, the following ten years saw an impressive improvement in efficiency with the average annual PUE for large data centers falling from 2.50 to 1.58 according to the Uptime Institute. Over the last five years, however, the rate of improvement has stalled, suggesting that PUE shouldn't be the only way of tracking a data center's energy efficiency.

Establishing Clear Accountability Around Climate Reporting

In response, we're now seeing a number of new standards, directives and rules aimed at providing organizations with a clearer accountability framework around climate reporting and the detailing of Scope 3 emissions. These include:

- **The SEC's new regulations on climate change** that require disclosure of Scope 1 and 2 greenhouse gas emissions and require public companies to comply with stated environmental claims such as net-zero target commitments.
- The **California Climate Accountability Act** that's focused on $1 billion plus revenue businesses that conduct business in the state. The act requires organisations to report on their Scope 1 and Scope 2 GHG emissions for their prior fiscal year starting 2026, and Scope 3 GHG emissions by 2027.

- The European Union's **Corporate Sustainability Reporting Directive (CSRD)** that requires large companies and listed SMEs to produce regular reports on their environmental and social impact activities. The directive takes effect on 1 January 2025, with data collection required to start from 1 January 2024. CSRD will require evidence-based reporting and precise measurement of GHG data and Scope 1, 2 and 3 ESG emissions.
- The European Commission's **Energy Efficiency Directive,** which was adopted in September 2023, is focused on reducing energy consumption. It includes a new obligation to monitor the energy performance of data centers, with an EU-level database collecting and publishing data. Data centers operating in the EU that use more than 2,780 MWh of energy each year will be required to report publicly on their energy performance.
- The **German Energy Efficiency Act – EnEfG** – came into force in October 2023 and sets special targets for energy consumption effectiveness. The act sets obligatory PUE targets for data centers based on when they first began operation. If your data center was operating before 1 July 2026, then it will need to have a PUE metric of 1.5 from July 2027 and 1.3 from July 2030. For those facilities operating from 1 July 2026, the PUE target will be 1.2.
- Additionally, the International Standards Organization (ISO) has defined and published its **ISO/IE 30134 series** of standardized data center resource efficiency KPIs. In addition to PUE, the series includes a Cooling Efficiency Ratio (CER), a Carbon Usage Effectiveness measure (CUE), and a Water Usage Effectiveness metric (WUE). Other relevant elements include an Energy Reuse Factor (ERF) and a Renewable Energy Factor (REF). At EkkoSense we see these ISO/IEC 30134 measurements as an important starting point for

organizations looking to measure their ESG performance.

Fundamentally Conflicting Challenges?

Data center operators are already coming under increased pressure to cut energy and carbon consumption to support corporate net-zero goals, and that's only likely to increase as organizations move to address their compliance obligations.

However, the key issue for data center operations will be how to resolve what appear to be two fundamentally conflicting challenges – how to reduce energy usage and secure quantifiable carbon savings while simultaneously delivering against escalating data center workloads.

Initially, this looks unresolvable. With the appetite for digital services continuing to grow rapidly, today's data center operations have never been busier. This should hardly come as a surprise, with facilities busy supporting all the "essential" technology services that we now insist on to support our personal and professional lives. Driven by trends that show no sign of slowing down, such as increased data usage associated with streaming services and 5G adoption, these escalating IT loads are clearly going to keep on impacting data center electrical loads.

And we're all responsible. As consumers we show no sign of kicking our data habit – video, for example, now accounts for over half of global data traffic thanks to our growing preference for hi-resolution viewing. It's a similar story from a business perspective, with more and more enterprises relying on multiple clouds to bring together their infrastructure, applications, core data and security workloads. With cloud computing growth scheduled to keep rising at a compound rate of approaching 20% through 2027, data center workloads will only keep on compounding.

This also precludes what's likely to become a further massive workload spike as organizations consider how the latest Generative AI applications can be supported with their likely demand on data processing performance and power consumption. Tirias Research, for example[4], predicts that improvements in neural networking and algorithm handling may help deliver a 400% increase in compute performance, but that this could be offset by a parallel 50x increase in processing workload volumes. Clearly, this presents a significant environmental challenge for organizations that are already tasked with cutting carbon consumption as part of their committed ESG programs.

Given that data centers were already looking at 20% plus increase in workload levels even before GenAI, it's imperative that operations teams now do everything they can to optimize their performance.

Acknowledging the Scale of the Challenge for Data Center Operations

Today's data center teams are under no illusion of the scale of the task they face when it comes to delivering on what can only seem like diametrically opposed goals. The impact of new energy efficiency and sustainability legislation will require quantifiable, evidence-based reporting around energy savings and carbon reduction across the entire GHG emissions chain. While carbon offsetting and trading have formed a significant component of many organizations' sustainability and ESG programs to date, the latest ESG directives will open this up to much more rigorous justification. Indeed at the COP27 Climate Change Conference in 2022, the UN recommended that businesses must reduce their own climate emission first before using carbon credits for "beyond value chain" mitigation.

Continued attacks on corporate "greenwashing" will shift the focus toward organizations needing to reduce their own Scope 1 and 2 emissions, while also requiring an additional understanding of how their activities impact other parts of their value chain through Scope 3 emissions. This will place increased pressure on data center teams as they look to deliver escalating workloads while at the same time identifying and securing energy and carbon savings.

What's clear is that this will require a comprehensive and

sustained commitment to data center performance optimization, with operations teams needing to unlock every possible area of improvement across their own data centers, that of colocation service partners, and edge facilities. Achieving this will require new levels of insight into existing thermal performance, power provision and capacity management – levels of insight that simply cannot be achieved by relying on traditional legacy Data Center Infrastructure Management (DCIM) and Building Management Systems (BMS) tools.

Why It's Important to Make the Invisible Visible

So what needs to change? Unfortunately, many data centers aren't starting from a good place, and that's hardly surprising when so many legacy facilities are over a decade old and often still operating to their original design parameters.

At EkkoSense we believe it's difficult to unlock the kind of performance improvements that are needed to handle greater workloads and secure energy savings unless you know exactly what's happening in your data center in real-time. We also believe that this won't be achievable unless data center management commits to bridging the gap between their IT and M&E functions.

While the latest digital services and core business applications may run on leading-edge platforms, it's still the traditional facilities management teams that manage and maintain the building and the critical supporting infrastructure within it. However, most IT teams have little interest in the underlying Monitoring and Evaluation (M&E) infrastructure that provides the power and cooling that enables their services to run. Because of this, it's not unusual to see expensive power and cooling resources being used inefficiently. Excess energy usage not only gets in the way of corporate net-zero initiatives but also potentially places organizations at risk when critical resources suddenly become depleted or unavailable.

This is perhaps why legacy DCIM data center management tools, which largely came from the IT side, often failed to address the very real M&E needs of data center operators – especially in terms of capacity management and overall energy efficiency. That's why EkkoSense takes a very different approach, with everything we do informed by engineering-first principles. Core heat transfer and thermodynamics disciplines are at the heart of our proposition, ensuring we are able to provide a deep understanding of energy efficiency and heat transfer across all aspects of today's data center operations from HVAC, building services and facilities management to the latest revolutionary clean tech and energy-efficient systems.

Creating a More Holistic Optimization Approach

This matters because it lets us create a more holistic data center optimization approach – one that works to bring together the IT and M&E spaces. By challenging traditional methods and incumbent software systems, we have been able to build up a very clear picture of why data center optimization matters. Analyzing over 50 billion software data points across over 500 sites has revealed a number of concerning issues.

With a typical BMS view, most data center teams only see their cooling unit temperatures. Rack inlet temperatures are largely unmonitored, meaning that their true status is effectively invisible. EkkoSense research has shown that only 5% of M&E teams currently monitor and report equipment temperatures on a rack-by-rack basis, confirming that the majority of data center operations are in the dark when it comes to performance optimization. This was alarmingly confirmed when our research found that some 15% of IT racks in the average data center were operating outside of ASHRAE's temperature guidelines. Given that the hardware contained within a server rack can range anywhere between $40,000 and $1 million in cost, it's clear that just hoping each rack is performing well introduces material risk and cannot be a sound long-term strategy.

This lack of real-time insight into actual data center cooling, power and capacity performance means that operations teams often have to over-cool because of this uncertainty. Adopting this approach on an ongoing basis effectively prevents data center teams from sensing the true levels of performance optimization that are achievable. In our research, we found that the current average data center cooling utilization stood at just 40% - implying that significant cooling capacity was effectively stranded as nobody knew how to release it and apply it elsewhere.

Need to Gather Massive Amounts of Data

The only truly reliable way for data center teams to troubleshoot and optimize data center performance is to gather massive amounts of data from right across the facility – with no sampling. This removes the risk of visibility gaps but also introduces a new challenge in terms of the sheer volume of real-time data that is being collected. ASHRAE still only advocates measuring just one out of every three racks. While this would lower monitoring hardware costs, it can also introduce risks. Data center operations teams simply can't assume that close proximity ensures they have a directly correlated relationship between different racks. Each single rack is a contained thermal environment, and as such, each has its own thermal reality.

The good news is that all the data is out there, ready to be collected – operations teams just need to capture it. That's why at EkkoSense we've focused on disrupting this process using ultra-low-cost Internet of Things wireless sensors that allow sensors to be deployed in much higher numbers across the data center. More sensors ensure much higher and more granular spatial resolution – right down to the rack level. By putting sensors on every rack, you can not only better optimize your environment, but also ensure that key operations team members are alerted when a threshold is breached allowing for quick response.

Translating Data into Operational Insights

Without a much more detailed, real-time view of how their facilities are actually performing, operations teams will find it hard to support their growing workloads – let alone make meaningful inroads on their sustainability and ESG targets. EkkoSense's distinctive Ekko-Soft Critical AI-driven SaaS solution and its ability to help operations teams gain a real-time view of their thermal, power and capacity performance, combine to create one of the few approaches that can deliver against both these goals.

Unlike traditional, IT-led DCIM-based approaches, EkkoSense's distinctive data center optimization approach is always informed by engineering first principles. Core heat transfer and thermodynamics disciplines are central to how EkkoSoft Critical helps resolve thermal challenges. We recognise that optimizing data center performance goes way beyond IT, hence our deep understanding of energy efficiency and heat transfer across all aspects of critical facilities – from HVAC, building services and facilities management through to the latest clean tech and energy-efficient systems.

The goal is to optimize data center performance while simultaneously delivering quantifiable sustainability results. This is achieved by bringing together an exclusive mix of technology and capabilities – including an innovative SaaS platform, low-cost Internet of Things (IoT) sensors, machine learning, gaming-class 3D visualization and digital twin capabilities, AI analytics and embedded advisory support – all backed by EkkoSense's PhD-level thermal and engineering skills and deep-rooted sector expertise.

The result is a data center optimization approach that has been developed and refined to be particularly easy for operational teams to implement, understand and use in-house – backed by exceptional ROIs achieved through reduced energy usage. Unrivaled levels of IoT sensing bring new levels of accuracy and granularity to data center operations – providing the core machine learning data that enables true real-time visibility of cooling, power and capacity performance.

Disrupting Traditional Data Center Optimization Through Machine Learning and Artificial Intelligence

Data center operations teams are busy enough without having to wade through over-complex optimization data. Humans simply are not good at staring at complex spreadsheets and trying to extrapolate what they are seeing. That's why EkkoSense provides an entirely new way for data center teams to understand the relationships between the potentially 100,000 new data points that EkkoSoft Critical collects for a data center room each day.

From a thermal management perspective, it's a lot easier to identify thermal issues quickly by using comprehensive 3D digital twin visualizations that allow information to be monitored and interpreted quickly – letting them see exactly what's happening in data centers across their enterprise. This visualization particularly helps in terms of highlighting potential anomalies and displaying suggested airflow and cooling improvements.

Artificial intelligence and machine learning at this level change the optimization game, taking all those complex datasets and crunching the numbers, doing in seconds what people would take weeks to attempt and most likely fail to achieve. With AI in place, data center teams benefit from fully correlated real-time data that's presented in a distinctive, actionable way.

Additionally, augmenting measured datasets with machine learning algorithms provides data center teams with easy-to-understand insights to support real-time optimization decisions, backed by data for significantly improved cooling optimization and airflow management. Expert data center operators still maintain control over decisions, recognizing that often they will have insights that simply weren't available within the data sets. And because optimization recommendations are presented each time for human auditability, data center teams are always on hand to ensure that any changes are delivering the expected results.

By following these steps, data center teams can benefit from an AI and machine learning-powered, software-driven optimization approach that unlocks significant benefits. Focused cooling performance recommendations and advisory actions help EkkoSense customers reduce their data center cooling energy costs by up to 30% - translating directly into quantifiable carbon savings. Ensuring 100% ASHRAE thermal compliance also helps to remove thermal and power risks for data center operations. That's why data center operations need EkkoSoft Critical - EkkoSense's SaaS-based M&E optimization and capacity management solution – to help unlock the potential of AI and machine learning-powered data center infrastructure management.

Helping Data Center Teams Get Closer to their Sustainability Targets

However, it's not only the ability to deliver quantifiable energy and carbon savings that makes such a difference – it's also our software's ability to equip data center operations teams and colocation service providers with the real-time insights they need to make smarter optimization decisions.

Unrivaled levels of sensing provide the core machine learning data that enables true real-time visibility of cooling, power and capacity performance. AI-powered optimization shows what's happening – but also why. Additionally, by introducing powerful algorithms that correlate the relationship between the critical infrastructure and IT load, teams can also materially reduce potential downtime events through continual optimization. The software observes changes in the environment in real-time, and will often inform you that a failure is going to occur long before it materializes – and invariably way ahead of when you might have received a BMS alert. This translates directly into key benefits for data center teams. Recent EkkoSense project examples include:

- Enabling rapid thermal optimization of connectivity leader Three's legacy data center sites, uncovering areas of thermal risk that weren't being picked up by BMS systems, securing initial cooling energy savings of 200 kW against a 196 kW projection, achieving a 12.5% data center cooling energy reduction in under ten weeks, and helping Three's data center team to meet corporate demands for a 5% total energy saving across its legacy sites.

- Working with global colocation provider Telehouse and CBRE to not only help to optimize cooling and thermal performance at the Telehouse facility in London Docklands, but also to provide the real-time operational visibility needed to secure a 750 tonnes reduction in CO_2 carbon emissions as well as 15% reduction in cooling energy usage.
- Virgin Media O2's Telefonica operation working with EkkoSense to help cool their data centers more efficiently and deliver energy savings. EkkoSense's software was deployed to achieve projected savings equivalent to one million kilograms of CO_2 year-on-year.

Given ongoing data center resourcing issues, it's also important for operations teams to take full advantage of optimization solutions that can help improve their productivity. Our EkkoSoft Critical tool helps teams stay on top of their escalating workloads and sustainability tasks – whether that's accessing proactive thermal advice through our embedded cooling advisory tool or automating the production of ESG and sustainability reports. And we're not stopping there – our next key development will be an entirely new tool that draws on our data lake to build precise simulation models that will take the guesswork out of data center capacity planning.

---

1. IEA. 2023. "Data Centres and Data Transmission Networks." July 11, 2023. https://www.iea.org/energy-system/buildings/data-centres-and-data-transmission-networks
2. Central Statistics Office (Ireland). 2022.- "Data Centres Metered Electricity Consumption 2022." June 12, 2022. https://www.cso.ie/en/releasesandpublications/ep/p-dcmec/datacentresmeteredelectricityconsumption2022/
3. Financial Times "The Looming Data Centre Crunch." October 5, 2023. https://www.ft.com/content/e597a8b5-f71a-4099-9add-d0e3c1613348
4. Colquhoun, Lachlan. 2023. "AI Is Forcing a Data Center Design Rethink." CDO Trends. September 18, 2023. https://www.cdotrends.com/story/18407/ai-forcing-data-center-design-rethink

About the Author

DEAN BOYLE

Dean Boyle co-founded EkkoSense, a rapidly-growing global SaaS company that's increasingly recognized as a smart choice for data center teams looking to take their operational performance to the next level. EkkoSense has a clear mission to help organizations resolve the thermal risks their data centers face from inefficient cooling strategies. As CEO he has driven the company's development to its current position as a global provider of a disruptive, artificial intelligence-powered SaaS-based data center optimization approach that minimizes data center cooling costs, helps data centers run leaner, and supports corporate ESG programs through quantifiable carbon savings and automated energy reporting.

Before setting up EkkoSense, Dean spent almost five years as Managing Director of 4energy, establishing a new VC-backed business focused on delivering energy savings in ICT rooms. Earlier he ran his own IBM infrastructure services business, building on his background in leading technical services teams supporting major IBM and ERP IT deployments.

SEVEN

Reviving Adaptive Reuse as a Sustainability Strategy: Gamifying Circularity with Carbon Accounting Credits

Sean Farney, JLL

Do you know what this is?

As my Chicago data center brethren know, it's the library that sits atop Digital Realty's storied 350 Cermak — one of the original carrier hotels. In my opinion, it's the prettiest 'data hall' in the world for a couple of reasons. First, because a library is the original data

Chapter Seven

center. From Alexandria to the Vatican, we've stored the history of humanity in versions of racks and cabinets for thousands of years. A fitting top floor of the facility, this library in 350 Cermak pays homage to the 21st century's metaphorical second transformation of the nature of knowledge: from books to bytes (the first being verbal to written, enabled *en masse* by Gutenberg's printing press in the 15th century).

The second and maybe more significant reason I see this as an important data center image is that it's an adaptive reuse project; it was formerly where R.R. Donnelley printed the Yellow Pages and Sears Catalog, both seminal artifacts of 20th century communications and commerce. The century old building is a fortress, its warren of dark hallways and beefy floors housing over 100MW of capacity. Access to the library was one of the best customer fringe benefits — I miss the team meetings in its rarified environs and the mass quantities of Lou Malnatti's pizza consumed there.

Thinking about 350 Cermak and the countless raised floors I've crawled around across the globe — I estimate I've managed, built, or leased space in over 100 facilities — I conclude that we are quite good at adaptable reuse.

In fact, our industry is rife with examples:

- **60 Hudson**'s beautiful red brick once housed Western Union's telegraph operations. Nicknamed the 'Telegraph Capitol of the World' it traded dots and dashes for bits and bytes when it became a carrier hotel in the '90s.
- **400 S. Akard** in Dallas, built in 1921, housed the city's original Federal Reserve.
- **529 Bryant Street** in Palo Alto, built in 1929, was once a telephone operations site but is now an active data center.
- **1 Wilshire** in Los Angeles, a former Class A office building, became a carrier hotel due to the mass of telecom cabling running into Pacific Bell's switching station down the street and MCI's brash installation of a competing microwave dish on the roof.

- **9377 Grand Avenue**, Franklin Park, Illinois, was home to Matsushita Electric Corporation equipment. I recall touring the site with my industry colleague and friend, Steve Holland, and marveling at the volume of gear stored there. In previous lives, the facility was owned by Motorola, who inventoried its console televisions there.
- **QTS Atlanta** is a former Sears distribution center.
- **The Switch Pyramid** is a repurposed Steelcase research facility in Grand Rapids that will support over 100MW of load.

Adaptive Reuse as a Value Proposition

In 2012, edge data center company Ubiquity Critical Environments was founded with adaptive reuse at the core of its value proposition. Ubiquity sought to leverage the massive 250,000,000-square-foot Sears & Kmart real estate portfolio to house a network of connected 600kW-1.5MW edge sites in Tier II and Tier III (non-NFL) metropolitan statistical areas. Partnering with Schneider Electric's nascent cloud and service provider division, Ubiquity planned to deploy data center modules into the existing environment to drive both cost and time to revenue down. An idea far before its time, Eddie Lampert's ESL Investments, Inc. — owner of the assets at the time — ultimately decided to move the real estate into a small real estate investment trust (REIT) and shuttered the company. However, as Ubiquity's former COO, I still believe in the edge and the value of adaptive reuse. I also celebrated the news of Compass Datacenters' acquisition of the original Sears headquarters property in Hoffman Estates, Illinois,[1] with plans to build a massive data center campus earlier this year with just a wee bit of melancholic irony.

Chapter Seven

As an industry, we've been very successful at component piece and part adaptive reuse too. Case in point: is Microsoft's 120MW Northlake, Illinois, facility. On July 20, 2009, it celebrated its 'go live' date after months of blood, sweat, and tears building, testing, and commissioning its 707,000 square feet of state-of-the-art mechanical, electrical, and plumbing infrastructure. Hosting Microsoft's new Bing browser, Office 365, Maps, and Xbox, the facility was not only significant for its size and scale — the largest in the fleet at the time — but also for its bold basis of design. CH1 was an adaptive reuse project, housing a majority of its critical load in off-the-shelf 40' ISO shipping containers. I am very proud to have managed this facility and loved showing it off, despite the barrage of jokes and occasional derision for such an unorthodox approach. The criticism and jokes abruptly stopped when we released our sub-1.2 container PUE and bragged about the record-breaking eight-hour installation time for 2,000 servers.[2] Not only were we sustainable in our reuse of the shipping containers, but the supply chain carbon reduction from avoiding server packing, shipping, cardboard, and pallets was immense.

Now the irony of this giant adaptive reuse experiment was that we spent $500M to build a traditional facility around these shipping containers.[3] But huge kudos still goes to Microsoft for investing in such an aspirational, needle-moving, revolutionary idea. Working with industry titans Christian Belady, Mike Manos, and Dan Costello on such a bleeding-edge skunkworks project was an honor and privilege. We proved not only that moonshots are worth the investments, but that they also provide the needed escape velocity that ushers in paradigmatic shifts. There are hundreds of containers of storage and compute still alive in the wilds of the internet, and the modular concept is the *de facto* standard now for many elements of facility electrical and mechanical deployments. In recent years, pioneers like Compass Quantum, Vertiv, Redivider, and Schneider have developed incredibly innovative modular data centers that are both ultra-efficient and portable.

Driving Change

Since the data center industry, by and large, is not so good at recognizing, celebrating, and marketing our sustainability achievements, I'll pause to do just that. The data clearly demonstrates that data center companies lead all sectors of commercial real estate in use of renewables — fundamentally an adaptive reuse concept — over the last decade. Solar, wind, and hydropower are some of the greenest sources of energy we have, and they are firmly and visibly entrenched in every single data center provider's sustainability program.

Big thinkers like Apple's Tom Jacobik, among other luminaries in the data center power design world, drove the radically different thinking necessary to employ big change starting in the early 2000s. I recall a conversation I had with Tom years ago atop the Pure Nightclub at a particularly famous data center party some readers may have heard of or even attended. I remember being absolutely floored as he retold how Apple decided to build solar arrays and a fuel cell adjacent to its then new iCloud data center in Maiden, North Carolina, to augment power and sustainability planning.

Even farther back, in 2008, Microsoft's San Antonio data center went into production. The company's second hyperscale facility, run by Nic Bustamante (now Corscale's CTO), was designed with conventional raised floors but achieved unconventional industry-leading sustainability due in part to leveraging the municipal grey-water program to create water adaptive reuse.[4]

Speaking of water, we cannot overlook the use of hydropower in the establishment of the Quincy, Washington, data center cluster.

First identified by Microsoft as a source of green, reliable, and ultra-low-cost hydro power, after it opened its first phase in 2007, a long list of data center providers invested more than $10 billion in the small agricultural town in the subsequent 10 years.[5] Today, this makes the sometimes treacherous trip from Seattle through twisty mountain passes worth it.

An Example of Circulatory Solutions Inspired from Nature

It's apparent that between sun, wind, and water, nature is an excellent source of adaptive reuse inspiration. As the original circular organism, having endured long periods of global cooling, extinction-level events, and even an atmosphere of ammonia and methane, she wastes nothing and thrives because of it. Perhaps there are more examples in nature from which we can draw creatively inspired circularity solutions? Take dead trees, for instance.

I am blessed that my backyard is 30 acres of Wisconsin hardwoods. It's a haven that charges my spirit and soothes my soul. It also heats my home. In an indubitably circular manner, I burn forest deadfall in the winter for heat. The natural cycle of forest death and rebirth furnishes as much reusable carbon as my chainsaw and log splitter can harvest. If you haven't seen a woodburning stove since your grandpa's noxious one down in the basement in 1972, you'd be pleasantly surprised by how advanced, efficient, and clean they've become. The ability to tightly control oxygen burn and modulate the conversion rate from potential to kinetic energy makes the long, slow burning of wood akin to an array of batteries. Plus, my Jotul stove's 79%/85% HHV/LHV efficiency and low 0.5 g/hr emissions rate qualifies it for the Inflation Reduction Act's Biomass Tax Credit.

Chapter Seven

Because I'm employing adaptive reuse of fallen timber as heating fuel, the carbon impact of my heating is very, very low, rewarding me with the great altruistic value that comes with having a small carbon footprint. Dropping my energy bill by two thirds is also nice. But one of the most surprisingly compelling aspects of this adaptive reuse approach to home energy use reduction is its gamification. We all love games and competition, right? Well, data center operators whose bonuses were tied to PUE scores especially love energy gamification.

I was fortunate to be at Microsoft during the formative era of hyperscale establishment, in the thick of efficientizing facility management, working with PUE's progenitor himself, Mr. Belady. Due to gargantuan power bills, we were incentivized to be more efficient to reduce OpEx and given a standard metric with which to measure its pursuit. The effect was exactly what you'd expect when giving a group of high-achieving, super Type-A operators something to compete on: results! It was a period of unfettered innovation. Hot/cold aisle containment, curtaining, air side economization, containerization, chicken coops, adiabatic cooling — all table stakes efficiency tactics and technologies today — were developed and ruthlessly optimized during this time. All because we gamified PUE and displayed the numbers on a very public scoreboard. Although we were pridefully competing with our hyperscale brethren, the deliverables made the world a better place. Instead of a dominant strategy game, we ended up creating a benevolent Nash

Equilibrium. As Dean Nelson likes to say: "We don't compete on the environment."[6]

Circular Ideas Learned from Dandelions

To add some game theory engagement to my woodstove experiment, I registered my home as an Energy Star node — and what fun it's proven to be! Because my furnace sits idle during winter, I earn county-leading Energy Star ratings or, minimally, I trounce my neighbors at sustainability. It's a testament to the power of gamified innovation.

Are there any circular ideas to be learned from dandelions? You betcha.

Chances are, if you have a lawn, you have dandelions — or used to. Most people find them to be undesirable and kill them using glyphosate or some similarly nasty chemical which also harms people, critters, and the purity of the glacial aquifer residing 230 feet under my home from which I drink. But as a guy who enjoys and grows a lot of native pollinator plants and moonlights as a flower arranger, I think dandelions are beautiful. Shakespeare agrees. What most people don't know about this 'weed' is that it has a robust nutritional profile. High in vitamin A, C, potassium, antioxidants and anti-inflammatories, the greens and flowers are edible raw and the stems make wonderful tea. I maintain a patch of dandelions in my herb garden and throw the greens in salads and omelets until snow falls. I think there are analogs in the data center business. In the U.S., Crusoe has a fleet of sites that utilize natural gas flaring to power facilities. In Germany, where there's regulatory pressure to reuse exhausted heat and meet Blue Angel requirements, first-movers like maincubes and DATA2HEAT, as well as giants like Equinix[7] and Digital Realty[8], are all working to connect to district heating networks in order to — like the lesson learned from our lowly dandelion — find value in what others discard.

Walking through the nascent history of our field, it's easy to see the demonstrable success we've had with adaptive reuse. With the increasing importance of sustainable building and operating practices vis-à-vis ESG goals, I'm shocked that the adaptive reuse concept is not more widespread. What better way to be sustainable than to reuse the built environment? Add in the lessons and inspiration from nature's circularity and you'd think we'd be rushing to adopt adaptive reuse practices to meet our Boards' sustainability needs. After all, adaptive reuse is simply recycling, which has become enculturated both at the office and at home. But with the rise of search engine solutioning and now AI, I fear it's getting easier and easier to fall into the intellectually lazy trap of assuming that increasing technological complexity and 'newness' will automagically provide better answers. This thinking has created a society with a disposable mindset.

At the same time, the size, importance, and complexity of data centers has increased, driving a reliance on net-new facility builds. Both the required time-to-revenue and certainty of technical performance has driven out the desire for building 'recycling'. Not only have we seen an increase in the number of general information services running over digital infrastructure — there's a good chance your home, car, watch, and certainly phone require a data center to function — but an accelerating general rate of information creation. Statista tells us we create around 330 million terabytes of new information every day![9] Furthermore, we are now trusting more critical services with true life and safety impacts like autonomous vehicles and medical wearables to live on digital infrastructure. The value of this data and the requirements to service it with always-on Service Level Agreements have added elements of hyperscale shareholder risk that, seemingly, has mandated build-to-spec.

Chapter Seven

The Time is Now for a New Approach

To combat the siren's call of throwaway culture, we need to think differently, moving beyond evolutionary and incremental perspectives to revolutionary, epochal ideation. We need 'Creative Destruction', a term coined in 1913 by a colleague of famed economist Joseph Schumpeter.[10] He used it to describe the natural and desirable process of innovation destroying the existing way to make way for new products, services, and ideas. Schumpeter championed the term, doing brilliant work on the nature of free market capitalism. Also called 'Schumpeter's Gale', it was this very force which launched the massive energy efficiency innovations we witnessed in the pioneering days of PUE.

What suffers when we don't 'recycle' buildings, though, is circular sustainability. As we've quietly taken adaptive reuse off the table in the interest of perceived risk and speed, we've added massively to environmental impact, chiefly in the form of concrete and steel embodied carbon. For when we build new, we forgo leveraging the existing carbon impact of the built environment. When Digital Realty bought 350 Cermak and converted it into a data center, it continued to 'amortize' the investment in embodied carbon made by R.R. Donnelley 100 years prior when it erected the building.

Why the huge missed opportunity? I believe it's because we generally lack the true line of sight into the carbon savings involved in adaptive reuse and, therefore, the incentive. I propose we measure both the embodied carbon used in original construction (scope 3) and the embodied carbon avoided in *not* building new. This does not just include concrete and steel, but the entire construction value chain; manufacturing, shipping, installation, build, and even the environmental impact of *not* paving over an entire new site (Doug Mouton at META is doing amazing things with site development in this regard). Armed with these numbers, we then need to gamify adaptive reuse — just like PUE — and issue a carbon accounting credit to companies who make the circularly sustainable choice to recycle a building. Imagine the optics of finishing a project carbon negative, going into a sustainability audit or CSRD reporting period with carry over, or scanning your carbon tag and seeing zero carbon impact numbers from the building? I'm certain that this would change behavior.

Change has never been needed more. We've been saying 'reuse and recycle' for a generation" now let's do the same at scale for the digital economy! The accelerating trajectory of the data center build pipeline not only has a huge carbon footprint, but it outpaces the inventory of sites with power and the land to erect new structures on them.

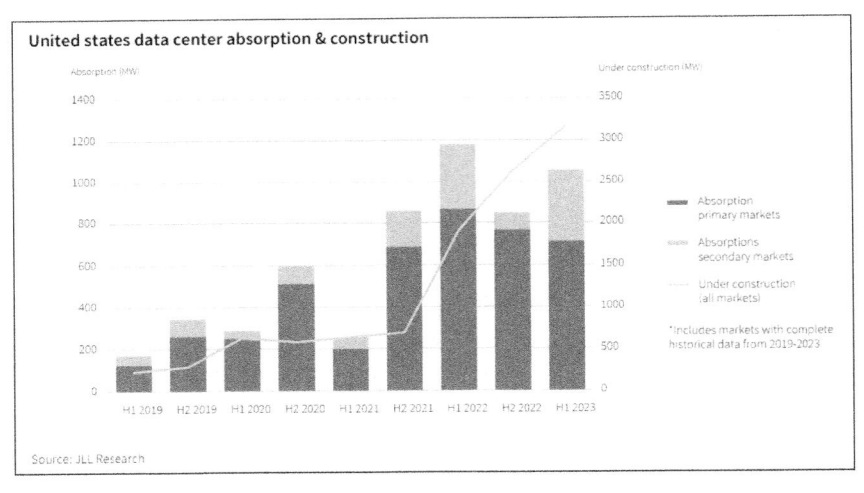

United States Data Center Absorption & Construction. Source: JLL Research

This land and power war is exacerbated by public commitments to shareholders to deliver both revenue and capacity. The 20 largest data center developers have the deep pockets to box everyone else out of the market and keep a firm grip on the waning supply of real estate. Throw new AI demand on top of this already constrained market, and we have a serious shortfall. Digital Bridge CEO, Mark Ganzi, estimates 38GW of accretive digital infrastructure demand due to artificial intelligence![11] These exogenous market factors make

Chapter Seven

adaptive reuse the perfect strategy to alleviate site shortages and weighty new construction carbon demands.

I'll use Ganzi's number in a thought exercise to illuminate the impact of adaptive reuse. Conservatively taking 10% of his 38GW as opportunities for adaptive reuse and assuming 10MW per 10,000 square feet for a high-density modular AI facility, we could recycle and future fit 380 buildings using modular deployment of storage and compute. Not only would we eliminate the carbon that would have been deployed to build new, but we'd see amazing reductions in time-to-revenue and relieve power constraints — a win for all involved! Plus, with 30 billion square feet of commercial real estate in the U.S. alone, there's no shortage of applicable sites.

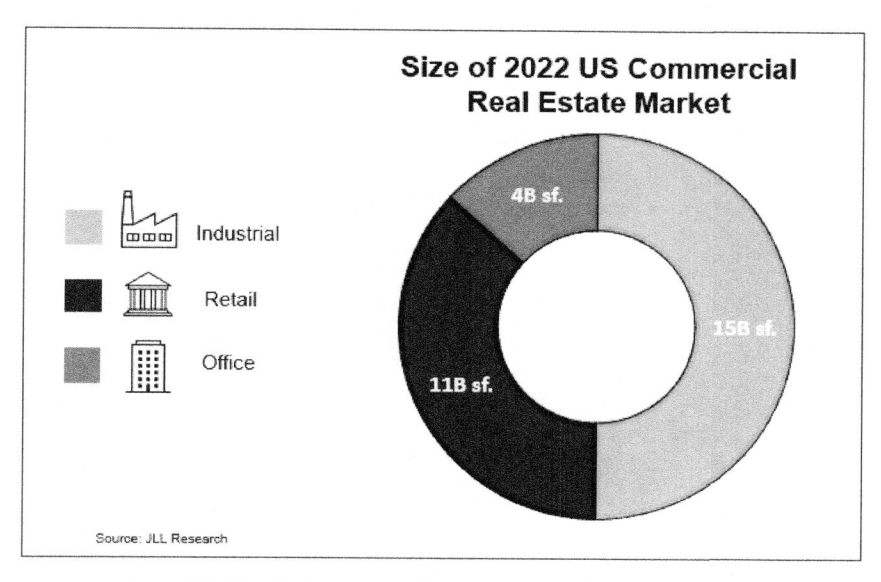

Size of 2022 US Commercial Real Estate Market

- Industrial: 15B sf.
- Retail: 11B sf.
- Office: 4B sf.

Source: JLL Research

Size of 2022 US Commercial Real Estate Market. Source: JLL Research

---

1. Butler, Georgia. "Compass Datacenters acquires Sears HQ in Illinois." Datacenter Dynamics. September 15, 2023. https://www.datacenterdynamics.com/en/news/compass-datacenters-acquires-sears-hq-in-illinois/
2. Miller, Rich. "Microsoft Unveils Its Container-Powered Cloud." DataCenter Knowledge. September 30, 2009. https://www.datacenterknowledge.com/archives/2009/09/30/microsoft-unveils-its-container-powered-cloud.

3. Miller, Rich. "Microsoft Plans $500M Illinois Data Center." DataCenter Knowledge. November 5, 2007. https://www.datacenterknowledge.com/archives/2007/11/05/microsoft-plans-500m-illinois-data-center.
4. Miller, Rich. "Microsoft: Grey Water Swayed Site Location." DataCenter Knowledge. December 7, 2007. https://www.datacenterknowledge.com/archives/2007/12/07/microsoft-grey-water-swayed-site-location.
5. Qunicy Data Center Market. Baxtel. https://baxtel.com/data-center/quincy.
6. JLL Data Center Forum 2022 Keynote presentation
7. "Repurposing Heat for Community Use—Heat Export Project Powered by Equinix Sets Stage for Further Cooperation." July 13, 2023. https://www.equinix.co.uk/newsroom/press-releases/2023/07/repurposing-heat-for-community-use-heat-export-project-powered-by-equinix-sets-stage-for-further-cooperation
8. Swinhoe, Dan. "Digital Realty partnering with Mainova for district heating scheme in Frankfurt." January 23, 2023. https://www.datacenterdynamics.com/en/news/digital-realty-partnering-with-mainova-for-district-heating-scheme-in-frankfurt/#:~:text=Data%20center%20firm%20Digital%20Realty,developing%20in%20the%20German%20city.
9. "Worldwide Data Created." Statistica. https://www.statista.com/statistics/871513/worldwide-data-created/
10. Kopp, Carol M. "Creative Destruction: Out With the Old, in With the New." Investopedia. https://www.investopedia.com/terms/c/creativedestruction.asp.
11. Lima, Joao Marques. "DigitalBridge CEO: 'We believe the opportunity set for AI is close to 38 gigawatts'. August 9, 2023. https://thetechcapital.com/digitalbridge-ceo-we-believe-the-opportunity-set-for-ai-is-close-to-38-gigawatts/.

About the Author

SEAN FARNEY

As Vice President of Data Center Strategy for the Americas, Sean helps clients operate more than 900 data centers sustainably and efficiently. He enjoys sharing his lifelong passion for critical environments by learning and evangelizing about digital infrastructure.

Prior roles, include Director of Data Center Marketing at Kohler, Founder and Chief Operating Officer at Edge data center startup of Ubiquity Critical Environments, data center manager for Microsoft's 120MW Chicago facility, and operations director at low-latency trading MSP 7ticks.

A Chicago native, Sean escaped to rural Wisconsin to live circularly; he hunts, grows, or harvests a majority of his food and burns deadfall to heat his home. A retired amateur boxer, he stays active kickboxing and rolling Brazilian Jiu Jitsu. Sean holds a master's degree in information technology from Northwestern University.

Part II

RENEWABLE & CLEAN ENERGY SOLUTIONS TO CUT CARBON IN THE DATA CENTER

EIGHT

Low Carbon Solutions: Pathways to Energy Maturity in the Data Center

LEAD ANALYST: MARY ALLEN, INSIGHTAAS

Report Contributors: Jeffrey Barber, Bloom Energy; Michael Donohue, Cumulus Data; Brian Jabeck, Enchanted Rock; Ehsan Nasr, Microsoft; Anand Ramesh, EdgeConneX; Sindhu Sharma, Nxtra by Airtel

Energy transition is widely viewed as the surest and most rapid path to decarbonization, the core input to creation of a climate-safe future. As UN Secretary-General António Guterres noted, "We face a moment of truth... how we produce and use energy is the main cause of the climate crisis.... We must start today and together realize the potential of energy as a crucial enabler for the achievement of the SDGs and the objectives of the Paris Agreement, ensuring a more prosperous, equitable and sustainable future for people and the planet."[1]

The transition Guterres refers to is the shift away from reliance on carbon-intensive fossil fuels and their replacement with low carbon energy solutions. A process that involves the development and use of 'green electrons' – electrons produced using renewable resources like wind or sun; 'green molecules' made up of green electrons stored in media such as hydrogen and other synthetic fuels; and increasingly, 'green bits', defined as digital services that support the optimization of energy systems and efficiency management across strategic sectors, including buildings, transport, and manufacturing. As a significant consumer of energy and a provider of the digital infrastructure needed to effect change in other sectors, the

Chapter Eight

data center industry has a key role to play in the clean energy transition.

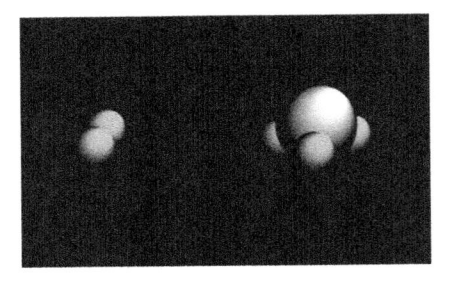

Over the past decade, efficiency innovation in IT hardware, along with the migration to large, more sustainable cloud environments, has resulted in modest increases to power usage in the data center – which today account for 1 to 2% of global electricity consumption.[2] But recent workload expansion has translated to significant increases (10-30%) in energy consumption on a y-o-y basis, a growth trajectory that demands a renewed effort to decarbonize the industry. To achieve recommended Net Zero scenarios, the International Energy Agency states that carbon emissions in the data center must halve by 2030.[3]

The data center's environmental profile is best managed through a lifecycle approach that takes into account a facility's impact from cradle to grave and across the ecosystem. This provides a more complete picture that can uncover new opportunities to drive sustainability; performance improvement is available through better management of the supply chain, innovation in the built environment, and through the introduction of circularity principles in component design. But the energy consumed in operations, estimated at ten times per square foot of that used by the typical household, remains a key contributor to the data center's environmental footprint.[4]

Essentially, there are two ways to tackle carbon emissions: through efficiency improvements to IT and facilities infrastructure, and through the consumption of clean energy. While ongoing OEM innovation in server and other data center equipment continues to prove out the first tactic, limits are beginning to emerge: how far can server density be pushed before cooling fails, and what level of investment is needed to improve on a PUE of 1.1 when 1.0 is perfect? The most direct way to improve environmental impact is to reduce consumption: a MW of power that is not consumed translates directly to carbon emissions reductions. But efficiency improvements will never deliver zero carbon, unless the power source is green, so the goal going forward is to ensure that the maximum amount of energy consumed is carbon-free.

For many data centers, the ideal sustainability scenario remains elusive. Factors, such as climate, location-based requirements including market need for proximity to data services, relative access to renewable resources, the regulatory environment, operational parameters, and investment budgets may each introduce constraints on the implementation of the net zero, green-fueled data center from day one. For most operators, and brownfield sites in particular, green energy implementation is more evolution than revolution. It develops over time, and may involve the use of interim solutions, including bridge technologies such as hydrogen, biogas or even natural gas that reduce carbon, as standalone solutions or in combination with other energy options. Given the residual value in acting sooner rather than later to reduce carbon emissions, interim fuel solutions can act as important contributors to sustainability strategy as the data center moves along the path to energy maturity. While keeping an eye on longer term, net zero renewable implementations, operators may also productively explore the art-of-the-possible through rapid install of shorter term, low carbon energy solutions.

Back to the Future? What Accounts for Renewed Interest in Green Energy?

The data center industry is doubling down on sustainability efforts. Most of the hyperscale companies have launched ambitious programs: of the top 30 US technology, media, and telecom companies, 25 have announced carbon neutrality or net zero targets within the 2050 window that IPCC scientists mark as a turning point in

Chapter Eight

our ability to manage climate change. For many of the leading data center operators, notably Google, Microsoft, Amazon, Meta, Apple, Virtus, Switch, Digiplex, and Tencent,[5] green energy is a focus in sustainability strategy, which will be achieved through clean power purchases and the construction of high profile renewable projects that could speed energy transition if implemented at scale. But what accounts for this bubbling of commitment to the adoption of clean energy solutions?

Crisis

Growing recognition of the need to do more to avert climate disaster is a top-level answer. Despite international agreements on carbon reduction enshrined in the Paris Agreement, a recent IPCC report[6] has explained that even if governments meet current climate targets, the carbon budget that could limit global warming to 1.5C by 2050 will be largely spent by 2030 – and the remainder spent in the following two years. In the figure below, the gray area represents carbon already emitted, blue represents carbon that will be emitted, based on countries' current climate plans, and the black shows the budget remaining after 2030.

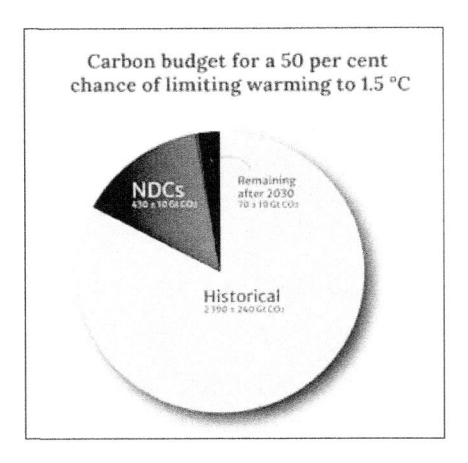

NDC = Nationally Determined Contribution. Source: UNFCCC 2023.

This climate reality has led to increasing social and business pressure from data center customers, shareholders, partners, regulators, and employees for better environmental performance.[7] The industry has been demonized in the past, with data center operations characterized as energy-hungry hogs. To address this perspective, several leading operators have launched mega renewable projects aimed at reducing carbon and recovering reputation. Apple, for example, has built 200 MW of solar for the company's data center in Reno, Nevada, and Google has two projects in Alabama and Tennessee that will produce 300 MW of solar energy. Other global providers, such as Microsoft, focus on the large-scale purchase of renewable energy through PPAs (13.5 GW of carbon free energy), while developing partnerships for small renewable projects that also deliver social justice benefits.[8] In the chart on the next page, from the Intergovernmental Panel on Climate Change (IPCC) Sixth Assessment Report, the importance of renewable deployments in the energy transition is clear.

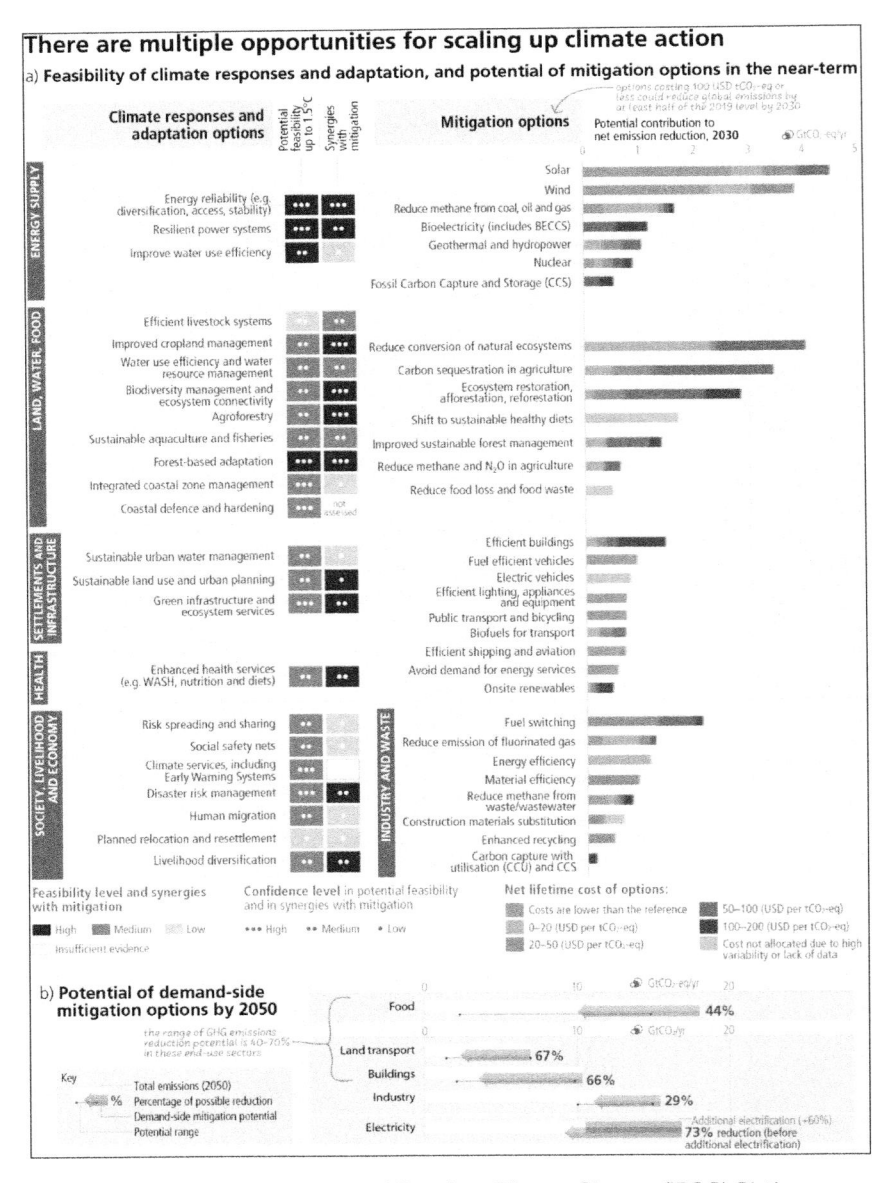

Chapter Eight

There are multiple opportunities for scaling up climate action

a) Feasibility of climate responses and adaptation, and potential of mitigation options in the near-term

Source: Intergovernmental Panel on Climate Change (IPCC) Sixth Assessment Report.

Cost

Another consideration is cost. Increased demand for renewable energy generation across industries and countries has driven production at scale, and with it, more affordable alternative energy solutions. The price of solar energy, for example, measured in kilowatts per US dollar, has declined 85% over the past decade, while the cost of onshore wind power – more cost effective at the outset than other renewables – has declined 56%, positioning wind as the cheapest source of energy today. Relative to other renewables, including hydropower, biomass, and geothermal, wind and solar emerge as the most affordable energy sources, while most of the other alternatives listed above are also cost competitive relative to energy derived from fossil fuels.[9] Declining prices mean that the data center operator looking to install renewables directly, or to use PPA purchasing power to drive renewable integration at the grid level, can establish better financials, while working to achieve carbon and human health targets. And post installation, barring infrastructure maintenance costs, the actual energy is limitless and free – a not insignificant benefit in the calculation of Total Cost of Ownership (TCO).

Going forward, financial incentives for the installation of renewables are likely to drive further uptake. In the US, President Biden's $369 billion USD Inflation Reduction Act, passed in August 2023 and aimed at incenting private investment in clean energy and boosting US production, represents the largest single climate investment the country has made. It offers support in the form of tax incentives for the development of a range of technologies, including nuclear, a carbon-free source of energy that is gaining strength as an attractive alternative to fossil fuel due to its ability to deliver baseload power. Currently, capital costs for building new nuclear facilities mean the cost for this energy source remains high[10] compared to coal, or natural gas sources; however, more competitive economic variants are surfacing in Small Modular Reactor (SMR) technology, which features a small footprint and mobility, and in the potential to reuse stranded assets. Depending on market conditions, the use of existing nuclear assets may be competitive from both cost and carbon perspectives – Scope 3 emissions are low relative to the impact produced by new builds – and innovations in these areas are redefining the nuclear outlook.

Continuity

A third factor driving interest in alternative energy sources is the potential for grid development. Ultimately, even total transition of the data center industry to carbon free energy sources would have limited impact on decarbonization of electricity generation: today, data center industry accounts for 1-2% of global electricity consumption and is growing at an annual rate of 3-4%. However, as industrial-scale consumers of electricity, data centers can lead by example, paving the way for other operators and other carbon dense sectors to embark on their own low carbon energy journey, while encouraging dialogue that can push utilities past traditional reliance on fossil fuels. For many electricity providers, the introduction of renewables entails investment and risk; while requiring significant land and capital purchases, there may be technical issues with integration of distributed resources, as well as issues with intermittency. But the potential for multi-year contracts with large purchasers is encouraging more forward-thinking power providers to seize the renewable opportunity. Today, large data centers are the largest purchasers of green electricity. With 20 GW of renewable purchases through 401 projects in 22 countries,[11] Amazon vies with Microsoft (13.5 GW in 135 clean energy projects in 16 countries)[12] for title as largest corporate purchaser of renewable resources. Generating low carbon energy 24 hours a day, 7 days a week, nuclear represents another reliable option that can help promote grid stability, and even support the introduction of a diversity of alternative energy sources to the grid.[13]

Chapter Eight

Source: Kaveh Aflaki. Unlocking Green Electrons for Decarbonization of the Grid.

For most data centers, the key priority is reliability and resilience – operational attributes that trump other considerations like corporate social responsibility, sustainability, or even energy cost. While electricity rates are a determining factor in siting decisions, access to adequate reserves of reliable power is an operational prerequisite. At a micro level, power requirements are inspiring the creation of new kinds of partnerships between the data center and local utilities, which expand basic notions of supply and demand. In Dublin, Ireland, for example, pressure on local energy supplies from an active data center sector has recently led the local utility provider, EirGrid, to impose a moratorium on new power connections for a 2 billion Euro planned expansion of data center capacity.[14] However, leading operators such as Microsoft are innovating to address issues with power shortages: for example, drawing on advanced storage systems – large battery banks that enable a "grid interactive UPS" at its Dublin data center – Microsoft is delivering power back to the grid, stabilizing fluctuations introduced by wind power, and supporting further integration of renewable resources.[15] In other regions, communities are demanding that data centers operate with clean fuel technologies to alleviate carbon and air pollution issues. In the US, for example, AWS gained permits for the construction of three data centers in Oregon, based on the use of fuel cell technology, which produces far less carbon than traditional diesel generators or solutions powered by energy derived from other fossil fuels.[16]

Closer integration between utility providers and data centers to support the use of renewable energy in the grid is not a new concept. Foundational infrastructure for the ground breaking microgrid at the University of California San Diego (UCSD) campus was installed back in the 1960s. Today, the advanced energy platform combines a natural gas cogeneration plant for heating and cooling, a 3MW solar installation and a 2.8 MW fuel cell that uses methane from the local wastewater facility to produce electricity at a fraction of the cost of grid power as well as heat that is recovered for district heating, a 2.5 MW storage system, and EV6095 charging. As it powers the entire campus, including the university's supercomputer, UCSD also has a demand response relationship with San Diego Gas & Electric, where it is paid to reduce energy demand at peak times and pays the utility to "wheel" the grid power it does use – all while providing backup to the electrical grid in emergencies.

This kind of installation offers several important benefits from the perspectives of both cost and resilience. Renewable energy resources are now viewed as a reliable backup source of power that can reduce reliance on overloaded or aging utility grid systems. The opportunity for energy arbitrage, where the data center optimizes energy costs by consuming either onsite resources or grid power depending on market pricing, will become critical, particularly in regions such as Europe where grid costs are increasingly variable.

Onsite generation can provide additional savings via the redesign of components that can reduce electrical losses through improved energy density, and reduced transmission and voltage conversions. Sustainable Digital Infrastructure Alliance (SIDA) researchers have pointed to significant power losses as power is converted to AC, to DC and vice versa, multiple times as it travels to the IT equipment, resulting in unnecessary cost and carbon.[17] SDIA also notes the potential for improved power quality that onsite generation can deliver when combined with small power storage systems: "Harmonics, voltage sag, frequency variations and momentary outages (enough to trip expensive computers) are all increasingly common on the electricity grid. The power electronics inside data centers are more sensitive to such grid imperfections than ordinary consumer items. Data center operators can therefore improve power quality and hence equipment reliability through onsite generation."[18]

Reduced cost, enhanced reliability and stability of power delivery, improved efficiency, and less dependence on increasingly overcrowded, centralized grid infrastructure, which may be achieved through onsite green energy production and storage bode well for data center uptime and long-term sustainability. This model is well aligned with the vision of a decentralized grid that many researchers advocate for the future: building "large constant base loads could be a burden in the future, especially as prices fluctuate. It is imperative that energy be consumed with proximity to supply and in a flexible manner. Data centers can be proximal, flexible energy suppliers." And as a former CRO for the CANARIE Network put it, it is cheaper and easier to move data to the source of power, than it is to move electrons to the data center.[19]

Pathways to Ideal: Low Carbon Challenges and Opportunities in the Current Crisis

A key question emerges from the renewable scenario drawn above: do we have time to build the ideal onsite generation future, or can we make productive use of "bridge" energy solutions that are readily available today? The incremental benefit of immediate action on carbon reduction,[20] set against ongoing challenges associated with direct integration of renewables in the data center argue for the rapid deployment of all available technologies – and the sooner the better.

Buying Green

A first line of attack in executing sustainability strategy is the purchase of green energy, typically through Renewable Energy Credits (RECs) or Power Purchase Agreements (PPAs) with local utility providers who contract to deliver power derived from renewable resources, to compensate for emissions generated by the data center. This approach is well suited to the needs of the large, urban facility that may not have adequate real estate for renewable installations. It may also serve to drive renewable adoption in the utility sector. Critics argue, however, that purchasing carbon forgiveness allows the operator to shift responsibility rather than work constructively to reduce emissions at source. Another issue is size: utilities will typically contract only with large corporations who can offer steady and substantial income, leaving the average consumer to pay for the downside of PPAs in increased variability and higher grid fees.[21] In addition, the smaller data center is effectively excluded from this activity. Though aggregate buyers exist who may represent multiple, smaller purchasers, these brokered contracts tend to be complex, and further obfuscate the relationship between contractual purchases and the physical consumption of green energy.

In the case of offsets, a key goal is to aim for grid equivalency – so that carbon emissions from the data center hub in the US state of Virginia, for example, are not offset by RECs 1,000 miles away in Texas – in order to drive real emissions reductions in a specific region. Establishing the provenance of 'green electrons' serves another purpose: it helps ensure that the energy consumed does in fact come from renewable resources. Increasingly, data center providers are turning to 'green bits' to fine tune the tracking of green energy consumption, extending control beyond the annual matching of RECs to power consumption. In a recent Carbon Free Energy pilot in Houston, Texas, for example, EdgeConneX has worked with AI-enabled power marketer Gridmatic and local wind assets to test out the business case for 24/7 hourly matching of green energy consumption.[22] While providing greenwash-free data for carbon reporting, the pilot has also demonstrated competitive financials, with better costs relative to reliance on local power rates, which are expected only to rise going forward.

Direct Connect

An attractive alternative to tracking and offsets is to build a baseline model that provides direct, or onsite, connection to clean energy. Today this proposition is difficult to achieve through reliance on solar and wind resources alone. Space constraints in the data center limit the installation of solar (that is not likely to deliver more than 30-40% of data center needs even in large installs) and wind generation capacity. At the same time, dependence on daytime production and weather variability mean that these sources are intermittent, and struggle to deliver dispatchable power at the level required by the data center when needed. When using local renewable energy, the data center must contend with real-time balancing of energy supply and demand, the need to ensure a reliable supply of power to support quality of service commitments, and load fluctuations around peak usage times.[23]

To help manage renewable challenges, data centers need to develop significant storage capacity. While battery costs have dropped significantly in the past five years,[24] and newer technologies such as lithium ion promise greater efficiency, data centers require a good deal of redundant power – 10s of hours to multiple days' worth of emergency power – in order to support IT service delivery and to maintain tier status. Data centers relying on renewable resources need multi-days of long duration storage, such as hydrogen-based solutions, or a lot of batteries that may be big but have a short number of discharge cycles. Ultimately, battery costs may impact the financial feasibility of renewable energy, while presenting an e-waste challenge for the facility.

Today, nuclear energy is gaining recognition as a reliable, carbon free energy solution that can deliver the base load data centers need to ensure service levels. Construction outlays for new build are high, in terms of both cash and carbon (concrete is carbon intensive); however, operators like provider Cumulus Data are putting a new twist on recycling – taking advantage of the zero carbon nuclear power generated at the Susquehanna Steam Electric Station in Northeast Pennsylvania to collocate a 48 MW data center that is directly connected to Susquehanna, with an ultimate goal of bringing 475 MW of capacity online. According to Cumulus Data, there are many existing nuclear plants throughout the US that can easily match the 24/7 demand of data centers. While waste storage may be an ongoing issue, the nuclear plant delivers "always on" power; it is especially well adapted to facilities that require hundreds of megawatts of power and that support workloads which are less latency sensitive – meaning that data can be moved for processing to the energy source location. For smaller facilities, a more viable option may be found in SMRs, which range from 10 MW microreactors to 12 unit clusters of "standard" 50 MW,[25] which were approved for research and development by the Nuclear Regulatory Commission in January 2023 and can now be located closer to high density population areas.

Microgrid

Combining various resources is another approach that is increasingly valued for its flexibility. Microgrids, as noted above, can integrate rooftop solar, biofuel, batteries, and fuel cell technology to create the steady power that will extend the role of renewables in the data center. They can operate independent of the grid or in tandem with grid infrastructure to provide an alternative source of energy to boost data center – or grid resilience. Factors such as climate, local utility provider fees, access to renewable resources, sustainability targets, and the local regulatory environment will determine which energy source is used. In California, stringent air quality regulations have led to a partnership between resiliency-as-a-service provider Enchanted Rock and Microsoft for development of the largest RNG-powered microgrid in the state,[26] which will deliver backup power for the cloud provider's San Jose data center. The project will outperform tight California emissions requirements for distributed generation, with hourly local emissions estimated to be 80%-96% lower than Tier 4 diesel standards.

Chapter Eight

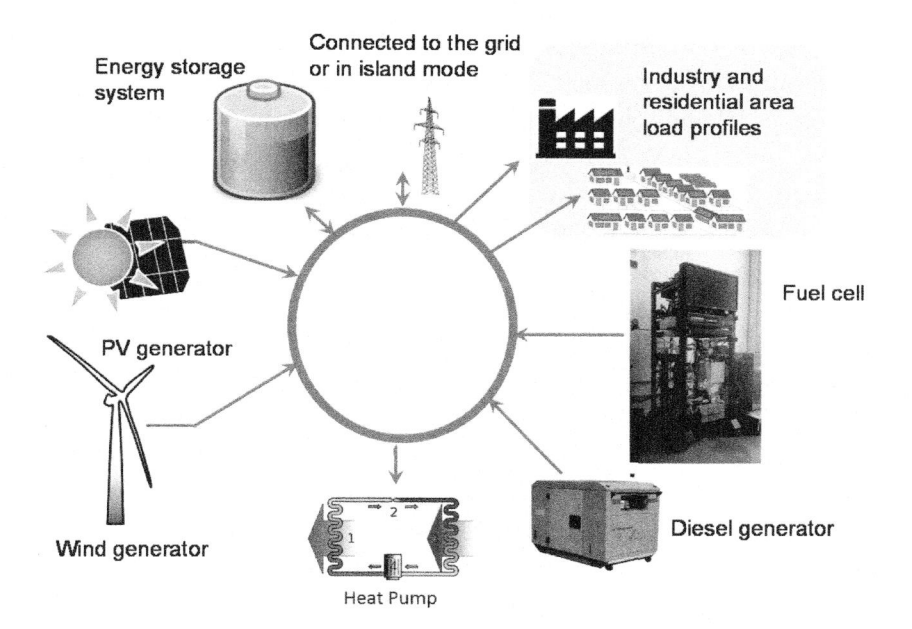

Source: Microgrid, Skoltech Center for Energy Science and Technology

Available for rapid deployment, fuel cell is another technology that is quickly gaining traction in data center markets. Fuel cells may be installed for storage – as in the figure above – as 'green molecules' when they store electricity in a hydrogen medium for later use by the data center, or even the grid. Fuel cells may also serve as the primary power source, offering the data center energy independence when grid power is unavailable, or is reliant on carbon intensive fossil fuel. In the AWS example cited above, the company chose solid oxide fuel cell technology to deliver 24.3 MW of energy to three proposed data centers in Oregon (seven planned in total) when the local utility was not able to deliver adequate electricity for the project. Powered by natural gas, these fuel cells rely on fossil fuel; however, since there is no combustion in the conversion of natural gas to electricity, their use is estimated to create 99% less smog-forming pollutants and 50% less carbon emissions than electricity supplied by the regional grid provider.[27]

Fuel cell providers are bullish on opportunities to further

improve the sustainable profile of the technology, largely by replacing natural gas with other energy sources, such as RNG or hydrogen. Widely viewed as the most promising clean energy source, hydrogen is produced either through natural gas reforming or electrolysis.[28] Solar power has been used to produce hydrogen from water by electrolysis, however, this approach has proved inefficient relative to natural gas (40% less efficient) due to electricity transformations involved in the process. A lack of distribution infrastructure – materials science precludes the use of natural gas pipelines due to fuel characteristics – introduces another limitation on broad-based deployment of hydrogen fuel cells. Today, natural gas functions as an interim fuel cell solution that supports data center reliability or even the use of other renewables. But a next step could be the fuel cells powered by RNG, consumed as an offset, or harvested through partnerships with industrial and food waste companies, and delivered as part of a blend in a Liquid Natural Gas (LNG) processing facility. Essentially, fuel cell technology takes molecules and turns them into electrons, but depending on the source, it is also possible with existing technology to reverse that process, turning green electricity to molecules (for energy storage) to create green hydrogen for zero carbon data center operation. Microsoft, for example, has deployed a 3 MW hydrogen fuel cell generator to provide emissions free backup for the data center;[29] however, sober estimates put the scale of green hydrogen solutions (or even hydrogen/gas blends) at ten years out.

Aimed at specific use cases, these single energy source microgrid solutions illustrate the enormous potential for microgrids to help data centers achieve sustainability goals. As the figure below shows, organizations across the globe are realizing this potential at a rapid rate.

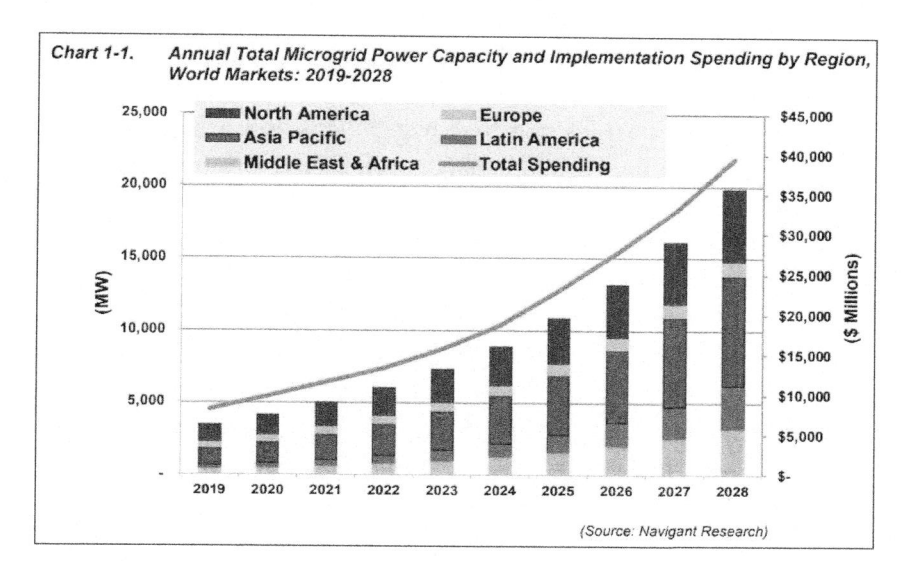

Chart 1-1. Annual Total Microgrid Power Capacity and Implementation Spending by Region, World Markets: 2019-2028

(Source: Navigant Research)

Building Low Carbon Energy Strategy: Expert Guidance

In building pathways to energy maturity, data center operators will encounter market, location, and industry constraints. For example, hyperscale provider projects have located operations next to renewable resources; however, public law in some jurisdictions requires that the data centers locate facilities in close proximity to the customers they serve. The concentration of digital industries in economic hubs like London, Frankfurt, Amsterdam, and New York City mean these areas will continue to be compelling data center markets.

This market reality, along with cost competitiveness, means the traditional grid is unlikely to wither away any time soon. But aging grid infrastructure, combined with massive new demand for digital services, means that power hungry data center organizations must seek to work collaboratively with local grid providers – building green energy solutions that buttress grid capabilities, while offering energy independence when electricity prices, lack of grid or renewable energy resources, or utility/weather emergency demand it. And as flexible energy consumers, data centers represent new opportunity to manage fluctuation in renewable generation as it comes online in the grid.

Industry partnerships may also help to drive decarbonization. In Europe, for example, GreenDataNet is an optimization solution that mixes solar panels and batteries to supply urban data centers, while the EU's RenewIT program, which aims to have data centers source 80% of their power from renewables, offers a simulation tool that enables operators to select the best combination of efficiency measures and renewable technologies to improve energy consumption and carbon profile in several European climate regions. For ecosystem partners, as for individual data center operators, 'green bits' will have a huge impact on the industry's ability to build a more sustainable future.

For individual operators, there are multiple pathways to energy maturity, and a number of questions that must be addressed in planning for the integration of green energy solutions. What are the data center's reliability and resiliency requirements? What kind of IT load will the data center need to support? What role are renewables expected to play; will they serve as primary, complementary, or backup sources of energy, and do they address a specific use case? What renewable resources can be accessed remotely, or locally, based on climate, available know how, and existing infrastructure? How big is the facility, and how must the data center work with the grid?

The model transition to energy maturity is a three-part process consisting of buy, match, and build onsite. But each data center will answer these questions in their own way, based on a unique set of circumstances, and will likely combine a number of strategies at different times at individual sites or across the portfolio. The guidance that follows is designed to help operators weigh the advantages of various approaches as they work to ensure that green energy strategy delivers carbon benefit and additional value to the data center.

- **Purchase of clean energy through RECs and PPAs** is often the most direct route to achieving sustainability goals, but buying at scale may prove challenging. Contracting PPAs is a complicated legal and logistical task that is now available only to the largest buyer. Until providers templatize this process with an "easy button" for sign up on a self-serve portal, consider partnering with an experienced broker who can help track progress on clean energy purchases.

- **Connect renewable purchases with consumption** by matching all electricity used with clean energy sourcing for the same period. To support the grid and improve the facility's scope two emissions, time physical electricity consumption to when the energy supply is the most green – or shift compute load to a time when there would otherwise be little demand for renewable resources. The ultimate goal is near real time, carbon-aware energy consumption achieved through matching or the combination of clean energy purchases and energy storage technologies.
- **Location matters!** Due diligence on the local regulatory environment may uncover tax credits for renewable installations. Site the data center near renewable sources where market conditions allow. Generate low-carbon loads onsite that can build value through the creation of RECs, or the sale of surplus energy back to the utility grid.
- **Define the use case for green energy integration to identify the right resource.** Data centers may access green energy as the primary power source, to fill a gap, to address issues with base power, or for backup. For example, Microsoft chose to integrate grid interactive features in architectural design by utilizing batteries inside the UPS for data center backup and grid services. Deploying fuel cells to power the data center or grid in times of emergency is a sort of solution designed for different backup needs.

- **Access multiple solutions.** Develop a range of clean energy solutions that may apply across a data center portfolio, or combine different resources through technology-enabled solutions such as microgrid. Energy storage is a critical input to this planning that must be considered up front to enable the integration of renewables that can deliver controllable, uninterruptible power load.
- **Speed matters!** Natural pairings, such as the use of microgrids with interim "bridge" fuel solutions, or the direct connection to an existing carbon-free power generation source like a nuclear plant or renewable energy/storage installation can deliver rapid results. The compounding effect of quick deployment and the avoidance of carbon spent during a lengthy build process translates to additional carbon emissions benefits. The potential to quickly transition to next steps, such as the refueling of natural gas fuel cells with hydrogen, reinforce the value in immediate action.
- **Accept incremental change, but document it in a strategic plan.** Data centers are unlikely to consume 100% renewable capacity from day one, but through partnerships with the right developers, who can identify the best mix of resources for specific data use cases, may build and intensify emissions reduction impact. In this effort, outline specific steps, set achievement milestones, and track progress to document the success of your clean energy program.

---

1. Announcing the creation in 2021 of a global roadmap to effect rapid energy transformation, UN Secretary-General António Guterres pointed to energy as the critical input to the Paris Agreement goals.
   UN Secretary-General issues new global roadmap to secure clean energy access for all by 2030 and net zero emissions by 2050. https://www.un.org/en/hlde-2021/page/global-roadmap-press-release
2. Excluding energy to service crypto demand.

IEA. Data Centres and Data Transmission Networks, 2022. https://www.iea.org/reports/data-centres-and-data-transmission-networks
3. Ibid.
4. Josh Mahan. Understanding Data Center Energy Consumption. C&C Technology Group. June 2023.
5. World's Leading Data Center and Cloud Operators with Zero Carbon Goals. Sunbird.
6. Addendum to the synthesis report for the technical assessment component of the first global stock take. UN Framework Convention on Climate Change. April 17, 2023. GST_SR_23c_Addendum_Final_02230417.pdf (unfccc.int)
7. For a more detailed discussion, see Measure to Manage: Sustainability Metrics and Reporting in Data Center Networks. Greener Data Impact report from JSA. 2023..
8. Microsoft 2022 Environmental Sustainability Report. p. 12, 20. https://www.microsoft.com/en-us/corporate-responsibility/sustainability/report?ICID=SustainabilityReport22_MOI-ESblog
9. IRENA. Renewable Power Generation Costs in 2020, International Renewable Energy Agency, 2021, Abu Dhabi.
10. Nooreddeen Albokhari. Electricity: Nuclear vs. Fossil. Stanford University 2017.
11. Amazon remains largest corporate purchaser of renewable energy. Daily Energy Insider.
12. Microsoft 2022 Environmental Sustainability Report.
13. Ivy Pepin. Keeping the balance: How flexible nuclear operation can help add more wind and solar to the grid. MIT News. April 2018. https://news.mit.edu/2018/flexible-nuclear-operation-can-help-add-more-wind-and-solar-to-the-grid-0425
14. Amrita Khalid. Microsoft and Amazon reportedly halt plans to build data centers in Ireland. Endgadget, August 2022.
15. [12] Janne Paananen and Eshsan Nasr. Grid-interactive data centers: enabling decarbonization and system stability. An Eaton Microsoft White Paper. 2021
16. Caroline O'Donovan. Amazon, despite climate pledge, fought to kill emissions bill in Oregon. The Washington Post. April 2023. Amazon tried to kill emissions bill in Oregon despite climate pledge - The Washington Post
17. Reza Ahmadi Kordkheil et al. On-site Power Generation for Data Centers. Integrating Data Centers with Low Carbon Energy Assets. SDIA.2021.
18. Ibid, p. 8.
19. Bill St. Arnaud. Former Chief Research Officer, The CANARIE Network. https://www.canarie.ca
20. "Deep, rapid and sustained mitigation and accelerated implementation of adaptation actions in this decade would reduce projected losses and damages for humans and ecosystems (*very high confidence*), and deliver many co-benefits, especially for air quality and health (high confidence). Delayed mitigation and adaptation action would lock-in high-emissions infrastructure, raise risks of stranded assets and cost-escalation, reduce feasibility, and increase losses and damages (*high confidence*)."
 IPCC. AR6 Synthesis Report. https://www.ipcc.ch/report/ar6/syr/
21. SIDA.
22. EdgeConneX and Gridmatic. A Practical Approach to Implementing 24/7 Carbon-Free Energy for a Data Center. October 2022. ECX-GM_247CFE-

NE_Whitepaper_10-22(1).pdf

In another example, Microsoft has committed to having 100% of energy consumption matched by zero carbon energy purchases 100% of the time by 2030.

Made to measure: Sustainability commitment progress and updates - The Official Microsoft Blog

23. Rostirolla, p. 2.
24. SIDA, p. 4.
25. David Chernicoff. Nuclear-Powered Data Centers: Modular Reactors on the Horizon. Data Center Frontier. March 2023.
26. Enchanted Rock to Develop California's Largest Renewable Microgrid to Ensure Resiliency of Microsoft Data Center. Enchanted Rock. June 2022.
27. Peter Gross. Data centers and fuel cells. Datacenter Dynamics. February 2023.
28. US Department of Energy. Hydrogen Fuel Basics. https://www.energy.gov/eere/fuelcells/hydrogen-fuel-basics#:~:text=Today%2C%20hydrogen%20fuel%20can%20be,solar%2Ddriven%20and%20biological%20processes.
29. John Roach. Hydrogen fuel cells could provide emission free backup at datacenters, Microsoft says. July 2022.

About the Authors

Mary Allen is CCO at InsightaaS and Sustainability Lead for JSA. As journalist, analyst, and content strategist, she has covered the range of IT subjects for her own properties, and on behalf of clients. Mary created the GreenerIT and Sustainability Platform websites, capping this with a stint as sustainability columnist for Bloomberg BNA, to promote the environmental agenda within IT. She continues this work in partnership with JSA on the Greener Data initiative.

Jeffrey Barber is an experienced sales leader who boasts over two decades worth of experience with leading companies in the data center space. He has developed expertise across the entire storage stack, and is currently contributing to standards development in NVMe. Jeff now serves as VP, Global Data Center Sales at Bloom Energy, where he focuses on helping clients take control of all their data center power needs with greener, more reliable, more resilient, and more predictable onsite fuel.

Michael Donohue is an electrical power industry expert with 15 years of experience in marketing/commodity trading, risk management, generation dispatch for leading energy suppliers. As Managing Director for Cumulus Data, he works to promote the adoption of carbon-free nuclear data in data center operations. His current project is Cumulus Data's digital campus outside Berwick, Pennsylvania, which will be directly connected and powered by Talen Energy's Susquehanna nuclear generating facility.

Brian Jabeck is an onsite generation and resiliency expert who has built his professional career as a business leader focused on sales and marketing of energy and power generation solutions for data centers. As VP of Sales for Enchanted Rock, he leverages deep knowledge of the North American and European markets for mission critical and demand response applications utilizing natural gas microgrid solutions, helping data centers adopt cleaner onsite power generation to benefit the local grid and community.

Ehsan Nasr has applied his PhD in Electrical and Electronics Engineering from the University of Waterloo to ongoing research in power systems management for Smart Grid and the data center. With demonstrated skill in mathematical modeling, AI, and control systems design, he has led projects in distributed generation for the large grid and microgrids, and for the renewables/environment industry. Ehsan currently works for Microsoft as a Lead Scientist with the Datacenter Advance Development Team, devoted to developing and managing new energy technologies for the data center.

With advanced degrees in Mechanical Engineering, **Dr. Anand Ramesh** boasts a distinguished career in process development, NPI, computer-aided engineering, power distribution for grid and microgrid, storage, and mobility platforms. At Google, he was responsible for sourcing and architecting the provider's data center technology portfolio; projects included a rethink of standby power infrastructure focusing on ROI improvement and sustainability through use of zero carbon solutions. Anand has brought this broad experience to EdgeConneX, where he now acts as SVP, Advanced Technology.

Sindhu Sharma has combined business management and electronics training with focus on finance and energy in a career that spans projects in Smart Grid communications, prospects for solar installation in India, and the deployment of 150 MW of solar across Southeast Asia and Africa. He now serves as Head of ESG at Nxtra by Airtel, where he is responsible for driving strategy, planning and development of renewable energy sourcing aimed at achieving maximum utilization of green energy across all company data centers.

NINE

The Future of Data Centers - Absolute Zero

Susanna Kass, InfraPrime

With contributions from Dr. Alberto Ravagni

Clean Energy Powering the Future of Data Centers

Through my journey as a clean energy strategist for the data center ICT sector, I have fought for what I believe in and what the United Nations Sustainable Development Goals (SDGs) Environmental Program stands for: a carbon-free future within our generation, which is a cause of paramount importance. While the planet itself is resilient, humans are rapidly depleting our natural ecosystems in a linear economy model that dictates "grab, use, and toss." We must act now to pave the way for future generations of people, and to lead in ways that make each moment count. For our industry, the way forward is clear — through transition to Absolute Zero.

In the data center world, action revolves around energy — power is critical to operations and key to our efforts to improve the sector's environmental footprint. As a sector, data centers are exiting fossil fuels and engaged in a just transition to the clean energy economy. The adoption of renewable energy and energy storage is based on a breakthrough transformation in economics within the energy industry, which can now fulfill its promise to power the next generation of net zero data centers with affordable, clean energy.

Today, the hyperscale cloud providers are leading the way with renewable energy power purchase procurement that no other industry has achieved in the past three decades; AWS, Microsoft Azure, Google Cloud, Meta-Facebook, and Apple are each responding to clean energy requirements with massive gigawatt scale renewable energy purchases. As they track energy and report capacity needs in annual ESG statements, large data centers typically use Power Purchase Agreements (PPAs) as proof that they are meeting emissions reduction targets outlined in carbon neutrality pledges. This information is incorporated in aggregate views of the renewable industry. As the CEBA figure below shows, since 2014, corporate customers have purchased 64+ gigawatts of renewable energy, and 2023 was a banner year in terms of new activity, with a strong momentum continuing into 2024. Clean, renewable energy development projects offer pathways toward a carbon-free economy future, as they drive green jobs, economic growth, clean tech investments and greening the grid.

Figure 1: Renewable Energy (wind and solar PV) projects.

Figure 2: Renewable Energy projects with hydrogen storage

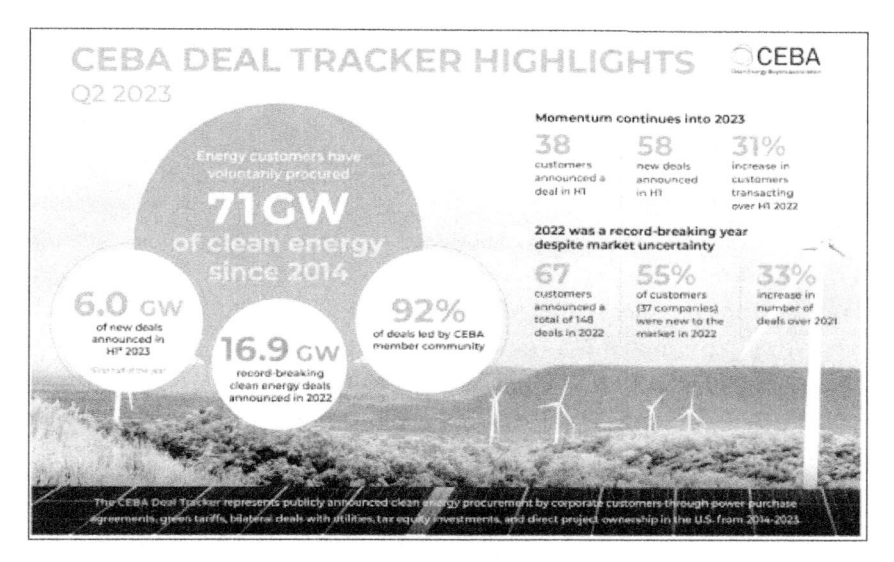

Source: CEBA Figure 3 Renewable Energy Deal Tracker

Meeting Power Availability Challenges in the Future of Data Centers

The data center industry is driven by electrical power. Currently, there is keen awareness of a lack of power availability in some regions, pressure to meet time of market requirements, and recognition of the need for access to a renewable energy supply to power data centers throughout the lifecycle and in the supply chain. At the same time, Artificial Intelligence (AI) technologies are causing a paradigm shift in advanced and sustainable computing, specifically using higher-density GPUs for Generative Pre-Trained Transformer (GPT) multi-modal, multi-domain computing models. AI technologies have demonstrated the ability to improve the accuracy of renewable energy generation to match consumption with clean energy sources by data centers. Conventional cloud computing is expected to embed AI technologies for productivity optimization that promises new scientific breakthroughs.

But this AI functionality comes at a price. With AI adoption, energy demand is expected to rise significantly. Numerous market studies; Gartner, Mission Critical Magazine, Data Center Magazine projected that AI will at the least triple the capacity demand for data centers within three to six years, as the industry's overall energy use soars to high heights.

Net-Zero Data Centers Support a Greener Grid

The hyperscale providers are pioneers on the renewable energy front. Over the past three decades, they have established a track record of driving the procurement of gigawatt-scale renewable energy projects. The additionality of their renewable energy projects has ignited the development of the green grid on a global scale. In addition, net zero data center designs based on clean on-premise energy generation can provide further support for the grid by offering backup power. When integrated with an energy storage function, on-premise renewable energy can act as a power grid stabilizer. At a time when renewable energies are entering into the power grid mix, mass frequency stabilizing mechanisms are essential. With megawatt scale baseloads, hyperscale data centers can operate continuously without connecting to the grid; net-zero architectures are designed to achieve resiliency with 99.99999% uptime performance. Net-zero data center designs deliver value by enabling operators to reach 100% green electrons, 100% of the time to meet carbon neutrality goals independent of green energy that may be accessed via the grid. Since the grid can be used as a reliable backup system, the expense and use of standby idle assets is alleviated, and diesel generators and other costly CapEx assets that are idle can be eliminated.

The Future of Data Centers - Bring Your Own Power (BYOP)

The Future of Data Centers is a new concept that allows the data center to act not only as an energy consumer, instead to become a contributor through continued leadership in gigawatt-scale renewable energy procurement and in clean energy investments, as a key enabler of the transition to green grids on a global basis. Based on reporting of time-matched clean energy consumption, the hyperscale data centers are transparent on their carbon neutrality results, and their ability to bring on-premise clean energy generation to supplement the grid with carbon-free sources of power. An increasing number of power utilities are making public the challenges involved in meeting current data center power demands and the anticipated growth in demand due to the rapid adoption of AI — let alone meeting this need with green energy. In recent years, rack power densities in data centers have grown substantially. Uptime Institute numbers from just over a decade ago put the average power densities per rack in the 4–5 kW range. By 2020, that was up to 8–10 kW per rack. Note, though, that two-thirds of U.S. data centers surveyed said that they were already experiencing peak demands in the 16–20 kW per rack range. The latest numbers from 2022 show 10% of data centers reporting rack densities of 20–29 kW per rack, 7% at 30–39 kW per rack, 3% at 40–49 kW per rack and 5% at 50 kW or greater.[1]

The new design for the *Future of Data Centers* includes BYOP when a new build is commissioned, with energy storage as a key element. While mainstream renewables (wind and solar PV) can introduce power density and intermittency challenges to conventional data center operation, if needed, onsite energy storage with lithium-ion batteries can deliver up to 4–6 hours of backup to address shortages.

Chapter Nine

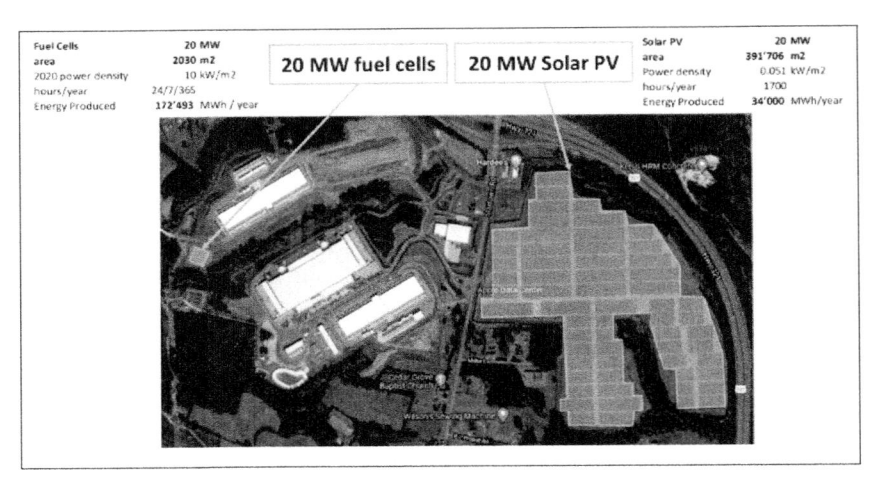

Figure 4: Onsite carbon-free energy sources comparison: fuel cells provide controllable, 24/7 energy, clean energy with hydrogen/ammonia RNG, generate 5x energy of 20 MW of solar PV, using193 times less land, fulfilling the requirement for onsite clean power generation. Source: InfraPrime

Deploying on-premise clean generation extends grid power to a grid that is not green 24/7. Green molecules in new energy storage technologies have energy densities that are substantially higher than traditional batteries, enabling longer-term operation without grid connection — or better grid support. Fuel cells (gas batteries) can be used for prime and backup power of clean energy generation. Technologies using green molecules and green electrons (produced by renewables), can play an important role in the *Future of Data Centers*, as the Apple Data Center illustration above shows.

Enter Absolute Zero

Absolute Zero is the most ambitious target set for the data center industry to date.

While net zero in the data center often relies on the use of offsets and/or use of on-premise clean energy generation with storage (grid is not green 24/7), Absolute Zero is achieved by eliminating carbon emissions from data center operations and physically removing the greenhouse gases (GHGs) from the atmosphere. With

Chapter Nine

Absolute Zero, no release of GHG emissions to the atmosphere can be physically verified. (Absolute Zero is a necessary term; there are no scenarios where there are no unavoidable emissions, hence "Zero" cannot be used.) Data centers can remove emissions through carbon removal processes during operation and in the supply chain to become carbon neutral; when the data center removes more carbon emissions than it emits, it is called carbon negative.

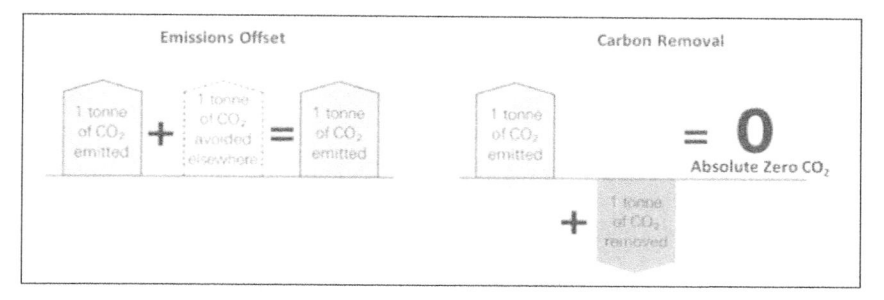

Figure 5: Comparison emission offsets versus Absolute Zero with emission removal. Source: Swiss Re, InfraPrime adapted

Absolute Zero – 24/7 Time-Matched Carbon-Free Energy Usage

With carbon-free energy sources in local grids, it is possible to utilize renewable energy sources – wind, solar PV, hydro-electricity — 100% of the time across different regions where data centers operate. Google and Microsoft have enabled their data centers to become more sustainable through hourly energy monitoring and matching with carbon-free sources from their clean-energy portfolios. Google's Time-based Energy Attribute Certificates, for example, have enabled data centers to be 90% carbon-free on an hourly basis, up from 61% in 2020. Their target is to achieve 100% 24/7 clean energy by 2030.[2] The 24/7 CFE efforts are designed to maximize Google's contribution to the decarbonization of power grids worldwide, a part of industry efforts that are coordinated in organi-

Chapter Nine

zations such as the United Nations' 24/7 Carbon-Free Energy Compact.

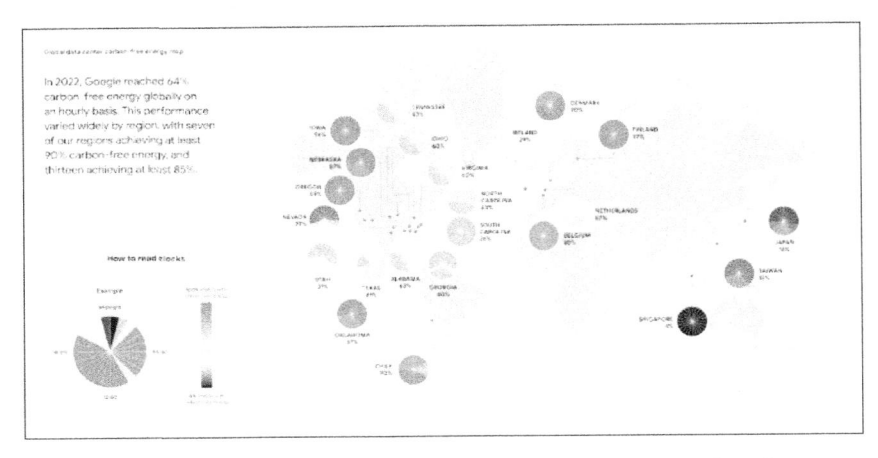

Figure 6: Global data center 24/7 carbon free energy map - Google. Source: "24/7 Carbon-Free Energy by 2030." Google. https://www.google.com/about/datacenters/cleanenergy/

Absolute Zero – 24/7 On-Premise, Carbon-Free Energy Generation

Data centers traditionally rely on UPS, batteries, and backup generators, which typically burn diesel, or other fossil-based fuels, causing carbon emissions to be released into the atmosphere.

Through the award-winning STARK architecture, which features zero downtime performance throughout its operations and duration, InfraPrime has collaborated with Microsoft to launch a megawatt-scale Absolute Zero resilient modular power system suited for on-premise carbon free primary and backup power systems using fuel cells. *The Future of Data Centers* are future proof; they enable the transition to carbon neutrality by achieving 24/7 carbon-free energy (CFE) with 99.9999999% uptime reliability, while simultaneously operating 24/7 on-premise power generation for clean energy primary and backup power.

Fuel cells are gas batteries that convert gaseous fuels into power and heat, operate without combustion, noise, or vibrations, and use traditional and renewable fuels such as biogas, hydrogen, renewable natural gas and ammonia. The system cooperates in reversible modes — from gas-to-power and power-to-gas mode — to enable the long-term storage of renewable energies, making intermittent renewable energies controllable and dispatchable.

Furthermore, Absolute Design is achieved as solid oxide fuel cells (SOFC) separate the carbon emissions, capture them in the process, and store emissions without releasing them into the atmosphere until the CO_2 can be reused. Data centers can transition to the carbon-free economy, and even negative carbon power generation, by choosing fuel sources that are not a fossil fuel.

InfraPrime and Microsoft are clean energy pioneers. Microsoft started to use fuel cell technology a decade ago. In 2013, they worked with the National Fuel Cell Research Center at the University of California, Irvine, to test the idea of powering server racks with SOFC systems for 24/7 on-premise prime power generation, created by InfraPrime co-founder.

The project was a success. It is an innovative design for the data center industry, earning Microsoft a prestigious DCD award for Mission Critical Power Innovation Design. In 2017 Microsoft inaugurated its own Advanced Energy Lab with a cable-cutting ceremony pictured below. The system has experienced no downtime performance, does not use grid power, and operates in island mode 24/7.

Chapter Nine

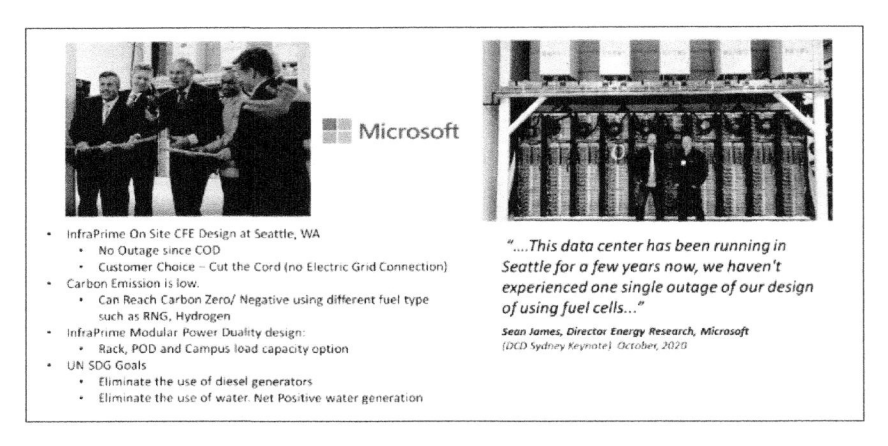

- InfraPrime On Site CFE Design at Seattle, WA
  - No Outage since COD
  - Customer Choice – Cut the Cord (no Electric Grid Connection)
- Carbon Emission is low.
  - Can Reach Carbon Zero/ Negative using different fuel type such as RNG, Hydrogen
- InfraPrime Modular Power Duality design:
  - Rack, POD and Campus load capacity option
- UN SDG Goals
  - Eliminate the use of diesel generators
  - Eliminate the use of water. Net Positive water generation

"....This data center has been running in Seattle for a few years now, we haven't experienced one single outage of our design of using fuel cells..."

Sean James, Director Energy Research, Microsoft
(DCD Sydney Keynote) October, 2020

Figure 7: Microsoft Advanced Energy Lab, powering server racks with SOFC fuel cells systems for 24/7 on premise prime power generation. Source: Christian Belady & Sean James. "Redesigning Datacenters for an Advanced Energy Future." Microsoft Green Blog. Sept 24, 2017.

This "Stark and Simple" architecture demonstrated superior energy efficiency and systems reliability without grid connection, and without the use of traditional backup diesel generators.

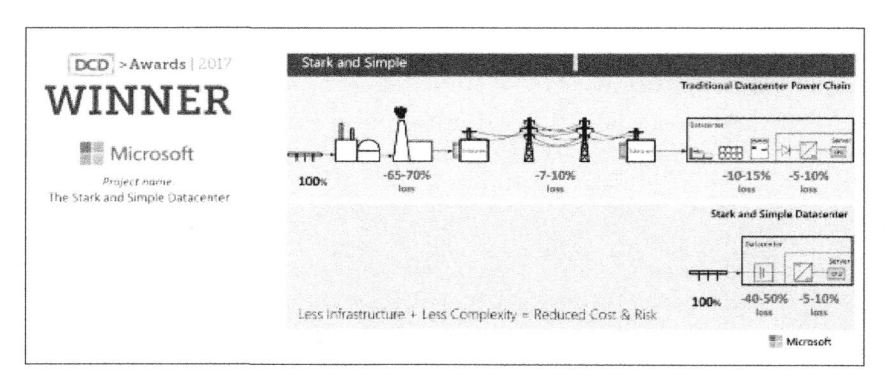

Figure 8: comparison of the primary power delivery efficiency between the traditional centralized power generation and the on-premise prime power generation with fuel cells. Source: Christian Belady & Sean James. "Redesigning Datacenters for an Advanced Energy Future." Microsoft Green Blog. Sept 24, 2017.

In 2018, Mark Monroe and Sean James from the Microsoft Advanced Data Center Energy Labs achieved another milestone, a

Chapter Nine

moonshot moment by introducing the use of Polymer Electrolyte Membrane (PEM) fuel cells to replace the backup diesel generator. PEM fuel cells are commonly used in the automotive industry because, like diesel engines, they are quick to turn on and off, and can follow a load cycle. The fast reaction and load-following capabilities are well suited to backup power needs at data centers; the project included the development of hydrogen safety protocols for the next generation of data center design.

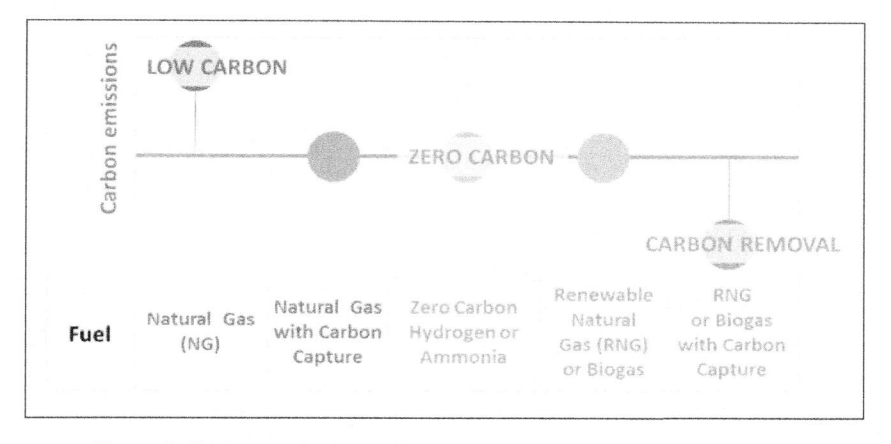

Figure 9: Carbon emissions of on-prem power generation depending on the fuel used. Source: InfraPrime.

Drawing upon InfraPrime co-founder's modular data center invention, InfraPrime has also developed a zero-design modular architecture that can integrate power generation technologies utilizing different fuels at scale. When green fuels, green molecules like biogas, hydrogen, ammonia, and renewable natural gas are used as energy input, the generated power has a zero carbon and negative carbon content. The capacity of a single fuel cell generator ranges from 60–240kW, the capacity of a fuel cell is at 1 megawatt in one module or it can be customized to hundreds of megawatt module. The system is ideal for AI to the edge builds and colo data center deployments. BYOP and megawatt clean energy generation modules add capacity to future proof The Future of Data Center AI factories and

Chapter Nine

support the continued growth of hyperscaler cloud data center deployments.

The architecture of the Absolute Zero data center is proven in its efficiency, functions well with microgrids, which delivers resilient, reliable, affordable carbon-free energy to the data center and grid resilience services to the community.

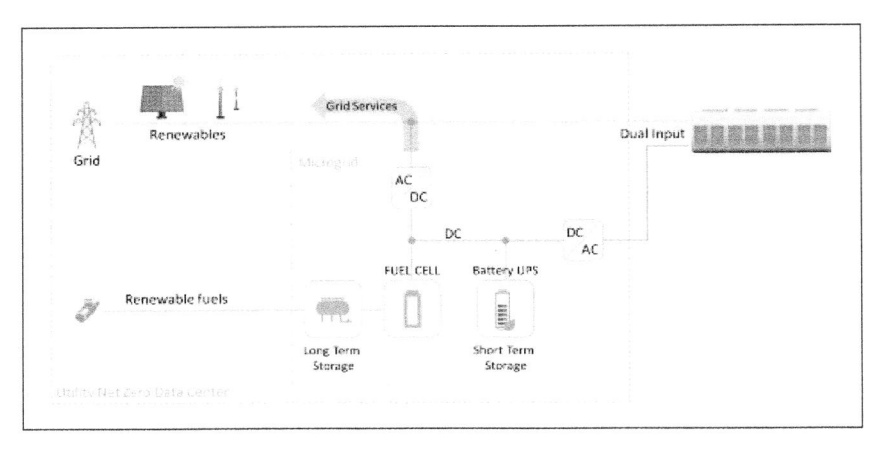

Figure 10: The Future of Data Center integrates grid-scale and on prem power generation and energy storage technologies, green electrons, and green molecules. Source: InfraPrime.

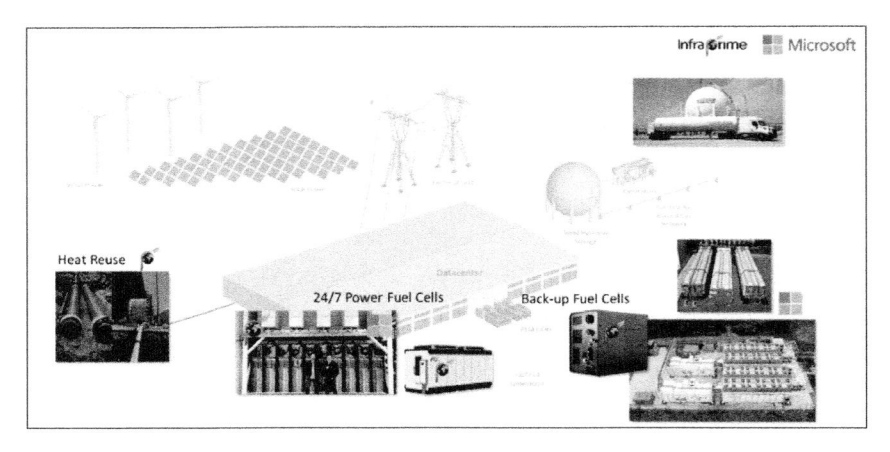

Figure 11: The data center of the future on premise wih grid-integrated power generation for back-up, 24/7 carbon free power generation and heat reuse. Source: InfraPrime.

The Future of Data Centers - Utility Net-Zero Availability Zones

The Future of Data Centers is a contributor to green the grid; it becomes grid interactive to ensure cloud and AI services add green energy generation to the grid, use the grid as backup power source; both systems are resilient, sustainable and affordable, and in so doing, future proofs their growth potential. The result is a triple bottom line of much lower CapEx for redundant assets, much higher utilization through multiple uses of common assets (ex. energy infrastructure), maximized investment efficiency for renewable power investments, clean energy generation, the elimination of the need for backup assets — and Absolute Zero with zero carbon content.

In this new model, data centers transition from an energy customer to a contributor to the local grid. When data center and utility grid operators each contribute to clean energy generation, a green grid is made possible.

The design concept of Availability Zones, which originated in the data center sector, may be applied to the utility grid. The electric grid assets operate to maximize power availability for all stakeholders to reach the full potential of power availability and concurrently, deliver cost efficiency at utility scale at Utility Net Zero Availability Zones by regions for each Energy Market.

Chapter Nine

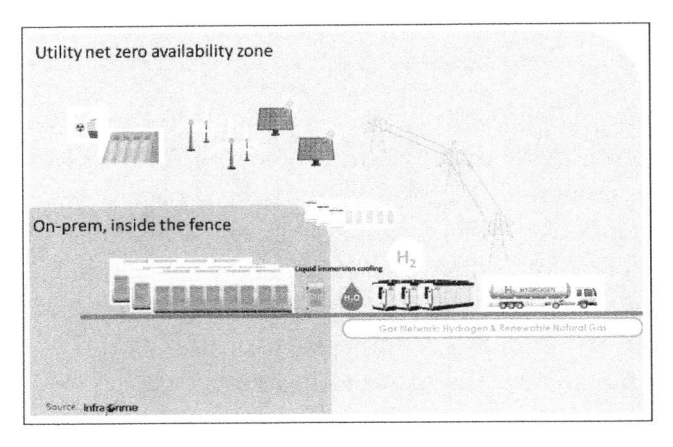

Figure 12: Zero design architecture of Utility Availability Zones

In an Availability Zone design, each zone operates to maintain resiliency. Utility Net Zero Availability Zones are designed with grid-interactive services for uptime performance to support hyperscalers' Service Level Agreements (SLAs). They are also designed to reliably power hyperscalers' mission-critical business operations, to enable load orchestration to shed data center load, to efficiently share resources to maintain data center resiliency, and to simultaneously maintain 99.99999–99.999999999% uptime performance. Both contributors — data center and grid — forecast demand, share resources, collaborate to shorten the time to resume normal operations from natural disasters or climate change events, and make continuous improvements through shared knowledge and technological grid resilience innovation across the region.

Utility Net Zero Availability Zones is an integral goal of the InfraPrime Absolute Zero design, aim to achieve net zero with clean energy development, produces economic returns for data centers' renewable energy investments, optimize time-matched carbon-free energy consumption monitoring and on-premise clean energy generation backup power, carbon dioxide removal solutions which all work interactively to green the grid to deliver net positive impact results of triple bottom line.

Chapter Nine

The Future of Data Centers - Circular Ecosystem Lifecycle

The Future of the Data Centers will take advantage of a circular ecosystem. The life cycle phases of data centers adhere to ISO 14040 and ISO 14044, which accounts for the environmental impact of different activities throughout the life cycle:

- Depletion of raw materials
- Process for manufacturing materials, products and construction
- Transport of materials to site(s)
- Consumption of materials, from operation throughout commissioning
- Decommissioning data centers and end-of-life materials

The Future of Data Centers consumes resources throughout its lifecycle and shares a symbiotic relationship in resources with the environment and the communities.

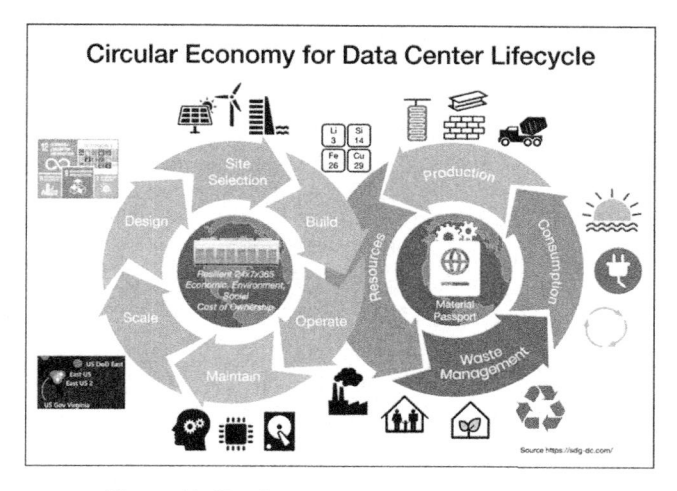

Figure 13: The Future of Data Centers circular ecosystem, adhering to the life cycle phases of ISO 14040 and ISO 14044. Source: InfraPrime.

Chapter Nine

The Future of Data Centers - Emission Reuse System

The Future of Data Centers looks to achieve a symbiotic relationship between the electric grid and the society of communities it serves. Each data center consumes massive energy, generating excess heat from compute servers. Millions of dollars are spent every year on power for the servers and to operate the cooling technologies needed to cool them. But it is possible to alleviate heat waste and emissions into the environment. In fact, the European Commission has enacted legislation that imposes heat recovery as a mandatory requirement for the building of new data centers.

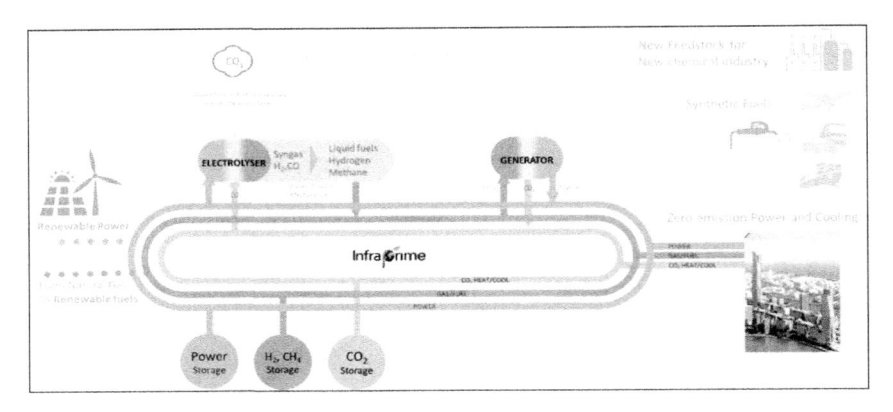

Figure 14: InfraPrime multi-energy zero architecture, integrating power and gas grids. The CO2 emission reuse network system provides Absolute Zero energy to the community. Source: InfraPrime.

InfraPrime as a clean energy pioneer, its net zero architecture extends beyond power to include heat energy. It has developed an innovative emission reuse network system using CO_2 emissions as a medium to transfer heat waste captured from the data centers to provide district heating and cooling services to communities. The system can save millions of dollars in energy expenses for the data centers and communities, while also reducing the use of grid power by the communities; instead become off-takers of data center heat energy.

Susanna is an academic lecturer on Urban Sustainability

Chapter Nine

Design, she and her students' research found circular CO_2 emission system fits well to facilitate off-takers at academic institutions, retailers, and businesses where the future of AI edge data centers are located. The use of CO_2 (R744) is considered a natural refrigerant and is rapidly being adopted for cooling in commercial, industrial and transportation applications. It has an Ozone Depleting Potential (ODP) of 0 and a Global Warming Potential (GWP) of 1. It uses no water and is more efficient than a traditional water system. As a thermal carrier, CO_2 transports eight times more energy per kg than water. It uses standard equipment and smaller, flexible pipes, resulting in at least 60% cost savings in installation time and equipment cost, and requires no unique skills for construction or operations.

In *The Future of Data Centers* circular ecosystem, heat regeneration is a standard operation.

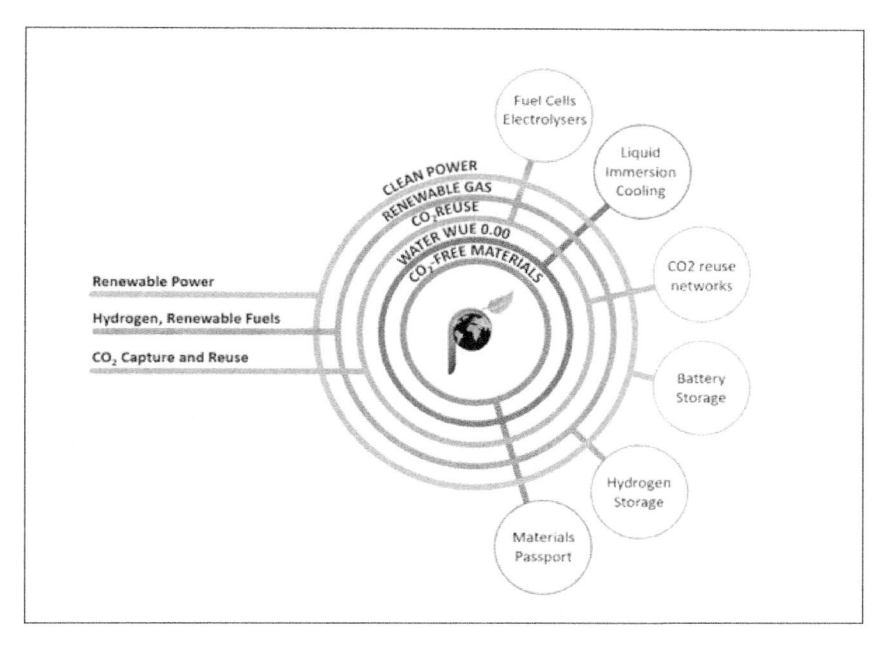

Figure 15: InfraPrime Absolute Zero pathway, zero carbon, zero emission, zero water, zero waste, zero embodied carbon materials

Chapter Nine

Absolute Zero - Leading Sustainability Innovation

Absolute Zero architecture provides the blueprint for a holistic approach to sustainable computing. *The Future of Data Centers* will be deployed with a full stack comprised of hardware, software, networking, and data storage systems and interfaces to support compute capacity needs, even in the case of AI factories running high-density GPUs. While it has huge potential to be used for social good — to optimize clean grid operation or to model different climate change scenarios — AI is a disruptive megatrend. AI has proven it has escalated the power demand growth and has the potential to jeopardize the energy infrastructure. In the future, it will continue to be a disruptor as well as the progress of digital transformation.

Absolute Zero promises a sustainable lifestyle for the energy and data center sectors that enables a just transition to the use of carbon-free energy sources (100% green electrons, 100% of the time), allowing data centers to reach their full potential for carbon neutrality, while simultaneously greening the grid and transitioning captured emissions to new value for the communities.

The climate-positive features of an Absolute Zero data center include:

- Resilience (anticipate, adapt, resolve, resume) at normal operation measured by zero downtime of the data center lifecycle; delivering on results with the most affordable, time-to-market advantage with 100% of electrons, 100% of the time delivered from clean energy sources for on-premise facilities on a global scale.
- Reduce (capture, store, eliminate, reuse) emissions at gigatons scale across digital infrastructure; design for responsible consumption and generation of energy in a circular system, build and operate with measurable results.
- Effectiveness (performance, sovereignty, security) of technologies is deployed for breakthrough results and the

use of good science and evidence-based framework for accuracy and consistency; machine learning is the foundation model used by leading scientists and data center experts that is improved by humans to integrate AI into best-in-class sustainability practices; this step includes optimization for resource usage effectiveness and achievements on a carbon density index.

The Future of Data Centers and AI DC

The Future of Data Centers is a circular ecosystem that achieves Absolute Zero results, operating at all times using clean energy sources, as it regenerates heat and electronics waste to create new value for communities and to the environment. The impact is measured by its ability to:

- Improve social access to renewable power generation through the additionality of renewable energy project developments. This will green the grid and support renewable energy project investment.
- Increase the resiliency of the local grid and ignite Utility Net Zero Availability Zone in regions across nationwide energy markets to achieve SLA uptime performance, with data center and grid operators as co-contributors.
- Eliminate massive heat waste to the environment and reduce millions in energy costs and millions of tons of emissions by regenerating district heating (and cooling services) for local businesses and communities, and through emission reuse systems for heat waste and carbon capture technologies.
- Optimize productivity improvements and efficiency breakthroughs with AI technologies for renewable energy generation to green the grid.
- Increase the accuracy of time match clean energy consumption.

- Enable new capabilities; including nowcasting of grid interactivity, complex weather mitigations and climate change simulations.
- Through Generative AI (GAI), radically transform visualization of Absolute Zero reporting and clean energy data impact analysis.

Aligning Sustainable Compute Capacity with Sovereign Policy Strategies

To ensure a just energy transition in the industry, sustainability leadership in the data center sector actively works with climate scientists, policy makers, regulatory governments, developers, grid operators, energy service providers, and digital infrastructure investors to meet the clients' requirements. The UN SDGs Environmental program, climate experts, and researchers at the Intergovernmental Panel on Climate Change (IPCC) can help influence the creation of effective environmental policies and economic models that can align sustainability policy with national clean energy standards and craft policy guidance on AI Nations. These discussions are not exhaustive, and they vary according to national contexts and needs, but they are the outcome of extensive work on evidence-based frameworks compiled by expert group members and exemplify a science-based approach to systematically measuring and planning sustainable computing for the current AI needs and the future of the Digital Envoy.

Each government's AI technical envoy is considering an AI Factory to protect its national investments related to AI policy objectives, including public-sector budget, national allocations, and private-sector investments. Policy is needed to shape and advance sovereign AI plans that will be increasingly critical to economic growth, cutting-edge science, national-scale resilience to natural disasters and to embracing the country's AI context as an ecosystem. Such an approach is strategic, as it includes the use of AI investments and partnerships with the Nvidia AI Nations leadership team to develop sovereignty amongst AI providers. Policymakers can consider how public- and private-sector investments provide *The*

Chapter Nine

Future of Data Centers AI computing capacity and how they can advance distinct types of AI policy objectives for their countries. Scaling out AI-enabled sustainability computing can future-proof investments and enable national agility and growth at scale. The scaling out approach is proven and commonly seen in countries where multiple inference data centers are being installed and replicated as AI to the Edge Availability Zone(s) that broaden access with the continued growth of Generative AI and ignited by the AI personalization digital assistant devices.

> "With Absolute Zero, we in the data center industry become the guardians for future generations that come behind us, so that they too can make the responsible choices that will shape the future of data centers." Susanna Kass

---

1. "Uptime Institute Global Data Center Survey 2022". Uptime Institute. https://uptimeinstitute.com/uptime_assets/6768e-ca6a75d792c8eeede827d76de0d0380dee6b5ced20fde45787dd3688bfe-2022-data-center-industry-survey-en.pdf
2. Texier, Maud. "A timely new approach to certifying clean energy". Google Blog. March 1, 2021. https://cloud.google.com/blog/topics/sustainability/t-eacs-offer-new-approach-to-certifying-clean-energy

About the Author

SUSANNA KASS

Susanna Kass is Co-founder and BOD at InfraPrime. Currently, she is Operating Partner, Digital Gravity Infrastructure Partners, focus on discovering AI technology to accelerate performance, energy efficiency, for sustainability investments. Susanna is also a Board member at Stanford University Graduate Management Board (GMB) Women's Circle, a data center advisor to the UNSDG Programme, a lecturer on Urban Sustainability Design at Stanford University, Cornell University, National University of Singapore, DTU, UCLA, UC Berkeley and SDSU, a researcher at CE4A and a Climate 50-member of the topmost Climate Change global leaders, an inventor with clean energy patents. Susanna was COO for eBay International, held 33 years of executive roles in data center global business, managed innovation and sustainability operations at HP, Sun, NextEra Energy, and Baselayer. She has led over 3.8 GW of renewable power contracts and clean energy project with clients including Google, Meta Facebook, Microsoft, Equinix, Goldman Sachs, Amazon, Apple, Akamai, John Hopkins University, Stanford University and Walmart that use clean energy, Net Zero design for site selection, and 24/7 zero carbon energy build and operations. Her passion is leading a Carbon Free Economy.

TEN

Zero-Carbon Future: How Data Centers are Leading Innovation

Raj Chudgar, EdgeConneX

How much electricity do data centers use around the world? The International Energy Agency reports that data centers used between 240 – 340 TWh of electricity in 2022[1]. Even with that margin for error, these figures give us a starting point for relevant, practical comparisons.

For example, in 2021 the greater Tokyo region used 284 TWh. And in 2022, the UK collectively used 320 TWh, the state of California used 278 TWh, Shanghai used ~175 TWh, Dubai used 53 TWh, and New York City used ~51 TWh. Worldwide, over 25,000 TWh of electricity were consumed[2], with a CAGR of 2.4% growth between 2012 and 2022.

It's clear that data centers use a lot of electricity, and play an important role in the move to clean energy sources. Still, given their critical role in the world's digital infrastructure, communications and economy, it's important to remember that, even using the high-end range from the IEA's figures above, data centers around the globe are estimated to use less than >1% of the world's electricity. [*For more information on data center power utilization, see our chapter in the earlier Greener Data - Volume One book.*]

Collectively, data center providers are at the forefront of innovation and efficiency in operating facilities that are commonly located in environments that are about as diverse as anyone could find on Earth. Extreme cold, extreme heat; mountainous elevations and at or below sea level; close to reliable sources of water and in arid regions where water is precious and scarce. As a result, no single solution will work for data centers everywhere.

There are, however, a number of pathways that providers are pursuing with documented goals and commitments to achieve 100% carbon-free energy sourcing within the next decade. In this chapter, we are going to explore the innovations, the challenges, and the promise of low- and zero-carbon solutions that can be deployed in new, greenfield developments as well as in existing data centers, some of them built a decade ago or more. We will also look at the importance of energy suppliers and grid operators partnering with data center operators to ensure the supply and availability of low- and zero-carbon electricity in markets around the globe. And lastly, we will review some success stories with real-world results that offer both hope and practical guideposts for going forward.

Supplying Clean Power: Utilities and Power Grids

Historically, data centers haven't generated their own power. In cases where a provider elects to construct a solar farm, wind farm, or other power generation platforms for a given data center, they often also enter into a Power Purchase Agreement (PPA) with a local utility to, over time, sell excess power to the utility so it can be redistributed to nearby cities and towns. So, it does happen and is seen in more cases each year. And, as an added benefit, it can result in additional renewable, carbon-free energy for the affected markets.

But in most cases, data centers rely on the utilities or grid operators to deliver power. This can result in limited power availability and/or local concerns that power needed for other residential and commercial needs might be affected if data centers consume too much of the energy supply. Either way, while utility-supplied power is essential, in these markets, data center operators have less influence on the availability and mix of renewable and carbon-free energy sources used to generate the electricity they need.

In some markets, coal is the easiest, most accessible power source available, and for a variety of reasons a utility may rely heavily on that source for some time into the future. Other utilities, however, are investing in and supplying cleaner energy by relying on wind, solar, geothermal, hydro, nuclear, and other low-carbon sources.

However, even in cases where the utility is moving aggressively to cleaner energy, there are challenges in accessing and transmitting those power sources.

An example: As of November, 2023, California has seen 56.4 feet of snow, the second-snowiest year on record. Including the heavy rains the state has experienced, the November 2022 to November 2023 season was among the wettest ever documented. Why is this relevant to a discussion of clean energy? Well, up until 2023, California was under drought conditions, quite severe in some places. And that meant that the ability to generate hydroelectric power via the region's dams was declining instead of increasing. There simply wasn't enough water to generate more electricity year over year.

2023 changes that trend. The state forecasts a 72% rise in hydroelectric power in 2023. However, it doesn't fully reverse the trend because there are critical needs for much of the available water for reservoirs, agriculture, and other residential and industrial services.

In this example, no matter how many dams are constructed, or where they are located, hydroelectric power still requires adequate rain and snow to fall throughout the year. In their own ways, wind and solar can encounter similar challenges. The environment doesn't always provide resources exactly where and when utilities and data center providers might like.

The most important factor about the major suppliers of electricity worth noting here is the effort they are putting into sourcing and delivering renewable and zero-carbon power to customers in diverse markets. These efforts include but are not limited to updated transmission infrastructure, power storage held in batteries and distributed as needed at a later date, and diversification in an array of energy sources. In the California example above, if there are drought conditions for some period of time, that might mean there is more solar energy that can be collected and distributed.

To cite a few recent examples in the United States and Europe, we can look at the ERCOT grid in Texas and the California and European power platforms.

- In Texas, between 2015 and 2022, carbon-based energy declined from generating 76% of the state's power to 60%. And carbon-free energy's contribution rose from 24% to 40%.
- In California, over the same period, renewables rose from 25% of the state's energy sources to 37%. Energy analysts note that the wet conditions across the state in 2023 promise to help generate more hydroelectricity and increase the levels of renewables, but only year-end analysis will be able to confirm or correct that working assumption.
- In Europe, the picture is encouraging but serves as another example of some practical complexities in migrating to clean energy. Carbon-based coal and gas declined to a combined 36% of consumed power in 2022 while cleaner hydroelectric, nuclear, wind, and solar contributed 55%, with solar and wind growing rapidly over the past few years.

Now, while this isn't an exhaustive report on the progress of grids around the world, we can see that the general trends point to zero-carbon sources contributing to more electrical power in global markets. So, for our purposes, the question becomes: How does all of this information factor into the goal of a carbon-free future for data centers?

Chapter Ten

Bridging the Gap from Fossil Fuels to a Zero-Carbon Future

Data center providers are benefitting from a number of improvements and innovations in their efforts to decarbonize their power consumption. Higher efficiency levels are reflected in lower PUE (Power Utilization Efficiency), cooling solutions are smarter and more optimized, design and operations have improved, chipsets in customer servers used in data centers have been optimized, and even concrete and other construction resources have been innovated to reduce the carbon footprint for new facilities, to name a few.

But when it comes to using renewable and zero-carbon energy, plans and goals are not the same as transparent, documented results. And the journey to a zero-carbon future will not be a straight line. Intermediate bridge technologies may help facilitate the move away from power sources that generate carbon emissions and toward carbon-free energy.

Hydrogen with fuel cell technologies and commercial generator platforms offer clean energy solutions, some of their solutions residing on-premise and others partnered with power utilities. These solutions may be especially useful in markets where renewable energy is scarce and there remains a heavy reliance on carbon-intensive fuel sources while utilities ramp up the development and use of cleaner energy solutions. Many of these providers have delivered proven, successful deployments but have also encountered challenges at scale. So, while they offer bridge solutions for many large customers, it can be difficult to judge their feasibility for specific applications and deployments.

The 24/7 Carbon-Free Energy Approach

A new approach, 24/7 Carbon Free Energy ("CFE"), which entails tracking carbon-free energy supplies in near real-time hourly or even more precise increments, can reduce the consumption of carbon-based energy and can be applied to both new and existing data centers. For older, less efficient facilities, CFE enables them to take better advantage of cleaner energy, reducing their carbon footprint without requiring new construction. So, even though 24/7 CFE does not improve the efficiency of an older data center, it can mitigate the environmental impact for old and new data centers by reducing the local use of fossil fuels and delivering electrical power generated with wind, solar, hydro, or virtually any available combination of renewable and carbon-free sources. This approach is separate from using EACs (Energy Attribute Certificates, also known as Renewable Energy Credits) and uses clean power delivered from utilities to help achieve ESG goals and foster greater acceptance within local communities.

24/7 CFE emerged as a response to the urgent need for the elimination of carbon emissions and the adoption of cleaner energy sources to address climate change. In 2021, the 24/7 Carbon-free Energy Compact[3], developed in partnership with the United Nations, was published and signed by a group of major energy buyers, governments, system operators, solutions providers, investors, and other organizations. The definition of 24/7 CFE is simple: every kilowatt-hour of electricity consumption is fulfilled by carbon-free electricity generation and measured hourly or in even smaller time increments.

By committing to the 24/7 CFE Compact, signatories agree to the following five principles:

1. Time-matched procurement: 24/7 CFE focuses on the time-sensitive matching of electricity consumption with carbon-free electricity generation.
2. Local procurement: 24/7 CFE means purchasing clean energy on the local/regional electricity grids where electricity consumption occurs.
3. Technology inclusivity: 24/7 CFE recognizes the need to create zero-carbon electricity systems as fast as possible, and that all carbon-free energy technologies can play a role in creating this future.
4. New generation enablement: 24/7 CFE focuses on enabling new clean electricity generation, in order to support the rapid decarbonization of electricity systems.

5. System impact maximization: 24/7 CFE focuses attention on maximizing emissions reductions and solving for the dirtiest hours of electricity consumption.

The U.N.'s end goal is to cut CO2 emissions by 50% from 2010 levels by 2030 and achieve net-zero emissions economies by 2050.

24/7 CFE vs. Energy Attribute Certificates / Renewable Energy Credits (EACs / RECs)

RECs originated at the turn of the 21st century and are well established, with standards and markets for trading. A single credit is awarded to the generator for each megawatt hour of renewable energy produced (typically wind, solar, geothermal, or hydro). If an organization consumed 100 MWh of load for the year, to offset its carbon footprint it would buy 100 RECs corresponding to renewable energy produced by generators annually.

There are two important differences between RECs and 24/7 CFE: (a) 24/7 measures carbon-free energy rather than renewable energy, and (b) 24/7 requires time matching. An organization committing to the 24/7 pact doesn't match usage annually but on a time-based increment, typically hourly, and the energy must be carbon free and produced locally during that time period. The time-matching requirement of 24/7 CFE targets is more difficult to meet than annual RECs because an organization may only claim generated energy which is carbon-free when consuming energy for that matched time slot.

A Real-World 24/7 CFE Pilot Project

EdgeConneX has placed a strong focus on reducing the carbon footprint of its data centers and is a signatory to the United Nations Global Compact [https://unglobalcompact.org/]. EdgeConneX elected to pilot one of its facilities on the 24/7 CFE solution with an eye to scaling this effort to other data centers within its global fleet.

Chapter Ten

After evaluating various onsite energy solutions including solar and storage units, EdgeConneX determined that working with a vendor who could provide offsite CFE was the best option. The company researched vendors and found Gridmatic, an AI-enabled power marketer who applies years of success in financial trading in energy markets using AI-optimized bid curves to enable its partners to source renewable and carbon-free energy more easily and economically. EdgeConneX found that Gridmatic had the closest alignment to its goals, with a combination of technology and a focus on carbon-free energy.

More details on this pilot may be found in the white paper developed jointly by EdgeConneX and Gridmatic on the Sustainability page of the EdgeConneX website[4].

The lesson learned from the earliest stages of the pilot is that there are some guidelines and metrics that can help ensure a successful deployment of a 24/7 CFE solution:

- **Targets:** set targets for the minimum acceptable mix of renewable and carbon-free electricity. An example might identify a baseline of 60% CFE with a stretch goal of 75%, helping to displace fossil fuel-based power.
- **Costs:** negotiate power costs upfront with providers, but note that prices will vary from market to market depending on the availability of carbon-free energy sources. In some markets, pricing may indicate that the utility or grid is not prepared to deliver reliable clean power at scale.
- **Reporting:** define timely, auditable reporting that shows the share of renewable energy consumed in hourly or other time increments to ensure that your suppliers are meeting your goals and their commitments.
- **Select Facilities:** select a facility equipped to monitor and measure power loads for tracking energy sourcing, including IT load, cooling units, awareness of breaker ratings, generator, UPS, mechanical plant capacity, and more.

- **Utility History:** determine whether your utility can provide historical data for up to a year, allowing you to refine modeling predictions.

Everyone has a role and an obligation in the effort to reduce or even reverse global warming trends associated with carbon emissions and fossil fuels. No single solution will work in every region or apply to every business around the globe. But everyone can do something to help.

The data center industry holds significant influence owing to its scale, its reliance on TWh of energy, and its presence in virtually every country worldwide. By working in tandem with local utilities and grid providers, to increase the distribution and consumption of carbon-free energy from solar, wind, hydro, and other sources, the goal is to prove that there is demand for cleaner energy and that cleaner energy can be provided reliably at both normal and peak levels.

Looking Ahead

Different industries face different challenges in their progress to a zero-carbon energy future but, because electricity is absolutely critical to their business and operations, data centers can and should offer paths forward that other industries can benefit from.

Because of the pivotal role they play in the world's digital infrastructure, and given the explosive pace of innovation in content, cloud, and now AI and other emerging technology services, we can expect data center capacities to continue to grow rapidly for decades to come.

What we know from the past 20 years is that data center computing and storage have grown orders of magnitude faster than data center energy consumption over the same period of time. As noted above, this divergence is due to an industry-wide emphasis on efficiency and optimization throughout every aspect of data center construction and operation.

Chapter Ten

Artificial Intelligence will demand more capacity, more storage, more computing power, and more data centers. It's important to note that AI is also a powerful tool that is helping to deliver 24/7 CFE deployments, manage optimal mixes of energy sources and predict market conditions. AI also promises to help improve data center design, construction, cooling, layout, and operations, likely to once again help data centers increase performance and capacity while simultaneously optimizing energy consumption and impacts on our environment.

Data centers are already playing a role in identifying, trialing, and rolling out low- and zero-carbon solutions that other industries will be able to adopt. As we have laid out in this chapter, there are many providers who are committed to growing smarter, cleaner data centers that will deliver more data, more computing power, more knowledge, and many more contributions to a carbon-free future.

---

1. Not including cryptocurrency mining operations, which are typically not permitted in commercial data centers.
2. Statista. 2023. "Net electricity consumption worldwide in select years from 1980 to 2022." 2023. https://www.statista.com/statistics/280704/world-power-consumption.
3. United Nations. "24/7 Carbon-free Energy Compact." https://www.un.org/en/energy-compacts/page/compact-247-carbon-free-energy.
4. EdgeConneX Sustainability. https://edgeconnex.com/company/sustainability

About the Author

RAJ CHUDGAR

As EdgeConneX Chief Power Officer, Raj Chudgar brings extensive experience in the international power and gas markets, technologies, strategies, and solutions. He has had over 25 years of extensive senior expertise through the power and gas value chain, including wholesale, retail, operations, renewables, demand response, trading, structuring, and value creation. Mr. Chudgar developed and implemented successful strategies at numerous employers covering all growth aspects, including fundraising, starting up, and selling multiple companies. He has worked extensively with end-use customers, utilities, technology companies, and regulatory bodies (PUCT, FERC, ERCOT, PJM, IESO, NYISO). He has led or been an executive at his last four start-up companies that were sold (Power Analytics, Power Generation Services, Viridity Energy, and Demand Power Group).

Mr. Chudgar holds Bachelor's and Master of Engineering degrees in Chemical Engineering from the J.B. Speed School of Engineering at the University of Louisville (Kentucky).

ELEVEN

How Masterplanning Data Centers Meets the Needs of Hyperscalers, Local Communities and Utilities

Bill Thomas, CleanArc

The world's largest hyperscalers have the unique challenge, and opportunity, of setting the tone for sustainability within one of the most power-hungry industries on the planet. Over the past few years, we've seen their ambition to lead this charge in the world's transition to a zero-carbon grid.

They're incentivizing the development of new renewable energy projects in the regions where they operate, contributing to lower-carbon grids. They've made incredible investments in renewable energy by bringing tens of gigawatts of new clean energy capacity onto electric grids every year.

But the same ambitious hyperscale operators know that they need to do more. While signing renewable power purchase agreements (PPAs) can help offset a hyperscaler's annual energy consumption, the goal has shifted to operating all of their data centers using carbon-free energy.

Google is aiming for net-zero emissions across its operations and value chain by 2030, with a specific ambition of running its data centers on 24/7 carbon-free energy, like wind and solar[1]. Microsoft Cloud has pledged to run its data center fleet entirely on renewable energy by 2025, with even back-up powered by non-diesel sources by 2030[2]. Amazon is working toward net zero by 2040, with a goal of powering operations with renewable energy only by 2025[3].

In fact, the digital infrastructure industry at large has done so much to "green up" our data, but we have to do more. The next generation of data center campuses *has* to evolve to meet modern compute-heavy needs while achieving ambitious sustainability goals.

Collectively, the industry is building the plane as we fly it toward net zero — which requires quick thinking, deep partnership and a lot of creativity. Merging the benefits of renewable generation with the consumption profiles of data centers where they operate requires new and sophisticated contractual power structures.

So, it's an understatement to say that we need to rethink data center planning. In fact, we need a completely different approach that takes scale to new heights while also delivering very intentional power sourcing. The next generation of data center planning must identify the best locations to build, incorporate deep collaboration with local authorities and power providers, and ultimately revise the way power contracting has been done in the past. Current data center demand simply does not fit the old paradigm. The next generation of hyperscale data centers needs to be master planned, with sustainability baked in from the beginning.

Clicking Clean

And as those of us in the industry know, the pace of change around here is set to "warp." The trend of information and communication technology (ICT) companies voluntarily buying up renewable energy assets first jumped out at me about a decade ago while working for a utility-scale renewable energy developer. (A recovering scientist brought up in the energy and financial worlds, I'm one of the many who followed market demand and interest to end up in the data center industry.) Around that time, Greenpeace had dispatched a proverbial stick in the form of an annual report on ICT energy usage. Its Clean Click Report Card shined a spotlight on how tech companies were using massive amounts of electricity to power their businesses, frequently using very "dirty" electricity accompanied by a colossal carbon footprint.

It was a wake-up call to the industry and provided a massive opportunity for renewable energy developers. In the early years of corporate renewable energy procurement (up until around 2015), ICT accounted for roughly 90% of all executed PPAs.

Greenpeace challenged the hyperscalers to step up and change the energy procurement paradigm, arguing they have a responsibility to the environment as the largest companies in the world. They responded in kind, but as we'll see later on in this chapter, it is an imperfect work in progress. Just a few short years later, a new approach is required to better serve hyperscalers, their customers, and the planet — and to give utilities a break, too.

Virginia As a Case Study

No other market illustrates the story and the potential solution better than the data hub of Virginia.

The Northern Virginia counties of Loudoun, Fairfax and Prince William have become something of a Bermuda Triangle for electricity. Data centers are to thank, of course, as they require massive amounts of power, the demand for which will only continue to grow as the physical world becomes ever more intertwined with the digital one and more compute power is required to unleash the power of emerging technologies.

As "Data Center Alley" has developed over the past quarter-century, power isn't the only thing running thin in the area. Opposition to new data center development has grown more vocal and organized in recent years as facilities have expanded. What were once desirable developments have become controversial, dividing communities. The Prince William County Board of Supervisors fielded 27 hours of public comment in December 2023 before deciding via a split vote to approve what's believed will be the world's biggest data center corridor, encompassing 23 million square feet of data center space over 2,100 acres.[4]

Meanwhile, the world's largest tech companies need data centers with a greater magnitude of capacity than the legacy facilities lining Northern Virginia. The nexus of these dynamics is where a new opportunity to masterplan the next generation of hyperscale data centers emerges.

Quick Virginia History Lesson

Several factors aligned to make Virginia the data center capital of the world. Its proximity to Washington, D.C., and all the associated federal operations and ancillary business put it ahead of the game in the industry from the get-go. Another catalyst came in the 1990s with the launch of Metropolitan Area Exchange-East (MAE-East), among the first Internet Exchange Points, in Washington, D.C., which was quickly linked with Northern Virginia. Then, Equinix opened its first data center in Ashburn, about 30 miles northeast of D.C.

From there, the industry snowballed, with startups coming to the area along with fiber builds that led to further investments in the region. Tax incentives and other elements combined to make Virginia home to more than one-third of all the hyperscale data centers in the world.

It feels a bit disingenuous to use the term "microcosm" to describe the home to the largest concentration of large-scale data centers in the world, but the situation in Virginia reflects the pressures on the industry worldwide. It offers insights into how to address the competing needs of tomorrow's data-driven world and our collective obligation to the environment. The main challenges facing Virginia right now are not unique to that state; the need to masterplan a new data center model is universal. The world's largest hyperscalers have said as much in whitepapers. They need new ways of contracting and a complete revisioning of business as usual. The only way to do that is by building a facility to the enormous scale at which they need to operate, using a deliberate, calculated process balancing all the pressure points.

Chapter Eleven

Breaking the Scale

The move to the cloud compute space has necessitated a completely different scale of data center. Everything about our modern, digital life generates data that needs to "live" somewhere. The pandemic accelerated the migration of computing resources to public cloud platforms, but the change was inevitable. This shift and the accompanying ongoing growth of data generation and usage means larger and more diverse data centers are at the heart of how humanity learns, lives, works, plays, loves — you name it.

On top of that, emerging technology has forced a major growth spurt in the industry. The year 2023 was the year of AI in a lot of ways and got people talking about it from all industries, not just tech. From Google's Bard to OpenAI's ChatGPT, these tools showcase just how powerful it can be to harness the immense amount of data the world creates and shares. I believe AI alone will add 25% to hyperscaler demand beyond 2022 established projections. It's hard to believe, but the application of AI technologies across search, information management, communication, finance, manufacturing, software development and business enablement will be as evolutionary over the next two decades as that of the internet, search and social networking. AI, however, is only part of the equation driving the demand for the next generation of hyperscale data centers.

Due to these swift changes, the dimensions of next-generation facilities are on a scale the market hasn't even contemplated before. It wasn't too long ago that facilities of 5-20 MW were considered massive. At CleanArc, our prototype facility is more than three times the large end of that range, and we're envisioning four or more of those facilities per campus. The only way to responsibly develop data centers of this magnitude is via a thorough masterplanning process that includes identifying a suitable location where electricity needs can be met. It's not only a question of utility providers being capable of handling the load, but also of how to supplement that power source with a comprehensive renewable energy portfolio.

Chapter Eleven

The Power Play

The first requirement to consider when assessing a site for a potential data center is physical power availability, which is exactly where Loudoun County and Ashburn in Virginia are jammed up. There is very little energy capacity available, and municipalities are trying to claw back some power (literally) to be able to serve their normal loads and load growth[5].

Masterplanning the next generation of data centers, on the other hand, means working directly with the transmission operators and host utilities to get into their long-term transmission planning process early on. For a 500 MW campus, the timeline spans six to eight years. The key is to align with what utilities are doing and what they need to do to conscientiously and responsibly build out high-voltage infrastructure to support loads that will be on their footprint. The sooner data center developers begin these conversations, the sooner work can begin to develop a comprehensive solution rather than something that's merely cobbled together, which is what's going on now in Northern Virginia. There are plenty of examples of poorly contrived experiments in data center siting, demonstrating the need for a holistic, masterplanned approach moving forward .

A New Approach to Renewables

The Federal Energy Regulatory Commission set the stage for today's energy market in 1996 with Order No. 888 reforming the Open Access Transmission Tariff — rules and regulations governing the access and use of electric transmission systems. OATT ensures all market participants, whether they are electricity generators, distributors or consumers, have equal, nondiscriminatory access to transmission networks.[6] Basically, it shifted utilities from generation companies to transmission companies. It opened the doors for companies to enter commercial contracts without being beholden to a host utility, or at least participation in the wholesale market. It democratized energy procurement in a way

Chapter Eleven

that allows hyperscalers to make a deal directly with a renewable energy developer to purchase electricity, and whoever operates the grid must allow access to it.

Previously, a customer would purchase electricity from the utility at the retail rate, and that was that. Because OATT changed the dynamic, hyperscalers were able to counter the findings of the Clean Click Report Card by entering PPAs with renewable energy companies. This allowed them to not only demonstrate to the world that they care about the environment and their impact on it, but also to effect change in the legacy fossil fuel grid. This change is bringing new, clean, more efficient generation online and advancing the retirement of coal.

As it stands now, hyperscalers can — and do — buy as much renewable energy from various sources as they consume in total. Which sounds great, but it doesn't tell the full story. They end up with solutions that address their annual electricity consumption, but not their hourly consumption. Renewable energy intermittency plays a major role here. You get unpredictable fluctuations in energy output from renewable sources for a number of reasons, e.g., the sun doesn't always shine.

As a result, hyperscalers must still rely on fossil fuels to fill in the gaps. In many ways, they're overprocuring renewables in places that aren't really offsetting consumed demand. It can go the other way, too, when there's, shall we say, too much of a good thing. Negative pricing occurs when too much of the same resource is generating power using the same type of fuel at the same time. It's a common occurrence where the price of electricity goes into the negative. California's Central Valley is a good example of this because of an abundance of sunshine during the day and installed capacity. Prices can become so inverted that grid operators need to curtail that resource. This is a "solution" that's adding to the existing problem of requiring more fossil fuel to mitigate intermittency.

So while virtual PPAs and renewable energy certificates have shown progress toward reductions in greenhouse gas emissions, reductions will only truly happen when renewable energy is generated from the same grid to the data centers. For hyperscalers to achieve their ambitious goals of carbon neutrality over the next several years, they need load following, fully vetted and quantified PPAs sourced through resource management processes and grid headroom analysis.

Strategic Siting

Let's take it back to Virginia, where our friends in the D.C. area are wary of further data center development, power constraints are a concern and space is at a premium.

One of the main reasons Northern Virginia became a data center hub is because it offers low latency. But adjacent areas can enjoy low latency without all of the challenges. Part of developing a master plan is identifying communities where people still want the benefits of data center development. There's a reason Loudoun County hasn't closed its doors to the industry. It draws hundreds of millions of dollars in tax revenue from data centers each year, not to mention the influx of high-paying jobs. People outside Data Center Alley and its immediate surrounding area are eager to welcome these facilities — so why go somewhere you're not wanted if you don't have to?

At CleanArc, we focus on finding data center sites where there's a nexus of community support, utility-scale power and availability. These areas aren't already inundated with massive power-hungry facilities. Don't get it twisted: It's a Herculean task to deliver the amount of power we're talking about here. But it's a different challenge in an area outside of the Loudon County concentration of DC capacity. A comprehensive renewable energy portfolio, baked in as part of the masterplanning process, lowers the overall strain these facilities place on utilities, which still benefit from the revenue stream of a large, consistent customer.

When talking about facilities of this scale, it's not just about the buildings themselves. The idea is to bring on board large-scale renewable energy developments that can feed into these data centers, and those need plenty of space. A 100 MW solar development can require up to 1,000 acres, and the equivalent in wind-powered generation needs even more space. Once again, location comes into play not only because of size, but also in identifying lands where it is appropriate to develop renewables. All land is not created equal, and it makes no sense to destroy pristine farmland when there are places where renewable infrastructure is far less damaging.

Powering Hyperscalers' Clean Energy Transition

We launched CleanArc in May 2022 to offer a different approach to the data center industry: fully packaged data center turnkey program management, design and construction, bundled with operational commissioning and robust power structuring. It's a complete revisioning of data center power, where we've pre-solved the challenge of carbon offset.

CleanArc works with local utilities and renewable energy developers far in advance of siting a project, to create contractual structures that allow our hyperscale customers to achieve their sustainability goals. We analyze grid headroom, historical clearing pricing and use predictive modeling to provide valuable due diligence to hyperscale energy teams.

CleanArc's approach is to develop a comprehensive portfolio that approximates a facility's consumption and avoids the issues of intermittency, transmission and curtailment. The goal is to deliver more green electrons and displace more fossil sources because the portfolio varies in technology, leveraging a combination of wind and solar and potentially battery storage and hydro, if available.

A balanced portfolio taking into account changes throughout the day delivers electricity at a flatter rate, with fewer peaks. Our approach seeks to provide the highest hourly content of renewable energy to facilities that we operate. Part of the masterplanning process involves developing diverse portfolios of renewable energy and bundling those portfolios as part of the siting stage, and then complementing it with a "last mile" structure allowing delivery of the highest hourly renewable content possible in the most financially responsible way. This harmonizing of the procurement process benefits hyperscalers, and it also makes life easier for utilities.

Bringing It All Together

At CleanArc, we have found that the best way to serve hyperscalers is to identify where their needs for performance, power and scale overlap, to develop a renewable energy portfolio unique to the site and build out the facilities accordingly. For the latter, we have taken a step back from the kludgy, business-as-usual stick-build approach. At the scale we're building, we can manufacture the mechanical and electrical rooms completely off-site and bring them in on skids when it's time to install them. It saves in terms of transport, labor and materials.

All in all, the master plan is the key. The CleanArc model, which we believe is the secret to responsibly answering hyperscalers' call, is all about delivering a solution for all stakeholders:

- Hyperscalers have access to data centers big enough to meet their needs with a robust renewable energy portfolio already baked into the facility's design
- Power companies get additional revenue without being overwhelmed by the demands of a hyperscale-level data center
- Communities that want it get the economic development benefits of facilities moving into their area

Gone are the days of quickly greenlighting a new data center build that relies entirely on fossil fuel–fed power sources. The unique challenges we're facing in the data center industry today require a unique solution.

---

1. Google. "Net-zero carbon". https://sustainability.google/operating-sustainably/net-zero-carbon/
2. Burton, Graeme. "Microsoft: This is how we're going to get to net-zero by 2030 – and then take back all the carbon we've ever emitted". DatacenterDynamics.

May 5, 2021. https://www.datacenterdynamics.com/en/marketwatch/microsoft-this-is-how-were-going-to-get-to-net-zero-by-2030-and-then-take-back-all-the-carbon-weve-ever-emitted/
3. Amazon. "The cloud". https://sustainability.aboutamazon.com/products-services/the-cloud?energyType=true
4. Peters, Ben. "Prince William supervisors approve PW Digital Gateway, expected to be the world's largest data center corridor". Inside Nova. Dec. 13, 2023. https://www.insidenova.com/headlines/updated-prince-william-supervisors-approve-pw-digital-gateway-expected-to-be-the-world-s-largest/article_48f6e8f2-99bf-11ee-95fc-efa85aff87a0.html
5. https://www.datacenterfrontier.com/energy/article/11436951/dominion-resumes-new-connections-but-loudoun-faces-lengthy-power-constraints
6. Federal Energy Regulatory Commission. "History of OATT Reform". https://www.ferc.gov/industries-data/electric/industry-activities/open-access-transmission-tariff-oatt-reform/history-oatt-reform

About the Author

BILL THOMAS

An accomplished renewable energy executive, Bill has held leadership positions in energy trading and project origination at the world's largest renewable energy developers.

Prior to joining CleanArc, Bill concentrated on wholesale energy trading as Vice President of Energy Marketing at RWE Renewables Americas. He also served as Chief Commercial Officer at LevelTen Energy, where he led efforts to aggregate corporate and institutional ("C&I") demand and syndicate renewable energy solutions for all classes of C&I buyers. Previously, Bill served as Director of Global Commercial & Industrial Origination at First Solar. Prior to First Solar, Bill was Vice President of Development and Energy Marketing at E.ON Climate & Renewables Solar PV and led the company's utility-scale solar development and commercial contracting efforts in North America. Before entering the renewable energy industry, Bill was a Senior Energy Trader at Xcel Energy. Bill began his career at AIG, where he was a foreign currency and interest rate derivatives trader.

At CleanArc, Bill is responsible for delivering comprehensive energy solutions CleanArc TrueAdditionality. His team sources and structures renewable energy products for CleanArc's hyperscale data centers. Bill holds a BS in Geology from the University of Colorado-Boulder and an MS in Hydrogeology from Dartmouth College.

TWELVE

Dual Rules: Microgrid Flexibility Powers Grid, Data Center and the Community

Brian Jabeck, Enchanted Rock

Time for Change

A data center's success is built on three energy imperatives – the adequacy, stability, and reliability of its power supply. But satisfying these power requirements is becoming increasingly difficult as climate change takes hold. The growing frequency, length, and intensity of extreme weather events is having a direct impact on data centers, via collision with aging grid infrastructure.

From 2011 to 2021, the annual number of weather-related power outages across the US increased by approximately 78% as compared to the decade before: from 2000 to 2001, 83% of major power outages were attributed by US utilities to weather-related events.[1] According to the US Department of Energy, "Extreme weather events like the Dixie Wildfire, Hurricane Ida, and the 2021 Texas Freeze have made it clear that America's existing energy infrastructure will not endure the continuing impacts of extreme weather events spurred by climate change."[2] In the US, the most recent widespread weather-related outages have occurred in Texas followed by California -- states that are densely populated and also home to active data center hubs, such as Dallas or Silicon Valley.

Chapter Twelve

These weather-related outages can have devastating consequences for the communities that are affected – the failure of the Texas grid during the winter storm of 2021 is just one tragic example[3] – as they jeopardize industrial production, including data center operations. Armed with batteries or backup generator systems, most data centers are prepared to operate without grid power. Depending on size and power demand/capacity, different facilities can run with backup fuel reserves for 8 hours (a smaller operation) or up to 48 hours (a larger operation). However, adapting to more frequent and longer-duration power outages that may last a week or two poses real challenges for the data center operator. In any one location that may be experiencing a long-duration outage, the logistics involved in refilling diesel fuel tanks and delivering reserve fuel to the facility can be problematic. Refueling difficulties, truck limitations, environmental conditions, and the volume of data centers clustered in certain markets can all compromise a data center's backup fuel supply, and hence its ability to withstand these longer outages. Across multiple locations, countries, or continents, the likely impact of the increasing intensity and frequency of outages is alarming.

Unfortunately, climate scientists and weather experts anticipate only increased incidence of severe weather events as temperatures rise on a planetary level. Experts agree that the time to act is now, with an energy transition that totally eliminates, or at least reduces, carbon emissions.

Today, much of the energy discussion focuses on the use of renewable resources backed by advanced battery technology or the introduction of hydrogen-powered solutions. In the data center industry, many of the large operators have made commitments to the use of renewables, generally through the purchase of RECs or PPAs and occasionally through onsite installations that function as part of a hybrid power strategy.

While there has been significant uptake of renewables at the grid level (22% of US electricity is now generated through renewables[4]) and in the data center industry, which accounts for approximately two-thirds of renewable capacity contracted by the corporate sector in the US,[5] scaling these solution approaches in industrial settings is still a challenge. Recognizing the need for technology development to ensure consistent, reliable power and competitive cost structures, market observers put the widespread use of renewables in data center environments out at least a decade. Similarly, the widespread adoption of hydrogen-based solutions is constrained by the current lack of distribution infrastructure, the cost of onsite storage, and adoption know-how in user communities.

Can we afford to wait? And what if the data center could contribute now as an active participant in the grid-wide transition to a cleaner energy future? For the data center, being prepared and adaptive to an evolving climate and energy dynamic in the marketplace is critical. For the planet, quick action on the environment can deliver incremental benefits. As the IPCC's Sixth Assessment Report on mitigation of climate change noted, "strengthened near-term action... can reduce and/or avoid long-term feasibility challenges of global modeled pathways [to a 1.5- or 2-degree Celsius global temperature increase]."[6] In other words, a stitch in time saves nine; the effect of intensifying action today can accelerate our ability to address climate risk tomorrow.

Grid Challenges

The root of the decarbonization challenge lies in the electricity grid, which in the US was built in the 1960s and 70s. Much of the power transmission infrastructure is at the end of its shelf life (typically 50 years), while the power plant fleet is similarly mature. Contributing to the outages noted above, issues with aging infrastructure are compounded by competition for power resources within the data center sector and from other heavy power users. Price hikes, combined with power shortages in many jurisdictions, will constrain new builds or even pressure existing operations. Electrification, which is needed to fight climate change, will only place additional demand on grid structures – think the EV revolution – while modern information technologies are expected to aggravate problems with spiking power demand from the data center. Major industries and modern society are embracing digital transformation, and the proliferation of energy-dense capabilities like AI or quantum computing will demand new levels of electricity supply that were previously unimagined.

At the same time, the need to decarbonize the grid poses additional issues. While country profiles vary, on a global basis, electricity production in 2022 accounted for approximately 40% of energy-related CO2 emissions, which in turn account for the largest share (80%) of all anthropogenic emissions.[7] And while investment in renewable energy sources has improved the carbon profile of the grid – today, renewable sources generate about 20% of US electricity – integrating these resources in a way that ensures power quality and reliability continues to elude many utility providers. Spiraling demand, combined with calls for decarbonization, mean the grid needs help. Going forward, the data center/grid supply and demand relationships that have been in place for 20 years will no longer be viable – an energy reckoning is expected within five years.

Dual-Purpose Microgrid

The good news is there is flexible technology that can address the dual challenge posed by the need to cut emissions and improve reliability in a climate-constrained world. Microgrids, for example, can operate at multiple levels to solve power grid and data center power issues. In its infancy, microgrid technology was deployed to support 'islanded' consumers, generating and delivering power off the grid to areas where power was unavailable. Examples include rural regions, islands like Malta in the Mediterranean, scarcely populated regions in the north, or military battle ships and submarines.

But today, microgrids also work within grid environments to deliver reliable onsite power generation when the grid fails, and supplemental energy to the grid at critical times, while also helping the utility to achieve sustainability goals. Enchanted Rock, a pioneer of the dual-purpose microgrid, provides natural gas-powered microgrid infrastructure to protect data centers from grid outages and to help grid owners balance supply and demand at a time when more and more renewable resources are being added to the grid. By delivering backup energy at the right time to compensate for power delivery interruptions and by providing grid services in periods of grid stress, the Enchanted Rock microgrid solution helps to address solar and wind intermittency, a key challenge with greater deployment of renewables in utility systems. And by boosting the reliability of the electric grid and supporting the green energy transition, microgrid technology works to support the productivity and health of the broader community.

Microgrid Onsite

Grid Collaboration

In efforts to stabilize power delivery, utility providers are looking to an additional channel – the data center. While microgrids provide a clear technical use case for the grid operator, installation can involve a complex mix of implementation prerequisites that may stymie rapid adoption. For equipment installation, the utility may need additional land, fuel storage facilities, permits from local authorities, as well as the ability to address regulatory requirements and other contractual necessities. These administrative and cost considerations can translate to disinclination, delay, or deferral. Data centers, on the other hand, have many of these assets at hand, as well as experience with processes around installing and maintaining backup generation infrastructure. By collaborating with a data center with an installed microgrid, the utility may contract for power in critical periods, leveraging data center microgrid investments to access hundreds of hours of metered resources without needing to build a peaking plant. When partnerships with several large data center customers are established, the advantages of sharing are even more compelling.

Data Center Gains

The benefits of this shared approach to ensuring power reliability are available to the data center as well. Grid challenges mean that data centers can no longer rely on traditional relationships where electricity was delivered with the flip of a switch; rather, shortages and/or high cost will be the increasing norm as growth in demand puts increasing strain on grid infrastructure. Data centers that can collaborate with their utility provider may secure microgrid-enabled consistent supply, while also realizing cost savings through reduced Capex for the technology provided by the microgrid vendor. In addition to the security of power supply, this direct financial compensation can be an important contributor to the economic proposition for hyperscalers and non-hyperscale services providers alike who must consider all sources of advantage in today's highly competitive marketplace. The indirect benefits – customer acquisition and retention through the reputation and marketing advantage of ensured uptime – can also deliver intrinsic value in a competitive environment.

In each jurisdiction, a range of market variables will demand unique contractual agreements. But shaving cost offers a clear opportunity. In Texas, for example, Enchanted Rock has created a resiliency solution for a data center involving grid interactivity in which the company installs a microgrid system fueled by natural gas that is the same price or less than a Tier 2 or Tier 4 diesel-equivalent solution.

Greening Data Center Backup

For many data center operators today, the financial argument for transition to a microgrid solution is critical, as the push towards sustainability can meet a financial wall. In general, and in the absence of grid services contracts, diesel is often cost competitive. That said, a natural gas dual-purpose microgrid provides a much greener and cost-competitive solution – a growing imperative for the data center operators and the corporations that back them.[8] The Enchanted Rock system described above produces up to 90% fewer local emissions than even 'clean' Tier 4 diesel-powered backup.

While some operators have argued that diesel fuel is burned in emergency backup situations only, this logic ignores fuel consumed in generator testing, which occurs in well-run facilities on a regular basis. It also neglects to account for the anticipated intensification of emergency weather events – a likely response to power shortages or blackouts will be the need to run much longer periods on diesel. With a lower carbon solution like natural gas in place, this crisis may be avoided.

Solution Evolution

A key advantage of the gas-powered microgrid is that it is shovel ready – a low-carbon solution that is ready to install today, rather than a decade out when other onsite renewable alternatives have achieved technical performance and adoption scale. Another important attribute is flexibility that can support technology evolution. Today, most Enchanted Rock microgrid installations consume natural gas. However, the technology can utilize a renewable natural gas (RNG) offset, which offers additional sustainability benefits with net zero carbon for backup power.

The EPA defines RNG as anaerobically generated biogas produced from landfills, wastewater treatment plants, organic-waste management systems, and livestock manure systems. When burned, RNG can significantly reduce methane and other emissions as compared with fossil fuels.[9] In vehicle fleets, the use of carbon-negative RNG produced from dairy manure in just 25% of inventory can offset emissions from the total, and is 500% cleaner than diesel, while offering potential to be carbon negative.[10] When the possibility of accessing carbon offsets related to the use of RNG over a period of time is factored into the microgrid financial equation, the outlook for RNG is improved considerably.

For leaders in the tech industry, cost is not the only consideration in technology adoption, rather, many operators have embarked on significant programs to achieve aggressive environmental targets. For example, as part of efforts to become carbon-negative and to source 100% of its energy supply 100% of the time from zero-carbon resources by 2030, Microsoft is building a data center in San Jose, California that will use RNG to power 60-megawatt of backup generation hooked to a microgrid. When it comes online in 2025, the solution will support Microsoft's sustainability goals on two fronts: when the data center needs to use its emergency backup generators, the RNG can offset carbon emissions from natural gas; and by using fuel created from animal waste, the solution keeps methane, which traps more heat per molecule that carbon dioxide, out of the atmosphere. California's largest microgrid, the Enchanted Rock installation at the San Jose data center is intended to act as a template for Microsoft work with the company on future fully decarbonized data center microgrid projects. Microsoft expects the project will outperform California's stringent emissions requirements for distributed generation with local emissions that are 80% to 96% lower than Tier 4 diesel standards.[11]

Going forward, microgrid flexibility may enable users to future proof against the need for even more dramatic approaches to carbon reduction. To address increasing climate impact, the integration of more green sources of energy, such as hydrogen, will grow apace; Enchanted Rock gensets are tested today with a methane blend that is up to 20% hydrogen. Identified as a central technology in the energy transition, hydrogen emits only water vapor and oxygen when burned, and the production of green hydrogen is essentially carbon neutral.

Today, hydrogen distribution infrastructure faces challenges. Since hydrogen is lighter and a much smaller molecule than natural gas, existing pipeline infrastructure is not completely leakproof. And when leaked into the atmosphere, hydrogen interacts with other GHGs such as methane, ozone, and stratospheric water vapor to cause global warming.[12] Similarly, trucking hydrogen to the data center site and storing required volumes is not feasible from safety, efficiency, or sustainability perspectives. In the near future, a blended (10-20% hydrogen) pipeline may be the most practical approach. For data centers, once hydrogen is available commercially, it can be used as fuel for the dual-purpose microgrid technology; the Enchanted Rock package is hydrogen-blend ready today.

The dual-purpose microgrid can be deployed to support data center and grid reliability. But it also responds to our current need to battle climate change on two fronts: adaptation and mitigation. By helping the grid and the data center rebound from the impact of a growing climate emergency, the microgrid functions as adaptive technology. At the same time, microgrid technology works to mitigate climate emissions by supporting grid integration of ever-cleaner energy resources.

Connecting with Community

The data center industry has a long-running public relations problem with the local communities it serves. Consuming much more power on a square-foot basis than commercial office space or residential structures, data centers are perceived as energy hogs that compete for an increasingly constrained resource. When they run on backup diesel or dirty grid power, data centers can be viewed as a primary polluter. In some jurisdictions, permitting for new data center capacity has become more exacting, as local authorities look to see better energy management and carbon reduction programs within facilities. But as the alternative-fuel microgrid demonstrates, data centers can operate more responsibly – by consuming cleaner fuel, the data center can reduce local pollution impact.

Through collaboration with the local electricity grid, data centers can also support system stability in the grid and in their own operations, extending power reliability to the broader community. Enabled by dual-purpose microgrids, the data center can provide power back to the grid in critical times to keep lights, heat, or A/C on in local homes and businesses. This ability to stabilize power supply will become increasingly important – in case of brown outs during fire season or extreme cold, or through intensified storm activity, which are becoming more common as the country and the planet experience warming. Planning for these disruptions means fewer emergencies in a climate-challenged world. We have the technology and the use case. Let's do it cleaner and greener.

Chapter Twelve

1. Analysis of major power outages 2000-2021 was based on data collected from the US Department of Energy's Form OE-417 reports.
   Surging Weather-related Power Outages. Climate Central. https://www.climatecentral.org/climate-matters/surging-weather-related-power-outages
2. Office of Energy. 2022. "DOE Launches New Initiative From President Biden's Bipartisan Infrastructure Law To Modernize National Grid." Energy.gov. January 2022. https://www.energy.gov/oe/articles/doe-launches-new-initiative-president-bidens-bipartisan-infrastructure-law-modernize
3. The Texas deep freeze is attributed to climate change weakening of the polar vortex, which has historically kept cold air at the North Pole. 2021.
   "How Climate Change is Driving a Deep Freeze into Texas." EARTH.ORG. February 2021. https://earth.org/climate-change-is-driving-a-deep-freeze-into-texas/#:~:text=The%20Texas%20deep%20freeze%20began,air%20at%20the%20North%20Pole.
4. U.S. Energy Information Administration (EIA). 2022. "U.S. energy facts - data and statistics. " https://www.eia.gov/energyexplained/us-energy-facts/data-and-statistics.php.
5. Adam Wilson. "Datacenter companies continue renewable buying spree, surpassing 40 GW in US. S&P Global Market Intelligence."March 2023. https://www.spglobal.com/marketintelligence/en/news-insights/research/datacenter-companies-continue-renewable-buying-spree-surpassing-40-gw-in-us.
6. Referring to state-level commitments, IPCC report highlight statements focus on transition to low-carbon fuels, and include: "Strengthened near-term action beyond the NDCs (announced prior to UNFCCC COP26) can reduce and/or avoid long-term feasibility challenges of global modelled pathways that limit warming to 1.5 °C (>50%) with no or limited overshoot. (high confidence)".
7. "Carbon Dioxide Emissions From Electricity". World Nuclear Association. Update 2022. https://www.world-nuclear.org/information-library/energy-and-the-environment/carbon-dioxide-emissions-from-electricity.aspx.
8. See "Low Carbon Solutions: Pathways to Energy Maturity in the Data Center," Greener Data - Volume Two.
9. EPA. An Introduction to Renewable Natural Gas.https://www.epa.gov/system/files/documents/2022-11/RNG_Intro_Guide.pdf.
10. Roche, Greg. 2021 "3 Reasons RNG is Decarbonizing Trucking Today.". October 2021. https://finance.yahoo.com/news/3-reasons-rng-decarbonizing-trucking-145820681.html
11. "Microsoft's San Jose Data Center: An Important Step on the Road to Net-Zero. An Enchanted Rock, Energy Tech Case Study." https://enchantedrock.com/wp-content/uploads/Enchanted-Rock-Microsoft-Case-Study.pdf?ref=briolink
12. CICERO. 2023. "New Study estimates global warming potential of hydrogen." June 2023. PHYS.ORG. https://phys.org/news/2023-06-global-potential-hydrogen.html#:~:text=Hydrogen%20is%20not%20a%20greenhouse,lack%20of%20direct%20radiative%20properties.

About the Author
BRIAN JABECK

Brian Jabeck is an onsite generation and resiliency expert who has built his professional career as a business leader focused on sales and marketing of energy and power generation solutions for data centers. As VP of SalesData Center Sector Saless for Enchanted Rock, he leverages deep knowledge of the North American and European markets for mission critical and demand response applications utilizing natural gas microgrid solutions, helping data centers adopt cleaner onsite power generation to benefit the local grid and community.

THIRTEEN

Solid Oxide Fuel Cells: Historic Innovation to Future Clean Energy Solution

Jeffrey Barber, Bloom Energy

Space is considered the final frontier of human exploration, an opportunity to discover the depths of our universe and the secrets it may contain to illuminate or improve our existence on Earth – or on another planet such as Mars if we so choose. Here on Earth, a new form of energy has been developed with Bloom Energy's pioneering hydrogen fuel cell technology; while working on NASA's Project Gemini in the 1960s, Bloom created what is often referred to as the "bridge to the moon" – and what NASA now considers "the bridge to the future."

In the 1980s and 1990s, Bloom's co-founders engineered electrolyzers and life support systems for NASA's space shuttles, missions and space stations. Over this time, there was growing interest in someday sending astronauts to Mars. Enter Dr. KR Sridhar, Bloom Energy CEO. Dr. Sridhar expanded electrolyzer research at the University of Arizona in the 1990s to make this vision a reality. While Project Gemini marked the beginning of Bloom's decades-long collaboration with NASA to engineer critical systems for space travel, it also marked Bloom's launch into providing more reliable and resilient fuel sources for life on this planet.

Chapter Thirteen

In 2001, Dr. Sridhar's team developed an electrolyzer that could convert Mars' atmospheric carbon dioxide into oxygen. Initially designed to enable future human missions to Mars by leveraging resources available on Mars, this technology would utilize oxygen produced from its CO_2 to support astronauts once they arrived on the planet. Dr. Sridhar realized this electrolyzer technology had powerful applications here on Earth and adapted it to create an innovative solid oxide fuel cell (SOFC) capable of delivering affordable, sustainable and reliable energy generation. Through a reversal of Dr. Sridhar's process — using fuels like natural gas to generate clean electricity via a highly efficient electrochemical reaction — Bloom became a leading provider of modular SOFC systems that produce reliable, resilient, and low-carbon power.

Today, our founders' vision for space travel and dedication to sustainable energy continue to drive breakthroughs — and real-world applications that can support our efforts to reach net zero in the digital infrastructure and technology industries. Data centers and other industries can lead the journey toward a cleaner and greener tomorrow by harnessing the potential of SOFCs powered by natural gas, biogas or hydrogen.

Natural Gas + SOFC Technology: Bridging the Gap

According to the U.S. Energy Information Administration, natural gas currently generates 39.9% of U.S. electricity. Replacing coal generation has substantially reduced emissions and, if used thoughtfully, can serve an essential transitional role to reliance on renewable energy sources. The Center for Climate and Energy Solutions notes that natural gas emits 50 to 60% less CO_2 than coal when combusted for power. This significant advantage has led many utilities to convert coal generation to natural gas, dramatically lowering emissions. Over 500 million metric tons of CO_2 reductions in recent years are attributable to this shift from coal to gas, per the International Energy Agency.

Natural gas combustion provides impressive benefits over coal and oil. As mentioned, it cuts CO_2 emissions by half per megawatt-

Chapter Thirteen

hour generated. Harmful air pollutants like sulfur dioxide, nitrogen oxides, soot and mercury are reduced by over 90% compared to coal, according to the Rocky Mountain Institute. These significant cuts in greenhouse gasses and health-harming contaminants make natural gas a valuable transitional energy source. Natural gas complements the growth of carbon-free renewables, as it provides reliable backup power when the sun or wind is unavailable, enabling greater grid penetration of intermittent resources like solar and wind. Natural gas facilitates an affordable, reliable transition to a decarbonized grid — a crucial goal for the digital infrastructure industry, which may be achieved sooner rather than later.

Although natural gas combustion contributes to approximately one-fourth of the U.S. CO2 emissions from fossil fuels, as reported by the U.S. Energy Information Administration, there exists significant opportunities to mitigate its environmental impact during this pivotal transition towards cleaner energy alternatives. Technologies like SOFCs allow natural gas to generate electricity efficiently via electrochemical conversion without combustion. SOFCs nearly eliminate air pollutants while capturing over 90% of CO_2 for sequestration or industrial reuse. SOFCs can also transition to biogas or green hydrogen over time.

With proper safeguards and declining coal utilization, natural gas and SOFCs can play a temporary role in clean power generation, buying crucial time for renewables, storage and transmission to scale affordably. Natural gas remains a powerful interim solution to zero-emission electricity. Investing in transitional technologies like SOFCs can help bridge the gap during this shift, though they complement rather than replace the need for dramatic renewable energy growth.

The reason for using natural gas is simple: green hydrogen distribution and production do not exist at scale. Natural gas is abundant, reliable and affordable, making it the perfect bridging solution to a zero-carbon future. The option to utilize natural gas future proofs on-site power generation for the customer, as moving to a pure hydrogen platform when this becomes feasible can be as simple as upgrading the energy server during a routine maintenance cycle. Bloom power modules are concurrently maintainable and highly redundant, meaning an upgrade to pure hydrogen can occur while the facility is up and running.

Microgrids: An Attainable and Plentiful Fuel Source for SOFCs

SOFCs have unique advantages as a bridge to a net-zero emissions future. Unlike intermittent renewable sources, they can generate uninterrupted baseload power. Bloom Energy's flagship product, the Energy Server®, is rooted in SOFC technology and offers a non-combustion alternative for converting fuel to electricity. SOFCs electrochemically convert natural gas, biogas or hydrogen to electricity through electrolytes, helping Bloom clients in their journey toward a cleaner today and greener tomorrow. Organizations can use the Bloom Energy Server® to form microgrids to island from the grid during outages and blackouts.

Microgrids containing SOFCs offer high reliability and clean on-site power generation: SOFCs reach 60% efficiency, nearly double that of legacy coal-based or hybrid power plants (35% to 45% efficiency), according to the U.S. Department of Energy. This increase in efficiency means less fuel is consumed to produce each kilowatt-hour. In the 1990s, government agencies, including the Department of Defense, funded SOFC microgrids at military bases and national labs, highlighting the technology's usefulness for critical infrastructure. Organizations and municipalities can implement low-emission systems sized for hospitals, data centers or neighborhoods faster than massive centralized plants. Modular or portable SOFC units can speed up deployment.

Chapter Thirteen

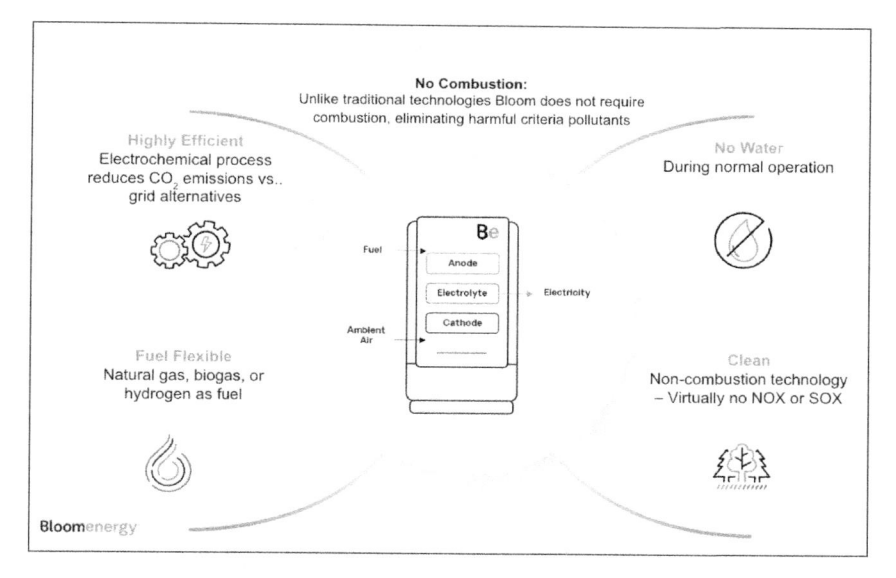

Source: Bloom Energy

As mentioned earlier, SOFCs can use hydrogen for power generation, but due to the lack of freely available hydrogen today, SOFCs typically use natural gas and biogas as fuel. But, because SOFCs are fuel-flexible, they fit into the long-term power generation strategy of organizations operating with natural gas or other hydrocarbons today and enable a pathway to zero emissions when hydrogen is readily available for power generation. And here's the sustainability kicker – since SOFCs don't burn the fuel, they produce virtually no particulate matter or air pollutants like nitrogen and sulfur oxides. Any excess heat from the cells can be captured and used, so nothing is wasted. Some may argue that SOFCs enable the continued use of gas instead of phasing it out. Still, others see it as a realistic bridge to help slash emissions from existing fossil fuel infrastructure as renewable energy scales up. According to NASA's Jet Propulsion Laboratory, avoiding emissions now matters because CO_2 accumulates in the atmosphere, taking more than 300 years to dissipate. Think of carbon reduction like a 401k fund. The less carbon we ingest in the atmosphere today, the greater the returns we'll see in the future from a health and climate perspective.

The Benefits of SOFCs in the Data Center

Businesses have received the message loud and clear — it's time to take action to meet net-zero goals. But the path to carbon neutrality isn't always clear, especially for energy-intensive industries like telecommunications and data centers. Renewables must be ready to power massive 5G networks or hyperscale data centers 24/7. However, SOFCs offer significant benefits for improving net-zero initiatives, specifically in the data center industry.

Data centers are notorious for high energy consumption, with estimated global data center electricity consumption 1 to 1.3% of global final electricity demand.[1] Addressing their carbon footprint is crucial for sustainability efforts. Known for the high efficiency of their energy conversion, SOFCs are typically 50% to 70% more efficient, with CHP-enabled fuel cells further increasing energy conversion efficiency to approximately 90% per the U.S. Department of Energy. A significant portion of the fuel's energy can be effectively converted into electricity by SOFCs. In data centers, where efficient and reliable delivery of electricity is the most critical function, this higher efficiency reduces fuel consumption and lowers greenhouse gas emissions.

Also, as mentioned earlier, SOFCs produce less greenhouse gas emissions than traditional power generation technologies like coal-fired plants or natural gas turbines. When using cleaner fuels or integrating carbon capture and utilization/storage (CCU/CCS) technologies, SOFCs can virtually eliminate CO_2 emissions. They can generate electricity and useful heat simultaneously, making them suitable for combined heat and power (CHP) applications. In a data center, the waste heat generated by SOFCs can be used for space heating or cooling, improving overall energy efficiency by up to 90% compared to traditional heating and cooling systems and reducing the need for additional HVAC systems.

Lastly, SOFCs are known for their robustness and reliability.

They can operate continuously for long periods, requiring minimal maintenance. This reliability is crucial for data centers, which demand an uninterrupted power supply to ensure data integrity and continuity for business facilities, ranging from small server rooms to extensive hyperscale facilities. This scalability allows data center operators to deploy SOFCs in a way that best suits their needs and growth patterns. SOFCs can operate independently of the grid or in conjunction with it. This flexibility provides data centers with a vastly more reliable primary power source than that offered by the traditional grid, reducing the risk of downtime during utility outages or disruptions. By diversifying the energy sources for data centers, SOFCs can enhance energy security. This advantage is especially significant in regions prone to energy supply disruptions or unreliable grid delivery — unfortunately, a reality for substantial swaths of America and the globe. Driven by concerns over energy security and climate change, organizations may utilize SOFC microgrids to reduce carbon footprints and electricity costs.

Advancing SOFC Technology

To develop the technology needed for extended space travel, NASA and Bloom's founders were forced to rethink energy at a fundamental level. How could they provide consistent, reliable, resilient power to sustain current and growing demands? The solutions were found via solid oxide electrolyzer cells. The research and extensive testing for NASA missions laid the foundations for Bloom's distinctive approach on Earth. Bloom's platform is unique in that it utilizes this technology to support net-zero energy reliability while being commercially available to organizations making efforts toward carbon neutrality. For over fifteen years, we've demonstrated that the current fuel cell is approximately 60% efficient, converting more molecules (input) to electrons (output). This efficiency is roughly 25% to 30% better than combustion technologies, translating to lower fuel costs per megawatt and zero particulates (NOX/SOX). Bloom has monitored every cell and subcomponent of these cells throughout this time, making use of predictive analysis that enables

Bloom to constantly refine the design, manufacturing and serviceability of fuel cells in the field.

The legacy of NASA's early SOFC development persists as Bloom's technology is continuously improved to enhance efficiency, durabilit and design for manufacturability. With ongoing improvements, microgrids based on SOFC technology can fulfill their potential as sustainable and resilient power solutions.

As mentioned earlier in the chapter, Bloom's SOFC technology separates hydrogen from carbon with a steam reformation process inside the system, typically using natural gas as the fuel input. The platform is flexible with hydrogen-ready and dependable fuel inputs and energy output, with 99.998% availability across the global installed base. It currently operates on biogas from organic waste, providing carbon-neutral electricity and is easier and more effective in carbon capture tech solutions than combustion-based generators.

An essential feature of this platform is its flexible design, which allows it to function independently of the grid and as a supplement to existing utility power when necessary. The design is modular and redundant across all aspects, with concurrent maintainability being core to the product. The ability to provide a much lower carbon solution, with or without grid infrastructure, translates to the customer being able to provide power where and when necessary within months versus years if relying on new grid connections. Bloom's platform offers a benchmark against which next-generation power supply solutions can be measured, combining flexibility, efficiency, redundancy and environmental responsibility — models other companies can adopt to meet greener initiatives and ESG goals.

As of 2022, Bloom has installed over 1 GW of fuel cell capacity across more than 900 customer sites globally, generating over 20 billion kWh of greener electricity. These systems provided reliable failover power for 597 hours across 436 grid outage events in 2022. By generating power at the point of use with high-efficiency fuel cells, these systems avoided over 941,000 metric tons of CO_2 emissions in 2022 while conserving more than 37 billion gallons of water compared to other power sources. This process has also maximized sustainability through 98% product recycling and ambitious emissions reduction targets while supporting local communities through initiatives and clean energy jobs. With exceptional power generation efficiency, low environmental impact and proven reliability, these statistics illustrate how SOFC microgrids present a compelling solution to meet sustainability goals and resilient energy needs.

Transitioning to SOFCs could reduce the natural gas industry's carbon footprint. One Harvard University study found that swapping out all conventional gas power plants for SOFCs in the U.S. would decrease CO_2 emissions by over 60% in under 15 years while cutting other air pollutants by more than 90%.[2] Those are substantial environmental gains. And SOFCs' long-term potential is even more significant. By switching infrastructure away from unabated fossil fuels toward hydrogen, the natural gas industry can lead to building a clean energy economy. Hydrogen makes substantial environmental progress possible in the near term while offering a bridge to a deeply decarbonized future. The energy industry could send a powerful signal by investing more ambitiously in hydrogen.

As the world's largest network-neutral colocation provider, Equinix is taking steps towards powering its global data center operations with 100% clean energy. The company previously announced the testing of a 1MW fuel cell system from Bloom to help power its SV5 data center. According to Equinix, this fuel cell project supports its sustainability goals, benefiting 8,000 customers looking to trim carbon inventory.

With over 145 data centers in 40 major markets across 21 countries and five continents, Equinix has an enormous data center footprint. By testing innovative clean energy solutions like the Bloom SOFC system, Equinix is working to transition its extensive operations toward renewable energy sources over time. The upgraded 50MW system represents the company's commitment to exploring and deploying new technologies to achieve its goal of 100% renewable operations. As a leader in the colocation industry with data centers spanning the globe, Equinix has the scale and influence to make a meaningful impact on sustainability through clean energy initiatives.

Chapter Thirteen

A Path Forward

SOFCs present a viable pathway for slashing emissions from existing natural gas infrastructure as cleaner energy sources become available. Their speedy and affordable deployment means SOFCs can be a critical step along the path to net zero achievement. That makes SOFCs a promising technology for better utilizing natural gas supplies and reducing their environmental impact during this crucial transition period.

Many renewable energy sources like solar and wind have yet to be ready for intensive commercial demands, and their intermittency cannot always meet baseload power demands. SOFCs bridge that gap, enabling businesses to meet ambitious net-zero timelines while the grid plays catch up. They align sustainability with reliability and affordability – a win-win.

Just as Project Gemini paved the way to the moon in the 1960s, breakthroughs in resilient and renewable power sources blaze a trail to an abundant future on our home planet. By witnessing the genesis of this progress firsthand, we will be able to marry humanity's reach for the stars with environmental stewardship on planet Earth. So, business leaders aiming for net zero, tech titans striving to improve upon a greener data ecosystem and corporations across sectors can look to SOFCs for affordable, 24/7, clean power today. Innovative businesses and data centers will adopt SOFCs and reap those climate and economic benefits first. This technology enables companies to walk the walk on climate action now with existing infrastructure, not years down the road. That's how you lead.

---

1. International Energy Agency. Data Centres and Data Transmission Networks. https://www.iea.org/energy-system/buildings/data-centres-and-data-transmission-networks
2. Gerhardt, Michael R. "Solid-oxide Fuel Cells: Using familiar fuel in a new way." Harvard University: Science in the News. November 16, 2015. https://sitn.hms.harvard.edu/flash/2015/solid-oxide-fuel-cells-using-familiar-fuel-in-a-new-way/

About the Author

JEFFREY BARBER

Jeffrey Barber is the Vice President of Global Data Centers at Bloom Energy, where he drives transformative change in the industry. A global leader with more than 20 years of experience in the digital infrastructure markets, Jeff held key roles at EMC/Dell, Oracle and Prime Data Centers prior to joining Bloom.

At Bloom Energy, Jeff oversees the data center vertical supporting businesses in meeting their mission-critical power needs. In his role, he is dedicated to empowering data center developers, tenants and operators to take control of all their data center power requirements and is passionate about paving a more sustainable path forward for data centers. His dedication to reliable, sustainable and efficient power remains at the forefront of his work, enabling the industry to take control of its most critical asset: access to power.

FOURTEEN

Green Data Centers: Nurturing Sustainability in the Digital Age

Sindhu Sharma, Nxtra by Airtel

Embarking on the path to digital maturity involves businesses navigating the intricacies of the digital paradox. As businesses increasingly rely on data centers for digital expansion, unfortunately, they represent the primary source of greenhouse gas emissions within the IT industry. As a result, there is a heightened focus on sustainable data centers, which are expected to operate with optimal efficiency; recognizing the environmental impact associated with maintaining constant online connectivity across a range of devices, businesses are placing a great emphasis on digital sustainability.

In the Indian context, companies harboring ambitious digitization goals are increasingly turning to collaboration with hyper-scale data centers. This strategic move is designed to fulfill business requirements for agile, resilient, and modernized technology and operations, with a key focus on ensuring sustainability. As the Indian data center industry is projected to achieve significant growth in market size in the coming years[1], there is a parallel and significant opportunity to strive towards achieving 100% "green interconnectedness".

Traditional data centers, while pivotal in supporting the digital landscape, have raised concerns due to their substantial environmental impact. One of the primary issues is the energy consumption of these data centers. The extensive hardware infrastructure required for data processing and storage demands a significant amount of power. This, in turn, contributes to a substantial carbon footprint and exacerbates the global energy consumption challenge.

The acknowledgment of environmental challenges posed by traditional data center models serves as a catalyst for transformative change. It propels us towards embracing sustainable, energy-efficient, and environmentally conscious approaches to data processing and storage, ensuring harmonious coexistence between technology and the planet. Collective awareness will pave the way for a greener and more responsible digital future.

This chapter delves into the realm of green data centers, exploring innovative strategies and practices that range from designing energy-efficient infrastructure to finding new ways to power it with the goal of mitigating the ecological footprint of these essential hubs.

Energy-Efficient Infrastructure

Data centers consume massive amounts of electricity to power servers, cooling systems, and other equipment. This makes energy-efficient infrastructure for data centers a critical aspect of addressing the environmental impact and sustainability challenges associated with the rapidly growing demand for digital services. Designing and implementing energy-efficient solutions not only contribute to environmental conservation but also result in cost savings and improved operational performance.

Chapter Fourteen

Below is a list of several key strategies that facility operators can put in place to improve the energy efficiency of their data center infrastructure:

1. Optimized Server Hardware

- Choose energy-efficient server hardware, including processors, memory, and storage components.
- Implement virtualization technologies to increase server utilization rates, reducing the need for idle servers.

2. Advanced Cooling Systems

- Employ innovative cooling technologies, such as liquid cooling or direct-to-chip cooling, to minimize the energy required for temperature regulation.
- Optimize airflow management within the data center to reduce cooling energy consumption.

3. Energy-Efficient Lighting and Power Distribution

- Utilize energy-efficient lighting systems, such as LED, and implement smart lighting controls to minimize unnecessary energy consumption.
- Deploy efficient uninterruptible power supply (UPS) systems and power distribution units (PDUs) to reduce energy losses.

4. Data Center Consolidation and Virtualization

- Consolidate servers through virtualization to decrease the overall physical infrastructure footprint.

- Implement cloud computing and edge computing strategies to distribute workloads efficiently.

5. Energy Monitoring and Management

- Implement comprehensive energy monitoring systems to track and analyze energy usage in real time.
- Use intelligent energy management tools to optimize resource allocation and reduce energy waste.

6. High-Efficiency Data Center Design

- Design data centers with energy efficiency in mind, incorporating features such as hot/cold aisle containment and efficient layout planning.
- Consider modular designs that allow for scalability and efficient resource utilization.

7. Lifecycle Management and Decommissioning

- Adopt sustainable practices for equipment procurement and disposal.
- Regularly assess and update technology to incorporate the latest energy-efficient solutions.

8. Employee Awareness and Training

- Educate data center staff on energy-efficient practices and the importance of minimizing environmental impact.
- Encourage a culture of sustainability and continuous improvement within the organization.

A Case Study on Successful Implementation of Energy-Efficient Strategies

The implementation of energy efficiency and conservation measures has proven beneficial for Nxtra Data Limited ('Nxtra'), resulting in the handling of increased workloads without exponential increases in energy consumption. Over the past five years, Nxtra saw a remarkable 20% improvement in Power Usage Effectiveness (PUE), enabling it to make the most of its infrastructure and strengthen operational efficiency[2]. In addition, improving energy efficiency has helped Nxtra to reduce operational costs, minimize environmental impact, and enhance sustainability. These energy efficiency efforts have also allowed Nxtra to maximize its data center capacity without needing to constantly expand its infrastructure, leading to better space utilization and reduced capital expenditures.

Nxtra has prioritized the reduction of electricity consumption, and the adoption of energy-efficient measures and optimal power usage through many of the strategies previously mentioned, including:

- Implemented advanced cooling techniques such as hot/cold aisle containment etc. to improve cooling efficiency.
- Optimized the data center layout for efficient airflow and heat distribution, reducing the need for excessive cooling.
- Installed LED lighting with motion sensors to ensure that lighting is only active in areas where needed, minimizing unnecessary energy consumption.
- Performed regular maintenance and upgrades to ensure that all systems are running optimally, reducing the risk of inefficiencies and failures.
- Arranged racks to avoid hotspots and ensure uniform airflow, improving cooling efficiency.

Nxtra has also secured ISO 50001:2018 certification for its core data centers. This is an attestation to the company's adherence to the rigorous Energy Management System (EnMS) guidelines.

Harnessing Renewable Energy Sources

Once a data center's infrastructure is optimized for energy efficiency, the transition toward use of renewable energy is a pivotal next step in addressing environmental concerns, reducing carbon footprints, and fostering a sustainable approach to digital infrastructure. As the demand for data processing and storage continues to escalate, the traditional reliance on non-renewable energy sources becomes a significant environmental challenge.

Transition to renewable energy is not only an environmental imperative but also a strategic and economically sound decision for data centers. It positions them as responsible and forward-thinking entities, contributing to the development of sustainable and resilient digital infrastructure.

Key reasons why data centers should consider the shift toward renewable energy include:

1. Environmental Sustainability | Traditional data centers that are heavily reliant on non-renewable energy sources contribute significantly to carbon emissions. Transitioning to renewable energy helps operators lower their carbon footprint, mitigating the advance of climate change.

2. Climate Change Mitigation | Transitioning to renewable energy aligns data centers with global efforts to mitigate climate change, as outlined in agreements such as the Paris Agreement. It demonstrates a commitment to sustainability and responsible business practices.

3. Energy Cost Stability | Investing in renewable energy sources provides data centers with a more stable and predictable cost structure over the long term. This is in contrast to fossil fuels that have volatile, and rising prices; renewables offer financial benefits in the form of reduced energy expenses.

4. Economic Competitiveness | Adopting renewable energy can enhance a data center's market competitiveness. Businesses and consumers increasingly prioritize environmentally conscious choices, and being a leader in sustainable practices can attract environmentally-aware clients.

5. Regulatory Compliance | Many regions are introducing stricter environmental regulations and emissions standards. Transitioning to renewable energy helps data centers stay compliant with evolving environmental laws and regulations.

6. Resilience and Independence | By generating their own renewable energy, data centers can reduce their dependence on external power grids, enhancing resilience during power outages or grid disruptions.

7. Public Relations and Reputation | Operating on renewable energy fosters a positive public image. Not only consumers but also other external stakeholders including regulatory bodies, government departments, lenders, etc. are increasingly supportive of businesses that prioritize sustainability, enhancing the reputation of data centers.

8. Innovation and Technological Advancements | The transition to renewable energy stimulates technological advancements in energy storage, efficiency, and renewable technologies. This fosters a culture of innovation within the data center industry.

9. Employee Morale and Recruitment | Employees, especially the younger workforce, are often drawn to companies that embrace sustainability. Demonstrating a commitment to renewable energy can enhance employee morale and attract top talent.

10. Social Responsibility | Embracing renewable energy aligns with broader corporate social responsibility initiatives. It reflects a commitment to ethical practices and responsible corporate citizenship.

Transitioning to Renewable Energy

Increasing renewable energy consumption is now good hygiene for data centers. While most data center players are heavily invested in exploring alternate means of supplying power, in India they are looking to develop their own captive solar, wind, and hybrid plants for energy. As many of these data centers are not large-scale they can follow more of a hub-and-spoke model or operate as part of an edge data center cluster, opting to procure renewable/clean energy from various private and government-owned real estate sources.

The exploration of renewable energy for data centers represents a significant stride towards a sustainable and eco-friendly digital future. As technology advances and the cost of renewable energy continues to decrease, the transition becomes not only an ethical choice but also an economically viable and forward-thinking strategy for the data center industry.

Key aspects to consider when transitioning a data center to renewable energy include:

1. Motivation for Transition

- The primary motivation lies in mitigating the environmental impact associated with conventional energy sources, reducing greenhouse gas emissions, and combating climate change.
- Aligning data center operations with environmentally responsible practices helps organizations meet sustainability goals.

2. Integration of Renewable Sources

- Power Purchase Agreements (PPAs): Entering into PPAs with renewable energy providers allows data centers to buy electricity directly from renewable sources, supporting the growth of the renewable energy market.
- Onsite Renewable Energy Generation: Deploying onsite renewable energy infrastructure, such as wind or solar farms, enables the generation of power specifically for the data center.
- Energy Storage Solutions: Integrating energy storage systems, such as advanced batteries, to store excess energy generated during peak renewable production allows for operation during periods of lower production.
- Hybrid Energy Approaches: Implementing hybrid energy solutions that combine renewable sources with traditional backup systems helps to ensure uninterrupted power supply.

3. Government Incentives and Policies

- Leveraging government incentives and policies that encourage the adoption of renewable energy, including tax credits and subsidies, can support capex commitments.

4. Public Awareness and Communication:

- Communicating the commitment to renewable energy to stakeholders, clients, and the public enhances transparency and builds a positive brand image.

Challenges of Renewable Energy

While the adoption of green data center practices is crucial for sustainability, several challenges can impede the process, including:

1. High Initial Costs | The upfront investment in green technologies, such as energy-efficient infrastructure and renewable energy sources, can be substantial. Many organizations find it challenging to justify these costs, especially if they have existing infrastructure that is not yet end of life.

2. Return on Investment (ROI) Concerns | Organizations may be hesitant to invest in green practices if they are unsure about the timeline for realizing a return on investment. The long-term cost savings and environmental benefits might not be immediately apparent, leading to reluctance to adopt.

3. Legacy Infrastructure | Older data centers may have legacy infrastructure that is not inherently energy-efficient. Retrofitting or upgrading such facilities to meet green standards can be complex and expensive, posing a significant challenge.

4. Complexity of Implementation | Integrating green technologies into existing data center operations can be intricate. Implementation may require downtime, reconfiguration of systems, and employee training, causing disruptions to regular operations.

5. Lack of Standardization | The absence of standardized practices and guidelines for green data center implementation can make it challenging for organizations to navigate the diverse options available. Lack of clear standards may also hinder comparison and benchmarking.

6. Limited Renewable Energy Availability | In some regions, access to reliable and affordable renewable energy sources may be limited. Data centers located in areas with inadequate renewable energy infrastructure may face challenges in sourcing clean energy.

7. Regulatory Barriers | Regulatory environments vary globally, and some regions may lack incentives or regulations that encourage green practices. Conversely, stringent regulations might pose compliance challenges for data centers looking to adopt specific green technologies, example implementation of fuel cells for energy storage etc.

Despite these challenges, the growing awareness of environmental issues and the long-term benefits of green data center practices are driving organizations to overcome these obstacles. As technology evolves and sustainability becomes a higher priority, solutions to these challenges are likely to emerge, making green data center practices more accessible and widespread.

Chapter Fourteen

A Case Study on Shifting to Green Energy

Nxtra is dedicated to reducing its use of fossil fuels and increasing the proportion of renewable energy in its data centers. The company has a goal to create a sustainable and green data center brand for itself in the industry. To achieve this, Nxtra sources and invests in green power for its data centers, while also installing on-site solar rooftop plants. These measures have resulted in numerous benefits, including lower costs and decreased carbon emissions, all while moving closer to reaching a net zero carbon footprint.

Transitioning to clean energy is critical to addressing climate change and renewable energy, and Nxtra has found success in India by sourcing through an open-access route. Nxtra, along with its parent company, Airtel, has committed to invest in fourteen companies that develop renewable power plants, enabling the sourcing of over 425,320 MWh of green energy for its data centers. Rooftop solar plants have also been installed at Nxtra's data centers and edge sites in 30 different locations. Out of the total electricity consumed in Nxtra's core data centers, 33% came from renewable sources in the Indian 2023 fiscal year.

Nxtra has also partnered with Bloom Energy to introduce solid oxide fuel cell (SOFC) technology, making it the first data center company in India to adopt this low environmental impact solution. The installation of fuel cells at the Karnataka data center marks a significant milestone in providing clean and sustainable energy. By deploying SOFC technology, Nxtra aims to reduce carbon emissions and unlock cost and sustainability benefits. The initial phase involves powering the fuel cells with non-combusted natural gas; looking ahead, the company plans to transition to a 50% hydrogen supply without the need for substantial investments. These natural gas-powered cells may serve as the primary source of energy generation, with the utility electrical grid and backup generators acting as additional support.

Chapter Fourteen

Looking Ahead to the Future of Green Data Centers

Embracing green data center initiatives is imperative in navigating the intersection of technological growth and environmental responsibility. The adoption of renewable energy sources, energy-efficient hardware, and innovative cooling systems are fundamental strategies to reduce carbon footprints and enhance operational sustainability. Beyond environmental benefits, embracing green practices often leads to long-term cost savings, increased energy efficiency, and enhanced corporate reputation. As the world becomes more digitally connected, the imperative to align technological progress with ecological well-being underscores the pivotal role of green data center initiatives in fostering a balanced and sustainable digital future.

As we look ahead, with data usage on the rise it is imperative that industry leaders, technology innovators, and policymakers join forces to drive environmentally conscious solutions that go beyond those shared in this chapter. This entails investing in cutting-edge technologies, to reshape the landscape of data management. Moreover, fostering collaboration and knowledge-sharing among organizations is essential moving forward to establish industry-wide standards and best practices.

The urgency of this call lies in the opportunity to not only mitigate the environmental impact of data management but also to pave the way for a more resilient, efficient, and sustainable digital ecosystem. By collectively embracing innovation and collaboration, we can ensure that the rapid expansion of data-driven technologies occurs harmoniously with a commitment to environmental stewardship.

---

1. Data Centers 2024 Global Outlook. JLL.
2. Nxtra Data Limited Sustainability Report. 2023.

About the Author

SINDHU SHARMA

Sindhu Sharma is an accomplished sustainability professional with a diverse background in the realms of low-carbon growth strategies and technologies, renewable energy procurement, water and waste management, risk assessment, disclosure practices, and operational governance. Additionally, Sindhu possesses extensive experience in cultivating strategic partnerships, executing sustainable solutions through fostering policy dialogues, and orchestrating capacity-building training initiatives to promote community development.

His collaborative efforts have spanned a spectrum of stakeholders, encompassing investors, consultancy firms, developers, and Independent Power Producers (IPPs), fostering the acquisition of a multifaceted skill set spanning technology, regulatory compliance, valuation, structuring, and corporate strategy.

His educational background encompasses studies in both management and engineering, with a specialized focus on finance and energy.

Currently, Sindhu holds the position of 'Head - ESG' at 'Nxtra by Airtel,' the data center business division of the Bharti Airtel Group.

FIFTEEN

Subsea Cable Sustainability

Erick Contag & Nicole Starosielski, PhD, SubOptic

Over the past ten years, researchers, policy-makers, and organizations have all sought to assess and reduce the CO_2 emissions produced by digital infrastructure. Efforts have largely focused on data centers, while subsea telecommunications cables, which transport over 99% of all transoceanic data traffic via 1.4 million kilometers of fiber optic cable globally, have remained almost entirely absent in this discussion.[1] This omission is in part due to the relatively low level of CO_2 generated by the ongoing operation of subsea cable systems.

Even though their power usage is minimal compared to many data centers, individual companies and organizations in the subsea cable industry have been developing their own approaches to assessing sustainability and implementing best practices across scope 1, 2, and 3. Up until 2021, however, these efforts remained ad-hoc and were pursued largely independent of one another. In this chapter, we describe some of the recent research conducted by the SubOptic Foundation's Sustainable Subsea Networks (SSN) research team to bring together these disparate efforts and facilitate industry-wide cooperation to enhance the sustainability of subsea cable networks.

Chapter Fifteen

For the past two years, from 2021-2023, the SSN research team has documented existing CO_2 emissions mitigation efforts of subsea telecommunications cable companies. These companies' activities range from standard practices such as accounting and disclosing CO_2 emissions and setting targets, to more specific efforts around sustainable design and operations, and recovery and recycling. By gathering information on these efforts, our *Best Practices in Subsea Telecommunications Cable Sustainability*[2] report provides insight into sustainability initiatives that can be scaled and replicated across many parts of the industry worldwide.

In the chapter below, we describe some of the report's findings, highlighting many sustainability efforts that are unique to the subsea cable industry, specifically in cable design, manufacturing and supply, and in maritime operations, two areas that typically lie outside existing digital infrastructure sustainability research.

The Emergence of Sustainability in the Subsea Cable Industry

Over the past several years, subsea cable companies have begun to put forward green agendas and initiatives. Japanese cable supplier NEC, who had committed to science-based targets in 2017, formulated *Eco Action Plan 2025* to increase the company's sustainability. French cable supplier Alcatel Submarine Networks (ASN) developed a Green Charter to address climate change and to take a leadership role on environmental matters, documenting its work in the first video on the topic.[3] The consulting company WFN Strategies developed an environmental roadmap and a set of internal policies. Red Penguin Marine, who provide subsea cable engineering and marine consulting services, convened an environmental group within the company to discuss how they could move toward net zero. Corning, the leading fiber optic manufacturing company, focused their bi-annual summit in 2023 on the topic of sustainability and challenges facing the glass industry. Ciena - a global leader in optical communications technology and software - created an Environmental Steering Committee in 2020 to manage its environmental programs, plans, and policies. Such efforts - which intensified from 2021 to

Chapter Fifteen

2023 - mark a transition period in the fiber optic submarine cable industry and technology toward developing sustainability initiatives and goals.

While some companies have positions dedicated to sustainability, others lack a coherent sustainability plan and dedicated sustainability officers. A few companies that the SSN team interviewed had no sustainability initiatives or policies in place. There are several reasons for this variation. Economic margins have been eroding in the industry, especially in the marine sector, and there are generally no excess resources to funnel into sustainability. The low carbon footprint of the industry as a whole has generally kept this from being as pressing a concern, as it is for the data center sector. The subsea cable industry is also global, stretching across diverse geographic and environmental contexts where sustainability is more or less of a concern. Although there are companies dedicated to subsea cable development, in many organizations subsea systems are merely one part of a broader set of telecommunications operations, and other more energy-intensive infrastructures take precedence in sustainability work.

Nonetheless, even without coordinated efforts, sustainability initiatives abound in the subsea cable industry. For a few companies, these initiatives are seen as providing a competitive advantage and contain knowledge to be safeguarded. Aside from these outliers, we found that most companies in the sector see more value in a collaborative approach; for over 30 years this industry in particular has embraced and even thrived from collaboration and co-opetition.

We are, however, in the early years of the subsea cable industry's sustainability movement, and today initiatives remain largely independent of one another and driven by a variety of influences. As our research has shown, while substantial coordination has occurred across the industry in marine sustainability – in part facilitated by the International Cable Protection Committee (ICPC) – many of our interviewees remain unaware of what others are doing specifically to mitigate carbon emissions. Communicating and sharing best practices is an essential first step for future development.

In our chapter featured in *Greener Data: Actionable Insights from*

Industry Leaders, we asked ourselves "How do we put connective thinking into action?" Through the SubOptic Foundation's Sustainable Subsea Networks project, we have started to engage and collaborate at a global level, and to facilitate industry-wide cooperation for the benefit of all. These initial steps should not be underestimated – through connective thinking, based on broad industry contributions, and commitment to a greener future, we have published our first industry report.

In what follows, we will highlight an array of ongoing activities, technologies, and practices that the industry has embraced to reduce our carbon footprint. We draw from the data and research in the *Best Practices Report* to highlight the contributions across the industry, ranging from sustainable design manufacturing to end-of-life cable recycling.[4]

Sustainable Design and Manufacturing

Subsea fiber optic cable design, manufacturing, and supply is a difficult area in which to assess specific sustainability data and information. The exact composition of cable materials is generally kept confidential since it can be used to calculate the cost of a cable. Although cable manufacturing is limited to only a few companies, these suppliers generally modify cable design to meet the specific needs of individual subsea cable systems, including the amount of strength and armoring. From the supplier's perspective, if customers were to ask for different cable compositions - including less carbon-intensive designs - they explicitly stated that they would be interested in meeting this demand.

While sustainable cable design - aside from energy efficiency - is not yet in high demand from subsea cable customers, suppliers have been doing many things to improve the sustainability of their own operations as well as the systems they are building. This includes connecting their facilities to carbon neutral and renewable energy; developing energy efficiency strategies at their facilities; and advancing eco-design.

There are several cable manufacturing facilities around the

world that are powered by carbon neutral or renewable power. ASN's site in Calais, France, is equipped with a surface of 1,781m² of solar panels, inaugurated in October 2022. ASN has also installed a heat recovery system and uses thermal emissions from their operations to heat their facilities. NEC has solar installations across its network of facilities, including its head office building, data centers, and factories. It has installed a 0.5MW solar power plant at the Ōtsuki Repeater/Branching Unit Factory and also has renewable energy at its OCC Cable Factory in Kita Kyushu. Both ASN and NEC have committed to purchasing green electricity in addition to that produced in these installations. The Hudiksvall plant of cable manufacturer Hexatronic is powered by 100% renewable energy from hydropower. Like ASN, Hexatronic has similarly installed a district heating system, powered by bio-based sources; in addition, the factory and other premises are partially heated with the excess heat generated by machines.

Corning, a supplier of optical fiber, has conducted life cycle assessments (LCA) for its major products. Corning's LCA study for optical fiber confirmed that the electricity required in manufacturing is the main source of impact, contributing 70-80% to the overall carbon footprint. As a result, the value of continued energy efficiency efforts and a greener electricity mix is clear and being pursued. Since 2006, the company has reduced the energy intensity of its global fiber and cable manufacturing facilities by over 50%, including the facilities used to manufacture optical fibers for subsea cables.

Fiber and cable manufacturers and suppliers have also begun to think about sustainability in cable design. In 2022, Corning piloted a *Design for Sustainability* program and is now developing sustainable design guidelines and tools for product developers. ASN has been intentionally working to develop slimmer cables, which helps to reduce materials and therefore both cost and carbon footprint. A slimmer cable design also helps to optimize loading of vessels, which in turn may reduce the number of trips a vessel takes to deploy a subsea cable system. Depending on the type of project and the kilometers of cables, the fuel consumption of the ships might also be reduced in the process. Most importantly, with slimmer cables, the quantity of raw material is reduced. Hexatronic has also been working to develop slimmer cables. The company has recently adopted a slimmer design using a fibrin metallic tube or loose tube design, based on a thin stainless-steel tube with slimmer fibers with a core diameter of only 190 μm instead of traditionally 250 μm, and thus further reducing their carbon footprint.

One new technology currently under consideration is the powering of subsea cables by ocean wave. In this model, wave buoys would be located on the surface of the ocean along the cable route and connected to the cable below. The motion of waves would be converted into electricity, as buoys rise and fall and move back-and-forth. Buoys could also be outfitted with solar panels to supplement the wave power. In 2022, GEPS Techno announced that they were partnering with Meta to investigate remote powering of high-capacity subsea cables.

Sustainable Marine Operations

Marine operators face some difficult sustainability challenges. We found that companies generally want to adopt sustainable practices, but face economic constraints. As noted in the *Best Practices* report, Bruce Neilson-Watts, CEO of Global Marine, told us that "it's really difficult for our industry to change…we are hamstrung because we sunk a lot of CAPEX into equipment and technology which is decades old." For the last 15 years, since the dot-com and infrastructure bust and industry collapse, it has been a customer's market with very low pricing. The "price point investment has not moved far enough" to be able to build new $90 million ships, he observed.

BT also stated that they would like to adopt additional measures for sustainability on cable ships, but this is difficult since the technology is still far from where it needs to be in order to be feasible. This is especially true because much sustainable technology has not been developed specifically for cable ships, with their significant size and specialized equipment.

Chapter Fifteen

In this economic climate, it is particularly notable that Orange Marine decided to build a new cable ship, the Sophie Germain, which reduces CO_2 emissions by 20% and NOx (nitrogen oxide) emissions by 80% as compared to its predecessor, the Raymond Croze. The company achieved these reductions through the use of new technologies. The vessel is a hybrid, combining generators and batteries in order to limit the use of generators on cable operations. The energy and propulsion systems are at "the cutting edge of technology": POD type propulsion engines (azimuthal with a submerged electric motor) and thin management of the efficiency of the generators (multi-stage power, semi-fast diesel). NOx emissions are reduced by installing a system comparable to a catalytic converter on the exhaust of the diesel engines.

In construction, new ships can take advantage of new computational systems for designing new hull forms, and in turn, produce more energy efficient vessels. Orange Marine's Sophie Germain has an optimized hull design, with lines designed for energy efficiency, for repair cable loading, and a transit speed of 12.5 knots. Global Marine is looking at hull design as well.

In Nokia's 2021 environmental report, the company noted that - in line with its marine strategy - ASN has been rejuvenating its fleet over the past three years.[5] It has sold three older vessels and bought three new vessels with lower tonnage and lower fuel consumption.

Despite the obstacles to building new ships, we found many creative initiatives to increase efficiency and decrease emissions. These fall into three main categories: efficiency strategies; connecting to shore power; and fuel conversion.

Efficient management of ships in installation and maintenance increases sustainability. Some companies are doing multiple installs at the same time, which saves fuel. Running a tight program enables economic efficiency alongside positive environmental impacts. The least amount of time that the vessel is out, the better for the environment and the less expensive for the company. This is why effective planning - and having a day-to-day plan in place - is so important. Fugro, a leading geo-data specialist company, has been using route optimization tools and economic speed models, and ASN has been

Chapter Fifteen

optimizing transit routes using routing software. The company also mobilizes regional-based chartered vessels to reduce transit. NTT also optimizes route selection in relation to ship speed, ocean currents, and weather conditions, based on a Ship Energy Efficiency Management Plan.

One key parameter that companies have debated is transit speed. Vessels burn less fuel when they run at an optimal speed for energy efficiency, often at a slower than maximum speed. Global Marine specifically asks its customers if they would like the vessels to go at a more efficient speed. A slower transit time leads to less fuel burned, but in turn the company has to pay more for the crew on the ship. Obviously, this is a less viable option when time is of the essence, such as transiting to repair a broken cable or install a new one, but might be a consideration for the return voyage when time is less pressing. Takahiro Kashima of NEC cautioned, however, that "speed optimization does not always lead to carbon reduction." If the marine installation is not completed during the workable season due to the adoption of speed optimization, additional vessel mobilization could be required, which would result in additional CO_2 emissions.

Another key sustainable technology for marine vessels is shore power. Shore power enables ships to connect to the electrical grid while docked, reducing emissions and air pollution, assuming the grid is clean. The on-shore infrastructure of shore power can be set up in different ways, depending on where the power converter is placed and the existing vessel infrastructure, but its advancement requires investments from ship owners as well as from ports. On the other hand, retrofitting existing vessels with shore power is more cost-effective than building and buying new ships. Notable organizations such as the US EPA, the United States Navy, and the Commission of European Communities have acknowledged the potential of shore power and advocated for its implementation, economic incentives, and the exchange of best practices.

Although shore power can offer significant emissions benefits, it is not always available for cable ships. "The truth is most major ports do offer shore power, but it's usually reserved for cruise liners, ferries, large cargo ships, and the like," said Steve Arsenault, Director of Global Submarine Solutions at IT International Telecom. "Cable ships are typically given berths away from those main areas, without shore power access."

The sustainability of the maritime sector will eventually rely on the transition from fossil-fuels to clean energy-based fuels. The maritime sector, however, poses unique challenges to some of the more common renewable sources, such as wind or solar, since shipping is time-bound and requires the ability to effectively store energy in fuel both at port and on the ship itself. Alternative fuel sources most amenable to marine transport are methanol-based (which has been available for some time), hydrogen (increasingly common), and ammonia (still expanding). Hydrogen and ammonia fuel sources are not yet operating at scale, though this does seem to be changing, especially as the price of hydrogen is becoming more affordable.

Another area in which new technologies are making a difference is in the marine survey. Traditional marine survey methods have long relied on large vessels and a crew. These vessels use diesel fuel, which increases the level of carbon emissions. This has implications not only for the environment, but for the economic cost of a system.

One new development, which poses opportunities for sustainable marine operations, increased efficiency, and reduced costs and risks, is the development of Uncrewed Surface Vehicle (USV) technologies for mapping trans-oceanic subsea cable systems. USVs have a low or non-existent carbon footprint. The adoption of USVs in the industry could potentially reduce reliance on traditional vessels, while significantly reducing the emissions of the survey process.

Lastly, and perhaps most importantly, one of the most significant things that can be done to reduce emissions in subsea cable maintenance is to minimize repairs. An adequately protected cable requires fewer repairs, less utilization of ships, and the emission of less CO_2.

Chapter Fifteen

Cable Recovery and Recycling

One carbon-intensive process in the subsea industry is the manufacturing of cables, which encompasses the mining and processing of cable materials, especially aluminum and steel. One direct way to mitigate this impact is through cable recovery, recycling, and the reintroduction of materials in a circular economy approach. We have learned from recovery and recycling companies Mertech Marine, Subsea Environmental Services, and OEC that approximately 99.9% of subsea cable materials can be recycled. Recovering and recycling cable, as well as dry plant Submarine Line Terminal Equipment, provides cable owners with an opportunity to incorporate sustainable practices into their ordinary business operations, improve environmental outcomes, and better reflect the sustainability of the subsea telecommunication cable industry as a whole.

With many 1990s and early 2000s subsea cables starting to reach the end of their economic and design lives, opportunities for recovery and re-lay or recycling of such older systems will increase in years to come.

A Call for Collaboration on Sustainability

Many of the practices outlined above are being undertaken by a relatively small group of companies. Our research, however, has found that the future of sustainability in the industry requires not only connective thinking, but active collaboration. Such collaboration should take place around the development and harmonization of metrics, especially for the design and marine elements of CO_2 emissions reduction that exceed the scope of the data center industry. The implementation of industry-wide metrics, some drawn from other sectors, could significantly improve companies' ability to develop and sustain environmentally friendly policies and practices internally. Metrics will also be essential if sustainability practices, targets, and standards adopted by the industry are written into contracts - in procurement agreements, vendor contracts, lease agreements, among others. In 2024-2025, the SubOptic Foundation

Sustainable Subsea Networks team will broaden its efforts and work to facilitate such collaborations around sustainability metrics and initiatives. We invite you to join us in this important work.

This chapter is an output from a SubOptic Foundation project funded by the Internet Society Foundation.

---

1. TeleGeography. "Submarine Cable 101." TeleGeography website. https://www2.telegeography.com/submarine-cable-faqs-frequently-asked-questions
2. Nicole Starosielski, et. al. "Best Practices in Subsea Telecommunications Cable Sustainability." SubOptic Foundation 2024. https://suboptic.org/page/sustainable-subsea-networks-report
3. Alcatel Submarine Networks, "Connecting the World Responsibly: ASN's Commitment to Sustainable Submarine Cable." https://www.youtube.com/watch?v=RZRZQ1hW4TU
4. All data and citations from this article are drawn from Nicole Starosielski, et. al. "Best Practices in Subsea Telecommunications Cable Sustainability." SubOptic Foundation 2024. https://suboptic.org/page/sustainable-subsea-networks-report
5. Nokia, "Nokia People and Planet 2021 sustainability report." https://www.nokia.com/sites/default/files/2022-03/nokia-people-and-planet-2021-sustainability-report.pdf

About the Author
ERICK CONTAG

Erick Contag is a strategist, who is passionate about building and operating sustainable digital infrastructures. He has over 30 years of executive management, entrepreneurship, marketing & sales, and business development expertise. Mr. Contag has been responsible for managing C-level relationships and telecommunications / high-technology projects for start-up enterprises through large multi-national and Global 100 companies. He has proven success in starting, building, and operating telecommunications / subsea networks, and colocation / data centers infrastructure and high-tech businesses. In 2011, and again in 2013, Mr. Contag was awarded the Global Telecoms Business Power 100 Award, an honor bestowed upon the most powerful 100 executives in the telecom industry. Mr. Contag has held executive positions in the U.S. and Latin America and serves on the Board of Directors of several companies and industry associations. Erick believes in giving back to society through education and research programs. Mr. Contag holds a degree in Electrical Engineering from the University of Tulsa, U.S. and an Executive Engineering Management certification from Instituto de Estudios Superiores de Administración (IESA). He recently attended the Executive Program at Singularity University.

About the Author
NICOLE STAROSIELSKI, PHD

Nicole Starosielski, Professor of Film and Media at the University of California-Berkeley, conducts research on global internet infrastructure, with a focus on the subsea cables that carry almost 100% of transoceanic internet traffic. Starosielski is author or co-editor of over thirty articles and five books on media, infrastructure, and environments, including *The Undersea Network* (2015). Starosielski's most recent project, Sustainable Subsea Networks (https://www.sustainablesubseanetworks.com/), works to enhance the sustainability of subsea cable infrastructures. The project has developed a catalog of best practices for sustainability in the subsea cable and a carbon footprint of a subsea cable.

SIXTEEN

Sustainability is Complicated

Loren Long, 3TAG

The goal of conservation and guarding our natural environment, while also providing for the sustainment of humanity, is fraught with trade-offs, conditions, and unintended consequences that deny the ability to easily choose solutions that address all the challenges that we face. The solution to one problem is often a contributor to another problem. A new technological innovation that is introduced to positively contribute to the reduction of carbon in the atmosphere is then discovered to adversely affect biodiversity. An agricultural advancement that reduces global hunger adversely affects life on land due to the toxicity of chemicals. *In almost every situation, we must balance the goal attainment of one against negative consequences elsewhere.*

The seventeen United Nations Sustainable Development Goals (SDGs) outline all the issues facing the global community that must be addressed to create a world where sustainability is achieved for all. Depending on the perspective taken, some goals may be considered as having a higher priority. However, upon further investigation, the interconnected nature between the goals shows that advancement across all of the SDGs is important for the attainment of each of them individually.

Considering that, the goal of this chapter is to offer a wider view of a topic that is central to all industries, but particularly to the data center industry: renewable energy. Renewable energy is currently regarded by many as the path towards a lower carbon future that can help to mitigate the effects of climate change. There are undeniably positive aspects, however, there are always adverse consequences that must be understood and mitigated. The purpose of this chapter is not to criticize current efforts toward the advancement of renewable energy; it is simply to offer a considered view of both the positive and negative aspects in hopes of driving towards continually better solutions. To put it simply, it's complicated.

Renewable energy itself is attractive because it has little to no carbon emissions directly associated with energy generation. By definition, the resource used for energy generation is readily available and cannot be exhausted like fossil fuels. No matter how many solar panels or wind turbines are deployed, the sun will continue shining and the wind will still blow. For these two reasons, renewable energy is rightly an attractive alternative to fossil fuel-based technologies. However, it isn't that simple, and turning completely to renewable energy doesn't solve all of our issues and in some cases, it may even create new ones. Before discussing the interdependencies and complexities of renewable energy, it's important to have a baseline understanding of how the electrical system works.

Electrical Grids: A Baseline

The first thing to understand about electricity is that energy is utilized immediately upon its production unless it is fed into storage until it is needed. Otherwise, the grid itself has no capacity to store electricity for later use. Electrical generation, transmission, and distribution systems operate as a grid and not as individual circuits or connections between energy generation and energy utilization. There are exceptions, like households that deploy solar panels on their roof to feed a battery in the house. However, when talking about large fields of solar power or wind generation farms, they are connected to the grid.

All sources of energy generation feed into the grid at their respective capacity and the users of the grid share in whatever mix is created at the time. This is referred to as the grid mix or carbon intensity and is used to help calculate the scope 3 carbon emissions associated with the manufacture of goods or the delivery of services based on the region in which the work was completed. Therefore, we need to decouple the concept of purchasing renewable energy from the reality of using renewable energy.

Another important concept is the idea of base load. The base load is the minimum energy required by the grid for operation. This requires that grid managers precisely match the demand with power generation instantaneously across all forms of power generation. Either too much power or too little power causes a situation of grid instability where grid managers are forced to either shed the load, meaning they will turn off power to certain areas, or curtailment of power, meaning they simply dump generated power off the grid. Traditionally base load is generated through fossil fuel, nuclear and renewables like geothermal, which have a constant rate of generation.

A Closer Look at Renewable Energy Options

There are essentially two different types of renewable energy. The first type of renewable energy provides a constant or reliable stream of electricity, for example hydroelectric, tidal, and geothermal energy. All these types of renewable energy are very location dependent, have limited capacity, and can potentially have significant environmental and biodiversity impacts. Dam-based hydroelectric energy has fallen out of favor in many countries for this reason and has been replaced by smaller-scale Run-of-the-River energy generation.

The other type of renewable energy generation is called variable renewable energy (VRE), whichis what most people talk about when they refer to "renewable energy". It is referred to as variable because it depends upon inputs that are not constant, specifically wind and solar.

First, let's discuss solar energy. There are various solar technologies, but they all share the same basic premise of transforming solar radiation into usable electricity using photovoltaic panels. While solar energy is predictable for the most part, it only happens during the hours the sun is shining. However, it is also dependent upon the latitude at which the solar panels are deployed, the time of the year, the angle of incidence and any atmospheric conditions that affect insolation, which is the amount of solar irradiation received per square meter. The cost of solar panels and the increased effectiveness of their ability to transform solar radiation into usable electricity are improving all the time. If we're only judging solar energy based on direct carbon emissions, it's great. But as stated at the beginning of this chapter, it's not that simple. Solar energy has limitations and negative environmental consequences, which will be discussed after discussing wind energy.

Wind energy immediately evokes the vision of massive wind turbines deployed across rural or coastal areas slowly turning huge blades that drive a generator that produces electricity. Unlike solar energy, wind energy is far less predictable. However, the capability to produce energy is only limited when there is no airflow. There is a great deal of science used in the placement of wind farms and wind farm managers use atmospheric data to predict the amount of electricity they will be able to provide to the grid. Wind farm generation varies both daily and seasonally, but small hourly deviations are mitigated by deploying many wind turbines across a large area. As with solar energy, there are no direct carbon emissions associated with wind energy. Also like solar energy, there are limitations and drawbacks to wind energy.

Zero Direct Emissions = Sustainable, Right?

On one hand, the answer is yes. Any technology that reduces the amount of carbon emitted into the atmosphere is a positive. According to the IPCC report of 2022, 64% of global emissions are due to fossil fuel and industry (IPCC, 2022). However, sustainability is about more than just climate change due to direct and indirect

Chapter Sixteen

emissions from energy generation. The embodied carbon of technologies must also be considered to truly gauge the magnitude of total greenhouse gas emissions. Embodied carbon, often referred to as scope 3 emissions, defines the energy required to produce a product starting with the extraction of raw materials through to fabrication, manufacture, and ultimately customer delivery. Therefore, to truly assess whether a technology is sustainable, we must assess it through multiple interconnected lenses carefully guarding against decreases in one area for the sake of improvement in another. It's complicated.

The first drawback for both of these renewable energy technologies is the quantity of construction materials required to deploy and operate. This figure based on data from a US Department of Energy report shows the relative amounts of major materials required compared between all the potential sources of energy generation on a material ton per terawatt hour basis (WNO, 2021). It's immediately evident from looking at the total, that both wind and solar are far less efficient in terms of embodied carbon emissions related to energy generation. It's worth noting a contributing factor to the discrepancy between the different technologies has to do with the expected lifespan of a particular deployment.

	Coal	Gas CC	Nuclear PWR	Hydro	Wind	Solar PV
Concrete & cement	870	400	760	14,000	8000	4050
Iron/steel	310	170	165	67	1920	7900
Copper	1	0	3	1	23	850
Aluminium	3	1	0	0	35	680
Glass	0	0	0	0	92	2700
Silicon	0	0	0	0	0	57
Total metals	314	171	168	67	1978	9430

Table 3: Materials requirements for electricity generation technologies, tonnes per TWh (source: US DOE)

In addition to the major construction materials used, renewable technologies are also much less efficient in terms of the critical raw materials required (IEA, 2021). Critical raw materials are those raw materials deemed to be economically or strategically important but have high risks associated with their supply. It is also worth noting that the same critical raw materials required for wind turbines are similarly required for the traction motors in electric vehicles. Therefore, as countries continue to encourage the electrification of transportation, the criticality of these materials will only increase.

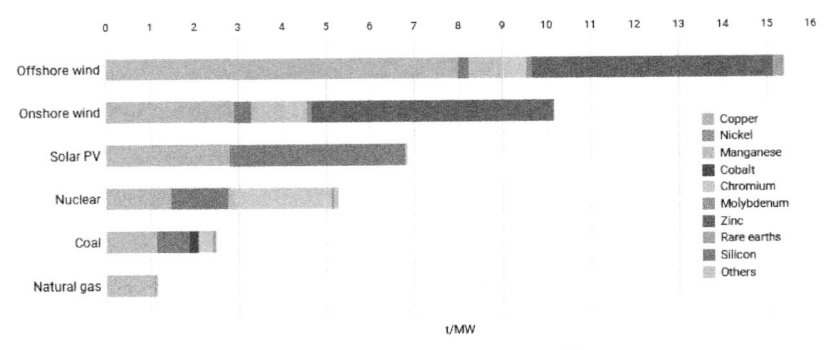

Figure 2: Critical minerals required for different generating technologies (source: IEA)

Unfortunately, the deployment of renewable energy sites is not the only contributor to the significant use of materials. The geographies that can support the substantial area required to deploy and have the conditions to maximize generation are generally in less populated areas. This means that the transmission infrastructure required to feed renewable energy onto the grid is higher due to both the distance and the distributed nature of the deployments. In addition, the transmission lines must be able to handle the current created at maximum generation even though they will on average carry less, as compared to more reliable energy generation technologies which operate at a constant level. Lastly, the local transmission network might also require upgrades to accommodate the increased capacity.

The last resource to consider, specifically as it pertains to solar, is land use efficiency and the local effects on biodiversity. As previously stated, large-scale solar deployments are generally deployed in more rural areas. As just one example, the Spotsylvania Solar deployment in Virginia uses approximately 3,500 acres (14 km2) to provide 618MWh of energy. According to data reported by the United

Nations Economic Commission for Europe, silicon photovoltaic (PV) requires 19m^2/MWh which is only slightly less than coal with CCS (carbon capture storage) at 21m^2/MWh. However, solar exceeds coal w/o CCS at 15m^2/MWh, natural gas w/CCS at 1.3m^2/MWh, wind at 0.4m^2/MWh, and nuclear at 0.3m^2/MWh (UNECE, 2021).

https://colonial-materials.com/portfolio/energy/spotsylvania-solar/

Using the data from above and comparing only solar to nuclear energy, both with zero direct carbon emissions, we find that solar requires approximately 56 times the amount of construction material, 1.3 times the amount of critical raw materials, and 63 times more land area to generate the same amount of energy. From a pure resource utilization perspective, renewable energy may not be the most sustainable option.

Don't Renewables Reduce Emissions?

Yes, but it depends. Peter Judge of Data Center Dynamics reported on a study by the Princeton University ZERO Lab that essentially found that current renewable energy procurement practices by large customers weren't leading to expected overall reductions in emissions globally (Judge, 2023). The article goes on to discuss the merits and challenges of volumetric versus temporal matching of energy usage through market mechanisms like power purchase agreements (PPA). Without going into too many details, a PPA is an agreement between an energy producer and a customer whereby the customer can show that the electricity used is directly attributed to energy produced by a renewable source. This is how companies can report

Chapter Sixteen

they have achieved Carbon Free Energy (CFE). The original idea of these programs was to encourage more investment in renewable energy, but as noted in the report by the Princeton team, "all or nearly all of the carbon-free energy procured by voluntary market participants pursuing volumetric or emissions matching strategies would have been generated anyway." In short, it's not working the way it was supposed to work for a very fundamental reason.

At the beginning of this chapter, there were three important points made that are salient to this question: energy is consumed immediately, all energy generation feeds the same grid locally, and supply or base load must always equal demand exactly. It is because of these three points combined with the fact that the two most prevalently deployed renewable energy sources are by nature variable that emissions won't decrease without further investment in technology and infrastructure.

The base load of any electricity grid fluctuates throughout the day. There are variations depending on location, but for the most part, it's low during the night, ramps up in the morning, comes down in the middle of the day, and then peaks again in the evening until returning to nighttime levels. Unfortunately, typical variable renewable energy doesn't follow that pattern. Solar generation is at its peak production consumption during the afternoon and then lowers and tapers off as the evening grid demand increases. If wind is available, it can fill in for some of that loss capacity. However, if neither wind nor solar are available, the demand is met through fossil fuel-based energy generation. Further complicating this equation is the fact that only natural gas has the ability to ramp up and down rapidly in concert with the fluctuation of renewable production. The other two baseload technologies, nuclear and coal, aren't able to vary their output as quickly and the economics that drive nuclear and coal-based power plants are dependent upon running at full capacity all the time. They are essentially either on or off.

So, one of two scenarios exist in a mixed grid. In scenario one, the grid mix contains nuclear and or coal plus natural gas and renewables. The energy produced by the constant generation creates a baseline level for the grid. When total power generation exceeds demand then the excess power on the grid is curtailed, which is another name for being dumped off the grid. Under the PPA, this power was paid for and used according to the agreement, but it never actually made it to the grid. In scenario two, the grid is only fed by natural gas and renewables. In this case, renewable energy is used whenever available and any additional demand is delivered by natural gas plants, as shown in the graphic comparing energy demand in Germany from the same week in 2012 versus 2020 (Energy Transition, 2018).

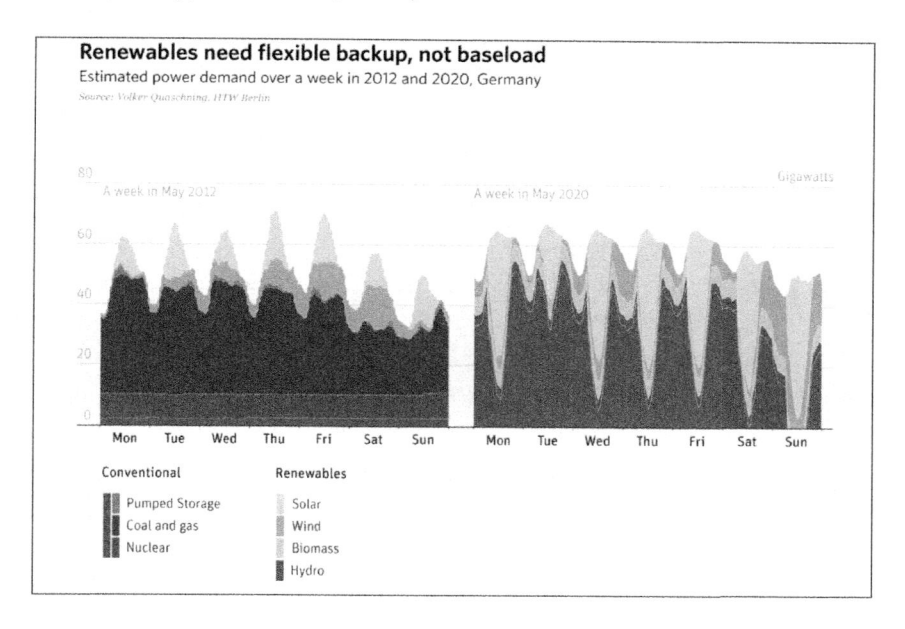

Renewables need flexible backup, not baseload
Estimated power demand over a week in 2012 and 2020, Germany
Source: Volker Quaschning, HTW Berlin

Conventional:
- Pumped Storage
- Coal and gas
- Nuclear

Renewables:
- Solar
- Wind
- Biomass
- Hydro

As the audience for Greener Data - Volume Two is predominantly from the telecommunications, media, and technology (TMT) sector, I wanted to offer an aside on power purchase agreements. At the risk of dating this book, there is a long-standing discussion within our industries about how best to collaborate with the communities in which we operate. Our operations take energy from the same grid that provides energy to the businesses, schools, and homes in our area. Purchasing all the green energy through PPAs, essentially denies anyone else the opportunity to claim carbon-free energy and may have unintended negative consequences on relationships. In a way, it's a bit like taking a piece of the cake but declaring that the data center's piece doesn't have any calories. It's all one big cake and perhaps sharing is better in the long run.

What About Storage?

There are many exciting advancements in energy storage technology. If there existed the capacity to store energy created by renewable energy and then feed the grid during times of low energy generation, it could offer an alternative to fossil fuel peakers (natural gas generating plants). There have been several large-scale battery deployments in support of VREs that have saved millions of dollars by avoiding curtailment of renewable energy. One current example is the Victorian Big Battery in Australia capable of storing up to 450 MWh of energy (MAC, 2021). There are however two potential challenges to using lithium-based batteries for large-scale storage. First, given its relative lightness, it's much better suited for portable usage. Second, the Victorian Big Battery contains over 2,700 tons of lithium. As lithium is on the EU's critical raw material list and is also being used for vehicle electrification, it's likely not the best long-term solution.

Pumped hydro operates much like an inverse dam where water is pumped to a higher reservoir using excess energy during the day and then comes back to the lower reservoir at night to provide energy via a turbine. Of course, this solution requires terrain features sufficient to support two reservoirs at different altitudes and is therefore not globally applicable. There are other projects involving large blocks that store mechanical potential energy much like weights in an old clock. Storing energy as heat that is then released as steam to power turbines like existing power plant technology has fewer geographical limitations. There are also chemical and electrochemical solutions under development. Green hydrogen is likely the current favorite potential solution because it has additional uses beyond just grid energy generation, like maritime, transportation, and microgrid generation. Unfortunately, experts have estimated that the infrastructure investment required to scale green hydrogen production and distribution is approximately $12 trillion dollars (Hydrogen Council, 2023).

The one critical component missing from the analysis is the increased investment required in renewable energy generation. In the case of solar, there would need to be enough panels deployed to not only power the base load, but enough excess panels to adequately charge the batteries to keep everything running until the sun came up the following day, assuming that it wasn't going to be overcast. Of course, anywhere north of the 40th parallel would require triple the required solar generation capacity and double the battery storage given those shorter days during the winter.

So Renewables Aren't Good?

No, renewable energy is great. Decarbonizing the world is imperative and moving away from fossil fuel-based energy is critical. This is especially true for the telecommunications, media, and technology industries where energy demand increases constantly as new energy-hungry applications and platforms evolve. However, greenhouse gasses are only one of the many problems we face and current renewable energy technology is not a panacea. One study analyzed the investment made by a certain European country in variable renewable energy and found that if the same level of investment had been made in nuclear energy, it would have enough energy to replace all fossil fuel and biomass in its electric generation sector and all the gas used for transportation (Shellenberger, 2018). That isn't to say that nuclear power comes without its negatives, simply that renewable energy can't be the only solution. It has a role to play in the race against 2°C, but it also has limitations and unintended negative consequences if not managed well.

The three most important factors we face when it comes to energy are:

1. We're all in this together. It doesn't matter if one company uses carbon-free energy if the rest of the world can't have access to the same technology.

2. In the race to solve one problem, we can't break something else. The 17 Sustainable Development Goals are aspirational and daunting, and they are also all interconnected.
3. The simplest way to positively help lower emissions and environmental impacts overall is to take less, make less, and waste less.

This chapter has only focused on the complexities of renewable energy, but the overarching theme is that sustainability is complicated. Anyone who suggests the "real answer" to any of the issues facing climate change doesn't fully appreciate the scope of the problem. Every solution has potential pros and cons and we must ensure that we fully understand all of the potential implications of the decisions we make. It's complicated.

---

1. Hydrogen Council (2023) *Global Hydrogen Flows – 2023 Update*, available at: http://www.hydrogencouncil.com
2. Shellenberger, Michael (2018) *Had they bet on Nuclear, not renewables, Germany & California would already have 100% clean power*, Forbes. Available at: https://www.forbes.com/sites/michaelshellenberger/2018/09/11/had-they-bet-on-nuclear-not-renewables-germany-california-would-already-have-100-clean-power/?sh=6b39bba8e0d4
3. Mines and Communities (2021) *Australia: Tesla 13 Tonne lithium battery fire fuels concerns*, available at: http://www.minesandcommunities.org/article.php?a=14643
4. Quaschning, Volker (2018) *Renewables need flexible backup, not baseload*, available at: https://energytransition.org/wp-content/uploads/2018/07/GET_en_Renewables-need-flexible-backup-not-baseload-.png
5. Judge, Peter (2023) *Most net-zero energy strategies have no real emissions benefits, researchers warn*, Data Center Dynamics,

available at: https://www.datacenterdynamics.com/en/news/most-net-zero-energy-strategies-have-no-real-emissions-benefits-researchers-warn/

6. UNECE (2021) Lifecycle Assessment of Electricity Generation Options. United Nations Economic Commission for Europe. Available at: https://unece.org/sites/default/files/2022-04/LCA_3_FINAL%20March%202022.pdf

7. IEA (2021), The Role of Critical Minerals in Clean Energy Transitions, IEA, Paris https://www.iea.org/reports/the-role-of-critical-minerals-in-clean-energy-transitions, Licence: CC BY 4.0

8. WNO (2021). Mineral Requirements for Electricity Generation. World Nuclear Organization. Available at: https://www.world-nuclear.org/information-library/energy-and-the-environment/mineral-requirements-for-electricity-generation.aspx

9. IPCC (2022) Climate Change 2022 – Mitigation of Climate Change. International Panel on Climate Change, Paris. Available at: https://www.ipcc.ch/report/ar6/wg3/downloads/report/IPCC_AR6_WGIII_SPM.pdf

10. Energy Transition (2018) Renewables overtake coal as Germany's most important fuel source. Energy Transition, Berlin available at: https://energytransition.org/2018/07/renewables-overtake-coal-as-germanys-most-important-fuel-source/

About the Author

LOREN LONG

Loren Long has almost 30 years of experience as a leader in technology and sustainability. Currently, he is Co-Founder of 3TAG which is creating the first-of-its-kind automated platform to enable manufacturers, enterprises, and regulatory agencies to improve the accuracy of embodied carbon values and communicate them throughout the supply chain from cradle-to-grave to ensure circularity and help achieve net zero. He is also a managing director with Clear Sustainability, an advisory practice to help data center operators, manufacturers, and governmental entities to create comprehensive, executable sustainability programs. Loren earned his BS in Physics and Nuclear Engineering from the United States Military Academy at West Point, MBA from the University of Texas at Dallas, and MSc in Environment and Sustainability from the University of London. He lives outside London with his wife and family.

Part III

POWER & COOLING INNOVATIONS TO SHRINK THE CARBON FOOTPRINT OF YOUR NETWORK INFRASTRUCTURE

SEVENTEEN

Green Fire: Innovation in Data Center Power and Cooling

LEAD ANALYST: MARY ALLEN, INSIGHTAAS

Report Contributors: Jon Summers, RISE; Maikel Bouricius, Asperitas; Maxie Reynolds, Subsea Cloud; Bill Kleyman, Apolo; Tate Cantrell, Verne; Bill Severn, 1623 Farnam; Melissa Reali-Elliott, DC BLOX; Benjamin Crawford, Kohler Energy

Mind the Gap

A defining trait of the technology industry is an enduring faith in the Promethean gift; by applying technology, humans are capable of solving even the most challenging problems. But as was Prometheus, this conviction is set to be tested by technology's inherent contradictions in a warming world. As our planet hurtles towards temperature increases that the IPCC scientists identify as the point of no return, will technology serve as a profligate consumer of resources or regenerative force, as a contributor to global warming or an important vehicle for climate mitigation? In the data center space, this drama will play out most actively in the realm of power and cooling.

Compared with other sectors, the data center industry accounts for a relatively small share of global carbon impact. According to the International Energy Agency (IEA), data centers and data transmission networks account for approximately 3% of energy demand, and .9% of energy related GHG emissions (.6% of total GHG). This assessment is expected to change quickly, however, in response to the widespread adoption of new compute-intensive services and tools, leading the research agency to call for emissions to decline by a half by 2030 if the sector is to achieve Net Zero targets.[1] For the IEA (others!) there is hope – a clear path to reduced emissions may be found through rapid innovation in digital infrastructure.

In data center environments, key tactics to improve carbon profile range from decarbonization of the energy supply to driving sustainability throughout the supply chain. But in between these approaches lie tactics that sit more closely within the data center operator's direct control, consisting primarily of efficiency improvements to reduce power consumption across IT and facilities systems. After servers, which are typically acquired direct from OEMs responsible for embedded carbon, cooling systems consume the most energy within the data center, and as such are often a first strike target for efficiency improvements. Depending on the data center, cooling can consume 40% of energy in a conventional enterprise operation, to 50% in a colocation environment, to 13% of energy in a highly optimized hyperscale facility.

This wide range in consumption behaviors underscores the opportunity for innovation in data center operations, but also begs an epic question. Given the enormous potential for carbon reduction through optimization of cooling and other systems, why is the adoption of new approaches to efficiency not more widespread? While each data center circumstance is unique – and levels of available investment resources and sustainability commitments fluctuate according to these – a variation on the *innovator's dilemma* suggests an additional answer. The absorption of disruptive innovations may be difficult for many data centers to achieve as cutting-edge technologies cater first to niche targets – the hyperscale facility, for example, with ample budget for continuous innovation. This adoption hurdle has been modelled in the *technology adoption lifecycle* concept, essentially a bell curve (presented in Figure 1. below), which outlines the advance of a new technology through the marketplace, based on different user characteristics that determine responses to innovation.

Chapter Seventeen

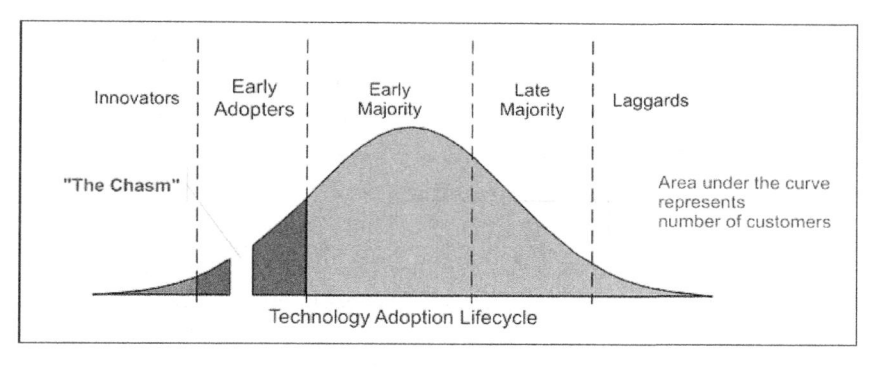

Figure 1. Technology Adoption Lifecycle

Adoption readiness can change over time, however, as market education and awareness work to bridge Moore's "chasm," which separates visionaries in the early adoption stage and pragmatists in the early adoption majority. As change relates to data center, increasing numbers of people are now coming to accept the reality of climate emergency, as well as our increasing dependence on more – and more advanced – data center capacity. With this growing recognition comes a greater sense of the urgency around the need for disruptive innovation in power and cooling. Through better understanding of the drivers of change, adoption imperatives, and the art-of-the possible in implementation, data center operators can look forward to achieving improved sustainability performance in this critical area.

Cost to Concentration – New Sustainability Imperatives

Historically, green data center initiatives have aligned with efficiency improvements aimed at slashing power bills. Energy savings that could be won were weighed against the potential for increased operational risk – shutting down idle servers, for example, rather than running them in 'just-in-case' scenarios – with sustainability outcomes thrown in as a nice-to-have, additional side benefit. The industry is accustomed to thinking about power, innovation, and conservation from a cost perspective that prioritizes energy inputs. Today, this cost imperative has only intensified, especially in areas like Europe that have seen dramatic increases in electricity costs over the past several years, but in North America as well, with regions that are thriving data center markets feeling the greatest impact. Competition in these markets, indeed in the industry as a whole, for scarce, high cost resources or for customers more generally, means that operators must find ways to improve operational efficiencies. After investments in build and IT provisioning, power is the most expensive item in data center facilities budgets, which serves as a bottom-line measure of efficiency across systems, and a key target for innovation that will reduce resource consumption.

In some jurisdictions – such as Europe or Canada – power costs are likely to increase with the application of staged increases in carbon taxes designed to discourage consumption of energy based on fossil fuel generation. But government influence on sustainability performance is not limited to taxation, rather increased regulation aimed at driving further innovation in the data center space is beginning to emerge. Singapore, the Nordics, and Europe are seeing energy efficiency directives designed to reduce consumption and associated GHG emissions. For example, to comply with the EU Code of Conduct for Data Centers, the recently published European Energy Efficiency Directive and the EN 50600 regulations, organizations must now report on data center energy consumption and emissions, develop an energy reduction plan, and implement measures to achieve energy savings/sustainability goals: the Directive will require data from 2023 on for floor area, installed power, data volumes, energy consumption, PUE, temperature set points, waste heat utilization, water usage, and use of renewable energy.[2] In Amsterdam, regulation now extends to PUE; absent a PUE of 1.2, new data centers will not receive a permit for building.

Close companion to cost is availability. With data creation on a steep upward trajectory in response to increasing digitization, the data center sector is booming; however, this growth is constrained by lack of power in key markets, including Dublin, Singapore, Frankfurt, North Virginia, and Tokyo. In Loudon Country, Virginia, which serves the US government, for example, the local utility supplier, Dominion Energy, announced in 2022 that it could no longer guarantee power delivery over existing powerlines due to spiraling demand in one of the most data center dense regions of the world.[3] Delivery shortfalls, combined with increasingly frequent power outages, serve to constrain new build as well as existing operations.[4] Against a backdrop of warming climate, which puts further strain on power supplies – and on data center cooling systems – the 'environmental pandemic' demands the implementation of new technologies that can provide emergency backup and/or reduce electricity consumption. In regions marked by new levels of increased compute demand – the Middle East or Asia Pacific – which tend to be warmer or higher ASHRAE zones, the consumption reduction imperative is even more critical.

Of greater concern from a sustainability perspective – in terms of sustaining data center operation *and* planetary health – is new energy demand that is attributed, ironically, to innovation in the IT/application world. The increasing use of artificial intelligence is an oft cited example of technology's potential to solve problems but also to create new management issues in the data center, and with good reason. AI may help parse satellite data on climate change, but what is the physical impact of training a large language model which may have 1.8 trillion parameters? While a simple Google search consumes approximately .3 kWh of energy (and there are 80,000-100,000 Google queries per second), a single ChatGPT instance is 50 to 100 times more powerful, and consumes 2-5 kWh of energy. Introduced in January 2023, ChatGPT hit a million users in five days and now has close to two million unique users. The rapid growth of data dense crypto mining, the spread of IoT applications, and the commercialization of quantum computing are putting similar strain on data center ability to process new volumes of data in increasingly complex calculations – or to power and cool the infrastructure that support these processes.

To address new processing demands introduced by compute intensive applications, silicon providers are innovating at the architectural level, configuring chips that are faster, fitter, and fatter (sandwiches between layers are deepening), while experimenting with materials such as glass substrates to engineer chips with vastly increased compute capacity. But there are limits to the results that can be achieved through densification. Intel, for example, has plans to put one trillion transistors on their microprocessors by 2030. Each of these switches would produce a small amount of energy (one attojoule or 10 to the minus 18), but a trillion would switch at a rate of 3 billion times a second (3 giga hertz), resulting in a 4 kilowatt microprocessor with a thermal design profile (TDP) that precludes cooling with currently available technologies.[5] Because the heat produced in this new chip would not be dissipated quickly enough, one solution is to light up only 20% of the transistor at any one time – leaving 80% as dark silicon, an unwelcome case of unsustainable overprovisioning.

For many operators, cooling requirements for infrastructure present challenges today: the AFCOM State of the Data Center Report 2023 survey found that only 46% of respondents believe they have adequate cooling capacity to meet current needs. The advent of increasingly dense computing is likely to dramatically shrink this group of confidents.

What is Old, New, Borrowed, and Blue?

Pushing Convention

For most data centers, the path to sustainable operation is more ongoing journey than destination. Over time, they have benefited from many techniques for improving energy efficiency, the key means to reduce power consumption, and with it, carbon impact, which are well established. Deployment of energy saving IT components, workload consolidation and the removal of idle servers, design for hot aisle/cold aisle containment or top of rack heat exhaust, raising environmental temperatures to push the limits of ASHRAE standards for servers, the use of advanced sensor monitoring platforms (DCIM), or even the use of 'free air' cooling are readily recognized tactics that operators can now implement without significant investment or disruption. In some cases, impressive results may be achieved by simply not running a component as often as in the past; less frequent backup testing of generators is just one example of an easy means to avoid carbon emissions.

At a next level, and in greenfield opportunities in particular, it may be possible to build sustainably-by-design, deploying innovation from the ground up to achieve greater performance improvements. Smaller, modular builds, for example, can take advantage of the latest efficiency improvements while right sizing capacity to compute needs – removing waste is a longstanding and good approach to achieving sustainable outcomes. Power management is another effective approach that can leverage TCO energy design modelling or SCADA monitoring and improvement software to provide transparency on operational improvements, such as the use of higher capacity, more efficient PDUs. In backup energy systems, diesel can be replaced with less carbon dense fuels like HVO to reduce emissions up to 90%, and battery/fuel cell powered microgrids can be deployed to reduce local air pollution and improve carbon impact.

But going forward, the goal must be to drive this intentionality with comprehensive sustainability strategies that can also address the power and cooling needs of the data center of the future. Today, energy system providers such as Kohler are seeing 3,000 kilowatt generators (and several of them) replace the 2,000 kilowatt standard for mission critical loads. And while GPUs can consume up to 700 watts and servers exceed 10kW in compute-intense applications (language model training may require hundreds of these systems), most data centers are built to manage 10-20 kilowatts per rack.[6]

Research into new models for power and cooling is a preoccupation of the hyperscale providers with large innovation budgets who compete on efficiency improvements as well as sustainability optics; it is also a matter of concern for research institutions focused on tackling large societal challenges such as the climate crisis. For example, ICE, a division of the Research Institutes of Sweden, is adjacent to and learns from one of the largest data centers in the world, running testbeds of new technologies that support the data center sector, ranging from liquid cooling, to the use of renewables, to new e-waste strategies.

Research, experimentation, and innovation are providing aspirational models for power and cooling management that can simultaneously address new compute demand and sustainability goals. For example, the climate neutral hyperscale provider Verne Finland has developed a hybrid approach to power and cooling that supports high density HPC at three data centers; one is located in a network of former military tunnels with a temperature of 8 degrees C that reduces mechanical cooling needs; the company runs on Finland's abundant green wind power and has built a 2,600 square meter solar plant at another facility; it makes extensive use of free air cooling while recovering waste heat for use in district heating systems (delivering heat for local housing), and engages in UPS/grid balancing to support the local green utility ecosystem.

AI Innovation

In building, integrating, and maintaining the kinds of systems highlighted in the Verne case, data – and analytics based on data modelling – play a key role. Leveraging data from IT and facilities systems, service providers like Neu.ro are working with large data centers that have high density racks in the 40 to 60 kilowatt range to optimize power through predictive analytics and to integrate cooling technologies for optimal thermal management. Using AI algorithms, the company is able to predict events with 98% accuracy, helping the data center move to competence-based predictive maintenance. In some client locations, the company is working to integrate a mix of different types of cooling environments, including air cooling, liquid cooling, immersion cooling and rear door heat exchangers.

Despite keen interest in the industry, in its most recent survey, the Uptime Institute has found that AI is currently used in data centers primarily for the dynamic optimization of power and cooling, anomaly detection, predictive maintenance and other types of predictive analytics, but that real life implementation case studies are rare.[7] However, AI can be applied to virtually all areas of data center operations, and may be especially useful in sustainability monitoring and reporting. Large multibillion parameter language models can provide deep insights into physical infrastructure, helping the operator to better understand issues with server density, resource scarcity, and cost, and to develop the most effective solution architecture based on this insight. They can also be tracked; the Neu.ro platform, for example, contains a green tracker that measures the carbon impact of different training models, which has proved sizeable in early cases. Researchers have estimated that training Microsoft's OpenAI GPT would take 30,000 (Nividia A100) graphics cards. In this exercise, the environmental impact of running 30,000 A100 GPUs for nine months, non-stop for 24 hours a day, seven days a week, would be significant. AI has huge potential as a modelling tool in the fight against climate change, but more research and education is needed to improve adoption rates and efficacy: a recent survey of decision makers in the AI and climate space, represented in Figure 2. below, has shown that few fully understand it, including technology CEOs. Responsible deployment of AI will require greater knowledge, and transparency around its carbon emissions impact.

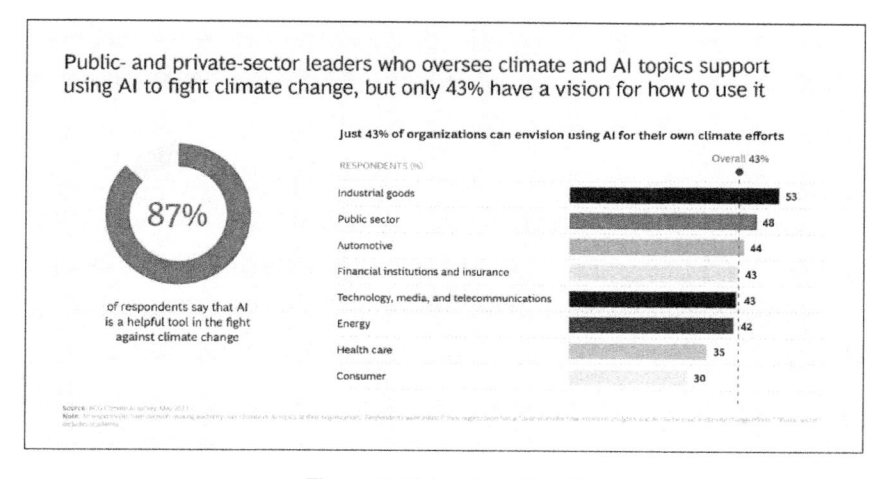

Figure 2. Vision for using AI

Running Hot is Not Cool

From a sustainability perspective, power and cooling are inextricably linked: the more power an operation consumes, the more heat it produces, and the more cooling it needs, which in turn requires additional energy. Beyond the detrimental carbon impact of this demand spiral, the uptake of data intense applications – IoT, quantum, AI – means that incremental improvements to conventional heat transfer techniques, including convection, conduction, thermal radiation, and or even evaporative cooling, which may have worked in the past are no longer able to keep up with computational advances. Space constraints in the data center, combined with latency requirements in advanced applications – where, for example, network devices are stacked on top of transistors – demand new approaches to thermal management.

To address this new requirement, many researchers, vendors, and operators are turning to liquid cooling, implemented as a sole solution or in hybrid scenarios. While deployments vary, as does the range of technologies that are available, liquid cooling has demonstrated its ability to dramatically improve power efficiency. In a high-density facility in Maryland, for example, Vertiv and NVIDIA researchers have found that direct-to-chip cooling produced a 10.2 percent reduction in total data center power consumed as compared with total air cooling, and that this outcome improved with the percentage of IT load cooled by liquid.[8] Another direct comparison of air vs. immersion cooling has shown a reduction of energy consumption by approximately 50% and a reduction of occupied space by two thirds, as immersion allowed for much higher rack densities.[9]

A key advantage of immersion cooling is the ability to cover all components in the data center, not simply the server chip. Immersion cooling itself is not homogenous, however, but comes in two forms – single phase where the liquid does not change form and transfers heat way through a heat exchanger, releasing it away from the equipment, and two phase where servers are sealed in a bath of highly-dense, engineered fluorocarbon-based liquid with a low boiling point that allows it to readily change to a gas, which then dissipates heat. Today, there is considerable debate on which approach is preferred. While two phase may support higher rack densities and provide greater efficiency, these cooling systems are more costly and complex to maintain, and are based on "forever chemicals" that evaporate quickly and have a high global warming potential (GWP). Though newer products present less environmental hazard – some are in the GWP range of 2 (CO_2 is GWP 1) – even this may not be acceptable in some jurisdictions with more stringent environmental regulation. And though single phase may consume energy for pumps to circulate the liquid, this approach is typically more affordable, features easy operation and requires less maintenance.

Recognizing immersion cooling as the best hope to manage growing thermal challenges in the data center, researchers and providers are working to mitigate key concerns with various approaches. Two phase direct-to-chip cooling, for example, may provide the containment needed to remove environmental hazards related to engineered fluids. With single phase, providers are innovating with simplified designs to further reduce energy consumption. A good example of innovation on this front is offered by Subsea Cloud, which addresses issues with heavy water usage in data center cooling by making use of sea water to dissipate thermal energy. In the Subsea solution, 16 racks are immersed in a liquid filled container, the pod is hermetically sealed, and sunk into the sea in shoreline areas close to metropolitan areas, that are as close as possible to sources of renewable infrastructure. Within the pod, active servers heat the liquid, which excites molecules to create an internal flow, vertical circulation that pushes hotter molecules to the edge of the container where heat is transferred through the wall and into the ocean. This simple, single phase system does not rely on energy for cooling, but rather on passive, free cooling provided by the ocean. According to Subsea, the specific heat of water is much lower than most elements; hence it can absorb much more thermal energy than air. Subsea claims impressive results: a 40% reduction in energy use as compared to conventional air cooling systems, and an equivalent reduction in CO2 emissions, zero spill of refrigerants or harmful chemicals in a closed system, and zero use of water – a looming challenge for data centers that rely on heavy consumption of this increasingly scarce resource.

Going forward, continued innovation in tank hardware, fluid engineering, IT infrastructure, and cooling systems is expected, including novel approaches that were not imagined yesterday. CMOS experiments, for example, which use liquid nitrogen to create really low temperatures have shown that significant energy savings are available when equipment is run at low temperatures. By dropping from 300 down to 77 kelvin (0 degrees Celsius equals 273.15 kelvin), which is where liquid nitrogen comes into its own, power consumption drops by a factor of eight, which would allow a future 4kW chip to consume / emit only 500 watts of thermal power.[10]

For many data center operators today, cryogenics remain in the realm of science fiction, and for those who are not running hyperscale environments immersion cooling may continue to represent next generation. As the adoption curve detailed above suggests, technology adoption is often more dependent on user readiness than on the intrinsic value of the innovation itself. To shift to a new cooling technology category, the operator must take an 'entrepreneurial leap' that depends on the state of ecosystem maturity and design services. To facilitate this process, astute providers such as Asperitas are developing the services and support that can help drive adoption readiness – education and services around service tooling, standard operating procedures, standards, guidelines, ecosystem development (in the area of remote sensing, for example), and even installation services. Fast ramp up of investment, education, and effort in these areas will be critical to helping operators cross the chasm, where they can make innovation work for them.

Success Metrics

In sustainability reporting, most data centers continue to focus on power consumption, as Figure 3. below from the Uptime Institute's 2023 survey of data center operations shows. Uptime researchers attribute this prioritization of energy consumption over carbon emissions variously to: focus on work that may be derived from a unit of power, or ease in tracking PUE or WUE as compared to carbon.[11]

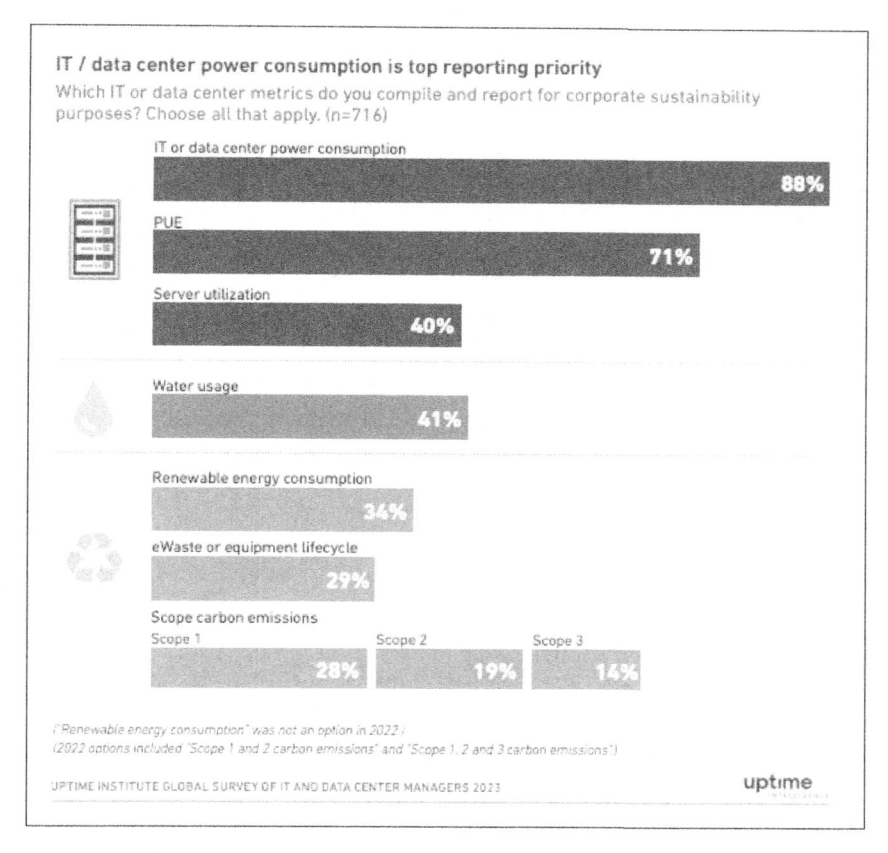

IT / data center power consumption is top reporting priority
Which IT or data center metrics do you compile and report for corporate sustainability purposes? Choose all that apply. (n=716)

Metric	%
IT or data center power consumption	88%
PUE	71%
Server utilization	40%
Water usage	41%
Renewable energy consumption	34%
eWaste or equipment lifecycle	29%
Scope carbon emissions — Scope 1	28%
Scope carbon emissions — Scope 2	19%
Scope carbon emissions — Scope 3	14%

("Renewable energy consumption" was not an option in 2022.)
(2022 options included "Scope 1 and 2 carbon emissions" and "Scope 1, 2 and 3 carbon emissions".)
UPTIME INSTITUTE GLOBAL SURVEY OF IT AND DATA CENTER MANAGERS 2023

Figure 3. Data center sustainability reporting priorities, 2023

Even though measuring power consumption remains challenging for some operators, it represents a first step for beginners, but not necessarily a desirable end for organizations which have made serious environmental commitments and who will face increasing requirement to report on a range of sustainability indicators. Single focus on these metrics may also offer an oversimplified view of operations that does not reflect overall progress towards sustainable outcomes. For example, running hotter is a popular technique used to decrease

PUE; if a higher environmental temperature in the facility is accepted, then cooling systems work less hard and consume less energy. But does this necessarily mean less consumption overall, when running hotter typically means drawing more power into IT infrastructure? Similarly, in evaluating the advantages of one type of cooling vs. another, new approaches to success measurement are needed. For example, liquid cooling effects both total data center power (the numerator in the PUE metric) as well as power consumed by IT equipment (the denominator), which makes PUE ineffective for comparing the efficiency of liquid relative to air-cooling techniques. As an alternative, Total Usage Effectiveness (TUE), which includes all energy used to support IT functions including that consumed by CPUs, GPUs, memory and storage, while separating out the power consumption of fans and other auxiliary devices from the measure of IT power (in PUE calculations) may present a more clear picture of IT power effectiveness, and hence total energy usage effectiveness.[12] Ultimately, the goal is to measure output relative to input – performance vs. watts – but to temper this with understanding that this calculation will vary according to the application. The goal of innovators going forward will be to use this ratio, optimizing for each use case.

Output, of course, is a crafty term. Is output exhausted heat, minus that reused in adjacent systems, measured by power consumption? Or is output measured by the relative value of the data that is produced in a data center – does data processed in streaming services carry less intrinsic value than a facility running HPC for bespoke medical research, and will we have to choose between these in a resource constrained world? Or can the industry find a commonly accepted means to ensure high exergy on power that enters the data center and low exergy on the heat that is emitted, eliminating waste as a first principle in sustainability, and neutralizing carbon as a second principle, with "Scope 4" or avoided emissions a third principle that can be usefully employed to drive further innovation in data center power and cooling.

As operators weigh the value to different approaches to power and cooling innovation, they may consider the following guidance.

- The future is now. When planning data center power and cooling system modernization, consider future requirements carefully. Data center density is quickly increasing, and all kinds of facilities, from hyperscale to enterprise, will have to respond with new capacity.
- Identify barriers to innovation. Knowing where innovation bottlenecks lie (cultural, institutional, investment budgets, staffing) is the first step towards removing them.
- Greenfield data centers may offer a unique opportunity to build best of breed in systems designed for maximum sustainability.
- In brownfield contexts, data centers may introduce incremental change, employing hybrid approaches to improve efficiency, while working with current infrastructure to maximize the sustainability potential of existing systems.
- Right size cooling to existing requirements, while preparing for liquid/immersion approaches.
- Educate for operational excellence, moving beyond "set and let be" for maintenance to fine tuning for optimal results. This counts as innovation.
- Exploit AI potential to optimize for sustainability, while being mindful of AI's emissions impact.
- Expand reporting beyond power consumption to include water and carbon emissions.
- Use new metrics that speak to value of work being done – avoid activities that are superfluous to improve Scope 4 performance.

---

1. IEA. Data Centres and Data Transmission Networks. https://www.iea.org/energy-system/buildings/data-centres-and-data-transmission-networks
2. These requirements are set out in Annex VII of the Directive.
   DIRECTIVE (EU) 2023/1791 OF THE EUROPEAN PARLIAMENT AND OF THE COUNCIL of 13 September 2023 on energy efficiency and amending Regulation (EU) 2023/955. EUR-Lex - 32023L1791 - EN - EUR-Lex (europa.eu)

3. Peter Judge. Dominion Energy admits it can't meet data center power demands in Virginia. DCD. July 2022. Dominion Energy admits it can't meet data center power demands in Virginia - DCD (datacenterdynamics.com)
4. For more discussion, see Low Carbon Solutions: Pathways to Energy Maturity in the Data Center. A Greener Data Impact Report from Jaymie Scotto & Associates. July, 2023.
5. RISE ICE Data Center research, courtesy of Jon Summers. August 2023. https://www.ri.se/en
6. Victor Avelar et al. The AI Disruption: Challenges and Guidance for Data Center Design. White Paper 110. Energy Management Research Center. Schneider Electric. 2023. The AI Disruption: Challenges and Guidance for Data Center Design (schneider-electric.com)
7. Uptime's 2023 survey of data center operators found that perceptions of AI's looming influence (on staff levels, for example) does not reflect reality, though the share of respondents who expect this in the short term has increased.
   Executive summary: Uptime Institute Global Data Center Survey 2023.
8. Ali Heydari et al. Power Usage Effectiveness Analysis of a High-Density Air-Liquid Hybrid Cooled Data Center. Proceedings Paper. ASME. December 2022. https://doi.org/10.1115/IPACK2022-97447
9. K. Haghshenas,, B. Setz, Y. Blosch, et al. Enough hot air: the role of immersion cooling. Energy Inform 6, 14. August 2023. https://doi.org/10.1186/s42162-023-00269-0
10. Courtesy of Jon Summers, citing: H. L. Chiang *et al.* "Cold CMOS as a Power-Performance-Reliability Booster for Advanced FinFETs." *2020 IEEE Symposium on VLSI Technology.* https://ieeexplore.ieee.org/abstract/document/9265065
11. Executive summary: Uptime Institute Global Data Center Survey 2023.
12. Fred Rebarber. Understanding the Limitations of PUE in Evaluating Liquid Cooling Efficiency. Vertiv. March 2023. https://www.vertiv.com/en-us/about/news-and-insights/articles/blog-posts/understanding-the-limitations-of-pue-in-evaluating-liquid-cooling-efficiency/

    Images from:

    Figure 1. https://medium.com/@shivayogiks/what-is-technology-adoption-life-cycle-and-chasm-e07084e7991f

    Figure 2. https://www.forbes.com/sites/markminevich/2022/07/08/how-to-fight-climate-change-using-ai/?sh=655991012a83

    Figure 3. Executive summary: Uptime Institute Global Data Center Survey 2023.

About the Authors

Mary Allen is CCO at InsightaaS and Sustainability Lead for JSA. As journalist, analyst, and content strategist, she has covered the range of IT subjects for her own properties, and on behalf of clients. Mary created the GreenerIT and Sustainability Platform websites, capping this with a stint as sustainability columnist for Bloomberg BNA, to promote the environmental agenda within IT. She continues this passion in partnership with JSA on the Greener Data initiative.

Research Lead in Data Centers at the Research Institutes of Sweden, **Jon Summers** is professor at Luleå Technical University, and visiting professor at the University of Leeds, where for two decades he chaired an HPC User Group. His work has involved building large compute clusters for various projects, and research into thermal management and energy flow within data centers. Since 2013, much of Jon's IT research has focused on liquid cooling at the data center and microprocessor levels. He now works within the ICE Data Center unit at RISE, exploring issues in the engineering of sustainable and energy efficient data centers.

Maikel Bouricius is CMO at Asperitas, an Amsterdam based provider that delivers immersion cooling solutions for high performance data centers on a global basis. Recognized several times in the past decade as one of the top 100/200 young professionals working on sustainability, design, technology and innovation, Maikel has worked in sales and marketing roles for Green IT Amsterdam, DURABILIT, a pioneer in the circular economy, and other media businesses. He is a frequent speaker on clean tech, sustainability, energy transition, and data center innovation.

Educated in computer science and underwater robotics, **Maxie Reynolds** has leveraged knowledge in these disparate fields and merged her expertise to create Subsea Cloud, a forward thinking startup that builds, deploys, and maintains sustainable, subsea data centers. Prior to founding Subsea Cloud, she worked on oil rigs as a ROV pilot, technical writer, and then in cybersecurity as pentester and social engineer. Her latest venture is designed to deliver dense compute capacity that replaces electrically driven cooling systems with zero carbon emissions cooling from ocean ecosystems.

Bill Kleyman is an award-winning data center, cloud, and digital infrastructure leader with a 20-year career at the forefront of technology. Ranked globally by Onalytica as one of the leading executives in cloud computing and data security, Bill is focused on advising organizations, training young talent, and educating global audiences about AI, machine learning, sustainable data center design, cybersecurity, and more. Today, Bill is the CEO of Apolo, an AI platform and infrastructure company. He is also the Chair of the Education Committee at Infrastructure Masons and the AFCOM Data Center World Program Chair.

Chief Technology Officer at Verne, **Tate Cantrell** has two decades worth of experience managing the full lifecycle of IT infrastructure, from data center development to DevOps. An electrical and biomedical engineer, Tate has been recognized for his industry-leading data center design and project implementations. He is currently focused on the impact of AI in data center design scenarios, on addressing increasing data center density through the optimization of cooling systems, the use of liquid cooling, and the redesign of security systems.

Bill Severn is CEO and President of 1623 Farnam and is Executive Vice President at BERKS Group. He leads the BERKS Group's business development efforts in technology infrastructure. Bill has deep industry experience in fiber networks, cable, broadband, data storage and cloud services. A sales, marketing and operations expert, Bill is now also a polished spokesperson for 1623 Farnam's edge connectivity and peering solutions, but also for sustainability activities in its data centers, ranging from air flow design, green fluid cooling, and utility partnerships on renewables.

Melissa Reali-Elliott is a marketing and communications specialist with a deep understanding of energy and power management systems in digital infrastructure. She began her career with TerraCloud, and has worked as content manager Kohler's data center unit, and as head of data center marketing at ABB. Melissa is currently content marketing manager at DC BLOX, a data center provider in the southeastern US. In her spare time, she is columnist for Mission Critical Magazine, where she lends her voice as an advocate for diversity and sustainability in the digital infrastructure industry.

With a BS in mechanical engineering and an MBA, **Benjamin Crawford** has embarked on a fast-paced career trajectory at Kohler Energy, a provider of power backup systems for industrial applications, including data center. He began work with Kohler as a mechanical engineer, advanced to senior project engineer for applications, and now serves as manager of business development for power systems. Benjamin is interested in alternative fuels for power generation, and is energized by his talks on the use of hydrogen to solve sustainability challenges.

EIGHTEEN

Sustainable Data Centers: Charting a Course through the AI Revolution

Kim Gunnelius, Verne

Sitting down to write this chapter, I'm struck by how the path toward sustainability has been a collective journey shared by many of us in the technology industry. The tech landscape has shaped not just our careers, but also our personal stories. It's a narrative woven together with a focus on innovation and a solid commitment to sustainability that goes beyond our professional lives — it resonates in who we are.

For me, the overarching 'why' of my career has always been efficiency — how to do things faster, smarter and how to waste less time and energy. I have always been fascinated by software and how you can leverage it to do almost anything, while always having to prioritize where to put in the effort. You have to be effective in addition to being efficient. During my time with Verne, my passion for efficiency has evolved into a passion for sustainability, which is perhaps conceptually similar — the goal of minimizing the resources used and maximizing the benefits.

Based on my experience of managing the operations of three data centers across Finland, I am proud to say we have been dedicated to implementing sustainable practices since Day One, and today, the environment plays a critical role in every business decision we make. However, as I reflect on our goals and accomplishments over the years, there have been notable changes in how we approach sustainability and how we go about adopting environmentally responsible solutions to transform our technological environments for the better.

One of the biggest challenges we face today is understanding and supporting the unprecedented growth of artificial intelligence (AI) and its ability to handle generative tasks. While AI is fueling innovation like never before, it also raises important questions about our environmental impact. These questions are fundamentally important when we consider that a failure to curb emissions would mean AI is part of the problem rather than the solution it should – and could – be. In this chapter, we will explore how AI affects data centers and how data centers can manage the density and scalability requirements it brings. Additionally, we will explore sustainable ways to power AI and how data centers supporting AI can contribute to society more broadly.

AI's Immense Impact across Industries

AI's capabilities are immense, driving innovations across nearly every industry, including transportation, banking, marketing, healthcare, manufacturing, and many more. In 2022, the global artificial intelligence market size was valued at over $136 billion. By 2030, the global AI market is expected to reach a staggering $1.8 trillion.[1] This extreme growth is intensified by the convergence of software and automation with various industries, signaling a monumental shift — we sit at the precipice of substantial change. The sheer numerical scale of this growth surpasses historical leaps in productivity, likely greater even than those witnessed during periods of rapid industrialization or the advent of the internet.

Driving the Density Dilemma

For data centers, the increasing adoption of AI means a significant increase in data processing, coupled with a rapid acceleration in data storage needs. This surge puts pressure on data centers to scale up quickly and efficiently, while addressing workload density challenges. AI affects data centers in many ways, impacting the virtual environment, connectivity, hardware and the related data center infrastructure.

AI workloads require power-hungry graphics processor units (GPUs), resulting in much higher power density requirements within data centers. This necessitates a reevaluation of data center design, in conventional enterprise-level operations in particular, where design is not always equipped to support power-dense workloads. The inadequacy is particularly evident in cooling systems, where traditional methods struggle to keep up with the heightened demands.

While data center operators have seen an increased demand for higher densities, AI is forcing them to focus even more on this area, prompting them to reassess existing data center designs and processes. As AI continues to drive demand and reshape data center design, these changes will also need to be made in a thoughtful and sustainable way. What's more, one of the major driving factors decision makers will need to consider when selecting a data center will undoubtedly be sustainability.

The Power Predicament

Generative AI models operate on GPU chips that require 10-15 times more energy than a traditional central processing unit (CPU). The implications of this energy consumption requirement are far-reaching, posing challenges to both current infrastructure and future sustainability.

For example, according to Danish scientists, in January 2023, ChatGPT (running on GPT3), reached power consumption levels that amount to the equivalent of all electricity used by 33,000 US households.[2] Additionally, it is estimated that a single search or query on ChatGPT uses 15 times more power than a basic Google search.[3] As data centers already consume 1-2% of all energy (depending on the study), the potential escalation of these figures in the coming years raises major concerns about grid strain, the increasing stress on power resources and carbon emissions impact.

Beyond issues around having adequate power, this new demand level turns the spotlight to the use of sustainable energy sources. The critical need to lessen the environmental impact of AI reinforces the importance of renewable energy sources like solar, wind, hydroelectric and geothermal power.

The emissions produced by large-scale foundational AI models, such as ChatGPT, are closely linked to where they are located, as the carbon footprint of the grid is a key factor. This intricate connection highlights that, beyond the amount of power used, the sustainability of that power is equally vital in molding the' environmental consequences of AI processes.

Assessing the Resilience of Renewable Energy

By leveraging renewable energy sources, data centers can significantly reduce their carbon footprint. In addition to enhancing sustainability, renewable energy can also reduce long-term operational costs.

However, renewable energy is not equally available worldwide. Solar, hydro, wind and thermal resources are unevenly distributed across the globe. Relying on a singular renewable source presents challenges, given variations in the reliability of supply, such as that experienced with solar availability during the night or hydro availability during dry spells. The optimal approach involves creating access to multiple sources to ensure consistent power availability.

The data center industry is not the only industry looking to leverage renewable energy. The green energy transition is gaining momentum across industries, with projects like green hydrogen or green steel demanding massive amounts of green power. On the positive side, there is a notable upswing in supply initiatives.

In Finland, for example, wind power capacity increased by 75% year over year in 2022[4] and another 25% in 2023, growing to approximately 18% of the country's total electricity generation.[5] Technological advances over the past decade have significantly improved the economic viability of wind and solar power generation, such as developments in turbine technology and ultra-efficient solar cells. The abundance of wind and solar resources present a massive opportunity, while there is potential for further support through a major green hydrogen initiative, which can help address the increasing global demand for energy as legacy fossil-based production is replaced.

Location Matters

As the data center industry strives to increase its operational energy efficiency and to adopt sustainable practices, the challenge is significant given the amount of energy that is required. Achieving a low CO_2 footprint is essential and choosing the optimal location for data centers is a key aspect of this effort. Selecting locales with access to sustainable power is crucial; the Nordics are a suitable and environmentally friendly option, boasting abundant green energy resources available at attractive prices. For instance, Iceland's abundance of hydro and geothermal energy and Finland's fast-growing wind capacity and low-carbon grid make the region a prime location for sustainable data center operations. In addition, the cool climate of the Nordics significantly reduces the need for extensive cooling within data centers. Leveraging naturally cool environments for cooling reduces energy consumption, resulting in cost savings as well as lower carbon emissions.

For most large-scale AI training workloads, physical proximity is not relevant for processing, which allows for the placement of data centers in environments that balance power optimization and efficiency. Verne's deliberate data center site location in Iceland and Finland underscores the distinct environmental advantages of these Nordic countries for organizations looking to align with the industry's sustainability objectives.

Chapter Eighteen

The Key Role of Advanced Cooling Technologies

As workload densities continue to rise, the demand for more efficient data center cooling solutions also continues to increase. Extreme demands of the latest algorithms are driving core compute components to be interconnected with faster, more tightly coupled networks. This has pushed more and more compute closer together, putting extreme pressure on the cooling requirements of the data center.

The intense computation in modern data centers generates substantial heat as a byproduct, necessitating a shift beyond traditional air cooling methods. Liquid cooling is a viable solution, but deployments can still benefit from a naturally cool environment. Even with liquid cooling, the energy needed for cooling is reduced, underscoring the benefits of harnessing the naturally cool air of Nordic climates.

Liquid Cooling Is Making a Splash

Liquid cooling is a collection of technologies designed to dissipate excess heat with liquid rather than air. This approach circumvents issues associated with inefficient air-based cooling systems where servers may blow hot air suboptimally.

Liquid cooling supports increased density in data centers as higher-powered processors can be cooled in a smaller space. Various liquid cooling methods, such as direct-to-chip, rear-door heat exchangers and immersion cooling, cater to different requirements.

Immersion cooling systems submerge servers and other components in the rack in a thermally conductive dielectric fluid, which absorbs the heat, converts it into vapor and then condenses it back to liquid. While the efficiency rate is high, there are a few drawbacks with immersion cooling, including maintenance complexity and the need for specialized hardware.

Direct liquid cooling utilizes flexible tubes to channel fluid to a cold plate situated above a processing chip. The fluid absorbs the heat, turning into vapor, which is then carried out of the equipment through the same tube. In a data center environment, airflow supports cooling the server at the same time.

For optimal versatility, a data center should be able to accommodate various liquid cooling types alongside traditional air cooling. Liquid cooling racks with higher density may be heavier, requiring robust flooring. They also occupy less floor space per megawatt, and notably, generate less noise compared to high-power, air-cooled servers. Verne has implemented a liquid cooling solution, the first DELL DLC 3000 in EMEA, at the Pori data center. It sits next to air-cooled racks, with additional piping implemented. The system is capable of reaching 80kW cooling capacity per rack.

While liquid cooling enhances sustainability through efficiency, it can introduce new challenges, such as environmentally compliant disposal, the need to protect data centers from liquid, and recycling of dielectric fluids and other chemicals.

Balancing Cooling and Connectivity

AI's substantial computational demands necessitate exceptionally low-latency, high-bandwidth connectivity between data center servers, particularly for tasks like training the models, which are high resource-intensive tasks. This results in precise specifications for cable length, capacity and the placement of racks. This is also the main reason for the densification of compute, which drives the need for liquid cooling. While one approach to handling cooling in air-cooled setups involves spacing racks widely to mitigate overheating, this conflicts with networking demands that require racks to be closely positioned and interconnected with high-throughput cables.

The Heat Reuse Revolution

While data centers traditionally consume large amounts of energy, there are additional opportunities for optimizing efficiency, including greater integration into the energy ecosystem through recycling the heat generated by servers.

Verne's data center in Helsinki innovatively employs indirect free air cooling to regulate server temperatures. Through sophisticated heat exchangers, excess heat from the server exhaust is transferred to water. This heated water, with temperatures hovering around 30°C, undergoes a transformation via high-efficiency heat pumps, elevating it to approximately 90°C — a temperature conducive to the local district heating company's needs, contingent on external conditions.

For every 1MW of IT power dedicated to servers, a notable 1.25-1.3MW of heat is produced. The heat pumps, demanding an additional 250-300kW of electricity, effectively raise the water temperature for the district grid, with the energy consumed by the pumps being efficiently converted into usable heat. Remarkably, the system incurs minimal energy losses, registering only a marginal percentage, even with energy used by the heat pumps factored into the equation.

In the context of liquid cooling for high-density AI servers, the potential for optimizing heat recovery expands, eliminating the need to transfer energy from air to liquid, further minimizing energy loss. The existence of an established district heating network significantly streamlines the integration of surplus heat from data centers, adding another layer of consideration. Connected to a heating utility, Verne's data center provides extra resilience to the utility, which is not solely dependent on a single business or application. Instead, the data center integrates seamlessly into a city-wide energy solution with consistent demand, a luxury not widely available.

Additionally, operating on 100% green energy and repurposing it as district heating elevates the environmental appeal of the data center. Beyond efficiency, this practice adds a social dimension by heating local residences, fostering a sense of community integration. Given the historical challenges of community acceptance of data centers in certain geographies, marked by protests or moratoriums, this integrated approach positions data centers as contributors rather than mere consumers of energy, redefining their role in the sustainability narrative.

Chapter Eighteen

Meeting the Escalating Demands of AI

The surge in AI requirements introduces complexities in data center design and poses new challenges for ensuring sustainable operations. However, amidst these challenges there are many opportunities. Strategic decisions regarding data center design and location have the potential to yield positive impacts.

When viewed through the lens of ESG — consideration for environmental, social and governance factors — data centers can contribute to a greener, more community-integrated, and transparent landscape. This becomes particularly crucial in the context of AI, where trust plays a pivotal role. Transparency in showcasing the sustainable production of AI and revealing how the data center, the technological core, integrates into and positively influences society becomes essential. Ethics in AI discussions extends beyond algorithms to encompass sustainable service delivery, forming an integral part of the overall user acceptance.

The nature of AI and its ability to handle massive workloads independently of data consumers allow for greater flexibility in data location. The criteria for selecting data center locations are extensive, ranging from political stability to natural disaster risks, and include connectivity, labor availability, and, increasingly, sustainability. Green power availability and the potential to reuse excess heat are emerging as top priorities in this selection process. Considering the significant expense power represents, the overall economic aspect also cannot be ignored.

In light of these considerations, the Nordics stand out as a promising hub for sustainable AI growth. Meeting diverse criteria, including green power availability and heat reuse capabilities, the region is poised to be a facilitator for sustainable AI, despite the potential environmental impact of its massive expansion.

Beyond Talk – It Is Time for Action

The blend of innovation and sustainability in our professional and personal lives aligns with the broader challenges faced by the data center industry in the era of AI. As AI becomes a significant force, not just technologically but environmentally, our exploration goes beyond technical details. It's a personal journey — a commitment to understanding the link between AI and data centers for a sustainable future. In navigating the complexities of designing for the AI era, I believe the key question is whether we can guide AI's growth while easing its impact on the environment. Together, with the team at Verne, we are working to answer this important question every day and continue to strive to achieve a greener path forward, especially as new technologies like AI emerge and compute demands increase.

It's time to move beyond discussions to concrete steps. Let's continue to share ideas, collaborate and collectively address the challenges and opportunities presented by AI and data centers. Sustainability isn't a far-off goal; it's a journey we started years ago. Today, let's engage in meaningful conversations and take actions to shape a sustainable future, where AI, data centers and environmental responsibility coexist seamlessly.

---

1. "Artificial Intelligence Market Size, Share & Trends Analysis Report." Grand View Research. https://www.grandviewresearch.com/industry-analysis/artificial-intelligence-ai-market
2. Cohan, Peter. "As ChatGPT And Other AI Tools Increase Energy Demand, Here's What Investors Need To Know." Forbes. November 9, 2023. https://www.forbes.com/sites/petercohan/2023/11/09/equinix-and-vertiv-stock-prices-could-rise-on-generative-ais-energy-use/
3. Reddit. 2023. https://www.reddit.com/r/aipromptprogramming/comments/1212kmm/according_to_chatgpt_a_single_gpt_query_consumes/?rdt=59417
4. Finnish Wind Power Association. "Finnish wind power year 2022: Wind power capacity increased by 75% and brought more than 2.9 billion investments to Finland." October 1, 2023. https://tuulivoimayhdistys.fi/en/ajankohtaista/press-releases/finnish-wind-power-year-2022-wind-power-capacity-increased-by-75-and-brought-more-than-2-9-billion-investments-to-finland
5. Finnish Wind Power Association. "Wind power production increased by 25% in 2023 - domestic wind power increases electricity availability." January 31, 2024. https://tuulivoimayhdistys.fi/en/ajankohtaista/press-releases/wind-power-production-increased-by-25-in-2023-domestic-wind-power-increases-electricity-availability

About the Author

KIM GUNNELIUS

As Managing Director Finland of Verne, Kim drives the operations and excellence of Verne's data center services. Having overseen the startup and early growth phase of Ficolo (now Verne Finland) as Chairman, Kim joined full time in 2017 as CFO and CCO. As head of Finland, he works with the largest technology companies in the world to cost effectively scale digital infrastructure while reducing the carbon footprint. Kim has overseen green certification initiatives that have helped the organization achieve several industry firsts, such as the first Dark Green-rated green bond for a data center company, as well as the first climate neutral label for a hyper-scale-level Nordic data center.

Sustainability efforts under Kim's leadership include directing excess data center heat into the district heating grid to enable the use of green energy not once, but twice.

NINETEEN

Unlocking a Sustainable, Digital Future through Power and Cooling Innovation

Robert Bunger & Marc Garner, Schneider Electric

In the world of data centers and digital infrastructure, many organizations today are conceptualizing technological solutions that are empowering cutting-edge advances in sustainable innovation. On one hand, critical power systems are enabling a greener and more resilient grid, advancing the green transition, and supporting both the adoption and generation of renewables.

On the other, new developments in processor technologies have accelerated the growth of artificial intelligence (AI) platforms, enabling manufacturers to experiment with water-based liquid cooling solutions which are directly reducing energy, emissions, and waste. In short, there has never been a better time to harness the power of technology and greener data to combat global warming.

Data Center Challenges

Today data center operators are experiencing a number of challenges, both in terms of operation and development to meet evolving needs. Much of this is taking place while the industry faces increased scrutiny from the public about energy demands and emissions, without an immediate understanding of how data centers fuel their daily activities. Taken together, these sentiments are compounding a misunderstanding of data centers' role as critical infrastructure. In many locations around the world, data centers have been highlighted as large energy consumers, spurring concerns about the impact on the decarbonization efforts of their respective host countries.

Despite publicized efforts to procure energy from renewable sources (RES) through measures such as power purchase agreements (PPAs) or significant investment in RES projects such as wind farms, solar, and more, as well as voluntary initiatives such as the Climate Neutral Data Center Pact[1], there is still a perception that data centers contribute little to either local or national economies, while consuming vast amounts of energy, creating waste and emitting carbon.

In this challenging environment, technological developments mean that data centers have an opportunity to help reduce emissions on an industrial scale and increase resilience and efficiencies, while also contributing to the green transition that will lead to accelerated adoption of renewables.

Renewable Energy Adoption

The International Energy Agency (IEA) has forecast that by 2025, more than 90% of global electricity expansion will come from RES[2]. This is a welcome estimate, as it predicts that 80% of global CO_2 emissions are attributable to the production and distribution of energy, which can be as much as 60% inefficient for current fossil-based end-to-end energy system losses.

In its pathway to net zero, the IEA also forecasts that almost 90% of global electricity generation in 2050 will come from renewable sources, with solar photovoltaic (PV) and wind together accounting for nearly 70%[3]. National targets vary from country to country, but some developed nations have set targets of 70-80% RES in energy generation capacity by 2030, with an overall net-zero grid by 2050.

This rapid expansion and adoption of RES comes with many

challenges, with the issue of variability being central. Wind and solar are referred to as variable renewable energy (VRE) sources because of their intermittence. An energy grid with a high proportion of VRE needs to accommodate situations when, for example, the wind blows and generates electricity, but demand is not there, as well as when there is demand but no wind. Through their critical power infrastructure, data centers and other large energy consumers are uniquely placed to help ensure supply meets demand.

Energy Storage

As large energy consumers with a requirement for resilience, data centers have large estates of battery-equipped uninterruptable power supplies (UPS). When specifically engineered, the battery systems associated with UPS can be used for energy storage, especially when RES generation exceeds demand. Another means to achieve this is through battery energy storage systems (BESS), where technologies such as flow batteries can store large amounts of energy in modular, scalable implementations when excess energy is generated either on-site or from the grid. Such capacity can work both ways to feed power back into the grid when demand exceeds supply. In this way, data centers could provide balancing energy storage capabilities that would otherwise have to be built out by the grid operator at great cost.

The two-way flow of energy is made possible by two key developments in technology: smart grids and microgrids.

Smart Grids and Microgrids

Much of the thinking around data center design historically evolved from implementations that supported the financial industry, where multiple redundancies and overcapacity were deemed necessary, and where abundant, reliable energy was a given and only ever envisaged as a consumed reource. Today, the industry is working beyond those parameters toward new approaches that mean resilience and availability can be achieved without the levels of redundancy that can be costly, resource intensive, and ultimately wasteful.

Smart grids utilize intelligent two-way communications between the utility and consumers, enabling grid capacity and resilience to be enhanced, for example, with the addition of on-site generators to meet peak demands and emergency requirements.

Microgrids are self-contained and self-sufficient power generation systems that are also connected to the grid and can enable data centers to meet their own energy requirements for certain periods. They also either relieve demand on the grid or support it by allowing that capacity to supplement overall supply. A complete departure from their historical forebears, microgrids offer many benefits, including the ability to increase resilience, reduce costs and improve data center sustainability.

A key feature of microgrids is their use of distributed energy resources (DER), or the ability to generate on-site power at one or multiple locations. This can be through direct generation, such as with fixed or mobile generators, or through renewable energy sources such as wind, solar or geothermal, but most often as a combination of the two, reflective of national energy mixes.

Data center stakeholders have been working with the supply chain to tackle emissions issues associated with direct generation by transitioning away from diesel and other fossil fuels for backup and supplementary power. The use of alternative renewable fuels is also being pioneered as another net-zero option. Hydrotreated vegetable oil (HVO) is projected to eliminate up to 90% of net CO_2 from generators while also reducing emissions of nitrogen oxide, carbon monoxide and particulates[4].

From our own research at Schneider Electric[5], we have established that microgrids go beyond fossil fuel-based power backup systems by enabling the use of combined cooling, heating and power systems, renewables, fuel cells and energy storage. They help increase resilience against grid disruptions, reduce energy-related operational cost, and ensure sustainability through advanced energy analytic capabilities.

Chapter Nineteen

Ultimately, a microgrid increases a data center operator's confidence in uptime and continuity, and helps both optimize and balance the use of grid versus onsite energy resources. From a technological standpoint, microgrid technology is mature, making solutions more affordable and easier to implement than ever. An optimized solution can be developed with the newest microgrid planning tools and modular architectures, along with energy as a service (EaaS) options to reduce financial risks while maximizing return on investment.

In the future, these combined efforts will be central to supporting requirements from some national authorities for new data centers to have on-site dispatchable power generation capacity equal to or greater than their demand as a precondition to be connected to the grid.

The capability of data centers to meet their own power requirements by generating green energy, and whose infrastructure can help provision a net-zero grid, demonstrates the central role that data centers can play in the transition to a greener, more sustainable digital future. Data centers and their operators must be responsible corporate citizens contributing to the transition not just to a greener data industry, but to a green energy future.

Digitalizing Energy

Each industrial revolution in history has been accompanied by a demand-led energy transformation. The current revolution is no different. The fourth electrical revolution has seen us moving out of the age of fire and into the age of clean, renewable power generation at scale, enabled by digital technology that drives greater efficiency.

At Schneider Electric, we refer to the concept of electrification through renewables and digitalization as Electricity 4.0 and we believe this is the fastest path to a net-zero future.

Electricity 4.0 can be thought of as the "fuel" for this new electric world—one which is more sustainable and more resilient. Electricity makes energy green because it is the most efficient form of energy, shown to be three to five times more efficient than other sources. It is also the best vector for decarbonization.

The digitalization of energy generation and distribution (with applied analytics and AI-optimization) works to make the invisible visible, driving efficiency and eliminating energy waste.

The IEA characterizes the digitalization of energy production and distribution as a key enabler of decarbonization, stating, "Digitalization—the application of digital technologies—could have a major effect on emissions as an enabler in accelerating clean energy transitions. Across the energy sector, digitalization can help cut costs, improve efficiency and resilience, and reduce emissions."[6]

The ability for data centers to cooperate with national grids has already been demonstrated by Aeven in Denmark. Working with the Danish Transmission System Operator, Energinet, Aeven developed a pioneering Fast Frequency Reserve (FFR) pool, whereby data centers and other energy-intensive industries could support the grid with frequency stabilization services. Aeven and Schneider Electric built an uninterruptible power supply (UPS) solution to deliver FFR and stabilize the local energy grid (DCD, 2023[7]).

Role of Data

Looking at wider decarbonization and net-zero efforts, data and analytics are vital. As every organization looks to gather the data necessary to assess their own environmental impact using frameworks such as the Scope 1-3 emissions, data becomes the foundation of any real assessment. Powerful analytics are also required to turn the data into intelligence and metrics that can form the basis of a coherent strategy to achieve net-zero.

Many modern data center facilities are leveraging digital design methodologies to ensure an efficient, expedited process to get from concept to operation. These sophisticated design models provide deep insights into how innovative facilities can operate, identifying issues or problem areas before they are committed to building infrastructure and ensuring the highest levels of operational efficiency from day one. However, the value of these models does not end there. Design models are being transitioned to digital twins, delivering further value through the lifetime of facilities they represent.

These models can provide specific insights on areas such as equipment usage and lifecycles, which can help with predictive and preventative maintenance strategies, for example. This not only increases the resilience of facilities and services, it also informs extended service lives for equipment, as well as assessment for repurposing, re-engineering and recycling, allowing the introduction and operation of circular practices that can keep vital materials in the system, reducing waste[8].

In operation, next-generation data center infrastructure management (DCIM) systems, that are capable of managing on-premises facilities, hybrid and multi-cloud environments, and edge computing deployments, provide the AI-assisted capability to ensure that operations are constantly optimized based on parameters such as costs, workload priorities and emissions.

Schneider Electric has coined the term DCIM 3.0 to characterize the generation of systems that can manage disparate and diverse resources across multiple sites and platforms, while drawing data from any relevant source and presenting optimization capabilities[9].

Metrics and Frameworks

With the ability to manage these sophisticated environments and provide consistent, comprehensive, granular data on emissions and environmental impact, it is important to have a common set of metrics to ensure that all data centers measure their environmental impact against common parameters. This feeds into common industry reporting frameworks that can allow operators to meaningfully compare their performance, giving further relevance to their efforts.

At Schneider Electric, this is an area where we have conducted extensive research and produced the industry's first standardized metrics framework for reporting sustainability. It comprises 28 key sustainability metrics in five categories: energy, greenhouse gas emissions, water, waste, and local ecosystem. It outlines these metrics across three reporting stages: Beginning, Advanced and Leading.

The beginning stage has six metrics that represent basic reporting for energy, water use and Greenhouse Gas (GHG) emissions—the core metrics required for every data center. The advanced stage includes more detailed metrics for energy, water, GHG emissions, and introduces two new categories including waste and local ecosystem. The leading stage adds even more detailed metrics to the existing categories[10].

With the data derived from these efforts, AI and machine learning (ML) algorithms can be applied to fully understand and map Scope 1-3 emissions implications. An assessment from the Stockholm Energy Institute shows that through digitalization, AI, big data analysis and deep learning, a green economy can be realized much more easily than without those technologies[11].

AI is already an important layer in the technology stack, turning data into intelligence and actionable insights from across the entire distributed digital infrastructure ecosystem. However, as AI is increasingly being used in production workloads, as well as assisting in operational and orchestration functions, it is also changing the way data centers are being designed and operated.

AI Impact on Data Centers

The boom in AI is expected to accelerate in the near term. Analyst firm IDC has estimated worldwide revenue for AI at $154 billion USD in 2023, with an expectation that it will surpass $300 billion USD by 2026[12].

This follows the broader adoption of digital technologies, including automation and robotics, electric and self-driving vehicles, and new elements of technology stacks such as blockchains, immersive digital environments and entertainment.

The rapid adoption of AI, in particular, has been made possible by advances and new techniques in combining CPUs and GPUs, and in increasing densities. At Schneider Electric, we estimate that AI represents 4.3 GW of power demand today and project this to grow at a CAGR of 26% to 36%, resulting in a total demand of 13.5 GW to 20 GW by 2028. This growth is two to three times that of overall data center power demand CAGR of 11%[13]

In our white paper on *AI Disruption: Challenges and Guidance for Data Center Design*[14], we outline four AI attributes and trends that underlie the physical infrastructure challenges these developments have for data centers: AI workloads (training and inference), thermal design power (TDP) of GPUs, network latency and AI cluster size.

These demands have exceeded the design parameters of previous architectures. In cooling, for example, the densification of AI training server clusters is forcing an evolution from air-cooled to liquid-cooled architectures to address their increasing TDPs.

While less dense clusters and inference servers will still use more conventional data center cooling, we have identified six key cooling challenges that data center operators need to address to harness the power of AI-enabled infrastructure with sustainability in mind. They include:

- Difficulty of air cooling management for AI clusters above 20 kW/rack
- Lack of standardized designs and site constraints that complicate liquid cooling retrofits
- Unknown future of TDPs increases the risk of cooling design obsolescence
- Inexperience that complicates installation, operation, and maintenance
- Increasing risk of leaks within IT racks when employing liquid cooling
- Limited fluid option exist to operate liquid cooling sustainabily

Chapter Nineteen

Liquid Cooling

Liquid cooling offers a more efficient, less wasteful, and more controllable set of solutions to not only meet the needs of AI workloads but to allow data centers to be optimized for them.

Our research has shown that rack densities higher than 50+ kW/rack simply cannot be managed by air cooling. Despite many colocation service providers being below 20kW/rack where the limits of air cooling are already being reached, they are increasingly worried about architecture.

As AI, the metaverse, and digital experiences drive structural changes in data center designs, cooling must take an end-to-end, agnostic approach that combines air and liquid elements with higher temperature heat rejection, and in a wide portfolio to accommodate varying server requirements.

These new cooling methods must also be sustainable by providing effective cooling while being highly efficient and effective at reducing waste and emissions. Based on our research, we recommend a four-step approach that minimizes energy use and facilitates heat reuse reduces GHG, has no water dependency and limits waste.

Although liquid cooling will greatly reduce the dependence on compressor based cooling, it still will be required. More environmentally friendly refrigerant options are being employed, comprising natural ingredients such as ammonia and others with a low global warming potential. Strong regulation in this area, such as F-Gas restrictions and the Kigali Agreement, ensures that new designs address the challenges of toxicity, capacity, flammability and efficiency, and help build toward a sustainable future.

Liquid cooling has the benefit of using much warmer water loops than air cooling systems which allows for increased economization hours and reduced evaporative water use. Zero water use is a goal for many, but the journey to get there is a balance of cooling system design, sizing, energy use and using evaporative cooling only when needed. The key is the right design coupled with operational flexibility. Cooling systems will be able adapt to environmental conditions and maximize water savings or energy used based upon what's best for the local water system and grid.

With these systems, a holistic, end-to-end view is possible. This gives a view across energy, land use, materials, management, potential pollution, transport, waste and water usage, as well as potential health and wellbeing impacts. Certifications, such as those under the BREEAM framework, assess the sustainability of a building or data center chapter according to such parameters, helping operators to establish and achieve targets[15].

Overall, liquid cooling offers a more efficient, controllable' and capable medium than air, with those liquid cooling benefits feeding directly into the overall sustainability capability of data centers. Operators must make this necessary transition to achieve the benefits and sustainability gains that will contribute to a greener industry.

Next Generation Requirements

This approach to cooling will facilitate the kind of liquid cooling that will be necessary for the next generations of GPU and CPUs. Our white paper on AI[16], which I previously referred to, goes into detail on recommendations for designing the cooling systems to accommodate air cooling and liquid cooling to scale up as needed and support different generations of accelerators.

For example, high-temperature chillers for air cooling that are used today can be easily switched to higher-temperature liquid cooling tomorrow. Another recommended practice is to design the chilled water piping system with tap-offs for future coolant distribution units. This will allow a transition to 100% direct-to-chip liquid-cooled loads combined with supplemental air cooling.

Direct-to-chip (or cold plate) liquid cooling for high-performance CPUs and GPUs is already seeing high rates of adoption as a means of achieving the same level of performance for significantly less energy consumed. NVIDIA claims its 100 PCIe GPU can maintain performance levels with direct-to-chip liquid cooling while consuming up to 30% less energy versus air cooling[17]. In research with data center service providers, NVIDIA estimates the liquid-

Chapter Nineteen

cooled data center could hit 1.15 PUE, far below the 1.6 of its air-cooled equivalents[18].

Overall, liquid cooling with direct-to-chip techniques offers opportunities to improve cooling effectiveness and efficiency. However, even has water-based liquid cooling has early market acceptance, developments in other technologies such as immersion techniques and two-phase direct to chip, will provide a rich a diverse portfolio of options in the future. These will be critical cooling methods in an improved cooling mix for future data centers with the major benefit of being optimized for AI workloads.

Sustainable Ambitions on a Journey for All

Data centers currently play a vital role in supporting increasingly digital economies around the world, which is a role that will only accelerate in the future.

To complete sustainable advances in power through smart, managed energy storage, green on-site generation, and new approaches to grid cooperation and support, data centers must be responsible corporate citizens that facilitate the accelerated adoption of renewable energy sources nationally. With those efforts measured through industry-standard metrics and common reporting frameworks, the vital journey to—and continued operation of—net-zero carbon is measurable and demonstrable.

Through sustainable liquid cooling infrastructure that is commensurate with the needs of tomorrow's high-density architectures and able to support emerging and future workloads, data center operators can continue to support digital transformation while playing an integral role in net-zero journeys, making the power of AI available to all.

It is imperative that every industry, sector, and vertical do what they can to reach and exceed climate change targets to ensure that we can collectively ensure warming stays within livable limits, while decarbonization continues apace.

Of the UN's 17 sustainable development goals, we believe that the measures outlined here directly affect success in 12 of those goals[19].

What's clear is that we have the tools, technology, and collective know-how to make these changes, and through our industry, we must provide a roadmap for other sectors to reach net-zero. It is our duty and responsibility to bring as many as we can on the journey, as fast as we can, to a true net-zero carbon future for the digital infrastructure that is such a vital feature of our modern world.

---

1. Climate Neutral Data Centre Pact, 2021. https://www.climateneutraldatacentre.net/.
2. IEA. 2022. "Renewable Power Growth is Being Turbocharged as Countries Seek to Strengthen Energy Security." December 6, 2022. https://www.iea.org/news/renewable-power-s-growth-is-being-turbocharged-as-countries-seek-to-strengthen-energy-security.
3. IEA. "Net Zero by 2050". May 2021. https://www.iea.org/reports/net-zero-by-2050.
4. Hannu Aatola, Martti Larmi, Teemu Sarjovaara and Seppo Mikkonen. "Hydrotreated Vegetable Oil (HVO) as a Renewable Diesel Fuel." SAE International Journal of Engines
    Vol. 1, No. 1 (2009), pp. 1251-1262.
    https://www.jstor.org/stable/26308354
5. Baumann, Carsten. 2020. "How Microgrids for Data Centers Increase Resilience, Optimize Costs, and Improve Sustainability." Schneider Electric, July 27, 2020. https://www.se.com/us/en/download/document/Microgrids_for_Data_Centers/
6. IEA. "Digitalisation." https://www.iea.org/energy-system/decarbonisation-enablers/digitalisation
7. Butler, Georgia. 2023. "Schneider Electric & Aeven to deliver excess power to Danish grid." September 5, 2023. DataCenter Dynamics. https://www.datacenterdynamics.com/en/news/schneider-electric-aeven-to-deliver-excess-power-to-danish-grid/ .
8. World Economic Forum. 2023. "Circular Transformation of Industries: Unlocking New Value in a Resource Constrained World." January 2023. https://www3.weforum.org/docs/WEF_Circular_Transformation_of_Industries_2022.pdf .
9. Brown, Kevin. 2022. "The DCIM 3.0 trend explained in 500 words." August 2, 2022. Schneider Electric. https://blog.se.com/datacenter/2022/08/02/the-dcim-3-0-trend-explained-in-500-words/.
10. Schneider Electric. "A guide to environmental sustainability metrics for data centers." https://go.schneider-electric.com/WW_202111_WP67-Sustainability-Metrics-EN_MF-LP.html

11. Capgemini Research Institute. "Climate AI: How artificial intelligence can power your climate action strategy." https://www.capgemini.com/wp-content/uploads/2021/05/Report-Climate-AI-4.pdf
12. IDC. 2023. "Worldwide Spending on AI-Centric Systems Forecast" https://www.idc.com/getdoc.jsp?containerId=prUS50454123
13. Schneider Electric. 2023. "The AI Disruption: Challenges and Guidance for Data Center Design." December 6, 2023. https://www.se.com/us/en/download/document/SPD_WP110_EN/
14. Schneider Electric. 2023. "The AI Disruption: Challenges and Guidance for Data Center Design." December 6, 2023. https://www.se.com/us/en/download/document/SPD_WP110_EN/
15. BRE Group. "How BREEAM works." https://bregroup.com/products/breeam/how-breeam-works/
16. Schneider Electric. 2023. "The AI Disruption: Challenges and Guidance for Data Center Design." December 6, 2023.https://www.se.com/us/en/download/document/SPD_WP110_EN/
17. Delaere, Joe. 2022. "NVIDIA Adds Liquid-Cooled GPUs for Sustainable, Efficient Computing." May 23, 2022. NVIDIA. https://blogs.nvidia.com/blog/2022/05/23/liquid-cooled-gpus-computex/
18. Delaere, Joe. 2022. "NVIDIA Adds Liquid-Cooled GPUs for Sustainable, Efficient Computing." May 23, 2022. NVIDIA. https://blogs.nvidia.com/blog/2022/05/23/liquid-cooled-gpus-computex/
19. United Nations Geneva. "170 Actions to Combat Climate Change." https://sites.ungeneva.org/170actions/climate/#allgoals.

About the Author

ROBERT BUNGER

Robert Bunger is innovation product owner in the Office of the CTO at Schneider Electric.

In 26 years at Schneider Electric, Rob has held management positions in customer service, technical sales, offer management, business development and across key industry associations, while also at the forefront of technological advances in the organization. He has championed Open Compute Project (OCP) principles within Schneider Electric, helping to develop OCP-Ready solutions, including Open rack and liquid cooling architectures.

Rob has been at the cutting-edge of data center sector-related research, helping to establish the industry's first environmental sustainability framework to help operators reduce their environmental impact. More recently, he contributed to the development of new tools and research reports that have enabled enterprise operators to fully quantify, model and develop strategies to address Scope 3 emissions.

Rob has lived and worked in the US, Europe, and China, and was formerly a commissioned officer in the US Navy Submarine force, with a BS in Computer Science from the US Naval Academy and MS in Electrical Engineering from Rensselaer Polytechnic Institute.

About the Author

MARC GARNER

Marc Garner leads the Secure Power Division for Europe at Schneider Electric.

In the current energy revolution and climate emergency context, Marc's mission is powering the path to a sustainable, digital future. He focuses on leading and developing a team of people from different backgrounds and cultures that supports customers and partners across Europe in their digitization processes.

Marc strongly believes in the convergence of digital and electric: while digital technologies improve energy efficiency, electrification speeds up decarbonization – leading to IT and data center sustainability, efficiency, agility, and resiliency.

With a business and sales background, Marc has had several roles in different companies throughout his professional career prior to starting with Schneider Electric through a graduate program. Marc likes to bring his sporting, adventurous spirit into business: ambition and hard work defining his professional path, while being competitive and results driven. He constantly engages his customers, partners and co-workers to address the energy challenge towards a net zero future.

TWENTY

The Dynamic Domino Effect of Energy-Efficient Direct Liquid Cooling

Ken Kremer, Involta

The digital infrastructure industry operates on the continuous hum of servers and the ceaseless flow of data. But beyond all the workloads, switches, routers and cables, there is a deeper purpose to what we do. It's about connection, progress, and making the world a better place through technology. It's what motivates me to go to work every day. It's even ingrained in my company's culture and core mission — to drive innovation and deliver outstanding experiences that enable our clients to change their worlds for good.

As I sit down to write this chapter, I can't help but think about how our work as an industry and our commitments to improving operational efficiency and sustainability have made significant strides — but that our work isn't done. We know that sustainability is not a choice, and it's not just a buzzword that looks good on an annual report, incorporated into a mission statement or written as an Environmental, Social and Governance (ESG) initiative. Sustainability is crucial, especially across the tech and digital infrastructure industries, where the demand for faster data processing and high-density workloads is unrelenting — and continues to require more and more power by the minute.

I feel every bit of this, and I deeply understand the importance of sustainable operations. I own this responsibility and lead efforts to ensure our company is putting in the work needed to create and adopt innovations to reduce emissions and improve effectiveness to achieve greener facilities and a brighter tomorrow.

But one thing's for sure. Being environmentally responsible is no small feat. As pressures mount for tech companies to deliver more innovation, keep costs down, and increase business growth, leaders across the digital infrastructure industry are juggling a mountain of demands. And while it may be tempting to hit the "easy button," we must proactively choose to take the path that will lead us to a more sustainable future. While this road may be more challenging and riddled with obstacles, the potential dividends are immense, especially when we think about the rich legacy of environmental efficiency we can pass on to future generations.

Throughout this chapter, I hope to inspire you to embrace the path less traveled. It's time to make the choice that will pave a greener way forward. As a CTO and a father, this chapter serves as a testament to my dedication — and to that of Involta, the company I co-founded almost twenty years ago — to build a better future for our children and our children's children.

It is an honor to share my experiences in shaping Involta's remarkable sustainability journey, where we continue to take a more challenging yet more meaningful path. Over the past several years, we have explored renewable energy technologies and cooling solutions in order to transform how our customers operate, helping them run high-performance computing (HPC) applications while achieving their own sustainability and ESG goals.

The Future Operates on HPC

We all know artificial intelligence (AI) and the HPC needed to support it are having an unprecedented impact on just about every industry worldwide. You could say it's an all-consuming, all-industry shift to a new way of thinking that has the potential to change our world radically. AI can process ridiculously huge amounts of data to glean real and useful insights. Just look at how ChatGPT is changing the way we learn, communicate and create. Currently, ChatGPT is considered the fastest-growing app of all time, reaching 100 million users in its first two months.[1] In October 2023, it generated an astounding 1.7 billion visits, and those numbers continue to grow like wildfire.[2]

Data means power. It will be used to pioneer scientific breakthroughs, drive transformative innovations and enhance the lives of billions globally. But as technologies evolve, the amount of data that organizations will have access to is growing exponentially. Much of the data will need to be processed in real time to carry out a range of tasks, such as tracking wearable medical devices, streaming live events, monitoring the weather, analyzing sales data and much more. The opportunities for innovation are endless — *if* a reliable IT infrastructure is in place to process and store the mountains of data. The data centers' ability to enable HPC will be key to making it all happen.

And the numbers illustrate projected growth. HPC is expected to grow rapidly over the next several years. The HPC market size is currently estimated at $56.98 billion and is expected to reach $96.79 billion by 2028, growing at a CAGR of 11.18%.[3]

In many ways, across multiple industries and organizations, the AI and HPC revolution has already taken hold. Let's take a look at the manufacturing industry, specifically.

HPC and the Fourth Industrial Revolution

Manufacturers have a new industrial revolution on their hands. The term "Fourth Industrial Revolution," also known as "Industry 4.0," refers to how IT advances, such as big data, advanced robotics, AI and machine learning, are disrupting industries and transforming how manufacturers test, develop, and produce products of all kinds — from cars to consumer goods to electronics.

As technology continues to advance, manufacturers are experiencing growing pains as they work to keep up with and embrace digital technologies to create "smart factories." Amid this ever-evolving landscape, IT teams in the manufacturing industry face the challenge of managing increasingly complex IT infrastructure, tighter uptime requirements and a growing number of audits and security breach concerns — all while keeping pace with a barrage of new technologies aimed at logistics, supply chain, connectivity, and IoT. That's where HPC comes in.

HPC powers the complex workloads of new Industry 4.0 technologies, and many manufacturers are leveraging it to carry out the following game-changing use cases:

Simulation and Modeling | With faster computing power, HPC empowers manufacturers to conduct complex simulations and modeling to optimize a product's design and performance more efficiently. Simulations of fuel dynamics, structural analysis, heat transfer and other processes allow manufacturers to achieve faster time to market.

Process and Supply Chain Optimization | HPC can analyze large data sets quickly, enabling manufacturers to streamline operations and reduce costs with more efficient demand forecasting, inventory management and logistics planning.

Materials Science and Research | Particularly in the aerospace and automotive industries, HPC can facilitate simulations of the properties and behaviors of materials at molecular and atomic levels to help optimize performance and fuel efficiency.

Quality Control and Inspection | HPC can help manufacturers ensure their products meet strict quality standards by analyzing large data sets for defect detection and image recognition.

Cyber-Physical Systems and IoT Integration | Real-time data from IoT sensors on the factory floor can be analyzed using HPC to enable faster decision-making and process optimization.

With so many groundbreaking uses, HPC is quickly evolving into an essential tool for manufacturers, empowering them to stay competitive, make better-informed decisions and optimize operations. Looking toward the future, there is no doubt that manufacturers will leverage HPC for nearly every aspect of operations — and having robust digital infrastructure in place to support such energy-intensive workloads is non-negotiable.

Challenges of HPC and Its Strain on Data Centers

While there are many benefits to reap from the advancement of HPC technologies, one major drawback is the amount of energy required to support it.

It is no secret that data centers are already energy intensive, consuming 10 to 50 times[4] the energy per floor space of a typical commercial office building. What's more, data centers account for approximately 2%[5] of the total U.S. electricity use, and as the demand for HPC increases at a record-smashing pace, data center and server energy will also grow by leaps and bounds.

While many data centers are designed to meet extremely high power demands, customers are asking providers to do more to enable even faster compute cycles to meet the demands of HPC technologies. Some of the world's most powerful supercomputers can consume tens of megawatts of electricity, equivalent to the needs of a small city!

Here's where it gets tricky. More power means more heat and a larger carbon footprint, leading to the urgent need for more effective cooling strategies. Today, many data centers with traditional air cooling solutions can't keep up with modern HPC workload demands, and data centers are seeking new, innovative ways to work

Chapter Twenty

more efficiently to address the issue. Enter direct liquid cooling (DLC) technology.

Meeting Manufacturing Demands in an Environmentally Responsible Way

Involta's path to installing DLC began with work with one of our large manufacturing clients, whose compute environment was growing exponentially, requiring ever-increasing amounts of power. To meet this client's need to run large, complex workloads, HPC and extremely efficient data center processing were required.

While our air-cooling systems adhere to ASHRAE® environment guidelines and were already energy efficient, they had reached their maximum cooling capacity. We knew our client needed us to do more. We made the decision to identify and adopt a more efficient, more sustainable cooling solution for our data center facility in Akron, Ohio. Investing in DLC infrastructure ensured we could continue to meet this client's growing needs.

The road to DLC was a multi-step, labor-intensive process. Through extensive planning, we mapped out an intricate strategy to overcome potential challenges and roadblocks along the way and set the wheels in motion. Over several months, we worked closely with the HPC manufacturer, designing the new cooling systems to integrate with our existing infrastructure. By understanding the client's specifications and redundancy needs, our engineers were able to leverage our current infrastructure, adapting it to the new requirements.

Exterior work began with extensive site preparation to create adequate protected space for a new chiller yard. After excavation and foundation work, we poured new concrete slabs to house chiller units and to construct an enclosure fence. The enclosure, made from galvanized steel tube structural posts and solid panels, resists both wind and weather and protects the chillers from the range of conditions the Ohio climate experiences throughout the year.

Chapter Twenty

Chiller enclosure fence structure installation

Inside the data center, we energized the electrical room with new uninterruptible power supply (**UPS**) systems that allow for increased power demands and protect equipment from damage in the event of power failure. Additionally, we installed HPC power modules to improve processing capabilities and capacity.

HPC power modules

We also installed a new piping loop that connects the data hall, mechanical room, heat exchanger/cooling distribution unit (CDU) and exterior chiller unit. This piping network is critical to liquid cooling systems as it transports the liquid through various stages of the DLC process.

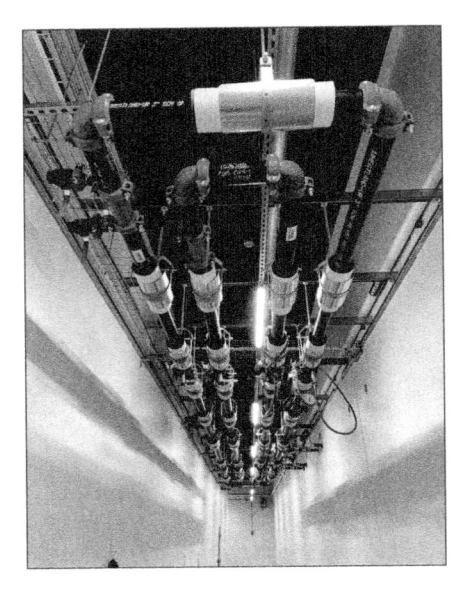

HPC clear water loop

The DLC Difference

With the new DLC infrastructure in place, Involta was positioned to manage equipment temperatures more efficiently, ultimately enabling our tech to operate at a higher capacity. With DLC in full swing, we continue to track power usage effectiveness (PUE) and energy consumption closely to manage critical loads and ensure our facilities remain highly efficient.

DLC solutions cool the central processing unit (CPU) with warm liquid, which has much greater (~4x) heat transfer capacity than air. The system is more efficient at extracting heat, reducing the burden on server systems and cooling infrastructure while significantly improving sustainability and reducing costs.

The many advantages of DLC are catching the eye of data center leaders and their clients. In fact, DLC is between 50 and

1,000 times more efficient than air cooling.[6] Also, DLC's cooling is targeted, and its capability is much more precise; it typically uses less water compared to air-cooling systems, equating to more energy efficiency and lower operating costs.

DLC is also compatible with existing data center rack infrastructure, resulting in simplified installation. For data centers that are new to DLC, an air/liquid hybrid cooling strategy is a viable option to explore, as both systems work well together. Plus, with DLC in place, data centers can say goodbye to loud, bulky air-cooling fans and pumps, which take up space and can generate significant noise throughout the facility.

Considering all of these benefits, it is no surprise that the global data center liquid cooling market is growing, projected to increase from $2.6 billion in 2023 to nearly $8 billion by 2028.[7] Global hyperscalers like Google, Intel, Alibaba and Meta are also employing liquid cooling technology to meet increasing computing needs and operate more efficiently.

The Ripple Effect of DLC

After Involta's initial shift to DLC, we determined the upgrade positively impacted our business, allowing us to keep energy usage and costs down while meeting our client's demands. By leveraging HPC technologies and adapting DLC solutions, we were able to achieve greater than 50% compute capabilities in 25% less physical space, realizing over 10% reduction in power consumption.

When we set out to install DLC, we knew it would improve efficiency, but we didn't realize how the impact would continue to grow. Our shift to DLC set off an incredible ripple effect, reverberating from the data center to the manufacturer and the value they pass along to their partners and customers.

The DLC upgrade allowed our manufacturing client to operate more efficiently, enabling it to make faster business decisions, establish data-driven go-to-market strategies and optimize products faster through more streamlined testing and production processes. With new insights gleaned from faster data processing, the manufacturer passed value on to its partners and customers, resulting in streamlined operations overall.

In addition, enabling DLC for HPC deployments allows manufacturing companies to be more innovative and produce more reliable products for better prices, giving them a competitive edge and positioning them as industry leaders. What's more, leveraging a data center equipped with DLC helps organizations meet ESG goals and attract environmentally focused investors, employees and customers.

What's Next? DLC Benefits Other Industries We Serve

Our team at Involta could not be more pleased with the success we achieved by implementing DLC at our Akron facility. Going forward, we plan to introduce DLC at all of Involta's data centers across the country, enabling more efficient and sustainable cooling to support HPC for more manufacturing clients and clients across other industries, including healthcare, financial services and technology.

Our Journey Has Just Begun

This sustainability story is just one of many from across our industry, and it's exciting to think that if we all work together, we truly have the power to drive meaningful change. Our shift to DLC shows that a single step toward a more efficient and sustainable future can have a huge impact across operations, teams, clients, overall productivity and a company's environmental footprint. Not only is DLC improving energy efficiency for Involta and our clients, but it's also enabling better performance and reliability, allowing our clients to report on their own ESG goals more efficiently and scale as their IT requirements evolve. It's a ripple effect that is resonating across our digital ecosystem and is inspiring us to do more.

I'm eager to see the progress we will achieve when we install DLC in all of our data centers. And that's not all. We are making other changes across our operations to drive positive change. We're tracking data center energy usage and measuring energy efficiencies,

Chapter Twenty

replacing end-of-life equipment with higher-efficiency equipment, establishing hot/cold aisle containment for higher cooling efficiencies in our data center halls, replacing incandescent lights with sensor-controlled LED lighting, recycling and disposing of electronic equipment and other hazardous waste responsibly, and much more.

Together, these measures have helped us achieve a 50% increase in energy efficiency across our flagship facility, commissioned in 2008, and our newest facilities. In 2023 more than 23% of our data center energy usage came from renewable sources, up from 17% in 2022. We will continue to contribute to a greener future through continuous energy efficiency improvement and greenhouse gas emission reduction by adopting sustainable practices and embracing renewable energy solutions.

Every action toward a greener tomorrow counts. We all need to do our part, and I'm so proud of the progress we have made on our journey toward sustainability. Our work is generating a more cost-effective, timely and impactful delivery of innovative products with the power to transform our clients' worlds. It's not always easy, but by overcoming challenges and navigating changes, our team has remained focused on our goal to change worlds for good — and it's working.

I'm looking forward to the next step in our sustainability journey, and as long as we keep moving forward to make a positive impact, we will continue building a legacy of a lifetime — one step at a time.

---

1. Porter, Jon. "ChatGPT continues to be one of the fastest-growing services ever." The Verge. Nov. 6, 2023. https://www.theverge.com/2023/11/6/23948386/chatgpt-active-user-count-openai-developer-conference.
2. Carr, David. "ChatGPT's First Birthday is November 30: A Year in Review." Similarweb. Nov. 30, 2023. https://www.similarweb.com/blog/insights/ai-news/chatgpt-birthday/.
3. "High Performance Computing Market Size." Mordor Intelligence. https://www.mordorintelligence.com/industry-reports/high-performance-computing-market/market-size.
4. "Data Centers and Servers - Department of Energy." https://www.energy.gov/eere/buildings/data-centers-and-servers.

5. Ibid.
6. Sheldon, Robert. "Liquid Cooling vs. Air Cooling in the Data Center." TechTarget. May 3, 2022. https://www.techtarget.com/searchdatacenter/feature/Liquid-cooling-vs-air-cooling-in-the-data-center?Offer=abt_pubpro_AI-Insider.
7. "Data Center - Liquid Cooling Market, Global Industry Size Forecast." Markets and Markets. July 2023. https://www.marketsandmarkets.com/Market-Reports/data-center-liquid-cooling-market-84374345.html.

About the Author

KEN KREMER

Ken Kremer, Founder and Chief Technical Officer at Involta, has been instrumental in the growth of Involta's national data center footprint. As one of Involta's co-founders, Ken's consistent leadership in technical services and operations has enabled the company to expand its data center and managed services portfolio.

Prior to Involta, Ken held leadership positions in high-tech companies focusing on operational efficiencies, innovative solution engineering and regulatory compliance issues. Ken's career has been focused on data center operations and managed services since 1997.

Ken leads efforts to achieve sustainable operations across Involta's nationwide network of data center facilities, contributing to energy efficiency, reduced environmental impact and a greener future. With a passion for community outreach and changing worlds for good through technology, Ken uses a methodical and measured approach to seamlessly integrate people, processes and services to ensure Involta fulfills its promise of "People Who Deliver."

TWENTY-ONE

When the Chips Are Down: Cooling Without Carbon

Maxie Reynolds, Subsea Cloud

A Little *Chip-Chat*

The modern world has been created by semiconductors or *chips*. A chip is a grid of millions or billions of transistors that remember and convert vast amounts of 1s and 0s into information we can understand and vice versa. Just a single smartphone today requires dozens of chips that each have billions of transistors. These transistors amount to the greatest volume of human-produced *things* on Earth[1], and they continue to determine the world around us. From military power and the financial markets to communication, personal interactions and expression, chips make up the modern world. And much of our modern world is housed in data centers.

It's the data center industry's job to keep much of today's world operational 99.999% of the time. To do this without further detriment to the planet, we know we can no longer cling to the status quo; we must move far away from air cooling technologies, both quickly and smartly. So, finally, the industry is looking toward immersion or *liquid* cooling. This chapter looks at a special type of liquid cooling, called *free liquid cooling*, along with its benefits, the roadblocks to using it, and the true costs of failing.

Chapter Twenty-One

Also known as liquid submersion cooling, immersion cooling is the practice of fully submerging servers in a thermally conductive liquid (dielectric coolant). Liquid cooling is far more efficient than air cooling due to thermal conductivities.

My interest in greener data is both personal and professional: my company has designed a product that is radically green; it uses no power for cooling and dissipates the heat very efficiently. It's my job to advance it commercially. There's also a humanitarian aspect to achieving greener data that's personally important, which I also consider in this chapter.

Completely Still

Most technology and devices draw energy and a conversion occurs. For example, a car motor, a complex mechanical device, converts chemical energy (fuel) into mechanical work (moving us around). The engine has an *efficiency factor* that describes how much of the energy we pump into our cars will be converted into useful work, such as moving the vehicle, versus what will be lost as heat waste. Energy conversions such as this happen with most of the things around us that draw power. But this isn't exactly true for a server. Servers mainly draw energy so that electrons can pass over their transistors, and nearly 100% of the energy going in comes back out as heat. Servers emit heat as a byproduct of managing and manipulating electrical energy and we in turn spend a lot of energy getting rid of this heat. Today, this is often accomplished through traditional air-cooling methods, which are expensive and use enormous amounts of electricity, which creates enormous amounts of carbon. We think there's a better way: free immersion cooling.

Chapter Twenty-One

How Our Free Cooling Works

In free cooling, natural fluids are used without air conditioning or mechanical or active components. Subsea Cloud places servers into submersible units and deploys them into bodies of water to benefit from free cooling. The servers are surrounded by a dielectric fluid that is dual purpose: it facilitates free, passive cooling and compensates against the pressure of the external water. The most significant outcome is the elimination of the power needed to cool, which is typically 40% of the total power consumption in a data center. This then eradicates 40% of the carbon emitted. This type of free cooling creates an optimal environment for the servers, as well as a low-cost maintenance model. How it works is relatively simple:

The Cooling Cycle

1. Servers are immersed in a dielectric fluid within a container, which is placed into a body of water.
2. Inside each unit the servers produce heat, just like on land.
3. At the molecular level, heat is essentially gets the molecules of the internal fluid excited, vibrating faster and expanding, which causes some separation in the fluid between temperature gradients (density).
4. This *excited fluid* floats to the top of the tank because it has a higher volume than cooler fluid, and a natural turbulent flow is created (due to more fluid rising within the unit as this process continues).
5. A heat exchange then takes place through the walls of the unit with the external water taking on the heat from inside; The free cooling component of the design ultimately takes place here.
6. The cooled internal liquid then shrinks again and is pulled back to the bottom of the unit.

7. The cooled fluid then naturally circulates back to heat-emitting parts where it is heated up again.
8. The heat itself is dissipated out of the pod in a continuous cycle.

The concept behind passive immersion cooling is simple yet highly effective. Within our first-generation unit, we can accommodate a rack density of 125kW+ (without cooling costs). It's a *cool* choice for getting rid of unwanted heat.

Convection and Free Cooling:

In convection, heat is transferred between a solid surface and a fluid (usually a gas or a liquid) in motion. We use natural convection (no fans, pumps, or other electrically driven devices) and because of this, the solution is both reliable and silent.

A Reframing of "Free"

Cooling: if it's not free, it's *very* expensive. In fact, every MWh of energy consumed from fossil fuel-generated power results in approximately half a ton of CO_2 in the atmosphere, regardless of where or how it's being consumed.

Our cooling mechanism reduces the amount of carbon emitted by at least 40% compared to that of a traditional data center as there's no power used for cooling, which results in near-perfect Power Usage Effectiveness (PUE). Although it may change in the future, most of the power consumed by data centers today is fossil fueled. To cool sensibly, free cooling should be utilized. Let's take a broad look at why with a quick comparison.

If we deployed 200 units (equal to roughly 200MW) on

Chapter Twenty-One

December 31, 2024, by December 31, 2025, we would have stopped 69,504 tons of carbon from being produced and emitted. In contrast, there are ~18 direct air capture plants operating globally and together they remove around 10,000 tons of carbon a year[2]. It's quite hard to remove carbon directly from the air and the same is true for storing it underground. All in all, there is no stronger alternative to actively and *actually* cutting emissions for the data center industry. Data centers are using more and more power; without free cooling, the costs are too high.

Environmentally Sound and Silent

There's an obvious external component to our cooling mechanism: a heat exchange takes place between the unit and the surrounding seawater. The seawater absorbs and then dissipates the heat. Using water in this way concerns many lay people and environmental advocates, too. My position is that it should.

Individuals and advocacy groups should take strong stances on behalf of the environment. We should raise questions and concerns around the practices of businesses in pursuit of profit relative to the environment. Equally so, evidence via scientific principles is the gold standard for assisting a change in perspective (alongside transparency). How our cooling mechanism works relative to its environmental effects is best shown through the principle of *specific heat*.

Specific heat is the amount of energy needed to raise the temperature of one gram of a substance by one degree Celsius. Water has a very high specific heat and warms up more slowly than air and can "hold" more heat. Put another way, water can absorb more heat before its own temperature increases by a single degree than the same mass of air can.

There are a couple of easy examples to illustrate this principle at work: Imagine you are on vacation and it's hot; you quickly tiptoe to the pool (you've forgotten your shoes); you get in the pool and you immediately feel cooler, but why? It's the same sun beating down on both parts of the resort, so surely the pool should be as hot as the poolside… It's not. But why? You feel cooler because it takes a lot more energy to heat the water (ocean or pool). Water can hold four times as much heat as the same mass of air. We can also think of this at a much larger scale: the sun strikes the earth continuously with ~173,000 terawatts (trillions of watts) of solar power and even this doesn't warm the ocean in an unsustainable way. Alas, it's mainly incremental and increasing human activity that is heating the planet in an unsustainable way.

Notably, whether on land or subsea, all servers and data centers produce heat. However, with our pods we aren't using power for cooling, which means less CO_2, whilst still maintaining optimal temperatures. Free cooling can be thought of as renewable cooling with no carbon, cost, or interference with the renewable resource. With free cooling, we essentially integrate ourselves with nature instead of manipulating it or trying to work against it.

Our toughest challenge, therefore, isn't to do with the environment given that when the solution is explained and inspected, we turn out to be environmentally sound. Our toughest challenge is subtle..

Our *Chief* Challenge

Our main challenge today centers around the many legacy companies that could move the needle by adopting greener solutions but are sometimes bureaucratically prohibited from doing so. These firms face the age-old predicament articulated in Clayton Christensen's 1997 book, *The Innovators Dilemma*. In it, Christensen asserts that maturing and legacy companies tend to strive for incremental improvements in their products and operations. Likewise, many incumbents must optimize for shareholders who often think almost exclusively in fiscal quarters. Even when staunch technical advocates exist within these organizations, adopting solutions that first seem too disruptive or unattractive in terms of profit and market share as compared to existing products, puts many shareholders on edge and often slows innovation overall.

At Subsea Cloud, our position is that free cooling with zero active water usage should be the standard to beat. Most of the industry agrees that incremental improvements won't support the near or distant future, and we know all companies should emerge from their constraints rather than in spite of them. Immersion cooling is becoming the front runner in our race to be better. There's a point to consider though: adopting immersion cooling doesn't necessarily result in a company becoming more environmentally friendly.

Standard Immersion vs Free Cooling

There's no denying immersion cooling is superior to air cooling. However, standard immersion cooling requires water to be pumped to remove the heat, and it can be energy intensive to pump water. To really understand immersion cooling and to save operators from making mistakes that aren't easily undone, it's best to look at the numbers.

To pump 1,000 cubic meters (one million liters/220,000 gallons) of water per hour requires a minimum 34kWh of energy if it is at a head of 10 meters (head here refers to the vertical height or distance through which water needs to be lifted) – not too bad. However, if the head is increased, and in most circumstances it is, it will take 340kWh to pump 1,000 cubic meters of water per hour (calculated at a head of 100 meters).

In other words, if the distance from the water source and/or the height of the water source is such that too much pipe resistance is encountered, it's no longer chiefly environmentally friendly.

So much energy is required to pump this water effectively, that, as far as the numbers are concerned, air cooling doesn't seem all that bad. Immersion cooling absolutely is the right direction, but it could also prove detrimental if our lens is too narrow, i.e., just getting away from air cooling without optimizing the height/distance from the water source. Free immersion cooling, by contrast, requires no active components for the cooling, which makes it an excellent choice.

Chapter Twenty-One

Human vs Data

Changing gears slightly, we can see that data affects humans in unintended ways. Because of how compute is spreading throughout society, we as an industry have an obligation to apply a humanitarian lens to our work, and many of us do.

Studies have shown that as global temperatures and sea levels rise, as the oceans acidify and precipitation patterns get rearranged, people living in poverty are the most severely impacted, in the following ways[3]:

- Wealthier national budgets can compensate their citizens when climate change harms livelihoods
- Higher incomes allow people to live in safer places, away from swelling rivers and tinder-dry wooded areas
- When weather affects food production, the prices go up which means it's less accessible to the underprivileged
- It's getting hotter; air conditioning is expensive and not prevalent outside of the western world
- Higher incomes allow people to buy water even in droughts (South Africa's Zero Day as an example)
- Higher rates of stunting in children occur in children nine months after the beginning of a drought event, which occur more frequently now
- When climate change affects where a person can live, it can reduce their access to health care and education

Whilst our industry may not be the primary cause of climate change, we obviously have a duty to act responsibly. We are in a unique position to mitigate our own environmental impact and that of all the industries we sustain. Our impact opportunity is huge.

But let's put a pin in that for now and assume most people reading this book are not disadvantaged, as described above, and want to look at the world through a more familiar lens. There's more bad news:

Chapter Twenty-One

1. If you use a computer at home, your power bills will rise due to the ever-growing power demands of GPUs and CPUs.
2. Renewables won't keep these costs down.

Literally millions (billions?) of people disagree, but we are decades away from having renewables effectively produce enough non-intermittent power to replace today's power generation fueled by coal and gas (including that used by planes, ships, and electric cars). There are technological and practical hurdles we just haven't solved yet. Without mass scale, long-term electricity storage that could offset renewable intermittent generation, or without robust and extensive grids to transmit electricity across the vast distances, we cannot rely on renewables in a more meaningful way. Adopting renewables as is required for our modern lives is very costly, very cumbersome, and very complex. To affect real change, the most promising course of action would be for all of us, citizens and businesses, to consume less. A lot less. Unfortunately, this is not something we are on track to accomplish in most parts of the world, with populations and energy-intensive activities tending to increase. Of course, we should continue to try to electrify our modern lives, but a full transition is too long into the future to lean on now. Exacerbating this is a huge sentiment issue around nuclear.

There's a little bit of good news: we could keep our home electricity costs down by connecting everything to the cloud, which is my genuine forecast. But we've just kicked the can down ~~the road~~ Data Center Alley. In relying more on the cloud, it becomes the data center industry's responsibility to get rid of even more heat at the same time as using more power and managing to do so without further detriment to the planet. However, when data centers *can* use renewables, it's a very good allocation of the power generated to its highest and best use. Used in combination with free immersion cooling, it's radically green.

Chapter Twenty-One

To overcome environmental, technical, and economic challenges in our company, we:

- Collocate with renewable providers
- Use renewable power where and when generated
- Completely circumvent attenuation issues
- Completely circumvent energy storage issues
- Use no water (actively) and have no adverse effect on the ocean or sources of water

Ultimately, the outcome of our design means we are using renewables and water in the most effective way possible. This brings us to something that warrants a lot of consideration in the pursuit of greener data: water usage. As we'll see, when a resource is underpriced, it often leads to overconsumption and inefficient use – a phenomenon known as the 'tragedy of the commons'[4].

Unsurprisingly, energy and water costs are not immediately evident to most users of data centers and not often talked about by providers. We do know though, that when resources are underpriced, we tend to waste them, and water might be the biggest victim of this phenomenon. Water usage in the data center industry alone has been controversial at best and an avoidable disaster at worst. Adequate drinking water is at risk in almost every country in the world and yet data centers use it to cool evermore powerful chips. A typical data center uses about the same amount of water per day as a city of 30,000 - 50,000 people, half of which is estimated to be drinking water[5] and this will naturally increase as the power required by the chip increases. It was estimated that in 2020, data centers in the United States consumed around 660 million cubic meters of water per year; in Europe, the consumption was estimated at 217.8 million cubic meters[6]. To put that into perspective, the average UK home is 212.5 cubic meters. Your home could be filled top to bottom more than four million times per year with the same amount of water data centers use per year, or 11,317 per day, in the USA and EU.

As discussed, free cooling can eliminate active water usage, without detriment to the body of water itself, or the rest of the biosphere. Of all solutions, ours can be used most readily and easily with renewables, creating an ecosystem that benefits both the asset owners and the public at large. Free cooling isn't a feat in engineering as much as a marvel of natural physics.

A Greener Conclusion

Arguably, the data center industry is responsible for two of the most voluminously produced things on earth: chips (transistors) and data. Reductively speaking, we are simply responsible for processing and storing data. Whilst some of this data is extremely important, and should be treated as such, the transition to proven (or provable) solutions should be prioritized over profits and corporate convenience. If you look at data relative to how our management of it impacts humanity, it quickly becomes critical to move rapidly toward real and environmentally sound solutions.

Where AI will be as pivotal to humanity as electricity was, the cooling mechanism most widely at work today (air cooling) is what coal was to homes in the 1970s, and our transition away from it is taking too long. The digital infrastructure industry finds itself in a unique position to underwrite the future of server and heat optimization in an impactful way, for the industry and the planet.

To move forward in a sustainable, responsible way the following at a minimum has to occur:

- Widespread responsible liquid cooling adoption
- Modular build outs
- More conscious placement of infrastructure
- More robust, integrated ecosystems
- More collaboration between intersecting industries
- More innovation and far less equivocation

Finally, the reason the current limits of renewables and the misuse of water have featured so heavily in a chapter about data center cooling is because it's vitally important for community and

Chapter Twenty-One

political leaders to understand that the pursuit of greener data isn't just a digital issue; it's also a humanitarian one.

---

1. Miller, Chris. 2022. "Introduction." Chip War: The Fight for the World's Most Critical Technology. October 4, 2022.
2. IEA. 2022. "Direct Capture 2022." IEA. https://www.iea.org/reports/direct-air-capture-2022/executive-summary
3. Wolfe, Deborah. 2021. "How climate change impacts poverty." World Vision. June 21, 2021. https://www.worldvision.ca/stories/climate-change/how-climate-change-impacts-poverty
4. Lehman, Bret. 2022. "Sustainability Spotlight: Data Center Water Usage." PCX. November 9, 2022. https://info.pcxcorp.com/blog/sustainability-data-center-water-usage#:~:text=Another%20source%20estimates%20that%20data,of%2030%2C000%2D50%2C000%20people.
5. Farfan, Javier and Alena Lohrmann. 2023. "Gone with the clouds: Estimating the electricity and water footprint of digital data services in Europe." Science Direct. August 15, 2023. https://www.sciencedirect.com/science/article/pii/S019689042300571X

About the Author

MAXIE REYNOLDS

Educated in computer science and underwater robotics, Maxie Reynolds has leveraged knowledge in these disparate fields and merged her expertise to create Subsea Cloud, a forward thinking startup that builds, deploys, and maintains sustainable, subsea data centers. Prior to founding Subsea Cloud, she worked on oil rigs as a ROV pilot and then in cybersecurity as pentester and social engineer, in which she published a best-selling book for cyber security professionals. Her latest venture is designed to deliver dense compute capacity that replaces electrically driven cooling systems with zero carbon emissions cooling from ocean ecosystems.

TWENTY-TWO

All Eyes on Efficiency: Engineering DC BLOX's Course to a Greener Digital Future

M. Reali-Elliott, DC BLOX

In an era driven by digital transformation, data centers stand as the unassuming pillars of our interconnected world. These vast complexes of servers and infrastructure quietly power our daily digital lives, from cloud computing to streaming entertainment. But as the demand for these services continues to soar, so does the energy consumption, environmental impact, and resource depletion associated with data center operations. In this context, sustainability becomes more than a buzzword; it's an imperative for both the industry and the planet.

Delving into the sustainability journey of DC BLOX, a relative newcomer in the data center industry, we have begun chronicling our early steps on the sustainability journey. We've also begun highlighting the ways even smaller data center organizations can make a substantial difference in the broader landscape of data center sustainability, from strategic planning to design and operations to certifications as a means of reporting. Our approach to efficiency in data center operations has been firmly rooted in ethical and environmentally conscious practices from the outset.

Sustainability in data centers encompasses a comprehensive approach that touches every facet of operations, from construction and design to daily efficiency and community engagement. In the pages that follow, we will share the story of how DC BLOX has strategically pursued sustainability, demonstrating the mindset we have undertaken, initiatives we have put in place, and technologies we have leveraged for a greener and more responsible digital future.

Our Journey Began with Efficient Power Utilization

Since the inception of DC BLOX, our data center design has been driven by the goal of reducing costs by utilizing power as efficiently as possible, which has the added benefit of being consistent with sustainability objectives. By prioritizing efficient power utilization as a core principle from day one, we align our practices to minimize environmental impact while optimizing operational expenses.

Our vision revolved around developing cutting-edge data centers and digital infrastructure that would continuously fuel the growth and connectivity of the Southeastern United States. This region, teeming with innovation and enterprise, was poised for digital transformation, and we aimed to provide the essential backbone for this revolution.

In 2017, we opened our first facility in Chattanooga, Tennessee, with a focus on optimal power utilization at the forefront of our minds. The selection of this site was intentional; we realized that for businesses to thrive in the digital age, they needed infrastructure that was reliable, scalable, and, importantly, built with a minimal environmental footprint. By building in close proximity to our customers, we have enabled smaller footprint data centers that also minimize emissions associated with customers driving long distances to manage and maintain the equipment within. Our goal was to ensure that as we fueled the digital transformation of our region, we did so responsibly, minimizing our energy consumption, carbon emissions, and overall environmental impact.

Chapter Twenty-Two

Efficiency from the Ground Up

As described with our first facility, at DC BLOX we've taken a proactive approach to building small, highly efficient data centers that use the latest equipment and technologies. We're not retrofitting existing facilities; we're starting from the ground up. The benefits of this approach to facility design are many, but most notably result in a reduction in energy usage for operations, cooling, lighting, and more that translates to a significantly lower carbon footprint and places less strain on the electrical grid.

This approach also allows us to maximize our resources more efficiently, not only in terms of servers and network equipment within the facility but also in terms of land and water use. By right-sizing our infrastructure and building from the ground up, we have more control over reducing energy consumption, emissions, and resource depletion.

Operational Efficiency and Management

DC BLOX's focus on efficient and cost-effective power management carries into deliberate actions across our system designs, operational processes, and workforce training. This involves both the adoption of energy-efficient hardware and equipment as well as the utilization of advanced power management tools to optimize energy usage.

Our commitment to reducing energy usage extends to both the design and operational aspects. In the design phase, we employ tools like Computational Fluid Dynamics (CFD) modeling and total cost of ownership (TCO) energy modeling to create efficient designs that meet the demanding requirements of our customers. We've made it a priority to optimize efficiency in our designs, from right-sizing equipment to considering mechanical efficiency.

In operations, we leverage our Supervisory Control and Data Acquisition (SCADA) system as a power management tool. This system allows us to actively monitor and review power usage effectiveness (PUE) and energy usage in our buildings, ensuring that they are optimized. We tune our cooling systems to align with the IT load in an efficient manner, avoiding any unnecessary energy waste. Our sites are designed with load considerations in mind, meaning there's no wasted energy; each facility is efficient for the IT load it supports.

In essence, our approach is not just about building data centers; it's about crafting environments where sustainability, efficiency, and environmental responsibility are at the forefront of our operations. Our journey to create a greener and more responsible digital future begins with a commitment to innovation and efficiency in every aspect of our data center operations.

Innovative Cooling Solutions for Waterless Data Centers

Efficient cooling is at the heart of sustainable data center design, but as with other design considerations, there are trade-offs between selections available, in this case between air- and water-cooled facilities. Each data center must strike the right sustainability balance to deploy energy efficient and sustainability-conscious options for the customers and communities they serve.

Currently, in the realm of cooling solutions, DC BLOX has striven to dramatically reduce cooling-related energy consumption while also preserving a precious natural resource—water. Traditional data centers often rely on water-intensive cooling methods, such as cooling towers or evaporative cooling systems. In contrast, at this time, DC BLOX has opted for the progressive approach to run waterless or closed-loop data centers. While it is often noted as a negative feature of waterless cooling that it uses more power than water-intensive systems, we must also counter-balance our considerations. Weighed against power use are the costs of implementing liquid cooling as well as the risk of leaks, so while more efficient, it may not always provide the best overall solution. We must always choose the most appropriate solution for our tenants based on the specific location. At DC BLOX, we've found that air-cooled solutions are improving and are efficient enough for many applications;

meanwhile our focus on energy efficiency has enabled us to make this selection for our existing facilities.

Our traditional, or core, facilities are equipped with high-efficiency direct expansion (DX) cooling systems. The DX cooling technology is recognized for its energy efficiency and effectiveness in maintaining optimal temperatures for data center equipment. What makes these designs truly forward-thinking is the flexibility they offer. The key feature of our approach is the ability to add economization in the future, further driving down PUE. By incorporating free cooling capabilities, we ensure that our data centers remain at the forefront of efficiency, continuously optimizing energy usage and reducing operational costs. Also with the employment of hot-aisle containment, we can increase the efficiency of our air-cooling operations .

Our DX cooling systems not only provide exceptional cooling performance, but do so without consuming a single drop of water. While one of our facilities does incorporate a closed-loop system, no additional water is used after priming the system. In the data center space, where cooling water usage can be substantial, DC BLOX is saving millions of gallons of water every year, per facility. By avoiding traditional water usage and employing cutting-edge cooling methods, we are taking steps to enhance the reliability and longevity of our customers' IT equipment while reducing energy consumption spent on cooling, making our data center operations highly sustainable and cost-effective.

However, we recognize that the need for high-performance computing is on the rise. To meet these demands, we continue to investigate whether waterless designs may be feasible, given spatial considerations, power requirements of equipment deployed, density per square foot, regional water supply, and of course, customer goals. Our recently announced, larger megawatt sites—while still on the design boards—will leave room for provisions to incorporate liquid cooling in our future high-density designs as we grow to serve the newest infrastructure demands for high-performance computing and AI.

Chapter Twenty-Two

Data Centers and Environmental Impact: Balancing Consumption and Production

Data center complexes, which encompass rows upon rows of servers humming with activity, are energy-intensive by nature. They fuel not only the computing equipment but also the extensive cooling systems required to maintain optimal operating temperatures. With a range based on various analyst reports, it's estimated that data centers consume anywhere from 1% to 3% of global electrical power, a figure that underscores their substantial contribution to overall energy consumption, and the reason most data center providers are focused on lowering their energy consumption through efficient practices, like those we have featured thus far.

We now take a brief look at the state of energy production. The data center industry, above all others, understands the complexities of the power production side of the equation. For data centers to generate their own renewable power, they'd need to embark on ambitious ventures such as microgrid development—a scale of undertaking that not all can pursue.

In the quest for a more sustainable energy supply, some data centers opt for Renewable Energy Credits (RECs) to offset their environmental impact. Others arrange Power Purchase Agreements (PPAs) to procure renewable power. These agreements often involve large-scale renewable energy projects to provide funding to the utility companies to aid their investment in developing renewable energy sources, so benefits are more easily achieved with large scale agreements. While the scalability of such projects doesn't always align with the operations of smaller edge data center facilities, procurement of renewable power on even a small scale is an option for tenants who desire this optionality, rendering these initiatives achievable by all who wish to sustainably invest in the future.

This leaves many data centers in the same category as other industries and residents of our communities when it comes to energy sourcing: reliant on our local utility provider to incorporate renewable power generation in the energy mix. In many regions, data center operators like DC BLOX don't have the luxury of choice when it comes to selecting power providers. The regulatory framework governing public utilities often leaves businesses tethered to local providers, with limited influence over the energy mix they receive (except by purchasing RECs and PPAs, which help them get there).

For these reasons, the environmental impact associated with data centers is, to a significant degree, driven by the energy companies that supply electrical power. As part of our strategic approach to site selection, and to the greatest extent possible, we seek out opportunities to collaborate with utilities that are actively investing in renewable power generation to ensure that our facilities remain part of the broader movement towards a more sustainable energy future.

As a concrete example, our facilities in South Carolina (Greenville, Myrtle Beach, and the latest in development, Charleston West), are powered by Santee Cooper, which holds the record as the first utility in the state to provide renewable power to customers.[1] Their energy mix includes sources such as solar, wind, landfill biogas, and agricultural biomass.

As another illustration of how our sites are aided by our utility partners, our facility in Chattanooga, Tennessee, boasts a strong utility provider, Tennessee Valley Authority, which draws from a diverse energy mix. The presence of six nuclear power plants in their jurisdiction[2] and Tennessee's status as one of the largest[3] producers of hydroelectricity[4] in the U.S. underscore the region's commitment to diverse and sustainable energy sources. This same utility also provides power to our Huntsville, Alabama, facility.

For DC BLOX, a primary focus is on minimizing energy consumption—an aspect within our direct control. Our approach to sustainability extends beyond efficient data center management to include strategic considerations in site selection. We closely manage relationships with local utility providers, aiming to align with their efforts in renewable power generation where possible. Through these measures, we aim to reduce our environmental impact while upholding our commitment to powering the digital world responsibly.

Sustainability Assessments and Certifications to Substantiate Our Commitment

As shared throughout this chapter, DC BLOX has always held efficiency and environmental considerations close to our heart. Yet, we recognize that there's no substitute for the expert eye of industry professionals who can assess our performance compared to other sustainability leaders.

This led us to solicit an assessment in accordance with the Data Center Energy Efficiency Program (DEEP). InformaTech selected our Birmingham, Alabama, facility for review. This thorough evaluation scrutinized every aspect of our data center operations, including energy and water usage, mechanical and electrical systems, and our overarching processes. It was an intensive process, and the results were enlightening for our organization to receive.

The DEEP assessment scrutinized vital areas integral to sustainability and efficiency, including:

Mechanical Systems | Efficiency in mechanical systems is vital for reducing energy consumption and environmental impact. In this category, InformaTech analyzed the type, number, and size of air-cooling systems, temperature sensors, monitoring, air and water usage economizers, HVAC power usage, and maintenance and optimization programs.

Electrical Systems | This comprehensive review of our electrical infrastructure ensured that it aligned with industry sustainability best practices. The evaluation encompassed power generation sources, backup power systems, power distribution, energy monitoring, management, and maintenance programs.

Airflow Management | Effective airflow management is paramount to efficient cooling. This assessment covered hot-aisle/cold-aisle containment, row and device temperature monitoring, airflow efficiency, and cooling load tonnage.

Processes | Once a data center design and construction is complete, the facility must still operate in an efficient manner. Accordingly, this assessment component evaluated our operational processes against the backdrop of leading practices in the industry —the use of Data Center Infrastructure Management (DCIM) and Building Management Systems (BMS) solutions, Power Usage Effectiveness (PUE) monitoring, heat waste reuse, carbon footprint monitoring, environmental training, and the implementation of a formal Environmental, Social, and Governance (ESG) program. It especially highlighted ways we recycled and reused discarded shipping containers that were on site from before and during construction, building our own adaptive reuse capacity even while the city had no formal recycling program.

At the conclusion of this in-depth assessment, DC BLOX's dedication to sustainable data center operations earned the prestigious DEEP gold-level certification for our Birmingham facility. This designation represents the highest tier available and affirms our strong predilection to sustainability-focused, industry-leading practices - while serving as a pivotal milestone in our sustainability journey.[5]

Community Engagement and Outreach: Nurturing Sustainable Bonds

At DC BLOX, our commitment to sustainability goes hand in hand with our dedication to the communities we call home. We believe that true leadership in our markets doesn't stop at technological innovation; it extends to ethical responsibility and acting for the social good.

In a world where data usage continues to surge, and the demand for connectivity rises, the need for smaller, local data centers like ours has become paramount. These centers bring time-sensitive digital services closer to consumer populations, minimizing latency and ensuring seamless digital experiences.

DC BLOX's deep-rooted commitment to making a positive impact on the communities we serve includes a holistic approach to sustainability that extends beyond the data center's walls. It transcends into the local communities where we operate. We're dedicated to making a difference and demonstrating our commitment to social responsibility, most especially through community involvement.

DC BLOX truly cares for the communities in which it does business. This care is not just a byproduct of our operations; it's a fundamental principle that drives our approach to sustainable data centers. It's about minimizing our environmental footprint and ensuring a brighter and more responsible digital future, not just for us, but for the communities we serve.

By fostering strong bonds with our local communities, we not only gain their acceptance, but also their support. We work hand in hand with them, ensuring that our presence is an asset rather than an imposition. This collaboration is a testament to our belief that true success in the data center industry doesn't just lie in technological prowess but in the positive impact we have on the world around us. At DC BLOX, we are committed to building a sustainable future, one community at a time.

A Commitment to Continuous Improvement

The foundation of continuous improvement is deeply embedded in our organizational culture. It's the driving force behind how we build, grow, and adapt every day. Our commitment to sustainability, too, is marked by the same unwavering attitude. We are resolute in our efforts to be better today than we were yesterday, to do more for our environment, our customers, and our communities.

The recent DEEP assessment was a pivotal milestone in our journey, awarding us their highest-tier mark, but the commitment to continuous improvement means that our journey doesn't stop here. The assessment highlighted not only the areas where we excel, but also some areas where we can improve. In the perpetual quest for improvement and a brighter, more sustainable future, the DEEP results have illuminated the path ahead, which will require ever-evolving technological and process advancements. The commitment to pursue new technologies and processes serves as an enduring pledge to make a positive impact and to shape a better, more sustainable future for all.

As we look ahead to the future, DC BLOX's commitment to sustainability will only grow stronger. We'll continue to seek innovative solutions, embrace the latest industry best practices and drive the change necessary for a more sustainable world. Every step we take, every endeavor we embark upon, will be a testament to our dedication to doing right by our planet.

---

1. Santee Cooper. "Renewable Energy." https://www.santeecooper.com/environment/renewable-energy/
2. Tennessee Environmental Council. "Nuclear Power in Tennessee." https://www.tectn.org/radioactivewastedraft.html
3. "Hydroelectric Power in the United States." https://en.wikipedia.org/wiki/Hydroelectric_power_in_the_United_States
4. Tennessee Valley Authority. "Hydroelectric." https://www.tva.com/energy/our-power-system/hydroelectric
5. Reali-Elliott, Melissa. Going DEEP on Sustainability in Birmingham." 2023. https://greenerdata.net/going-deep-on-sustainability-in-birmingham/

About the Author

M. REALI-ELLIOTT

Melissa Reali-Elliott has spent over 15 years marketing digital technologies and is a self-professed data center nerd. She holds degrees in Marketing, Economics, and Psychology from the University of Central Florida. Over her career, she has supported organizations specializing in software applications, IoT, RFID, industrial automation, and power distribution to utility markets, including smart grid, smart city, and microgrid applications, as well as critical infrastructure industries such as data centers.

She currently serves as the Content Marketing Manager for DC BLOX, a provider of tier III data centers throughout the Southeast US, along with connectivity and fiber solutions that further build digital infrastructure. Prior to this, she held senior marketing roles in the data center segment teams for Kohler and ABB. She is a regular contributor to many industry publications and authors the Data-Centered column for Mission Critical Magazine. She is also an Ambassador for the Nomad Futurist Foundation, which empowers and educates the younger generations through exposure to digital infrastructure technologies. As a result of her work, she has been awarded a 2022 IM100 by iMasons and a 2023 Top 25 Women in Technology by Mission Critical Magazine.

TWENTY-THREE

Navigating the Path to Carbon Reduction: Strategies for Effective Backup Power Generation

Nicole Dierksheide, Kohler Energy: Power Systems

The data center sustainability journey can be daunting. What are the benefits - and risks - of adopting a new technology? How do we know if one technology option is truly more sustainable than another? How do we make more sustainable choices that also make economic sense? Will something that seems like the right choice today still be the right choice tomorrow?

I'm here to tell you to breathe: the sustainability journey is not necessarily easy and each decision along the way may not be perfect. The important thing to remember is to take the first step and to maintain momentum.

The first step for most data centers is to focus on energy consumption. In this discussion, I'm going to take a deeper look at the solutions available to data centers now and in the future - and offer insight on how data centers can take the first step towards greener operations while managing risk and resiliency.

The Looming Energy Crisis & New Technologies

It is well known that data centers consume a lot of energy - after all, it takes a lot to keep our digital world running! With the adoption of artificial intelligence (AI), researchers anticipate that an exponential increase in global data center energy consumption is on the horizon[1]. Couple this increased consumption with an aging utility infrastructure[2] that can't scale fast enough or provide enough low-carbon energy, and you have a supply crisis.

While new and upcoming technologies, such as battery storage and hydrogen fuel cells, aim to address these foreseeable issues, the challenge lies in their inability to arrive quickly enough and the inherent risks they carry until proven over time.

Where does that leave us? Today, we have a huge opportunity to continue to improve existing technologies that have demonstrated the ability to limit risk, while having a significant impact on emissions reduction. These new technologies are exciting and promise to be major game changers. I can't wait to see how these solutions evolve over time, but I'm equally excited about what we can do now to make a major impact while we wait for new technologies to prove out.

A Traditional Solution: Backup Diesel Generators

A utility-based source of electricity paired with a backup diesel generator is a proven choice for establishing energy resilience, which offers numerous advantages that are hard to beat with other technologies. A generator entails simple onsite fuel storage that can provide an extended runtime of at least 24 hours, which t can extend up to 96 hours and beyond. The production and distribution of diesel is well established so adding fuel to the storage system is reliable and cost effective.

Diesel generators also have a fast start time, ready to accept load in under 10 seconds. Additionally, a diesel generator can accept up to 100% load step with minimal transients. This fast start time and large load step capability are difficult to match with other technologies. Finally, a diesel generator is a compact design. This can be described as energy density, a measurement of how much power is contained within a given square footage. Space costs money so the smaller the solution, the lower the cost.

Chapter Twenty-Three

When you evaluate other technologies in terms of these attributes, you find they do not meet all the same performance criteria. Where a technology may lack in performance, let's say in the length of runtime, for example, then you need to add another technology to offset that shortfall in performance. Overall, this means that there is not a single technology out there that will displace a diesel generator - it will take a combination of many to provide the same benefits.

A Closer Look at Battery Storage

The most common solutions for energy storage now discussed are batteries, hydrogen and fuel cells. Battery storage generates a lot of interest as it can pair well with other energy providers, such as utilities, solar, and wind generation, and provides a way to store excess generation for deployment during a peak time. Although this is a powerful combination, batteries have several challenges. First, since they rely on another generating source for charging, if your power grid is already strained, charging them adds further pressure on the utility. Ideally, battery charging should be put off to a low demand period to reduce this strain. If charging comes from a renewable source, such as solar, there is often variation in the availability so fully charged batteries may not be guaranteed.

Second, batteries have a relatively short run time. The most typical is 2-4 hours and they can stretch up to 8 hours. To extend beyond this requires more batteries which in turn require more space. In general, batteries have poor energy density compared to generators and the longer the run time required, the larger the battery system becomes. So, batteries have a place in the energy landscape but they do not provide long-running resiliency in an acceptable footprint.

Gaining Ground with Hydrogen Innovations

As a fuel source, hydrogen is promising but still immature in terms of mass production and distribution, and hence not ready to transform backup power to this source. The adoption of hydrogen will have to match the growth of the supply and distribution. Production and distribution are increasing each year, driving down the cost and making hydrogen a viable option in more and more situations.

The other challenge with hydrogen from a sustainability perspective is ensuring that the energy source for producing hydrogen is renewable so that the end product is truly a low-carbon option. Some hydrogen choices, such as hydrogen produced from natural gas (known as grey hydrogen), are not low-carbon choices. Alternatively, hydrogen produced through electrolysis using a renewable source, such as wind, has a minimal GHG footprint. This is referred to as green hydrogen and is the lowest carbon choice. There are many colors of the rainbow when it comes to the carbon footprint of hydrogen so operators need to be aware of the carbon profile of their hydrogen, and to opt for the lowest footprint, which is green hydrogen.

Once a low-carbon hydrogen fuel source is identified, the next choice is to determine what solution will use the hydrogen. The most common choice today is a combustion engine, with solutions already on the market today and more becoming available. Combustion engines are a proven technology and introducing hydrogen as a fuel source is a logical next step with minimal risk. However, there can still be tradeoffs to consider when you look at start time and load acceptance criteria depending on the engine design. As more hydrogen engines are available, it will be intriguing to see what options are available for a resilient backup solution versus what may be a better fit for a long running continuous application.

Another exciting option emerging for hydrogen usage is the fuel cell. There are two main types of fuel cell technologies: Polymer Electrolyte Membrane Fuel Cell (PEMFC) and Solid Oxide Fuel Cell (SOFC). There are some distinct differences in how these two fuel cell technologies perform which will determine the best application fit.

Regardless of application, a fuel cell is extremely attractive from

Chapter Twenty-Three

an environmental standpoint since it produces no emissions. The output of a fuel cell is heat and water. That's it.

PEMFC is most close in performance to a standby diesel generator. A PEM fuel cell has a fast start time - usually less than one minute - which is quite a bit longer than a generator's 10 seconds, but still much faster than SOFC. A PEMFC can respond to load steps quickly, providing a good transient reaction to large changes in load. A key difference from a generator though is the size. To obtain the same power output, a PEMFC solution is much larger than a generator. For sites that are already space constrained, a hydrogen fuel cell can prove to be challenging as a replacement for a diesel generator. As fuel cell technology continues to develop, it is reasonable to expect that the size will reduce but time will tell what is possible in a smaller footprint.

To help draw the comparison to generators, you can look at a standby generator versus a continuous generator. A standby generator, as discussed before, has a fast start time and can accept large changes in load, making it ideal for an emergency standby application. A continuous generator is typically used in a Combined Heat and Power (CHP) application, running thousands of hours each year. It is optimized for fuel efficiency but has a slow start time as well as a limitation on the amount of load it can accept in a load step.

A PEMFC is closer in performance to a standby generator with the added benefit of zero emissions and economic advantage for several hundred to a few thousand hours of operation each year. A SOFC is most like a continuous application, with slow start times and minimal load steps but is optimized for heat capture; running it for over 8,000 hours a year provides the most benefit.

Taking Action Now

As technologies continue to advance, creative solutions will prevail but while we wait for these new technologies to become viable and proven, let's look at some actions you can take today to have a meaningful impact.

Chapter Twenty-Three

First, let's challenge the notion of diesel as the only fuel source for the generator. If you have been paying attention to the generator offerings of the past few years, you will have seen the adoption of renewable fuels using today's technologies. Hydrotreated vegetable oil (HVO), also known as renewable diesel (RD), is a direct replacement for fossil diesel. HVO provides a 90% reduction in carbon emissions compared to fossil diesel through the lifecycle of fuel production and consumption. HVO is equivalent to fossil diesel in performance and can be mixed if needed. This means that you can add resiliency to your fuel supply by using both HVO and fossil diesel as you reduce your GHG emissions. This is a choice you can make today to have an immediate impact.

Future renewable fuels, such as hydrogen, are on the horizon for mass production and distribution. Until then, because you need a steady source of fuel for your energy needs today, you can supplement fossil diesel with HVO and make a full transition to HVO as it becomes available in your area.

Another option is to add an aftertreatment system to a generator to further reduce the GHG emissions. In some countries or regions, using the best technology or limiting the carbon output further than the standard offering is required. In some instances, there is a financial benefit to participating in demand response or peak shaving programs offered by your utility, but these typically require you to have an aftertreatment system.

When it comes to aftertreatment system designs, there are key factors to consider. In the simplest terms, the solutions involve three types of technology: selective catalytic reduction (SCR), diesel particulate filter (DPF) and diesel oxidation catalyst (DOC). To understand the relative benefits in these system designs, it is important to understand these systems look to reduce multiple emission contributors and solving for one can have an inverse effect on another. For example, if you work to reduce carbon monoxide (CO), the solution can cause nitrogen oxides (NOx) to increase. But the final solution needs to reduce both. Depending upon the engine technology, you will need to deploy multiple technologies to achieve the desired overall reduction.

Chapter Twenty-Three

An SCR will primarily reduce NOx. A DOC reduces CO and hydrocarbon (HC). A DPF filters out Particulate Matter (PM). To know what technologies you need, you need to understand the current emissions output of the generator and then identify what specific emissions you want to reduce and by what amount. That will determine the solution.

For example, the Kohler KD Series generators optimize combustion to minimize most pollutants and to address NOx as the primary emission. As a result, when designing an aftertreatment system, it may be necessary to deploy an SCR only to reduce NOx; the addition of a DOC or DPF may not be required. This can simplify and reduce lifecycle costs.

The challenge with aftertreatment systems is that they are an additional expense, in terms of both upfront cost and upkeep of the system. It is harder to justify the investment unless the generators are used to participate in a program, such as demand response, which can offer additional financial benefits. Without this additional financial benefit, you are reducing emissions but at an additional expense that is not offset elsewhere. Due to this, we do not see broad adoption yet of aftertreatment systems. However, as emissions reductions are mandated in more areas, adopting an aftertreatment system is becoming a requirement. Luckily, the technology exists today, and there are a few solution choices that you can make today to have greener data.

The Life of a Backup Generator

It is critical for a data center to be operational 24/7. While you may experience power outages throughout the year, a backup generator does not run 24/7. However, it has been common practice to test a generator once a month. Traditionally, this exercise lasts for 30 minutes to one hour and is run with at least 30% load on the generator. This exercise not only consumes fuel, it also generates GHG emissions. The more load, the more fuel and GHG emissions are produced. In challenging the notion of a required exercise, Kohler has shifted to providing several options

Chapter Twenty-Three

that significantly reduce fuel usage and GHG emissions for exercise purposes.

One option is to still exercise each month but do it for a shorter period of time and without load. For Kohler KD Series generators, we allow a no-load test to be run for as little as 10 minutes. Due to the combustion efficiency of the engine, the concern for wet stacking (hydrocarbon build-up in the engine over time due to unspent fuel in the fuel system) is not present and the generator can run without load and not have performance degradation over time. Switching the exercise from 30 minutes at 30% load to 10 minutes with no load reduces the fuel consumption by 44% for test purposes. Additionally, it reduces generator exhaust GHG emissions by 40%. If you look at the entire lifecycle, this lowers GHG emissions, including emissions released for the production and distribution of the fuel, by 70% in total.

Another option is to extend the exercise to every four months. This unloaded exercise can also be for as little as 10 minutes. Switching the exercise from 30 minutes at 30% load every month to 10 minutes with no load every four months reduces fuel consumption by 71% and reduces generator exhaust GHG emissions by 69%. For the entire lifecycle, the GHG emissions are lowered by 79% in total.

Additionally, the exercise can be performed in a low-speed mode that reduces noise and eliminates visible exhaust smoke at the start. Due to optimization of the generator performance for Kohler KD Series, the benefits add up quickly for a more sustainable maintenance program.

These savings are significant. Not only for the emissions impact but also the bottom line based on lowering fuel consumption. The best part is that this is available today. It is a great example of using proven technology and finding a way to make it more sustainable without adding risk. Another creative idea, which may feel like a small change, is to evaluate how you heat your generator. Just like a car, a generator will have a faster starting time if maintained at a minimal temperature for starting. Most generators have a generator heater installed to ensure the minimum temperature is maintained.

Considering that the heater is plugged in 24 hours a day and drawing power from the utility (which likely is not a very green source), the heater is a large portion of the lifetime emissions produced for an installed generator. Think about taking excess heat created by a data center and using that to heat the generator. You can reuse waste heat and reduce the power draw. This is an example of how a small change has a meaningful impact and further reduces the carbon footprint of a generator.

Finding the Right Fit for Now - and the Future

So, while we look towards hydrogen, long term battery storage, fuel cells and other new technologies to prove out for resiliency, performance, and affordability, you have choices today that can benefit the carbon footprint of a data center. For a backup generator, choose renewable fuel and adjust your maintenance practices while sustaining reliability and performance. Let's keep pushing advances on existing technologies as well as new technologies forward together!

---

1. McKinsey & Company. "Investing in the rising data center economy." https://www.mckinsey.com/industries/technology-media-and-telecommunications/our-insights/investing-in-the-rising-data-center-economy
2. Brooks, Chuck. "3 Alarming Threats To The U.S. Energy Grid - Cyber, Physical, And Existential Events. Forbes. February 15, 2023. https://www.forbes.com/sites/chuckbrooks/2023/02/15/3-alarming-threats-to-the-us-energy-grid--cyber-physical-and-existential-events/?sh=5f6bde58101a

About the Author

NICOLE DIERKSHEIDE

Nicole Dierksheide is the global category leader for Kohler's Data Center product line. She has broad experience over her 25+ year career that spans from engineering subsystems on locomotives to marketing test and measurement equipment. She has been with Kohler Energy for 13 years, focused on offering energy resilient solutions. Nicole holds a degree in electrical engineering from the University of Arizona and uses her technical expertise to work with customers on finding the optimal solution for their needs. She is a sustainability champion and passionate about driving green actions both at work and in her personal life.

TWENTY-FOUR

Achieving Energy Efficiencies At Cell Towers

John Celentano, Inside Towers

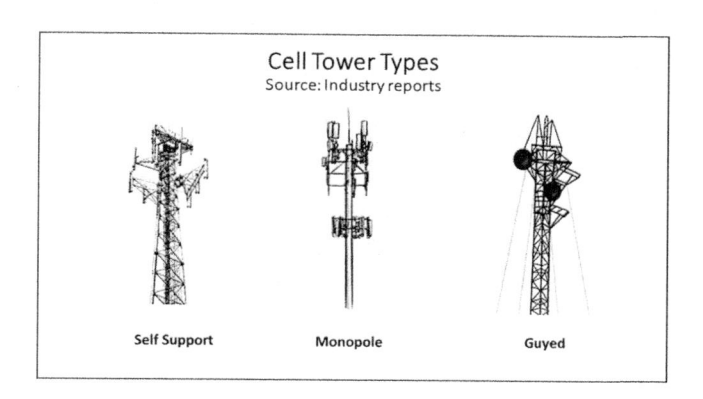

Cell Tower Types
Source: Industry reports

Self Support   Monopole   Guyed

They are everywhere, often hard to miss. Some are unseen, camouflaged in the landscape. They make our smartphones and other mobile devices work. We're talking about telecommunications towers that support cellular and other wireless network equipment. We simply refer to them as cell towers. And there are lots of them.

Worldwide, we estimate that there are over 1.6 million cell towers owned and operated by dozens of independent tower companies, and another roughly one million towers still owned and operated by mobile network operators (MNOs) in various countries.

Chapter Twenty-Four

These tallies do not count the more than two million towers in China operated by state-owned China Tower.

In the U.S., we estimate that there are roughly 185,000 towers registered with the Federal Communications Commission. This portfolio of towers is owned and operated by the so-called Big 3 public tower companies – American Tower, Crown Castle, and SBA Communications – and another 100 private, independent tower companies. The Big 3 public tower companies have over 100,000 towers, and account for over half of the total towers in the U.S.

Tower companies utilize a mix of self-support towers, monopoles, and guyed towers depending on what is required for high-performance wireless connectivity in a specific location. We estimate the U.S. tower installed base is growing at a rate of 2,000-3,000 new towers a year.

At each location, the tower company owns the tower structure itself and either owns or leases the land under the tower. Each cell tower supports multiple cell sites that are part of the MNO networks. One or more MNO leases space on the tower from the tower company in a shared infrastructure business model, similar to colocations in data centers. Here, tower companies are the landlords, and MNOs are the tenants.

In the U.S., the cell site equipment is owned and operated by MNOs like Verizon, AT&T, T-Mobile, DISH Wireless and UScellular. Cell sites make up the so-called radio access network or RAN portion of the overall cellular network. A cell site consists of several elements: remote radio units (RRUs) and antennas for transmitting wireless signals to and from smartphones and other mobile devices; the baseband unit (BBU) that converts those wireless signals into data streams (voice, data, or video); fiber optic transmission systems that transport those data streams between the cell site and the network core where voice, data and video signals are routed to other mobile devices or over the internet to websites.

With all that active equipment, each cell site continuously draws thousands of kilowatts of power from the electrical grid to support all the equipment used at the tower. When you extrapolate the power demand at each tower over the global tower installed base, we're talking gigawatts of power consumption every year.

The challenge for tower companies and their MNO tenants is how to make their sites as energy efficient and sustainable as possible.

The Cell Tower Sustainability Imperative

Cell towers are an integral part of the digital infrastructure ecosystem along with fiber optic transmission systems, data centers, small cells, edge infrastructure and in-building wireless systems. Keep in mind that mobile voice and data communications are only "wireless" from your cellphone to the nearest antenna on a tower. After that, the signal is carried through the terrestrial network to a MNO's switching/routing hub in a data center where voice and data cells are processed and routed. We like to say, "It takes a lot of wires to make wireless work!"

It is interesting to note the interplay and complementary roles that different infrastructure assets play. To wit, all the major U.S. MNOs have outsourced their core network switching functions to cloud providers – AT&T with Microsoft Azure and Google Cloud, Verizon and DISH with AWS, and T-Mobile with Oracle Cloud. And all cell towers are connected to data centers by fiber optic networks.

Given the growing level of infrastructure ecosystem integration, it is important for each infrastructure asset class to be optimized for energy efficiency to achieve the lowest greenhouse gas emission levels.

At a cell tower, the tower company, and its MNO tenants (and their equipment suppliers) have separate roles and responsibilities to achieve energy efficiency and sustainability goals of the site as a whole. It is important to distinguish which company owns what part of a cell tower installation and how they each contribute to the sustainability of the site.

Chapter Twenty-Four

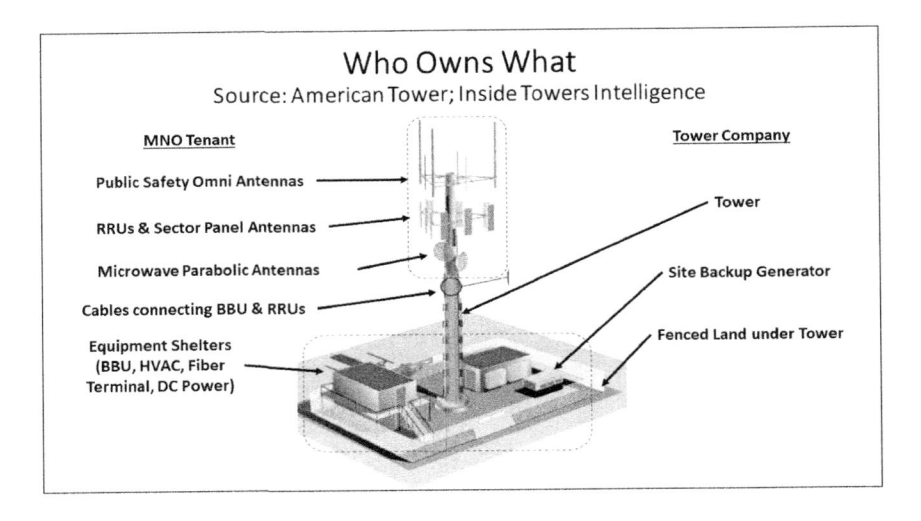

Who Owns What
Source: American Tower; Inside Towers Intelligence

MNO Tenant
- Public Safety Omni Antennas
- RRUs & Sector Panel Antennas
- Microwave Parabolic Antennas
- Cables connecting BBU & RRUs
- Equipment Shelters (BBU, HVAC, Fiber Terminal, DC Power)

Tower Company
- Tower
- Site Backup Generator
- Fenced Land under Tower

The tower itself is passive infrastructure that is owned and managed by a tower company. The tower companies are responsible for the construction and maintenance of the towers, as well as the plot of land at the base of the tower. The tower company also provides security for the site, generally with a secure perimeter fence. In many situations, the tower company supplies a generator as a backup power source for the whole site.

MNOs are the tower company's tenants. MNOs rent space on the tower and on the ground. The MNO rental terms are established in master lease agreements, in a shared infrastructure model that is similar to colocation in data centers.

MNOs install their RRUs and antennas in a specified area on the tower, known as a radiation center or RAD center. Most towers have several RAD centers stacked at different heights, one for each MNO operating at that site.

Each MNO installs their own equipment shelter or cabinet on the ground to house the BBU, routers, microwave or fiber transmission terminals for backhaul and DC power supply and batteries.

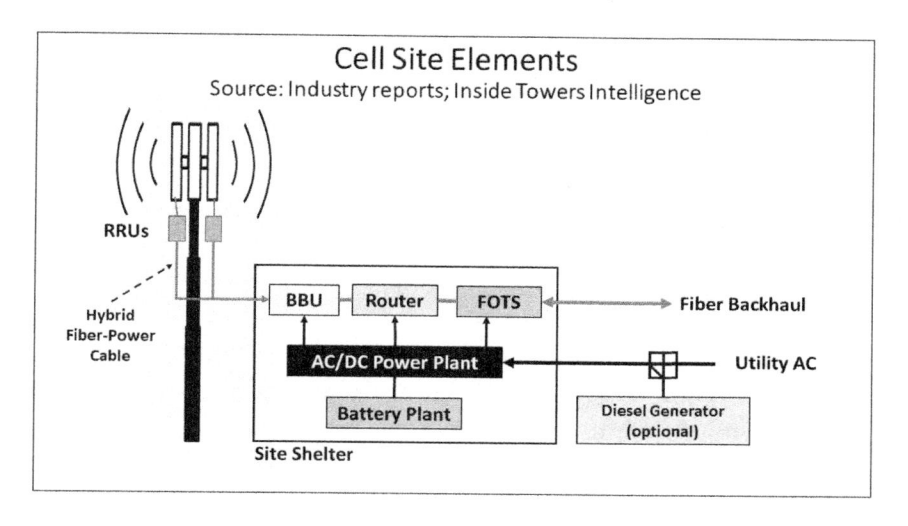

Cell Site Elements
Source: Industry reports; Inside Towers Intelligence

- RRUs
- Hybrid Fiber-Power Cable
- BBU
- Router
- FOTS
- Fiber Backhaul
- AC/DC Power Plant
- Utility AC
- Battery Plant
- Diesel Generator (optional)
- Site Shelter

RAN Needs Lots of Power

This discussion focuses on the RAN. Of all the active equipment needed at each cell site, the RRUs, BBU and ancillary gear consume about 50 percent of the total power, according to industry estimates. To give you an idea of how much power we're talking about, consider the following metrics using the U.S. wireless market as a model:

- Among the MNOs, including Verizon, T-Mobile, AT&T, DISH Wireless, UScellular and a couple dozen regional carriers, we estimate there are about 243,000 cell sites installed on the 185,000 tower base.
- In broad terms, we estimate that about 45 percent of all cell sites are located in urban markets, another 35 percent in suburban markets and the remaining 20 percent in small town and rural markets. This breakdown is important because the amount of radio equipment installed, and the corresponding power consumed, at the cell site varies with the number of mobile devices being served in a given area.

Chapter Twenty-Four

- Radios used in cellular networks consume roughly 500 watts. So, an urban cell site with a 3 120-degree sector configuration and 3-radios per sector would consume 4,500 watts. Similarly, radios in a suburban cell site with a 3-sector, 2-radio per sector configuration would consume 3,000 watts, and a rural cell site with a 3-sector, 1-radio per sector configuration would take 1,500 watts.
- Applying those figures across the number of cell sites by respective markets, at a national average cost of $0.1331 per KwH (as per the U.S. Energy Information Administration, August 2023), then the annual aggregate electricity costs, expressed in annual KwH usage, would be $600 million for urban cell sites, another $311 million for suburban sites and $89 million for rural markets. That adds up to a tidy $1 billion a year for cell site power consumption in the U.S.!
- Extrapolated to the worldwide installed base of cell towers, across all geographies and applications, using local energy prices, we estimate that the cell site global power consumption can be as much as 10 times greater than the U.S. level.

Our estimate may actually be conservative. Each MNO incurs energy costs that are specific to its network configuration and the geography in which it operates. Notably, new 5G cell sites tend to have more equipment installed than earlier 4G deployments. Even though 5G equipment is designed to be energy efficient, in that it is designed to use less energy per bit compared to earlier generation wireless systems, there are a lot more bits being consumed. The Ericsson Mobility Report shows that mobile data demand is escalating, doubling every two to three years, particularly at sites in heavily populated urban markets. More energy consumed means the higher the operating costs for the MNO.

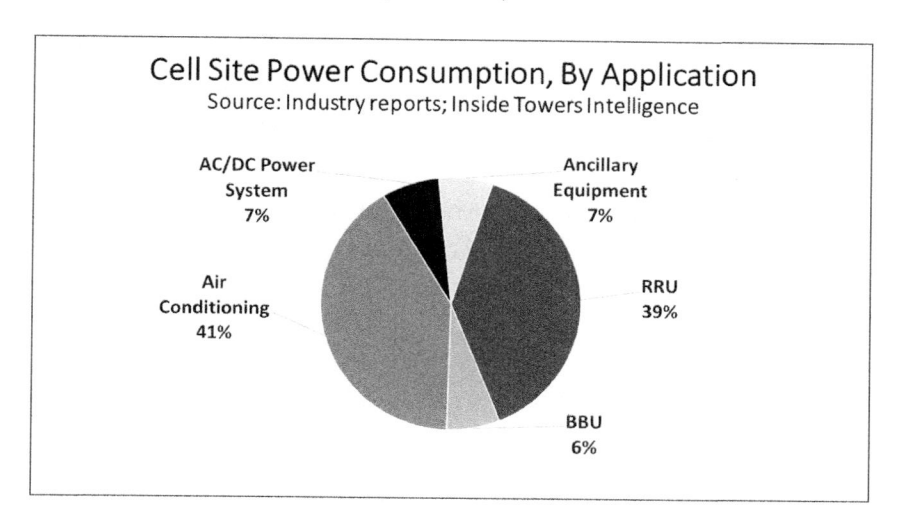

Cell Site Power Consumption, By Application
Source: Industry reports; Inside Towers Intelligence

- AC/DC Power System 7%
- Ancillary Equipment 7%
- Air Conditioning 41%
- RRU 39%
- BBU 6%

Making Towers Green

Given the power consumption level at cell towers on a global scale, even a 10 percent reduction in energy consumption can be significant. To achieve greater sustainability and net zero goals at cell towers is challenging, however. Tower companies, MNOs, and telecom original equipment manufacturers (OEMs) are all working towards achieving greater energy efficiency at cell towers, both on their own and through mutual cooperation. Here are some of the major steps being undertaken.

Product Innovation

The OEMs continue to develop energy efficient equipment used in the RAN.

Radio Design | Since the RAN consumes such a high proportion of energy consumption at a cell site, energy efficient radio designs have been an OEM focus for some time. Companies like Sweden's Ericsson, Finlanad-based Nokia, and Samsung Electronics of South Korea, are making their 5G RRU and BBU equipment more energy efficient and smarter by incorporating machine learning (ML) and artificial intelligence (AI).

Chapter Twenty-Four

Ericsson recently introduced the latest generation of processors in its Ericsson RAN Compute portfolio, which is built for the mobile network demands of 5G Advanced and enhanced AI algorithms. The company said at the launch, "As the industry works toward scaling 5G coverage and preparing networks for a surge in uplink demand, it is important to also keep in mind its net zero goals."

Sleep Mode | A wireless network is very dynamic. Mobile traffic patterns at every cell site ebb and flow throughout the day. Commuter corridors and urban centers tend to be busy during rush hours and throughout the workday. However, that high volume traffic moves to the suburbs in the evening.

Using ML and AI, MNOs can track usage at a cell site and adjust its operation for busy hours and slow periods. When mobile voice and data traffic slows down, the MNO can program a cell site to: reduce power to the RRUs during low traffic volumes; temporarily deactivate lightly loaded frequencies; or, put lightly loaded sectors into a "sleep" mode, that is, idling it without shutting it off.

Intelligent controllers and radios are learning to be more energy efficient by adjusting their operating mode according to the real-time usage demand.

Massive MIMO Antennas | Sector antennas connected to the radios generally are designed to operate in a static manner, continuously transmitting and receiving signals at specific frequencies, to and from all mobile devices within the coverage area surrounding a tower.

In contrast, Massive MIMO (Multiple In/Multiple Out) antennas operate in a dynamic manner and focus their signals on specific high connectivity demand areas using a technique called beam steering. This feature optimizes radio power consumption and provides better data rates to targeted connections. With 5G, MNOs are relying more and more on Massive MIMO antennas to handle the increasing mobile data volumes.

Equipment Cooling | At every cell site, RRUs are installed outdoors, high up on the tower near the antennas to take advantage of natural air cooling.

On the ground, the BBU and other networking equipment are installed inside a cabinet or a shelter. This equipment emits heat and needs to be cooled, typically with fans or an air conditioning unit installed on the shelter. Cooling is a big operating expense.

Rather than relying on air conditioning, Nokia has introduced its Liquid Cooling AirScale portfolio, which the company claims is the first-of-its-kind solution designed to make radio networks more sustainable and cost-efficient by reducing the energy required for cooling. The company claims that its cooling system reduces energy consumption up to 90 percent and base station CO_2 emissions up to 80 percent, compared to traditional active air-cooling systems.

With this design, the BBU is cooled by running an antifreeze liquid through the unit, thus reducing, or eliminating, the need for external air conditioning, and in turn, lowering utility power consumption.

What MNOs Are Doing

MNOs approach energy efficiency differently than the OEMs. Certainly, they are purchasing more energy efficient radios from the OEMs. More than that, MNOs look at how much operating expense they will incur at a given site based on the space they occupy and the rent they pay, and the energy consumption costs they incur with the equipment installed.

Cabinets Versus Shelters | As radio designs have become more modular with RRUs separated from BBUs, many MNOs have switched to ground mounted cabinets from larger, trailer-like shelters. A smaller footprint meant less ground space occupied, and less rent. Cabinets can be air cooled while shelters usually need air conditioning, thus saving energy costs. In sunny regions, the cabinets may be equipped with sun shields to reduce solar heating.

Multiband Radios | Both Ericsson and Nokia have introduced multi-band radios that can transmit and receive two RF signals simultaneously. In the U.S., for example, MNOs are deploying dual-band C-band (3.7 GHz) and 3.45 GHz radios. Operating both these frequencies in one unit occupies less space on the tower and consumes less energy than two discrete radio units. This way the MNO can install the two frequencies with just one tower climb, again reducing the energy it takes for the installation.

Battery Backup | In the U.S., all MNOs must maintain a minimum of 2-4 hours of battery backup at cell sites to address a utility power outage. Historically, the telecom industry has relied on lead acid batteries that must be maintained on a regular basis to ensure they will work when needed. Using IoT data gathering and data analytics, new battery monitoring systems help reduce operating costs by limiting maintenance crew dispatches to every site. With better data, battery maintenance has shifted from 'programmed and preventative' to 'as required or remedial' procedures, saving labor and energy costs.

In recent years, lithium ion and nickel cadmium batteries have found more use at cell sites. These types of batteries have appeal because they are compact and store more energy per unit volume, are environmentally friendly, require less maintenance, and have longer life cycle characteristics. The tradeoff is higher upfront costs compared to lead acid batteries.

What Towercos Are Doing

The tower companies themselves are doing their part to become more energy efficient, although they only manage the passive tower and land infrastructure, not the active RAN equipment belonging to their MNO tenants.

Tower Lighting | In the U.S. and around the world, flashing or blinking lights must be installed on any tower of 200 feet or more to provide a visual warning to aircraft. In recent years, tower companies have been installing energy efficient LED lighting that uses less electricity and performs reliably with less maintenance over longer periods than incandescent bulbs.

Grounds Maintenance | Tower companies have developed novel ways of grooming and maintaining the grounds at the base of the towers with more foliage and less grass coverage to reduce maintenance costs.

Chapter Twenty-Four

Generator Backup | As an alternative to more batteries, tower companies often install generators to keep the most critical sites operational during power outages. At the same time, tower companies use generators as another revenue source, referred to as a Power-as-a-Service, charging their MNO tenants for the energy they supply. Usually, one generator at a tower site is sized to produce enough output power to serve multiple tenants' needs.

The primary fuel for generators is diesel or propane. Gas is rarely used, due to storage and usage safety reasons. Other generators run on natural gas where a tower located near a public gas line. Hydrogen fuel cells are another consideration, although high capital and maintenance costs are still big decision factors.

Renewable Energy at Cell Towers

MNOs and tower companies around the world are realizing the benefits of solar and wind installations at cell sites.

Reducing direct scope 1 GHG and scope 2 indirectly at towers can be achieved with either solar or wind depending on the location. Renewable energy sources like these need adequate space (read, land) to produce sufficient power for the site. As a result, these renewable energy sources often are not feasible at urban and suburban cell sites where land is sparse, unless renewables are used as a small, secondary backup power source.

As discussed, cell sites require lots of power, especially in the U.S. where the power demand at most cell sites would exceed the capacity of a small-scale renewable power system.

For sites outside of metro areas and in rural markets, however, solar- and wind-generated power sources are being considered to a greater degree. Power demand at these sites is less than at urban sites, and usually there is available space.

Certainly, solar and wind applications are being used extensively in developing countries where the grid is unreliable or even non-existent, but where people still need wireless connectivity. Several small companies are making inroads with cell site power in developing countries. Caban Systems, based in Burlingame, CA, provides its MNO customers energy-as-a-service (EaaS) with solar arrays and cloud-based software management at over 500 sites in Latin America and the Caribbean. Two Canadian companies, ClearBlue Technologies and NuRAN Wireless, offer EaaS to MNOs in central Africa using Clear Blue's proprietary Smart Off-Grid technology with solar generated power. Crossflow Energy, based in the U.K., offers a novel monopole tower-mounted, small scale wind turbine design.

Long Term Sustainability Commitments

The drive for energy efficiency and achievement of net zero goals will only increase. As an industry, we're in this for the long haul. Tower companies, their MNO tenants and the OEMs worldwide are reporting progress in developing and applying energy efficient equipment and processes in their segment of the digital infrastructure ecosystem. Public and private tower companies and MNOs have adopted environmental, social and governance (ESG) initiatives as part of their overall corporate strategy and operations, and regularly update their investors on their progress. These companies believe that setting and achieving sustainability goals is not only the right thing to do, but it is good business.

A good example is Boca Raton, FL-based Vertical Bridge, a private tower company with over 11,000 towers in the U.S. In 2020, the company became the first telecommunications tower company to be certified as a CarbonNeutral company in accordance with The CarbonNeutral Protocol and re-certifies every year. The company says it strives to create a "culture of sustainability", from eliminating paper waste and single-use plastics from its corporate headquarters to replacing building and tower lighting systems with lower-energy consuming LED systems.

In the end, each company can only do its part, but collectively all the players in the wireless infrastructure ecosystem can make significant gains on energy efficiency and sustainability for decades to come.

Chapter Twenty-Four

1. Inside Towers Intelligence. 2022 Vol 4. "International Towers Rising." December 2022 www.insidetowers.com/intelligence.
2. Ericsson Mobility Report. June 2023. https://www.ericsson.com/en/reports-and-papers/mobility-report/reports/june-2023.
3. Ericsson. 2023. "Next-generation Ericsson RAN Compute breaks ground in network processing power." November 14, 2023. https://www.ericsson.com/en/press-releases/2023/11/next-generation-ericsson-ran-compute-breaks-ground-in-network-processing-power.
4. Nokia. 2022. "Nokia adds Liquid Cooling technology to latest AirScale Base Station portfolio outlining commitment to sustainability." March 1, 2022. https://www.nokia.com/about-us/news/releases/2022/03/01/nokia-adds-liquid-cooling-technology-to-latest-airscale-base-station-portfolio-outlining-commitment-to-sustainability-mwc22/.
5. Katherine Tweed. 2013. "Why Cellular Towers in Developing Nations Are Making the Move to Solar Power." Scientific American. January 15, 2013. https://www.scientificamerican.com/article/cellular-towers-moving-to-solar-power/.
6. David Lopez-Perez, Antonio De Domenico, Nicola Piovesan, Geng Xinli, Harvey Bao, Song Qitao and Merouane Debbah. "A Survey on 5G Radio Access Network Energy Efficiency: Massive MIMO, Lean Carrier Design, Sleep Modes, and Machine Learning." October 7, 2021. https://arxiv.org/pdf/2101.11246.pdf.
7. Sun-in-One. 2023. https://suninone.com/product-views/solar-powered-cellular-towers/.

About the Author

JOHN CELENTANO

John Celentano is a highly regarded analyst and consultant with over 25 years of engineering and business experience in telecommunications. He is Business Editor at Inside Towers, a daily newsletter that covers the wireless infrastructure business. Towers is in the name, but the publication covers all aspects of digital infrastructure – towers, fiber, data centers, small cells, edge infrastructure, power.

He is also Managing Director of Inside Towers Intelligence, a quarterly market analysis report that dives deep into the digital infrastructure business. He regularly writes and speaks on issues and trends in wireless and wireline infrastructure markets, and hosts the podcast, Tower Talks.

John has worked with telecom equipment manufacturers and service providers in network planning, and RF and power systems engineering. As a consultant, he has worked with tech companies developing and executing product launches and strategic marketing campaigns. He advises investors on telecom mergers and acquisitions.

John holds a B.Eng. degree in Electrical Engineering from McMaster University, studied Marketing at the University of California-Santa Barbara and has participated in many corporate technical and business training sessions.

A Canadian-American (Canada, eh!), he now resides in Baltimore, Maryland.

TWENTY-FIVE

Being Green to Make Some Green: The Many Business Opportunities Presented by Immersion Cooling

S. Jay Lawrence, Equus Compute Solutions

"Everything should be made as simple as possible, but not simpler." - Albert Einstein

In global conversations about climate change and environmental responsibility, the focus often shifts to strategies that restrict services, particularly concerning power consumption. However, limiting computing capabilities or scaling back data center operations isn't the only solution, nor is it practical or possible in many cases. Embracing new technologies like immersion cooling can offer both environmental benefits and economic opportunities.

Should the solution involve creating less computing, reducing the number of data centers, or limiting application development? While it's a possibility, it's not necessary. Consider the advantages: new AI systems assisting physicians in diagnosing and treating diseases; enhancing overall healthcare to improve quality and lower costs; automation filling workforce gaps and providing safer work environments; and preserving essential services that would be affected by output restrictions. This restrictive approach is not conducive to progress. Instead, as an industry, we should leverage

Chapter Twenty-Five

the free market and innovate technologies to tackle these challenges head-on.

In computing, we currently have a chance to enact meaningful change with immediate benefits for both businesses and the environment. Liquid cooling technology, utilizing thermally efficient liquids to draw heat away from servers and other equipment, outperforms traditional air-cooling methods. When implemented effectively and at scale, liquid cooling results in substantial power savings, decreased greenhouse gas emissions, extended hardware lifespan, and reduced real estate usage.

Liquid cooling solutions have been utilized in supercomputers since the 1950s. Today, smartphones boast computing power comparable to those early supercomputers, while even "smart refrigerators" exceed the computing capabilities of the Space Shuttle at its launch in 1981. Clearly, our initial liquid cooling methods are no longer sufficient, and it's imperative that we evolve them to meet the demands of modern computing. My company, alongside others, is actively engaged in this necessary evolution.

Although liquid cooling has a longstanding history, recent advancements in material science have revolutionized its potential. Today, we possess liquids that are fluorocarbon-free, resembling vegetable oil and boasting non-toxic properties for humans and animals. This stands in stark contrast to the potent greenhouse gases found in traditional air conditioner fluorocarbon fluids. With immersion cooling, we can minimize our carbon footprint significantly.

Immersion cooling fully submerges servers in a liquid that efficiently dissipates heat. This readily available solution provides measurable and sustainable benefits to individuals, businesses, and the environment, while also drastically cutting computing expenses.

Technology Trends Driving Us to Rethink Network Infrastructure

The rapid emergence of AI alongside 5G, and the imminent arrival of 5G Advanced and 6G, has ushered in a new era of applications, workloads, and demands, fundamentally altering our daily interactions with technology. However, this transformation comes with a substantial increase in power consumption to support the underlying computer infrastructure.

Since 2019, CPU and GPU thermal performance, also known as Thermal Design Power (TDP), have doubled. Presently, CPUs operate at nearly 400 Watts and GPUs at nearly 800 Watts. In data centers, 30-40% of total power consumption is dedicated to cooling systems to maintain optimal temperatures for servers housing these high-performance components. This trend is expected to escalate with the proliferation of AI, new media, and advanced data transmission systems.

Data centers remain power-intensive, with some forecasts predicting upwards of 20% of the world's power by 2030[1]. However, our power generation capacity hasn't kept up with demand, leading to a shortfall in new power stations. By favoring intermittent renewables like wind and solar over reliable zero-emission options like nuclear energy, we're facing challenges with maintaining consistent power output. This imbalance has resulted in rolling brownouts, blackouts, and increased power expenses.

Liquid cooling presents various advantages aligned with emerging trends, such as the imperative to shift computing capacity to the network edge. According to Gartner, by 2025, 75% of enterprise-generated data will be processed outside traditional centralized data centers or clouds.[2] However, cooling ultra-high-performance computing clusters at the edge poses a challenge without relying on large, air-cooled data centers. Immersion cooling emerges as the immediate solution, offering a viable alternative. Over time, further innovations may arise, potentially leading to the development of significantly smaller data centers, even as small as suitcase-sized, especially in commercial settings.

The convergence of 5G and computing has significantly intensified system complexity, pushing the boundaries of air cooling to its limits. From a cost-benefit perspective, we may have reached the peak of economic and environmentally friendly air-cooling solutions. To meet the growing demand for data centers and their associated services, embracing readily available alternatives like liquid

Chapter Twenty-Five

cooling becomes imperative, rather than persisting with conventional air-cooling methods.

5G-enabled application development is rapidly accelerating, introducing novel computing, hosting, and deployment challenges that strain existing infrastructure. Equus Compute Solutions, my company, is currently developing workstation servers with a power consumption of 4KW, surpassing the capacity of standard household circuit breakers. This highlights a genuine infrastructure weakness. However, it also underscores the ongoing industry-wide efforts towards reducing power consumption. Fortunately, we now have access to advanced tools to address these challenges more effectively.

The Many Benefits of Immersion Cooling

> "If your only tool is a hammer then every problem looks like a nail." - Abraham Maslow

Immersion cooling not only reduces power requirements in a server rack by 30-40%, but its advantages extend far beyond mere energy savings.

Chip Technology

As chip technology advances, traditional air-cooling methods are becoming inadequate to maintain semiconductors at their optimal clock speed and efficiency. This dilemma, akin to "buying a Ferrari to haul lumber," necessitates either effective cooling solutions or sacrificing the potential benefits of high-performance chips by underclocking them.

Massive Density Enablement in Server Racks

Today, an air-cooled rack comprising 52RU typically caps at around 30kW of total power, encompassing components like CPU, GPU, Storage, Memory, and Fans. In contrast, immersion-cooled racks boast capacities exceeding 300kW. While this might initially seem counterintuitive, it aligns with the escalating demand for greater compute workload capacity driven by increasingly complex systems, chipsets, and applications. Notably, air-cooled racks squander approximately 40% of their power on cooling, undermining valuable compute power. Immersion cooling, however, efficiently absorbs and dissipates heat from compute components, as validated in our test labs for customers and governments.

Image: LiquidStack™ Immmersion Cooling with ECS Server

Server Lifecycle Extension

Immersion cooling solves the common issue of dust accumulation in computer chassis, which can damage fans and lead to various problems on the motherboard. By maintaining servers at a steady temperature, immersion cooling prevents these issues. Additionally, it eliminates thermal fatigue concerns by keeping the environment stable, ensuring optimal performance for CPU/GPU components even under heavy use.

Noise Reduction

Imagine walking into a data center filled with air-cooled servers buzzing and whirring loudly, making it challenging to hold a conversation or concentrate. The noise generated by traditional air-cooled servers can be disruptive and unpleasant, affecting the working environment for technicians and other personnel. However, immersion-cooled servers offer a stark contrast. Submerged in a thermally efficient liquid, these servers operate almost silently. Without the need for loud fans or air conditioning units, immersion cooling creates a calm and quiet atmosphere within the data center. This noise reduction not only improves the working conditions for staff but also enhances the overall experience for visitors and clients who may need to spend time in the facility.

Elimination of Water Usage

Traditional data centers are notorious water consumers, guzzling an astonishing 3-5 million gallons of water on average.[3] This immense water usage poses significant environmental concerns, particularly in regions already grappling with water scarcity issues. However, immersion cooling technology presents a compelling solution to this problem. Unlike conventional cooling methods that rely heavily on water for cooling purposes, immersion cooling systems can operate without consuming any water. By submerging servers in a non-conductive liquid, these systems efficiently dissipate heat without the need for water-based cooling mechanisms. This revolutionary approach not only eliminates the water usage associated with traditional data centers but also reduces the strain on local water resources and minimizes the environmental impact of data center operations. As sustainability becomes an increasingly critical consideration for businesses, the water-saving benefits of immersion cooling make it a compelling choice for companies looking to minimize their ecological footprint.

Chapter Twenty-Five

The Economics of Immersion Cooling

Immersion cooling revolutionizes data center economics, leveraging market incentives to drive greener solutions. Traditional data centers operate at a PUE of around 1.5, where a significant portion of expenditure is wasted on cooling infrastructure. However, immersion cooling slashes this figure to a remarkable 1.013, ensuring that nearly every dollar spent directly benefits computing power. This translates to not only minimal power wastage but also maximized computing efficiency, yielding profound reductions in carbon footprint and resource optimization. Moreover, immersion cooling enables high-density computing within compact footprints, offering substantial savings in real estate and cooling costs.

As the demand for computing power continues to surge, immersion cooling presents an ideal solution for space-constrained environments, extending the life of facilities and facilitating the repurposing of existing infrastructure for edge computing. Furthermore, immersion cooling is tailored for high-performance computing tasks, effortlessly accommodating overclocked CPUs and GPUs without throttling. Beyond cost savings, immersion cooling aligns with corporate sustainability goals, offering a tangible way to reduce power consumption and environmental impact. Whether driven by space limitations, performance requirements, or environmental objectives, immersion cooling provides a versatile and efficient solution.

By embracing market-driven innovations like immersion cooling, businesses can achieve cost-effective and environmentally responsible data solutions, exemplifying the transformative potential of collaboration and competition in the private sector.

Final Thoughts

This publication delves into the pivotal question of our purpose: Greener Data. There's a compelling chance that the IT/Compute/Telecom industry could wield a comparable influence on carbon emissions, global temperatures, and air quality as the energy

Chapter Twenty-Five

sector. Unlike energy, which is merely consumed with pollution as a by-product, our industry has the potential to redefine its environmental footprint.

The IT industry has a unique opportunity to reduce waste, minimize pollution, and create tangible benefits for society and the planet through technologies like immersion cooling. By embracing sustainable solutions, businesses can not only reduce their environmental footprint but also enhance their bottom line in the long run.

---

1. Foy, Kylie. "AI models are devouring energy." Lincoln Laboratory - MIT. September 22, 2023. https://www.ll.mit.edu/news/ai-models-are-devouring-energy-tools-reduce-consumption-are-here-if-data-centers-will-adopt#:~:text=Escalating%20this%20energy%20demand%20are,world%27s%20electricity%20supply%20by%202030.
2. "What Edge Computing Means for Infrastructure and Operations Leaders." Gartner. October 3, 2018. https://www.gartner.com/smarterwithgartner/what-edge-computing-means-for-infrastructure-and-operations-leaders
3. "Data Center Water Usage Challenges and Sustainability". Sensorex. August 16, 2022. https://sensorex.com/data-center-water-usage-challenges/

About the Author

S. JAY LAWRENCE

Jay Lawrence is a seasoned executive and technologist with hands-on experience leading enterprises in diverse domains of the telecommunications sector including AI/ML, real-time control systems, semiconductor, system integration/networking, data center, immersion cooling and fixed broadband (5G) systems. He has operated in these areas of business in a leadership role, globally, for the past 25 years running business from start up to a billion dollars. Most recently, he has led the Technology Enablement business unit of Supermicro Computer, Inc., (NASDAQ: SMCI) and has been CEO of multiple public and private businesses leading successful turnarounds and exits.

TWENTY-SIX

A Year of Non-Stop Innovation: What I Learned, and Why We Were All Caught Off Guard

Bill Kleyman, Apolo

Welcome to my little section in this book. I love writing chapters. It's less time-consuming, and I don't have to think about writing a whole book. I greatly respect the fantastic authors who can put together a fascinating read. For me, I'm just grateful that you'll spend a little bit of time with me. That said, buckle up. We have a lot to discuss. And no, ChatGPT was not involved in the writing of my chapter. Although, we'll be covering the technology.

Let's start here ...

If you read the previous Greener Data book, which I highly recommend, you'll know I got my start interestingly. In Soviet Ukraine, my brother used to compete in large telegraph competitions.

He used an old telegraph switch that our grandpa had modified so that my brother could punch in Morse code a bit faster. When my brother was practicing, he'd let me sit on his lap and listen as code came in. He taught me numbers, letters, and how to communicate with people throughout the Soviet Union. It was a fascinating time for me. I became exceedingly interested in communication and bringing people closer at a young age.

Chapter Twenty-Six

So, there you have it, a millennial who started with the telegraph. We came to the United States in the early 1990s, and I remember being interested in technology courses from the start.

We've come a long way from the telegraph to Generative AI, which brings us to a critical point and the central thesis for this chapter. We are seeing a level of innovation that none of us were ready for. And there's a good reason for that.

"The data center industry loves innovation as long as it's ten years old."
　　Peter Gross, Industry Legend

A Year in AI: None of Us Were Prepared for What's Happening Today

My journey in 2023 speaks to the broader industry arc throughout the year. I remember it like it was just yesterday. Switch was just taken private for $11B, and I had the fantastic chance to step away post-sale and do something different. It was January 2023 when I told myself I'd take a long break.

That lasted about a week when my dear friend Uri called me and asked me to join an emerging AI company called Apolo (formerly Neu.ro). At that point, ChatGPT was just about to hit the market, and I was learning just how powerful the Apolo interoper-

Chapter Twenty-Six

ability platform would become in this industry. (At the time of this publication, I was named the CEO, and we rebranded into an evolved organization called Apolo. To give you a bit of background, Neu.ro was born in Ukraine in 2019 and brought all of its operations to the USA due to the war. The company was exceedingly successful during its inception because of the platform's open nature and powerful integration with infrastructure and AI tools.)

So, what is Apolo? I'll keep this brief, but it's essential to understand company basics, as will become clear in the rest of the chapter. Apolo was built by AI developers for AI developers. Today, we are an AI Platform and Infrastructure company that delivers AI infrastructure and MLOps platform capabilities that are sustainable, ethical, and transparent. As a platform and infrastructure, Apolo can be deployed as dedicated clusters, white label design, or even self-service.

Why is this important? When ChatGPT came out, data center leaders who wanted to capture this market realized that the Apolo platform would be able to save millions of dollars in development costs and years trying to build this ecosystem.

But, while we were ready for the data center industry, it was not prepared for us.

Generative AI: The Data Storm No One Predicted

For the past 25 years, all of us — everyone reading this — have been conditioned to interact with data in a certain way. Readers will go to their favorite search engine, type in a question, and get a blue link. It's been the same blue link on Yahoo, Ask Jeeves, Alta Vista, Bing, and Google.

Today, when you go to Bing or Google and ask a question, the first response is no longer a blue link. The first interaction you'll see regarding your query will be generative AI. This is not a fad. It's an evolution of how we, as humans, interact with data.

It took ChatGPT five days to hit one million users[1]. After only two months, there were over 100 million active weekly users[2]. There was only one other app in the history of humanity that hit one

Chapter Twenty-Six

million users faster than ChatGPT. Threads did it in about an hour, but how many of you are using Threads vs. ChatGPT?

Right after ChatGPT hit the market, there was a storm of activity, and data center leaders wanted to jump in. However, the industry wasn't ready for what adoption would look like. Working with generative AI and large language models differs from trying to support traditional SQL or Exchange databases. Here are some of the things we at Apolo have learned having worked with ChatGPT and designing GPT-like services:

Density | I will share some exclusive findings from the AFCOM State of the Data Center 2024 report. Eight years ago, when the first report came out, density was around 6 KW/rack. Our most recent findings[3] showed that the average density had doubled to 12 KW/rack. The good news is that our industry took notice and worked hard to double that metric. The challenge is that this is still not enough.

Let me put this into perspective. A single Nvidia DGX unit of 8xH100 GPU cards will take up six units in a 42U rack and consume between 10-12KW[4]. That means the average data center has enough density per rack to host just one of these compute nodes. That's not going to cut it. One of our biggest challenges is that many of our data center partners are perfectly happy supporting traditional workloads. And they are largely unprepared regarding model training and AI. Not just that, it will take them months, if not over a year, to catch up.

Power and Cooling | In 2023, the AFCOM State of the Data Center report indicated that 54% of respondents were either consistently running out of cooling capacity or were forced to look at other options to compensate for demand. The 2024 report found that[5] that metric improved, with about 40% of respondents reporting that their cooling solutions failed to meet all their requirements. That's still quite a bit. One way we've been working with partners is through hybrid solutions. You do not have to rip out and replace the entire infrastructure. Our partners have successfully adapted existing ecosystems, such as rear door heat exchangers (RDHx), with improved containment and airflow. Even small spaces can do a lot for an AI solution.

Education | A large language model, inference training, and AI work are different. While we still require the essential components of power, storage, compute, space, and so on, the way it's deployed and leveraged is entirely novel. For example, we don't need low-latency connectivity when training massive amounts of data. This translates to a new approach to deploying physical infrastructure where connectivity isn't the primary focus. Similarly, we have spent countless hours defining use cases and showcasing what customers want when adopting AI. Instead of just telling data centers to adopt AI, we have been working to showcase how their customers leverage AI and how it can be deployed within their facilities.

The contextual application of AI and LLMs has been paramount in helping traditional data centers adapt to their clients' new and emerging needs, which brings us to the next point.

Adopting New Services | Staying in your comfort zone is a great way to protect doing what you're already good at. In the traditional data center space, this translates to selling space, capacity, and power. Some will adopt tangential services like security, remote-hand support, and even telecommunications. However, adopting a platform architecture for AI and LLM services feels too far-fetched for some operators, even though their customers are asking for these services. The Apolo platform is specifically designed to allow data center leaders to continue doing exactly what they are good at.

Our interoperability platform is deployed on top of physical gear that the data center already manages. From there, we control the portal, the payments, how jobs are trained, and everything else flows from the software layer upwards. The portal is white-labeled

Chapter Twenty-Six

with the data center's logo, but the functionality is entirely independent of the data center's primary business. It literally becomes a service add-on. Think of it like a movie theater. The data center sells the tickets to the show, and Apolo manages the popcorn and candy stand.

Over the past year, we've shown data center partners how easy and critical it is to be a part of this AI movement.

Complacency | We learned from the previous point that many data center operators are happy with their business model. And they should be. After all, at the wholesale level, vacancy is at record-low levels, people are buying up capacity years in advance, and as of this writing, we are adding more than 100MW of construction pipeline every month. However, this is just chasing the same business without understanding the modern demand structure for AI. A recent McKinsey & Company report[6] indicated that GenAI could add $2.6 trillion to $4.4 trillion annually to the global economy. We want the data center community to be a part of this trend.

Many data centers happily support the AI market without becoming part of it. That said, some of our partners took the leap, bought the gear, and deployed AI-capable facilities to support existing customers and their emerging use cases specifically. Those who went on the journey with us learned they now have a new revenue model and stream.

They've increased the valuation of their organization, and much to their board's approval, they have created a new business line to support the overall organization. Outside of just discussing this as a high-level topic, I have a real case study[7] of where this happened. Scott Data Center in Omaha, Nebraska went on this journey and modernized their entire infrastructure to support AI, and run on Apolo. They went from traditional racks supporting 10-15kw/rack, to read-door heat exchanger racks now supporting 60+kw/rack.

Scott Data Center found that their existing clients want to work with a trusted partner. They just never had the opportunity to do so because of infrastructure and density limitations. Now, Scott Data

Chapter Twenty-Six

Center is offering the *platform* and the *compute* for their enterprise customers. The data center provider went from charging a few hundred dollars kilowatt per rack, to generating revenue in the thousands of dollars per kilowatt per rack. The process has revolutionized their business model and has created a roadmap to support some of the most advanced AI workloads in our market.

The other significant aspect of this learning process is what the enterprise and end-users demand from their infrastructure partners. I found this to be unique. Apolo isn't actually being driven by data center demand, although there is plenty of it. We're being driven by data centers' customers. Here's what we're hearing:

1. Companies want to have more control of their data. Clients are increasingly concerned about maintaining control over the AI/ML models they develop and the sensitive data used for ML model training and usage. This leads to a need for secure, in-house/private cloud AI infrastructure solutions.
2. Companies don't want their data to be used to train another large foundational model.
3. Companies require more control over costs, physical infrastructure, and resource use.
4. Companies want a more open platform that gives them control over development, LLM utilization, and the final models.
5. Companies are looking at more efficient and sustainable ways to deploy AI, train LLMs, and do inference.

It's certainly not all doom and gloom. I'm proud to say that as of this book's publication, we have several data center partners, like Scott Data Center, who went on the AI journey with us. For our data center operators that got started on this journey early, here's what we've learned together learned:

1. Customers want to work with their colocation partners.

Chapter Twenty-Six

2. Innovation requires discomfort.
3. There is a massive upside in adopting new services.

It's important to note that the integration of AI in the data center industry marks a paradigm shift, heralding a new era of efficiency, scalability, and innovation. As AI continues to evolve, its role in driving sustainability, reducing operational costs, and enabling data centers to meet the growing demands of the digital world cannot be overstated. The future of the data center industry, integrated with AI, is not just about technological advancement but redefining the very backbone of our digital infrastructure.

With all this in mind, let's shift to a crucial topic regarding generative AI and working with LLMs. The vast difference in the infrastructure required to support modern AI applications forces us to rethink deployment and infrastructure development. It also forces us to understand sustainability at an entirely new level.

"The cost of improvement is becoming unsustainable." - IEEE[8]

Environmental Sustainability and ChatGPT - It's Not Easy

Let me give you some essential sustainability metrics related to ChatGPT-like workloads and instances. Please note, the following data was compiled by our data sciences team at Apolo.

A single Google search can power a 100w light bulb for 11 seconds. This consumes about .3Wh of energy. Similarly, a single ChatGPT-like session is about 800-1000 more powerful than a Google search, consuming about 300-400Wh of energy. In context, this is equivalent to charging a smartphone (with a 5Wh battery) 60 times.

Similarly, if have ever used Dall-E to create an image, a single

Chapter Twenty-Six

process[9] to create one picture will consume as much energy as charging a smartphone.

Now for a couple of sizeable clarification points. The above Google search metric is from 2011, so it's likely they've improved the search capability since then. ChatGPT-like services run in multiple queries per single process. That means a single session could consume between 1-2KWh of energy every time it runs. Finally, many of these metrics are done with GPT-3 or GPT-3.5. This is important because now, we're using GPT-4 as the base model, which is nearly 1,000 times larger than GPT-3.

GPT-4 is also a multi-modal model. Unlike its predecessors, GPT-4 can take text and images as input and generate text as output. This gives it a huge advantage over previous models, which could only handle text. GPT-4 can perform more diverse and challenging requests by combining different data types. The increased capability of this model also increases its power consumption and dependency on more advanced hardware.

Over the past year, our organization has been training models for large enterprises and working with large data center partners to deploy AI solutions for their customers. Our organization was founded on three core principles:

1. AI Ethics
2. AI Transparency
3. AI Sustainability

Focusing on that last point, we aim to ensure our AI operations are as sustainable as possible. Within Apolo, we have a Carbon Counter that helps users understand the impact of their data models and inference training. We also allow them to intelligently modify training schedules or train during off-peak hours. Furthermore, as a distributed platform, we enable clients operating from our data center partners to shift and move workloads to more appropriate locations.

When working with data centers, we have made a concerted effort to ensure operations are sustainable. Here's what we've done:

Chapter Twenty-Six

1. Embed a green tracker (the Carbon Counter) into the software to help people visualize their carbon impact.
2. Work closely with data center partners that actively acquire their energy from sustainable sources.
3. When it makes sense, work with infrastructure partners that can supply second-life, circular economy gear to support LLMs and inference training. For example, some of our partners run on older **NVIDIA V100** cards. While they can't support some of the larger models, they're great for inference training and consume much less energy.

Let's Recap

Great job, you made it this far into my chapter. Thanks for hanging out with me! We covered so much, and there's so much more to discuss. The wild thing about writing this chapter is that as soon as I send it off to the publisher and it comes out in book form, there will be a million new updates in terms of AI, generative AI, and ChatGPT. However, the essential points I am making here will remain valid. So, let's recap our chapter:

1. **"Our industry loves innovation as long as it's ten years old."** This might not shock you, but we don't have ten years. We barely have ten months. Large hyperscale leaders have leapfrogged our data center industry and have taken the lead in the AI race. The challenge is that we had an enterprise customer base wanting to work with their data center partners, not just large hyperscalers. *Exploration of new AI solutions must start now.*
2. **A market that's *hungry* for on-premise GPU resources.** One of the most exciting learning points is that the end-user would love to work with their colocation partner. As mentioned above, the challenge is that traditional colocations don't have the capacity or

capability to deploy high-density workloads to support AI at scale.

3. **You MUST rethink your infrastructure.** While we are all afraid of change, change must happen, as change is a constant in our industry. To become a part of this market, you must look at higher-density gear, more power, and more capabilities to support emerging workloads.

4. **All data centers will become AI data centers.** Read this point as many times as you need for it to stick. I can't stress this part enough. Every single digital infrastructure facility will become an AI data center. It's just a question of how quickly you can get there.

5. **Adapt or experience revenue bleed to the cloud.** We have a market that wants to leverage on-premises facilities. So, they'll either work with you or go to a colocation partner that can support their needs. The traditional cloud provider is no longer the default answer here. Colocation and data center facilities must step up.

6. **This is not a fad. None of this is going away.** I get the chance to speak at many conferences all over the world. When I ask if someone in the room has used ChatGPT, well over 90% of the room raises their hands. This is not "Zoom will take over the Internet" or "connected cars will produce so much data that it'll take over the data center." The innovation around generative AI is truly industry-changing and here to stay.

One of the most significant points I want to end on is this. The massive shift in how we search and use data isn't necessarily technological. We are experiencing an enormous change in how humans interact with data. For the first time in our history, we can ask our data questions and get conscious answers. What we have here is a shift in humanity, not just technology.

As we stand on the cusp of a future defined by interconnectivity and digital innovation, the fusion of data centers, AI, sustainability, and digital infrastructure emerges as the cornerstone of this new era.

Data centers, the cerebral hubs of our digital universe, work harmoniously with AI to drive unprecedented efficiencies and insights, heralding a future where decisions are more intelligent, faster, and more data-driven.

The commitment to sustainability within these realms is not just an ethical imperative but a strategic necessity, ensuring that our digital growth is both environmentally conscious and enduring. The robustness of digital infrastructure is the backbone, supporting the ever-expanding web of connectivity that binds our world.

Together, these elements don't just shape our future; they are reinventing it, crafting a more connected, intelligent, and sustainable world. We must innovate, collaborate, and sometimes get out of our comfort zone to get there. If we can accomplish a more visionary approach to the power of AI, in this synergy lies the promise of a future that connects us more closely and respects and preserves the world we share.

---

1. Mollman, Steve. "ChatGPT Gained 1 Million Followers." Yahoo Finance. December 9, 2022. https://finance.yahoo.com/news/chatgpt-gained-1-million-followers-224523258.html
2. Hu, Krystal. "ChaptGPT Sets Record Fastest Growing User Base." Reuters. February 2, 2023. https://www.reuters.com/technology/chatgpt-sets-record-fastest-growing-user-base-analyst-note-2023-02-01/
3. "Eighth Annual State of the Data Center Industry Report Reveals How Power Design and AI Demand Has Forever Changed the Industry." Yahoo Finance. https://finance.yahoo.com/news/eighth-annual-state-data-center-150000005.html
4. "Nvidia DGX Superpod Data Center Design." Nvidia. https://docs.nvidia.com/nvidia-dgx-superpod-data-center-design-dgx-h100.pdf
5. Walker, James. " AFCOM AI Boom Fueing Data Center Construction, Design Innovation." DataCenter Knowledge. January 31, 2024. https://www.datacenterknowledge.com/design/afcom-ai-boom-fueling-data-center-construction-design-innovation
6. "Capturing the Full Value of Generative AI in Banking." McKinsey. https://www.mckinsey.com/industries/financial-services/our-insights/capturing-the-full-value-of-generative-ai-in-banking

7. "Scott Data GPU Service." Scott Data Center. https://www.scottdatacenter.com/gpu-service/
8. Thompson, Neil. Kristjan Greenwald, Keeheon Lee, Gabriel F. Manso. "Deep Learning's Diminishing Returns." IEEE. September 24, 2021. https://spectrum.ieee.org/deep-learning-computational-cost
9. Zeff, Maxwell. "Generating AI Images Uses as Much Energy as Charging Your Phone, Study Finds." Yahoo Finance. December 1, 2023. https://finance.yahoo.com/news/generating-ai-images-uses-much-150000379.html

About the Author

BILL KLEYMAN

Bill Kleyman is an award-winning data center, cloud, and digital infrastructure leader with a 20-year career at the forefront of technology. Ranked globally by Onalytica as one of the leading executives in cloud computing and data security, Bill is focused on advising organizations, training young talent, and educating global audiences about AI, machine learning, sustainable data center design, cybersecurity, and more.

Today, Bill is the CEO of Apolo, an AI platform and infrastructure company. He is also the Chair of the Education Committee at Infrastructure Masons and the AFCOM Data Center World Program Chair.

Uniquely comfortable in technical and business leadership roles, Bill worked with sustainable hyperscale data center environments while driving brand awareness as EVP of Digital Solutions for Switch. Bill has also served as Director of Technology Solutions for EPAM Systems, CTO for MTM Technologies, and Director of Technology for World Wide Fittings.

Every year, Bill speaks at several leading technology conferences. Thousands of his articles, blogs, whitepapers, and chapters appear in publications such as Data Center Frontier, Data Center Knowledge, ITPro Today, InformationWeek, and the Amazon Best Selling book "Greener Data."

As the 2021 iMasons Education Champion Award winner, Bill is passionate about digital infrastructure sustainability, democratizing powerful technologies, evolving the IT industry, and training the next generation of empathic technologists focusing on diversity, equity, and inclusion. In short, he works daily to build a more sustainable and inclusive future.

TWENTY-SEVEN

The Ghosts in the Tamarind Tree: Overcoming Resistance to Disruptive Ideas in a Risk-Averse Industry

Karim Shaikh, Cato Digital

Our Fears are Fed by Beliefs

Splosh.., splosh.., splosh!

"*Get off the field.*" *Nothing bothered my grandfather more than the sound of excited kids plodding in the muddy paddy fields, while he diligently oversaw the seeding of rice grains early in the summer. We did get off the field, but only for as long as he wasn't looking.*

The early days of summer were bright and we came out everyday for a few weeks to prepare the rice fields and seed them. Kids loved it - school was out for the summer, and we had plenty of time. We ran through acres of open fields with nothing but fun on our mind. But we also definitely got in the way. Some workers didn't mind and laughed at us, and others did mind and yelled at us. It was all part of the game.

We lived in the little town of Kandukur in India, and the fields were in the outskirts four miles from our house. Sometimes we would ride in a bullock-cart, but mostly we just walked to the fields and back. We would go early at sunrise and return at sunset. It was always fun to go there but returning home was a different story, at least for me.

"*Come on, let's go,*" *shouted my cousin as he headed down the path that would take us home. I followed him for a bit and stopped in my tracks. "Oh no...*

Chapter Twenty-Seven

not again," he exclaimed exasperated. Everyone knew. I looked up and saw the tamarind tree up ahead along the path. It was dusk and that meant, well, there are ghosts hovering around it. Believe it or not, I could feel them.

"You guys go ahead, I'll come by the main road." I know that was at least a mile longer but I will not risk walking under that tree in the dark.

"We're going to pick some tamarind fruit along the way." Hearing those words perked me up. I love ripe tamarind fruit. That particular tree had the sweetest fruit anyone had ever tasted. I knew I wanted some. But the ghosts...

The stories my grandmother and her friends talked about every night instantly came to my mind. Stories of people who had seen ghosts in that tree and went out of their mind, and woke up screaming from their nightmares. Stories of people who went down that path and were never seen again. Stories of people who saw ghosts luring others with sweet talk and gobbling them up. Everything felt so real at that moment.

"I love the fruit from that tree but I am definitely not going to risk running into the ghosts for that", I said to myself. Carefully, I went down another path that led to the main road and reached home. There was a sense of relief, but it wasn't a clean one.

Risks Feel Real When Rooted in Fear

"I don't know if we are ready for that." It was a response we had heard before. Sitting in the boardroom of a prospect, Dean and I did our best to explain what our software did to recoup stranded power capacity in data centers. Cato Digital, with Dean Nelson at the helm as its CEO, had just brought its flagship software product M9 to the market.

Data centers operate efficiently as REITs, but are quite poor in their performance as actual "data centers." The amount of power capacity investment is often two or three times what is consumed by their tenants. Data centers are profitable by the way leases with tenants are structured, but this is a significant waste of investment and resources. In most data centers, the utilization of the power infrastructure is under 50% - sometimes as low as 20%, leading to stranded power[1]. Over several years, Cato Digital, previously called

Virtual Power Systems (VPS), had developed a power orchestration platform that addressed just this problem.

In my chapter on "Autonomous Digital infrastructure" in *Greener Data: Volume One*, I wrote about the details and the incredible size of this "stranded capacity" that is wasted, and how Cato's ADI/M9 software works with generic hardware already in the data center to help recoup and repurpose this stranded power capacity through flexible SLAs. With this solution, data center operators can increase their average utilization to 80% or more by leasing out the recouped capacity to flexible SLA tenants while ensuring that existing tenants are supported at their critical SLA. The innovative software was based on multiple patents.

The response from potential data center customers was positively overwhelming. "This is a powerful solution and just what the industry needs to ensure data center sustainability." "It's going to challenge and revolutionize how we consume power in the digital infrastructure industry." "This will make it so easy for existing data centers to go green." What a great market response - we had apparently achieved a product-market fit.

We followed up with the next appropriate question. When can we deploy this solution and start generating ROI for your data center? As if on cue, the tone changed. "This is certainly an interesting option. However, it requires tenants who need flexible SLAs, and we have never had tenants ask for anything less than a five 9's SLA."

What if we brought such tenants to you?

"Relying on your software is a risk that we're not ready to take on," continued this data center executive. "We operate safely with the systems in place today. While I see your value, I just don't feel comfortable with deploying power orchestration software in my data center."

We were staring at an insurmountable mountain of historical beliefs and ideas. Compounding this issue was the financial accounting of data centers as REITs. There was no forcing function or incentive to drive higher utilization. Power utilization was a "tenant problem" and "out of their control".

Chapter Twenty-Seven

Data center operators were living in a fear similar to that of the ghosts in the tamarind tree. Despite seeing the value of M9, this fear of the unknown kept them from moving forward. Maintaining the status quo was a safe approach, and the ghosts would never get to them!

We were disappointed, and were no longer sure if Cato's innovative product would ever find broad production appeal. There are many published articles lamenting the inability of the digital infrastructure industry to push the boundaries of risk to take advantage of innovations. At every data center conference, new ideas are proposed by both new and existing players in the space – but they tend to remain ideas. At best, they may see action as a prototype. M9 might also remain an idea and a prototype.

Circular Economy with Excess Power

"You've got to hear this," said Dean, who called me on the phone with excitement. He had just finished a conversation with our largest investor. "I believe we have a customer for our product!" I was all ears. But, as we continued the conversation, I was not so sure. The idea sounded a little strange. The proposed customer of our product was… Cato. Us?!

I trusted Dean's instinct so I continued to listen.

Hyperscalers like Meta, AWS, Google and Microsoft are the biggest users of IT equipment. They constantly grow their compute capacity, sometimes exponentially. Adding more servers requires them to lease or build out more space. Instead, it is more economical to replace them with new servers which pack more compute capacity in a smaller footprint. Not too long ago, a rack consumed 3 to 6 kW of power, but now it is common to see racks that consume 10kW, 25kW, and even 50kW. But, disposing of replaced equipment at scale can be a challenge for these companies, and so they leverage IT Asset Disposition (ITAD) vendors to help them out[2].

ITAD vendors destroy drives and chips that hold sensitive data, extract reusable/recyclable components, and dispose of the rest as e-waste. In 2019, the world generated 53.6 million metric tons of e-waste, and only 17.4% of this was officially documented as properly collected and recycled[3]. Reducing the contribution of replaced servers to this number would be beneficial to all. Global Industry Analysts Inc. estimated that the global market for ITAD in 2020 was $17.4 billion and the projected growth by 2034 is $36.4 billion[4].

Though recycling is a useful practice, even this approach is premature and inefficient. It's like taking the engine out of a BMW 3 series and scrapping the rest of the car versus tuning it up and putting it back on the road. It still has a lot of useful life in it. While the ITAD vendors are effective in what they do, and it works well for their business model, the big picture view shows a lot of wastage and an unintended impact on the environment.

First, we're destroying equipment that has another 3 to 5 years of useful life. While the large platforms replace these servers more frequently to increase performance for their specific requirements, the "retired" equipment still meets market needs. This is evident by the fact that servers of the same model are still listed and fully rented on public clouds such as AWS many years after standard retirement. These servers are capable of supporting intense workloads of many high-demand customers and, by the nature of its power agreements with Colo providers, Cato can enable those customers to operate critical production workloads at a fraction of the cost of cloud.

Second, dismantling and recycling the servers within their useful life drives purchases of new equipment, adding more embodied carbon and exacerbating the issue. Even with net-zero carbon pledges from some of the biggest tech companies in the world, this practice is counter-productive.

Dean recognized a strong synergy between ITAD workflow and Cato's M9 product that could enable a unique solution. We could go to market with a bare metal cloud offering that beats the competition in four ways.

1. Low cost equipment - the servers repurposed from the hyperscalers have three to six years of life left in them.
2. Low embodied carbon - the original buyers of the equipment have accounted for the embodied carbon

associated with their manufacturing. Their second life is essentially embodied-carbon free.
3. Low cost power - Cato can use their M9 software to safely access stranded power capacity from colo operators that is not accessible to other tenants since Cato's customers only require 99.5% SLA.
4. Low carbon power - Cato would leverage partner data center clean energy contracts or negotiate new agreements where possible.

With this approach, Cato would be able to implement its vision of carbon free compute, while helping data center providers increase their utilization and lower their overall carbon footprint.

Logic Cannot Be Ignored Forever

"This is yummy," I exclaimed as I ate dinner with my grandparents. My grandmother was a great cook, and I especially loved her South Indian style tamarind pickle. When eaten with rice, it develops a unique taste - sour, as one would expect tamarind to be, but she mixed it with other spices so that a variety of tastes hit your tongue, giving a unique sensation.

"Your friends brought these tamarind fruit from the tree near our fields - you know, the one you will not go near." I knew that. Everyone loved the tamarind fruit from that tree. I've had it too, but I've always had to beg for them from my friends. I have been walking to the fields for four years, but I still haven't summoned the courage to pluck some fruit myself.

Of course, I knew there were no such things as ghosts - they were fiction. But our mind can latch itself on to strange superstitions that our logical side knows are not true. We all have some of those beliefs, and you do too, although it may not have to do with ghosts.

What if they were real, though? I certainly don't want to find out the hard way. That was not a risk I wanted to take. But if I could, just once, pluck those fruits myself, the satisfaction of having done that would make them taste so much better!

Cato Digital signed agreements with ITAD vendors to buy their circular economy IT equipment. Dean worked on partnership agreements with colo data centers for space and power. These agreements are for five-9's power, because that was the only type of agreement colos would sign. However, we overprovision power in the Cato rack and use our M9 software to ensure customer SLA.

Today, Cato bare metal is deployed across two continents and growing. We were able to deploy in the same data centers that were previously not inclined to use our software to unlock their power infrastructure. We have achieved the original intent of our M9 software by applying it to ourselves as the customer.

As we moved forward with our deployments in their space, the colos watched our bare metal cloud operation with intrigue. It is clear that their minds are turning and they're able to see first hand the benefits of leveraging stranded power capacity.

Check for Your Own Ghosts

I could no longer resist the temptation of the fruit. It was time to muster the courage to walk up to that tamarind tree. This was scary - it is not easy to let go of years of reinforced beliefs. Was I just tempting fate?

The first time, I walked quickly past the tree, relieved when I got to the other side. Each day, I got a little bolder until I was able to walk up to the tree and pluck the fruit. No ghosts came swooping down on me, and nothing chased me away. I emerged from under the tree with my body intact and my mind, although shaken, very relieved and excited! And, of course, the fruit tasted amazing!

As humans, we are prone to our beliefs and comfort zones that constrain us much like the ghosts from my childhood - they are easy to justify with apparent logic, though we are aware of the lack of a factual basis. As innovators that attempt to push boundaries, it was frustrating for us to work with a conservative industry. To its credit, it's just as challenging for the industry to ignore the historical decisions and beliefs that have kept its operations safe and reliable for decades.

If you are an innovator, you need to embrace the reality of these *"ghosts"*. Instead of expecting an instantaneous and dramatic change, extend your creativity to work around these challenges.

Chapter Twenty-Seven

Start with empathy and lead towards change, creating an effective path to success.

If you are a leader in the digital infrastructure industry, you are accountable to your tenants and may be compelled to make conservative decisions. As you evaluate these risks and fears, ask yourself if they are real or if they are just *"ghosts in your own tamarind tree."* You may be missing out on a delicious tamarind fruit!

---

1. Hassan Moezzi. October 2023. "Reduce Data Center Over-Provisioning and Stranded Capacity for Sustainability" https://community.cadence.com/cadence_blogs_8/b/data-center/posts/reduce-data-center-over-provisioning-and-stranded-capacity-for-sustainability
2. Gillis, Alexander. January 2022. "IT asset disposition (ITAD) - Definition." TechTarget. https://www.techtarget.com/whatis/definition/IT-asset-disposition-ITAD
3. Global E-waste Monitor. 2020. "The Global E-waste Monitor 2020 Quantities, flows, and the circular economy potential" https://ewastemonitor.info/wp-content/uploads/2020/11/GEM_2020_def_july1_low.pdf
4. Future Market Insights. 2024 "IT Asset Disposition Market Outlook from 2024 to 2034" https://www.futuremarketinsights.com/reports/it-asset-disposition-market

About the Author

KARIM SHAIKH

Karim Shaikh is the Chief Technology Officer at Cato Digital, where he drives patented hardware and software innovations in software-defined power to orchestrate data center power infrastructure. His work at Cato helps data centers achieve sustainability by tapping into stranded power capacity and maximizing utilization.

With a career spanning 30 years, Karim has a strong foundation in product management and engineering. His expertise spans across startups and publicly traded companies reflecting a diverse experience across a number of domains. While he enjoys getting into the technical guts of scalable and reliable technology products, Karim is also passionate about building high-performance teams by simplifying people and process interactions.

Karim is engaged in academia as a part-time faculty member in Carnegie Mellon University's Software Management program where he empowers students to adopt a futures-based approach to product development, combining machine learning and software architecture with design thinking and futures studies.

When he's not involved in all this, Karim likes to travel and immerse himself in nature, history and culture.

TWENTY-EIGHT

Innovations in Power and Cooling: Shaping the Future of Data Center Technology with Flexential

Chris Downie, Flexential

Data centers are the very foundation of today's digital transformation, enabling businesses to remain competitive, agile, and innovative through staggering technological advancements. As businesses increasingly leverage technology to empower their business capabilities, demand for data processing and storage grows. This mounting need for data center services is amplified by the intense high-performance computing (HPC) requirements of artificial intelligence (AI) and machine learning (ML) workloads. To harness the potential of these advanced technologies, businesses need modern data centers that can withstand the colossal computational demands these technologies impose.

While ensuring operational resiliency, performance, and reliability has always been paramount in effective data center operation, today, these core responsibilities must be balanced with sustainability. This requires data centers to adapt their data center infrastructure to deliver the sophisticated power and cooling capabilities necessary to support more intense power and thermal demands with sustainability in mind.

Chapter Twenty-Eight

Flexential Innovates a Path Toward Sustainability

Flexential's journey in the evolution of data center design has been marked by profound and continuous innovation spanning many decades. Driven by customer expectations and a desire to be a good steward of the environment, Flexential integrated innovation and sustainability into its data center designs and practices, undergoing significant transformations to make pronounced strides in data center efficiency.

In this chapter, we will explore the power and cooling advancements engineered by Flexential, a distinguished leader in the data center industry, to meet ever-increasing processing and storage demands while minimizing energy consumption and improving cooling efficiency.

High-density Workload Management: The Challenges of the AI and ML Era

As technology continues to advance, the demand for processing power, storage, and network bandwidth continues to grow exponentially. The rise of high-density workloads, driven by the increasing sophistication of AI and ML applications, has altered the modern computing landscape, placing new, more extreme power and cooling requirements on data centers.

AI and ML Demand High-performance Computing

AI and ML hold tremendous potential to improve business capabilities, solve problems, and drive competitiveness. However, these advanced technologies can use 300 to 1,000 times[1] more power per transaction than traditional workloads, generating exponentially more heat in the process.

To handle massive amounts of data effectively, these workloads require HPC capabilities. HPC is not a new trend; technologies such as grid computing, clustering, and large-scale processing have been evolving for decades, revolutionizing the way we approach research, development, and problem-solving. As an enabling force behind various computationally intensive tasks, HPC plays a pivotal role in shaping today's computing environment and helping organizations address the most complex challenges of our time.

Data center infrastructure must be prepared to meet the demanding power and cooling requirements of HPC at scale as AI-rooted power consumption is projected to grow at a compound annual growth rate (CAGR) of 25% to 33% between 2023 and 2028[2].

The GPU Revolution

The extreme requirements of HPC are driving the development of new technologies. Large graphics processing unit (GPU) deployments have emerged as the cornerstone of contemporary computing. Serving as the workhorses underpinning AI and ML applications, they empower the efficient processing of vast datasets integral to large-scale training and inference workloads. These powerful units also have greater power and thermal needs than traditional CPUs.

Not surprisingly, demand for GPU deployments is rising, with 20% of shipped processors expected to be GPUs by 2027—up from 10% in 2022[3]. This forecasted growth suggests a future challenge to data centers, compelling them to adapt their infrastructure to support the more extreme computational, power, and cooling requirements of these high-density environments to avoid high rack temperatures that can increase the risk of server failure and downtime.

Balancing Uptime, Performance, and Sustainability

Supporting HPC and GPU deployments requires that data centers evolve their infrastructure. However, in today's environmentally conscious climate, delivering the necessary power and cooling to ensure the reliability and performance of HPC in high-density environments is only half the battle. Modern data centers must offer next-generation power and cooling capabilities while being attentive to the environmental impact of their efforts.

Flexential addresses this challenge through a robust combination of innovative and eco-friendly data center designs and practices.

Efficient Data Center Cooling Enables High-Performance Computing at Scale

Flexential envisions data centers as hubs of both high performance and sustainability, and we have shaped our power and cooling strategies to keep pace with HPC and sustainability best practices. Recognizing the pivotal role of GPUs in enabling HPC workloads, we modified our data center designs to provide optimal support and performance for these powerful devices. By investing in advanced power and cooling systems, we lay the groundwork for a future that balances technological advancement and increasing demand for computing power with our deep commitment to environmentally responsible practices.

One Size Does Not Fit All for Data Center Cooling

At the core of Flexential's strategy is the commitment to provide flexible, efficient cooling. Our cooling innovations move beyond one-size-fits-all solutions. Instead, they are customized to suit the unique requirements of each deployment, considering the technical needs of the server configuration and the specific priorities of the company—whether cost-effectiveness, efficiency, or performance. This approach not only ensures optimal cooling efficiency for a variety of workloads, it also positions our data centers as adaptable, effective, and environmentally conscious leaders in the dynamic field of data management.

To achieve this flexibility, we offer a combination of advanced liquid- and air-cooling solutions, setting the essential foundation required to facilitate HPC at scale and ensuring that the computational demands of today and tomorrow are consistently met. Flexential's commitment to effective data center cooling solutions not only supports the performance and reliability of HPC systems but also fosters a sustainable approach to computational power. By applying precision cooling, our forward-looking method allows us to direct cooling load to the hottest parts of the data center to regulate and maintain ideal temperatures across the facility more efficiently.

Flexential Generation 4 and Generation 5 Data Centers with Advanced Power and Cooling Technologies

Focused on sustainability, efficiency, and adaptability, Flexential Generation 4 and Generation 5 data centers set new standards in resiliency and performance, demonstrating Flexential's dedication to innovative data center cooling.

Introduced in 2011, Flexential Generation 4 data centers set new benchmarks in the industry. Built with fault-tolerant electrical systems and featuring our SuperCRAC cooling design for Next-generation Scalable Cooling (NGSC), these facilities offer efficient temperature management and a Power Usage Effectiveness (PUE) of 1.40. Notably, they were designed to be water-free, delivering a Water Usage Effectiveness (WUE) of zero while supporting high-density workloads with a capacity of up to approximately 50 kilowatts (kW) per rack. These facilities are also liquid-cooling-ready, preparing them for future technological advancements.

Building on the success of Generation 4 data center designs, Flexential introduced Generation 5 data centers in 2022. This generation brought forth continued innovation with the first use of Power Module technology to support efficiency and repeatability and allow mechanical, electrical, and plumbing (MEP) infrastructure to accommodate customer density requirements. Liquid cooling is also available by design to manage the intensifying thermal demands of HPC workloads. Powered by high-efficiency technologies, these cutting-edge data centers also offer a WUE of zero to help customers achieve their own sustainability goals. The deployment of Generation 5 designs is already underway, with more than 110 megawatts (MW) under development across Atlanta, GA, and Hillsboro, OR.

Chapter Twenty-Eight

Flexential Generation 4 and Generation 5 facility designs also employ high ceilings to aid efficiency efforts. The ceiling height allows hot air to rise away from the servers, minimizing the energy required to cool and recycle the air near the infrastructure. This helps lower PUE.

Flexential's data center power and cooling innovations have supported customers' large-scale workloads, ensuring the availability and performance of their systems and minimizing their environmental impact. Flexential's proven track record of delivering high-density capacity on demand positioned CoreWeave[4], a specialized cloud provider of large-scale Nvidia's GPU-accelerated workloads, to maintain rapid growth by meeting the explosive demand for high-performance cloud infrastructure to power AI workloads. Expanding its data center footprint into Flexential Generation 5 facilities with cutting-edge power and cooling capabilities in the 40-50kW range allowed CoreWeave to establish a state-of-the-art computing framework to optimize its infrastructure efficiency. This high-density solution substantially curtailed compute costs by limited cabling and platform deployment costs and avoiding more expensive localized cooling in favor of air cooling at the rack level—all while maintaining the agility needed to meet customers' shifting needs.

Advanced Air Management: Tailored Cooling Strategies for Data Centers

With a history spanning approximately fifty years, air cooling continues to be a widely utilized heat management method. By circulating cold air around data center hardware, air cooling dissipates heat, exchanging warmer air with cooler air. The regulation and direction of airflow are facilitated by computer room air-conditioning (CRAC) units. However, traditional air-cooling solutions cannot typically provide the extreme cooling and efficiency required to meet modern demands.

To address this issue, Flexential revolutionized its air-cooling capabilities, allowing it to support rack densities of 50kW. Our advanced air management techniques meticulously ensure each piece of equipment receives the precise amount of cooling necessary to avert overheating and protect data center reliability.

Innovation is at the Heart of Flexential's Super CRAC System

To take air-cooling efficiency to the next level, Flexential introduced its proprietary Super Computer Room Air Conditioners (CRAC) system in its Generation 4 data centers. Utilizing a sophisticated and highly specialized system, the Super CRAC system represents a significant leap forward in cooling technology. Through a combination of advanced cooling technologies, such as variable speed fans and economizers, the Super CRAC system adjusts cooling dynamically based on the data center's current load and environmental conditions to stabilize temperatures and humidity levels. This allows Flexential to reduce hot spots and deliver greater energy efficiency within the data center. This adaptability is crucial in an era where fluctuating workloads and the need for scalable solutions are the norm.

The Super CRAC system also aligns with Flexential's commitment to sustainability. Its energy-efficient design reduces power consumption, contributing to a lower PUE rating. The use of free cooling techniques, through which external air or water sources are utilized for cooling under suitable environmental conditions, further underscores its eco-friendly approach.

Fungible Air Delivery for Ultimate Flexibility

Flexential data centers are also leading the industry with our innovative use of fungible air delivery. This unique approach enables us to tailor cooling solutions specifically to each client's needs, optimizing energy efficiency and reducing operational costs. Fungible air delivery's versatility extends beyond conventional cooling methods, effectively handling everything from standard applications to intensive HPC tasks. By customizing cooling for each situation, we enhance data center reliability and performance, while also lessening our environmental footprint to contribute to a more sustainable future.

The fundamental difference between various air-cooling methods is the control of air cooling, whether at the room level, row level, or rack level.

- **Room level** air cooling typically relies on air conditioning, circulating chilled air around the entire data center room. Many data centers have incorporated hot and cold aisles to better utilize energy. In its simplest form, the server racks are lined up in alternating rows with cold air flowing in on one side and hot air flowing out on the other side.
- **Row level**, also known as in-row cooling, utilizes a dedicated cooling system for each row of cabinets. This design improves cooling efficiency over room-based cooling, using shorter, more clearly defined airflow paths to address the actual needs of specific rows.
- **Rack level** cooling improves efficiency further, providing each rack with its own cooling unit. Although this offers higher precision and efficiency than the two methods above, this method requires a large number of cooling units, thereby increasing overall costs and complexity.

Liquid Cooling Technology Supports Intensifying Workload Demands

Liquid cooling solutions have emerged as a more efficient way to remove heat and support the thermal output of the most advanced AI technologies. This capability is critical as the industry expects rack densities for extreme GPU workloads to reach 200kW to 300kW per rack within this decade.

Closed-loop Liquid Cooling Systems | Flexential's newest data centers are designed to support liquid cooling and feature a chilled water loop for liquid-cooled servers. The closed-loop cooling system utilizes cooled liquid to regulate server temperatures, absorbing the heat of the server and then cooling and recycling it in a continuous loop to offer a WUE of zero and improved cooling efficiency.

Flexible Liquid Cooling Options | Flexential Generation 4 and Generation 5 facilities can support other liquid cooling technologies, including direct to chip and immersion cooling with a variety of scalable configurations and densities. By deploying specific liquid cooling architectures, organizations can meet the precise cooling requirements of specific deployments while also considering customer priorities such as cost and green initiatives.

Nvidia DGX-Ready Partnership to Support Customer AI Deployments

The true measure of an innovation's effectiveness is its real-world impact. Flexential's collaboration with NVIDIA, a technology company primarily known for its expertise in designing and manufacturing GPUs, strategically positions us as a leader in providing the indispensable infrastructure for the increasing demands of AI and ML applications.

This partnership allows customers to trust Flexential for the highest density workloads, optimized for power, air cooling, and future-proofed liquid cooling. Deploying the highest performance compute, network, and storage services requires careful consideration across the board, with focus on environmentals, maintainability, and even cabling. Optimizing deployments means faster time to results, which is key for customers to achieve and maintain a competitive advantage.

The NVIDIA partnership proved impactful for Applied Digital,[5] a company specializing in next-generation data centers for the HPC industry. At the recommendation of NVIDIA, Applied Digital leveraged Flexential, an NVIDIA DGX-Ready partner since 2019, to deploy high-density computing resources—including NVIDIA

Chapter Twenty-Eight

H100 GPUs—in record time to address the rapidly growing demand for AI-based cloud service solutions. Flexential offered the high-density capacity necessary to support 40kW to 50kW per rack deployments across three markets as Applied Digital expanded its presence and AI cloud services. The high-density capacity provided by Flexential ensures Applied Digital's AI initiatives can scale efficiently, meeting the unique requirements of its high-compute customers.

The powerful alliance between Flexential and NVIDIA not only speaks to our shared commitment to advancing technology but also highlights our determination to make a meaningful impact on the world. Together, we aim to lead the way in the world of high-performance computing and contribute to a better, more sustainable environment through our innovative solutions.

Managing Legacy Facilities for Continued Optimization

Flexential also recognizes our responsibility to improve the efficiency of our legacy facilities. For example, we performed an optimization review of our Collegeville, PA data center, which resulted in a 6% reduction in PUE. We also continue to upgrade our data center equipment with the most energy-efficient models. By operating our data centers at or near capacity, we can better distribute the electrical load across more deployments to lower PUE. Additionally, optimized data center capacity improves efficiency and minimizes waste by ensuring power is used to cool heat-generating servers, rather than open spaces. Our ability to tune cooling capabilities to target the hottest areas further minimizes energy consumption to help lower PUE. We can also deploy rack-based heat exchangers or cooling modules to make legacy facilities more power dense at the rack level, taking advantage of their locations and network densities to solve workload challenges.

Chapter Twenty-Eight

Pioneering a Sustainable and Innovative Future for Data Centers

Data centers are—and will continue to be—increasingly pivotal in global business as advancing technology heightens the need for power-efficient and sustainable facilities. As the industry shifts towards green computing, advanced cooling solutions become more essential to manage the intense heat generated by GPUs and HPC. Flexential's investment in advanced power and cooling systems exemplifies our commitment to supporting future demand sustainably.

Our vision to transform data centers into not only performance powerhouses but beacons of sustainability fuels our efforts to balance computing demands with environmental responsibility. In this spirit, we have committed to setting specific sustainability goals to drive efficiency improvements in our new data centers and updates in our more mature facilities.

Green Bond Financing Promotes Sustainability-focused Growth

Flexential's Green Financing Program demonstrates our market-leading commitment to align business growth and sustainability with transparency. In 2021, Flexential completed the largest-ever data center and green bond inaugural asset-backed (ABS) issuance to support rapid growth and development. Issuing the green notes under our new Green Finance Framework, we set a new standard for green eligibility in the data center industry. Through this innovative program, we invest in projects that support a more sustainable future. Flexential issued two additional series of green notes in 2022 to fund the development and expansion of more efficient data centers and liquid cooling innovations.

Future-focused Sustainability Partnerships

In alignment with the United Nations Sustainable Development Goals, Flexential created specific sustainability objectives, including preserving water, utilizing energy-efficient technologies in our data centers, reducing our environmental footprint, promoting responsible consumption, and improving recycling efforts within our office spaces. We continue to work with multiple organizations, including the Science Based Target initiative (SBTi) and Infrastructure Masons (iMasons), to set our direction and provide specific targets and guidelines for our sustainability journey, including achieving a PUE of 1.4 and a WUE of zero. We are also a founding member of the Climate Accord and follow ASHRAE standards for efficient cooling and heating. To remain transparent and accountable towards our goals, we have committed to publishing an annual ESG report.[6]

As a leading data center provider, we understand the escalating demand for data processing and storage and are poised to continue to address this need while minimizing our environmental impact. Our innovations are aimed at ensuring operational resiliency, efficiency, and reliability, while paving the way for the future—sustainably and forcefully. Our journey continues to be marked by a steadfast commitment to excellence and innovation that aligns our operations with ESG principles to push the boundaries in power and cooling solutions and lead the way in sustainable data center practices.

To achieve this, we continue to explore green or clean energy solutions that reduce carbon emission and are developing best-in-class reporting for our customers to meet the Securities and Exchange Commission (SEC), California, and the European Union (EU) reporting rules on climate impact and goals. Additionally, in conjunction with our industry partners, we are dedicated to furthering our sustainability conversations and goal development. To demonstrate this commitment, we recently held a Customer Advisory Sustainability Summit to understand the growing needs of our customers. Frequent meetings with our power suppliers and MEPs also help us understand the latest generation, storage, and transmission technologies to ensure we meet our customers goals for sustainability, reliability, and cost.

Looking toward the future of next-generation workloads and

innovative data center designs, we invite collaboration in building a more sustainable, technologically advanced digital world to position data centers as both performance and sustainability exemplars.

---

1. AFCOM Webinar. "The Race to AI: How Every Data Center Will Become an AI Data Center." October 3, 2023.
2. Schneider Electric White Paper 110 (version 2.1). "The AI Disruption: Challenges and Guidance for Data Center Design."
3. "Servers Market Insights." IDC. Updated December 18, 2023. https://www.idc.com/promo/servers
4. "CoreWeave Expands Data Center Footprint with Two New Flexential Colocation Facilities." October 10, 2023. https://www.flexential.com/resources/press-release/coreweave-expands-data-center-footprint-two-new-flexential-colocation
5. "Flexential Empowers Applied Digital's High-Perfermance Computing Solutions with FlexAnywhere Platform." August 29, 2023. https://www.flexential.com/resources/press-release/flexential-empowers-applied-digitals-high-performance-computing-solutions
6. "Flexential ESG Report 2022." https://www.flexential.com/system/files/file/2023-11/Flexential-ESG-Report-2022-hvc.pdf?t=1705681327

About the Author

CHRIS DOWNIE

Chris, who joined Flexential in 2016, is responsible for setting and managing the strategic priorities of the company to drive profitability and growth. He is a proven Chief Executive Officer with deep expertise in economics, delivery, and operations in the data center and hybrid IT industries. Chris is a well-known speaker at industry, business, and regional events.

Before Flexential, Chris was Chief Executive Officer at Telx Holdings, a leading interconnection and data center solutions provider based in New York City. He has more than 30 years of executive leadership experience in finance and operations, working for Bear Stearns, Daniels & Associates, BroadStreet Communications and Motient Corporation.

Chris holds a bachelor's degree in history from Dartmouth College and a master's degree in international business from New York University.

TWENTY-NINE

Sustainable Innovation in Data Centers, a Critical Mission by Scala Data Centers

Agostinho Villela & Christiana Weisshuhn, Scala Data Centers

In Latin America, you'll find a region filled with both the lush landscapes of the Amazon rainforest and technological hubs like the cities of São Paulo and Santiago. It's here that Scala Data Centers, a leader in innovation and sustainability, is rewriting the script on how data centers contribute to a greener planet. This chapter explores Scala's journey, the insights they have learned and implemented, and the bright, sustainable future that lies ahead.

A Strong Commitment to the Environment

Latin America (LATAM) is a region of diverse cultures and economic opportunities, shaping its identity of immense potential and growth. The region's natural bounty is matched only by its rich cultural heritage and vibrant communities. Latin America has demonstrated a history of commitment to sustainability, recognizing the critical role it plays in both the region's economic development and environmental preservation. This commitment is evidenced by a variety of initiatives and policies aimed at reducing carbon emissions, conserving natural resources, and promoting renewable energy sources.

Chapter Twenty-Nine

Brazil, for instance, has been a leader in the use of renewable energy, with hydroelectric power, wind, and biomass contributing significantly to its energy matrix. According to the Brazilian Ministry of Mines and Energy, renewable sources accounted for about 93.1% of Brazil's installed electricity generation capacity in 2023[1]. This emphasis on renewables is part of Brazil's broader strategy to reduce greenhouse gas emissions and combat climate change, aligning with its commitments under the Paris Agreement.

Similarly, other LATAM countries have made strides in sustainability. Chile has emerged as a global leader in solar energy, taking advantage of its vast Atacama Desert, one of the sunniest places on earth. The country has set ambitious renewable energy targets, aiming for 70% of its electricity to come from renewable sources by 2030 and complete carbon neutrality by 2050[2]. Mexico has also been proactive, with the government implementing policies to increase renewable energy production and reduce carbon emissions, targeting a 35% renewable energy share in its electricity mix by 2024[3].

These regional commitments to sustainability and renewable energy have significant implications for the LATAM data center industry, including how companies design and deploy facilities. Recognizing the region's abundant renewable resources and the growing demand for sustainable digital infrastructure, Scala Data Centers has strategically integrated these trends into their operations and growth strategies.

LATAM: A Land of Digital Opportunity

The digital transformation across LATAM over the last five years has been both rapid and powerful, fundamentally reshaping how people, businesses, and communities interact with technology and data. This transformation, driven by increased internet consumption, mobile device adoption, and a surge in digital services, is making data centers an essential part of the region's infrastructure to support future growth and innovation. The necessity of data centers is emphasized by the growing reliance on digital platforms for education, healthcare, e-commerce, and government services, which demand robust, secure, and scalable data processing and storage capabilities.

One of the primary drivers of digital transformation in LATAM has been the significant increase in internet penetration and mobile adoption. According to the GSMA Mobile Economy Report 2023, 70% of the region's population in LATAM were using mobile internet by 2022, with this number expected to increase to 77% by 2030[4]. This surge in mobile internet users has been instrumental in providing widespread access to digital services and platforms, thereby increasing the demand for data center services to manage, store, and process the burgeoning data traffic.

The e-commerce sector in LATAM has seen explosive growth, as consumers shift towards online shopping platforms. Online sales in the region grew three times between 2019 and 2023, from $117 million to $364 million[5]. Similarly, digital banking and fintech services have witnessed rapid adoption, with millions of unbanked individuals gaining access to financial services for the first time. This growth in digital transactions emphasizes the need for secure and efficient data processing infrastructure, highlighting the critical role of data centers.

Cloud computing adoption has been another significant trend, enabling businesses across LATAM to scale rapidly and innovate. Spending on public cloud services in LATAM was expected to reach $15 billion in 2024, demonstrating the region's increasing reliance on cloud infrastructure[6]. Furthermore, the Internet of Things (IoT) is transforming various sectors, such as agriculture and manufacturing, generating vast amounts of data that require processing and analysis. Governments across LATAM are also riding the wave. In some areas, municipalities have launched digitalization initiatives to improve public services and increase transparency. For instance, Brazil's Digital Government Strategy prioritized the digitalization of 100% of public services by 2022, facilitating access to government services for citizens and businesses alike[7]. These digital initiatives generate significant amounts of data, and data centers play a pivotal role in supporting these technologies by providing the necessary computing power and storage capacity to ensure secure, efficient, and reliable public services.

Despite these advances, LATAM's engagement with Artificial Intelligence (AI) is a noteworthy aspect that highlights both the region's digital aspirations and its challenges. While AI's global impact is undisputed, its relevance in LATAM particularly underscores the region's infrastructural disparities compared to leaders like the US, Europe, and Asia. This context does not diminish the importance or potential of AI in LATAM, but rather emphasizes the critical need for continued investment and development in digital infrastructure to close these gaps. By addressing these infrastructural challenges, LATAM can fully harness the transformative power of AI and other digital technologies, reinforcing its role in a globally connected digital future.

The Necessity of Data Centers in LATAM

LATAM's profound digital transformation has created a massive demand for data processing and storage. This trend is set to continue, with the region's digital economy expanding and hyperscalers such as Google, Microsoft, Huawei Technologies and Amazon Web Services (AWS) investing in the region[8]. Data centers, with their ability to support high-volume data traffic, ensure data security, and enable cloud and IoT applications, are becoming an indispensable component of LATAM's digital infrastructure.

As the region continues to embrace digital transformation, the need for sustainable, efficient, and scalable data centers will only grow. These facilities are crucial for supporting the region's digital economy, enhancing the quality of life for its citizens, and driving future innovation and growth. The ongoing digital revolution in LATAM underscores the importance of investing in data center infrastructure to support the region's vibrant digital ecosystem. But, the same data centers that are essential for processing, storing, and distributing the vast amounts of data generated daily, consume a considerable amount of energy, contributing to the global energy demand. In 2022 data centers used between 240 and 500 terawatt-hours of electricity, roughly 1-2% of that consumed worldwide.[9] As society becomes increasingly aware of environmental issues, the digital industry is under scrutiny for its carbon footprint and sustainability practices.

The landscape in LATAM is also uniquely shaped by the imperatives of data sovereignty and the accelerated digital transformation triggered by the COVID-19 pandemic. The pandemic significantly fast-tracked the digitalization of the economy, pushing more sectors online and amplifying the need for robust digital infrastructure. With increasing concerns over data privacy and security, the requirement for data centers to comply with data sovereignty laws—ensuring data is stored and processed within national borders—has never been more critical. These considerations add layers to the already complex landscape of digital transformation in LATAM, underscoring the multifaceted role of data centers as infrastructure components and essential enablers of regional resilience, security, and innovation in a rapidly evolving digital world. Moreover, given the energy scarcity in Northern Virginia, it might be necessary to "digitally reshore" workloads from other countries, contributing to more data center demand in Latin America. Finally, since AI training workloads have less stringent latency requirements, Latin America, given its abundant availability of clean energy, can be an ideal location to host data centers for this purpose.

The Imperative for Green Data Centers

Traditionally, data centers have been energy-intensive facilities, primarily focused on maximizing reliability and performance, often at the cost of increased energy consumption and carbon emissions. This traditional approach is quickly becoming unsustainable and unfavorable in the face of growing environmental concerns and the urgent need to combat climate change.

The shift towards green data centers represents a major movement in the industry, driven by a recognition of the urgent need to minimize the environmental impact of digital growth. Scala's green data centers aim to achieve high efficiency and performance while

Chapter Twenty-Nine

significantly reducing energy consumption and utilizing renewable energy sources. Scala stands out, championing the use of renewable energy and striving for a low Power Usage Effectiveness (PUE) ratio, in every one of its facilities across Brazil, Columbia, Chile and Mexico.

Occupying more than 21 million square feet across 57 properties throughout Latin America, our landbank inventory is strategically positioned near key connection points with cloud providers and submarine cables linking North America, Asia, Europe, and Africa. With over 100MW of operational capacity in its Latin American data centers—and an additional 145MW under construction or in the planning stages—Scala's commitment to advancing the digital revolution across the entire LATAM region is clear. Our company boasts the most efficient Power Usage Effectiveness (PUE) in the region, with a ratio of 1.35, a testament to its dedication to energy efficiency.

Map of Scala Data Center's LATAM footprint

The imperative for green data centers transcends the growing acknowledgment of climate change; it embodies a critical commitment to the future of our world, fueled by understanding our collective responsibility to forge a sustainable path that ensures the vitality and health of our planet for generations to come. Not to mention that it is also a strategic business decision.

Consumers and corporations are increasingly prioritizing sustainability, demanding that their data service partners not only be reliable and efficient but also implement environmentally friendly standard practices. This shift in expectations is giving green data centers a competitive advantage. Our commitment to sustainability, exemplified by our innovative approaches to energy efficiency and renewable energy use, not only enhances our reputation but also aligns with the broader industry trend towards environmental responsibility. As we move forward, the transformation of data centers from energy-intensive facilities to pillars of sustainability will be imperative in ensuring the digital industry contributes positively to the global fight against climate change.

Engineering Excellence for a Greener Future

Sustainable practices at Scala represent a cornerstone of our company's ethos. Central to this is Scala's renowned Center of Excellence in Engineering (CoE), an esteemed institution that boasts more than 400 engineers who are dedicated to pushing the boundaries of sustainable data center design and operation. The CoE serves as Scala's hub of expertise, bringing together a diverse cadre of professionals to pioneer groundbreaking solutions that redefine the standards of sustainability in the industry.

Our commitment to sustainability extends to every aspect of our data center operations and we strive to minimize our environmental impact at every opportunity. For example, the CoE is tasked with providing cutting-edge solutions that optimize our land usage to its fullest potential, resulting in the highest density per square foot in the market.

Take one of our newest facilities, located at its Tamboré Campus in the city of Barueri, Brazil. Once completed, the Tamboré Campus will have an IT capacity of 450MW, with an ensuing energy consumption of 600MW, which is equivalent to the consumption of the capital of Brazil. SGRUTB08, within the Tamboré Campus, stands as the tallest vertical data center in LATAM. Spanning an impressive 17,500 m^2, this vertical colossus is a testament to future-ready infrastructure, designed to scale with the rhythm of digital demands. Its sprawling capacity of 24MW, initiated with a potent 6MW, epitomizes the essence of adaptability, catering to the intricate requirements of AI and Machine Learning.

What sets SGRUTB08 apart is not just its vertical magnitude, but also that sustainability is woven into the very fabric of its operation. The facility's use of cutting-edge cooling technologies and its commitment to energy efficiency manifest in a projected PUE of 1.35, a figure that transcends the conventional benchmarks of environmental stewardship in the data center realm. Additionally, its Water Usage Effectiveness (WUE) stands at zero, underscoring a conscientious move away from water-dependent cooling methods, thereby aligning its operation with the principles of sustainable development.

The CoE also focuses on developing energy and water-efficient solutions, implementing equipment and cooling techniques with minimal energy consumption, thereby solidifying Scala's position as having the lowest PUE in Latin America.

Energy Efficiency through Cooling

Recognizing the environmental impact of traditional cooling infrastructures, our strategy encompasses the adoption of next-generation solutions designed to lower energy consumption and promote sustainability.

Central to our approach is the implementation of advanced free cooling systems, which utilize the external environment to cool facilities, eliminating the need for energy-intensive mechanical refrigeration. Additionally at Scala, we are assessing the use of AI in predictive climate control, optimizing cooling processes based on real-time data and forecasts. This innovative method not only enhances efficiency but also ensures a more responsive cooling infrastructure capable of adapting to varying demands.

Chapter Twenty-Nine

We are reimagining data hall designs to incorporate natural cooling features, leveraging the ambient conditions to maintain optimal operating temperatures. By transitioning to liquid cooling, Scala plans to achieve a PUE as low as 1.15, marking a significant improvement over the previous average of 1.35. This advancement will translate to a 50% decrease in infrastructure energy consumption, contributing to the global movement towards greener data centers.

The exponential growth of AI applications has dramatically increased power requirements, with racks soaring from 10kW to hundreds of kilowatts of power. This surge stresses the inadequacy of conventional cooling methods and highlights the necessity for innovative solutions. In response, Scala is embracing liquid cooling, to meet the thermal management needs of high-density computing, thus future-proofing them.

Our energy efficiency initiative also entails a thorough evaluation of traditional cooling components, such as air-cooled chillers and Computer Room Air Handling (CRAH) units. In line with some hyperscaler standards, we aim to optimize our cooling strategy by increasing the maximum Cold Aisle temperature and adjusting the Hot Aisle temperatures accordingly. This approach necessitates careful consideration of the physical limitations of cooling equipment and the thermal conditions of data center environments.

Through comprehensive Computational Fluid Dynamics (CFD) simulations and a commitment to innovative cooling solutions, Scala is paving the way for more sustainable and energy-efficient data center operations. Our ongoing efforts include enhancing aisle containment, optimizing rack layout, and continuously monitoring the impact of temperature adjustments on overall efficiency. By embracing these strategies, Scala is not only improving its environmental footprint but also setting a new standard for the data center industry in the era of green computing.

Exploring Sustainable Backup Power: The Case of Hydrotreated Vegetable Oil
At Scala, we're dedicated to leading in sustainable innovation,

Chapter Twenty-Nine

which includes our venture into alternative energy sources like Hydrotreated Vegetable Oil (HVO) for backup generators. This initiative underlines our commitment to environmental stewardship and ensuring a reliable power supply, crucial for data center operations.

HVO, made from renewable vegetable oils, is a sustainable energy alternative with a significantly reduced carbon footprint, offering an eco-friendly option for reducing ecological impact. Our venture into using HVO aimed at carbon neutrality, testing its integration into our infrastructure without compromising power reliability. This effort balances environmental responsibility with the need for dependable power solutions.

Using HVO in data centers cuts greenhouse gas emissions and releases fewer pollutants, supporting cleaner urban air quality and reducing reliance on fossil fuels. Our Proof of Concept showed HVO's efficiency over fossil diesel, though its higher cost has paused its immediate adoption. Despite this, the successful PoC lays the groundwork for future implementation, as we continue to explore renewable energy technologies, affirming Scala's leadership in sustainable data management.

Construction

Our Center of Excellence in Engineering (CoE) has also played a significant role in the ideation and development of the FastDeploy methodology of data center design. This cutting-edge technique harnesses the power of prefabricated, transportable modular components to redefine the efficiency and speed of deploying data centers. FastDeploy is our response to the industry's increasing demands for quick, scalable, and environmentally friendly data center construction solutions.

Rapid Deployment and Efficiency: FastDeploy significantly cuts down the time traditionally required for data center projects, which can range from 18 to 24 months from the planning phase to operational status. By enabling up to 50% faster deployment, FastDeploy ensures that projects transition from concept to fully functional operations in record time. This rapid assembly capability meets the immediate demands of the digital age and also introduces a higher level of precision and quality in construction through its use of pre-engineered modular components.

Environmental Sustainability: FastDeploy embodies our proactive approach to sustainability, aiming to minimize the environmental impact traditionally associated with data center construction. The methodology achieves this by optimizing design for reduced resource consumption and mitigating the potential for stranded assets, thus lowering the overall carbon footprint of new data center projects. FastDeploy showcases our leadership in data center innovation and paves the way for a new era of data center solutions that are fast, flexi

Redefining Data Centers with AI-Driven Sustainability

But sustainability isn't just about reducing our carbon footprint; it's also about planning for the future. Suppose data centers fail to adapt to the requirements of the AI-driven workloads of the future. In that case, they risk becoming significant contributors to environmental degradation rather than part of a sustainable solution. The exponential growth in data processing needs, coupled with the energy-intensive nature of AI algorithms, presents a formidable challenge for data center operators worldwide.

This intersection of AI and sustainability presents a complex challenge. The Scala team recognizes this challenge as an opportunity to lead the industry toward a future where AI and sustainability converge. Traditional data centers now face the daunting task of adapting to the energy and processing needs of AI. The shift towards AI-driven applications isn't just a trend; it's a seismic change in how data is processed, demanding more from the facilities that house these operations. Without a thoughtful recalibration towards sustainability, data centers risk becoming relics of an unprepared past.

Our AI engagement goes beyond demand generation. Our data centers harness AI's potential to revolutionize operational efficiency and design processes. From employing computer vision for enhanced security to utilizing generative AI for rapid conceptual design, Scala exemplifies how AI can transform traditional practices. The ability to review technical proposals and generate conceptual designs in mere seconds, as opposed to weeks, reiterates the transformative impact AI has on reducing time to market and improving responsiveness to client needs.

Additionally, the adoption of AI within Scala has prompted a shift towards a more educated workforce, capable of higher-order critical thinking. By automating routine tasks, Scala's engineers are freed to focus on innovation and complex problem-solving, ensuring that the human element remains at the forefront of technological advancement.

As Scala continues to blend AI innovation with sustainable practices, it paves the way for a future where technology and environmental responsibility go hand in hand, setting new standards for the data center industry worldwide.

Closing Thoughts

At Scala, our commitment to integrating sustainable practices into every facet of its operations illuminates a path for the industry, signaling that the pursuit of technological advancement need not come at the expense of the environment. Between now and the end of 2025, we plan to invest $2 billion in data center launches and expansions across Latin America in 2024-25, deploying 200MW of capacity – in the LATAM region that has 900MW of demand.[10]

Our journey has been marked by challenges and triumphs. From pioneering the investigation of liquid cooling systems to navigating the intricate landscape of renewable energy integration, every step has been a testament to our commitment. Challenges are not road-

Chapter Twenty-Nine

blocks; they are opportunities to innovate and redefine industry norms.

As we stand at the crossroads of digital transformation and environmental preservation, the team at Scala Data Centers exemplifies how our company's mission has illuminated the path for the entire industry. Sustainable innovation in data centers isn't just a roadmap for operational excellence; it's an example of technological advancement that will lead to a more sustainable world. Scala's achievements remind us that the true measure of progress lies in our ability to harness the power of technology in service of our planet.

---

1. "Brazil achieved 93.1% of power generation from renewable sources in 2023." EnerData Daily Energy & Climate News. Feb. 2024. https://www.enerdata.net/publications/daily-energy-news/brazil-achieved-931-power-generation-renewable-sources-2023.html
2. "How Chile is becoming a leader in renewable energy. World Economic Forum. Jan. 2023. www.weforum.org/agenda/2023/01/how-chile-is-becoming-a-leader-in-renewable-energy
3. "Worldwide Spending on Public Cloud Services is Forecast to Reach $1.35 Trillion in 2027." International Data Corporation. Aug. 2023. www.idc.com/getdoc.jsp?containerId=prUS51179523
4. "The State of Mobile Internet Connectivity Report 2023." GSMA. 2023. www.gsma.com/solutions-and-impact/connectivity-for-good/mobile-economy/wp-content/uploads/2023/03/270223-The-Mobile-Economy-2023.pdf
5. "Latin America – an emerging e-commerce powerhouse." Payments Industry Intelligence. Oct. 2023. www.paymentscardsandmobile.com/latin-america-an-emerging-e-commerce-powerhouse
6. "Public Cloud - South America." Statista.www.statista.com/outlook/tmo/public-cloud/south-america
7. "Brazilian Digital Transformation Strategy." Brazilian Government. 2020. www.gov.br/mcti/pt-br/centrais-de-conteudo/comunicados-mcti/estrategia-digital-brasileira/digitalstrategy.pdf
8. "Latin America Green Data Center Market - Industry Outlook & Forecast 2022-2027." Arizton. Dec. 2023. www.arizton.com/market-reports/latin-america-green-data-center-market
9. "Data centres improved greatly in energy efficiency as they grew massively larger." The Economist. Jan. 2024.www.economist.com/technology-quarterly/2024/01/29/data-centres-improved-greatly-in-energy-efficiency-as-they-grew-massively-larger
10. Scala Data Centers reveals plan to invest US$2bn in LatAm by 2025." BN Americas March 2024. www.bnamericas.com/en/news/scala-data-centers-reveals-plan-to-invest-us2bn-in-latam-by-2025

About the Author

AGOSTINHO VILLELA

Agostinho de Arruda Villela has worked in IT for over 30 years, with extensive leadership and hands-on experience in software (system and application) and hardware. He is currently the CTO and Conceptual Engineering VP of Scala Data Centers. Agostinho holds two US patents and is a member of iMasons and leader of the Brazilian chapter, a pioneering initiative in the country to promote innovation, education, and best practices among several peers, customers, and suppliers, in the digital infrastructure space. Agostinho was previously an IBM Distinguished Engineer, IBM Latin America Innovation Director, and IBM Innovation Studio WW Co-CTO.

About the Author

CHRISTIANA WEISSHUHN

Christiana Weisshuhn serves as the Senior Director of Communications and ESG (Environmental, Social, and Governance) at Scala Data Centers, directly reporting to the CEO. With over two decades of expertise in Program Management and Strategy execution, Christiana brings a wealth of experience to her role. She leads the implementation of Scala's sustainability strategy, a pivotal responsibility as a member of the Scala ESG Committee.

In addition to her ESG role, Christiana also spearheads Scala's communication and branding efforts, ensuring the company's image aligns with its core values and objectives.

She holds a distinguished track record in the digital infrastructure industry. Recognized for her exceptional contributions, Christiana received the iMasons 2023 Education Champion Award, highlighting her commitment to nurturing talent within the industry. In 2022, she was honored with the IM100 award for her outstanding achievements in the digital infrastructure sector. Additionally, in 2023, Christiana was named one of the Top 10 Sustainability Leaders in the Industry by Data Centre Magazine.

A graduate of Electrical Production Engineering from the Pontifícia Universidade Católica of Rio de Janeiro (PUC-RJ), Christiana is based in São Paulo, Brazil.

THIRTY

The Magic Trio: Industry Innovation, Customers, and Consumers Will Fuel Greener Data

Fredrik Jansson, atNorth

In the Eyes of a Child

As a parent, it's important to address every question fired at you from your children, even though sometimes the answer may not get the desired response. I well remember one such occasion. I was sitting at my kitchen table, working in the Stockholm winter sunshine, when a voice boomed up at me; *"Daddy, what do you actually do at work?"*

The question was posed by my young daughter who had just woken up and entered the kitchen, her auburn hair in tangles, a teddy bunny under one arm and an iPad under the other. Feeling quite happy at her vested interest, I launched into an explanation on data, power and cooling – until I saw her green eyes glazing over.

"Ok, I am going to watch My Little Pony now," she said as she walked out of the room.

Many of us can relate to this scenario – children don't necessarily understand what we do for a living, but that's not to say we shouldn't try and explain. I realized at that moment that if I cannot explain to a child (the next generation) what I (and our industry) do, then I (we) have a big problem.

Chapter Thirty

So, I asked her to come sit on my lap and I tried again. Looking at her iPad still in hand, this time I explained, in language she could understand, that when she carries out her digital activities on her device, the process starts in what is called a data center. If that data center is a power-hungry, coal-fired one that lets excess heat out into the atmosphere, then she is contributing to climate change. Her eyes widen:

"*Oh, so I am hurting the climate when I video chat with grandma?*"

Drawing a heat recovery and renewable energy comparison.

I now had her full attention! Not necessarily, I told her. I explained that data center where I work is energy efficient and runs on renewable energy, and that some data centers (like the one I'm employed at) even reuse excess heat to warm us, which I demonstrated by putting my hand on the radiator next to us. She jumped off my lap and stared at me, and said with pride in her voice: "*So, your job is to make the world a better place?*"

Without waiting for the answer, she took her iPad and rushed out of the kitchen. I heard her saying proudly, "*Grandma, did you know that dad makes the world a better place?*" As she ran up the stairs to her room, I could hear her passionately telling my mother the story of how watching My Little Pony heats her home.

Ever since that day, when someone asks me what I do at work, my standard reply is: "I'm helping to make the world a better place." I'm lucky to be able to do exactly this at atNorth.

Chapter Thirty

The Two Defining Trends of Our Time Meet in the Data Center

The two defining trends of our time — digitalization and sustainability — are intrinsically linked. As consumers (like my daughter), every time we browse social media, stream a movie, or shop online, a data-intensive process starts. Add to this the explosive use of artificial intelligence (AI) and high-performance computing (HPC) as businesses strive to automate processes, increase productivity, and optimize operational efficiencies, and the impact of data becomes a real concern. At the intersection of these two mega trends is the data center. Choosing the right location, site, and partner can not only future proof technological investment, but also significantly reduce a business's environmental impact.

It is not surprising that the data center industry is facing unprecedented challenges right now. On one hand, digital data consumption continues to grow at an exponential rate, while on the other, additional scrutiny continues from governments, regulators, mainstream media, lobbyists, and organizations on how we can address long-term sustainability and reduce carbon emissions.

As the industry responds to these challenges, we are seeing great innovation come to the fore with speed and tenacity, which truly is making the world a better place. Yet, there are also challenges in how our industry communicates this information and how it is perceived; most often not as an industry that is making the world a better place.

In this chapter, I zoom in on innovation transforming the data center industry before zooming out to address the critical factors which I believe will really fuel change. A hint: they are external to our industry.

The Digital Data Explosion Fuels the Need for High-Density Data Centers

In today's day and age, everything that can be digitalized will be digitalized. We are at a real tipping point where digital transformation meets the climate crisis with force. The data center sits at the

Chapter Thirty

intersection of these two mega trends, where the speed of digitalization is fueling floods of data — data that needs to be stored, processed, and analyzed in facilities that we know can be detrimental to our planet.

To put things into perspective:

- It has been estimated that data centers account for 1-3% of global electricity use[1], while digital technology represents 4% of all global greenhouse gas emissions.[2]
- The digital transformation market in Europe is expected to be worth $18.53 billion USD this year, with a predicted compound annual growth rate (CAGR) of 13.1% over the next 10 years.[3]

It is no surprise that the data center industry is set to grow in turn, with a market size estimated to reach $10.5 billion USD[4] this year. The IDC Global DataSphere, a worldwide measure of how much data is created, captured, and consumed every year, is expected to more than double in size from 2022 to 2026[5]. Meaning that, in the next five years, consumers and businesses will generate twice as much data as all the data created over the past 10 years. The resulting pressure on organizations to manage this data and meet increasing business requirements while also protecting the environment could be stifling. In addition to this, legacy systems and infrastructures will struggle to cope with the explosion in data and the surge in digital transformation projects, AI, and beyond as we look to the metaverse.

The role of IT sustainability has never been more critical, and our industry is fortunate to be in a position to protect our planet so that my daughter and future generations can rely on greener data at the core when they binge watch their next TV series or video call grandma.

In the data center industry, another major demand driver is the high demand for data-intensive digital transformation workloads from hyperscale customers. Research from Synergy Research Group[6] published earlier this year sees the average capacity needs of hyperscale data centers growing threefold, while new data center sites opening are likely to more than double in the next six years.

Companies are increasingly adopting emerging technology solutions like AI or automation in every part of their business. According to the IDC, global spending on AI-centric systems is set to rise by 27% this year to reach $154 billion USD, with year over year spending expected to exceed $300 billion USD by 2026[7]. This illustrates how essential high-performance computing applications are to maintaining competitive advantage.

As the demand for greater density and additional compute capacity increases in the data center in response to these innovations, so too will power consumption and cooling requirements as more heat is generated by the infrastructure. This increase in heat can lead to decreased performance, hardware failure, and efficiency challenges. Furthermore, it is at complete odds with the purpose of high-density deployments: to enable more compute resources and faster applications to run on servers.

For high-performance computing systems in particular, cooling is a considerable challenge. Infrastructure cooling has been estimated to account for 40% of the total electricity cost of the data center,[8] a share that is expected to grow as data center rack power densities, next-generation servers, and HPC and AI applications continue to put additional pressure on data center cooling.

High Density Requires Innovative Cooling and Favorable Operating Climate

The increase in ESG initiatives, coupled with a scarcity of power supply (in some regions) and increasing energy prices across most of Europe, have led organizations to also consider the physical environment of where their data center sites are located – both in terms of the weather as well as ability to lean into an existing, sustainably-minded infrastructure. For example, the Nordic region

Chapter Thirty

boasts a cool, consistent, and favorable operating climate that allows data centers to capitalize on more ambient temperatures to provide high density air and liquid cooling solutions that ensure temperature and humidity levels within the facility are maintained more efficiently. Moreover, most Nordic cities, regardless of size, have residential heating systems in place that strategically placed data centers can easily plug into to recycle residual heat.

atNorth has spent 15 years designing, operating and fine-tuning cooling systems that work in tandem with this cool and ambient Nordic climate – this allows us to air cool at high levels of density of up to 50kw per rack. Customers are increasingly requiring higher rack densities, which is where the benefits of liquid cooling can be experienced – not least the operating advantages it offers. Liquid cooling is a 'perfect fit' for heat reuse with the ability plug into an already existing infrastructure across most Nordic cities.

atNorth's ICE03 data center facility takes advantage of the cold climate and sustainable infrastructure.

Liquid cooling systems have significantly higher thermal conductivity and heat capacity than air, which means they can dissipate heat better and are a more cost-effective cooling method for high-density needs. It's little wonder this is one innovation gaining traction across the industry, most notably Direct Liquid Cooling (DLC), a novel approach that draws on the thermal conductivity of liquid to target cooling to exact areas of the data center. By capturing component heat in its liquid path, DLC allows for significant component performance and reliability, higher densities, and decreased data center operating expenses through the reduction, or altogether elimination, of chillers and computer room air conditioning units. DLC goes one step further to make heat recovery more efficient using warm air exhaust that goes into the cooling units to heat the temperature of the water before it is sent to the district heating network and from there, recycled to residential heating systems.

For enterprises and hyperscalers looking to safely house their most valuable asset — data — the Nordic region is poised to become the green location of choice. With Europe's climate warming at twice the rate of the global average,[9] many countries are experiencing increasingly extreme weather conditions such as droughts, storms, and flooding. Data centers already generate a considerable amount of heat, and prolonged periods of extreme hot weather mean that cooling systems will need to work harder, inevitably consuming more energy at a significant cost in order to ensure the infrastructure remains at an acceptable temperature. However, this risk is lessened in regions such as the Nordics where temperatures are consistently cooler and the existing infrastructure supports efficient sustainable reuse practices, which is likely why data center builds are seeing an outsized share of the demand for power-hungry workloads. CRBE, the global leader in commercial real estate, noted this in recent research predicting the Nordics will account for 8% of all colocation data center supply in Europe by the end of 2023.[10] Their findings predict data center capacity could double by the end of 2026 as many customers with large-scale needs look to the Nordics for the region's availability of purpose-built facilities and renewable energy sources at scale.

As many data centers are under pressure to reduce their environmental footprint, DLC is an important contribution, not just to improving efficiencies and performance, but also to meeting sustain-

Chapter Thirty

ability goals. By capturing heat in its liquid path, DLC yields substantial energy savings, decreasing power consumption and increasing the efficiency of heat reuse. And for those data centers located within the Nordic region, there is the added benefit of being able to tap into an infrastructure that supports sustainable, circular economic practices.

Forward-Thinking Design at Work: DLC + Heat Reuse = Circular Economy

At atNorth, we are putting this to the test across our Nordic sites — from Denmark and Iceland to Finland and Sweden — where all our facilities are DLC-ready. As an organization that benefits from the Nordics' environmental advantages, we offer sustainable, cost-effective, scalable colocation and high-performance computing services.

In 2022, atNorth integrated CoolIT's DLC technology at its new, state-of-the-art Stockholm facility, SWE01, which is unique in its design, with a primary cooling system created specifically to maximize heat recovery. CoolIT's technology uses a combined approach of DLC and warm water, which decreases the need for fans and air handling systems. This approach cools the IT load more efficiently, and delivers superior performance, reduced power use, a higher rack density, and greater control over the heat reuse process.

Many governments in the Nordic countries are driving large-scale initiatives to enable a circular economy and help businesses take advantage of the sustainable infrastructure across the region. In Finland, data centers can sell excess heat to the local energy companies to be reused within residential areas, while also benefitting from significant lower tax rates for electricity[11]. Similarly, atNorth has partnered with Stockholm Data Parks and energy provider Stockholm Exergi at its SWE01 facility to enable heat reuse. Here, atNorth captures the heat outputs generated by its data halls, recycling residual heat through Stockholm Exergi's district heating plant to provide heat and hot water for thousands of local residents. Instead of dispersing this heat waste into the atmosphere, this process can capture up to 85% of the heat outputs used in the data center to be captured and regenerated as heat and hot water for up to 20,000 homes in the local area.

The SWE01 data center has proven the heat reuse concept and now serves as a unique blueprint for all new atNorth data center sites, which are enabled with heat reuse capabilities and designed with more compute for a better world. It also illustrates the powerful role that data centers can play in driving sustainability and circularity principles, allowing me to tell the story of what I do with conviction: I'm helping to make the world a better place.

Heat recovery unit inside atNorth's SWE01 Stockholm campus connecting the excess heat from the data center to the district heating plant.

Critical Factors to Accelerate Sustainable IT in the Data Center

By communicating the positive strides we are making within the data center itself (from liquid cooling to heat reuse), we can start to truly come to terms with the carbon footprint of our digital transactions.

There is no doubt that the industry is transforming itself at pace — we will certainly see more innovative examples of heat reuse and cooling systems that evolve and go beyond what is currently possible. However, there are two critical factors that I believe will be the biggest accelerators for greener data — which I believe are external to our industry.

1. *Customers realize the massive location gains and that going green is not more expensive!*

The geographical location of digital infrastructure is becoming more important than ever. In addition to proximity to markets, there are still other perceived and very real risks for many businesses to address: data sovereignty and compliance, political and economic stability, connectivity, resilience and security considerations to name a few!

Sustainability is equally moving up the boardroom agenda. But to assess the environmental and energy footprint of its data, a company first has to uncover where its data is located. Is it on-prem or in the 'cloud', or is it outsourced to a managed service provider or a colocation partner? Regardless of solution, the data of course always physically resides in a data center. With this in mind, it's important to know what constitutes a good data center. Data centers located in regions that support the circular economy, including ample renewable power and reliable supply, international connectivity, low energy prices, and large-scale heat reuse alongside factors such as political stability and a skilled workforce will continue to prove why location is key to future proofing the industry.

The second step is to assess the digital environmental footprint by calculating the associated CO^2 emissions and Power Usage Effectiveness (PUE) of the data center that houses your data. This is necessary to establish what your current footprint looks like and to find a data center that can offer a decarbonization solution. The exercise may start with figuring out where your data lies, but the sleeping customer truly wakes once organizations understand their current costs and CO^2 footprint and how much they could be saving in money and carbon. This is the education that will force data centers to become more aware and more green.

BNP Paribas CIB is a leading example of why they moved to the Nordics. The global financial institution has looked at sustainability

Chapter Thirty

as a strategic initiative from the top of the company down to understand the overall footprint of its global operations, including its IT and digital footprint. By moving a portion of its data center footprint to an atNorth center in Iceland, BNP transitioned to renewable energy and achieved a reduction in energy consumption of more than 50% and an 85% decrease in CO^2 output.[12]

Another example is Shearwater (a global marine geophysical company) who has taken the stage to present its powerful story to the data center industry to encourage others to reduce their carbon footprint. The move from Shearwater's legacy UK data center to one of atNorth's facilities in Iceland resulted in an 84% cost savings and a reduction of CO2 that totalled 92%[13].

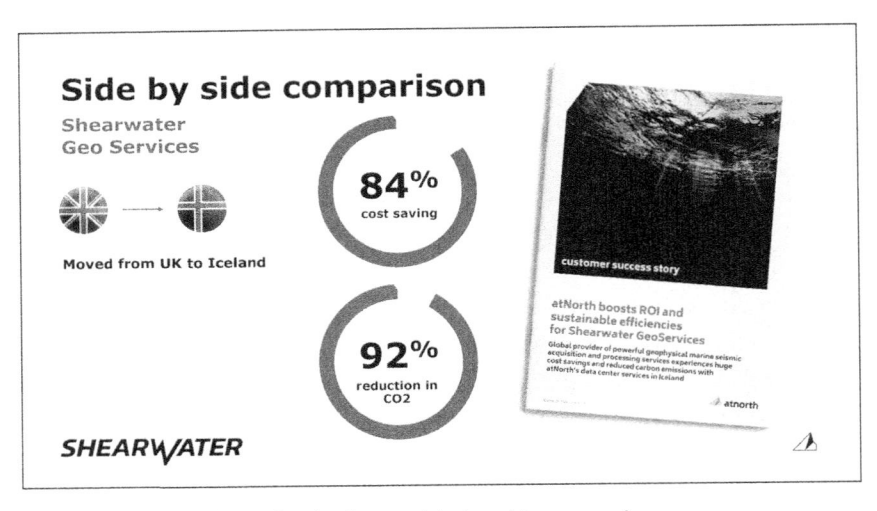

Decarbonization: a side-by-side comparison.

New, purpose-built facilities can allow renewable power and innovative cooling technology to deliver significantly lower total cost of ownership because the sites are designed to operate cost-effectively, optimizing energy, reducing waste, contributing to circular economy and minimizing the environmental impact. By utilizing Nordic high-density data centers as a decarbonization platform that offers both efficiencies and competitive advantage, more compute at a lower environmental footprint can be achieved. The current recession will accelerate this trend to Nordic hosting as businesses are also increasingly realizing the financial benefits of going green.

2. From Climate Culprits to Climate Champions: Consumers Will Drive Change

Consumers have a huge responsibility and pivotal role to play in driving more sustainability outcomes in the data center industry. Most consumers today are acutely aware of the climate crisis and the negative impact on our environment. As individuals, we all have a power akin to superheroes — with every purchase, we can positively impact the environment.

Consumers today are not only savvy, but hot-wired to take action and create change. They seek information about companies with every purchase they make — from values to sustainable practices. Education will go a very long way. Most consumers would probably pick a streaming service, internet bank or video chat with a lower carbon footprint if they were given the choice.

While every business faces challenges with implementing sustainable practices in the right way, being honest, transparent, and communicative with their customers is crucial. By first recognizing that digital activities do carry a carbon footprint and then communicating and visualizing this to end consumers, companies can take actionable steps to improve their sustainability initiatives and create long-term value for their business.

More importantly, businesses can begin to enable the consumer to make an active choice when it comes to their digital carbon footprint. Despite strong buying power, consumers are not truly being given a green option in most digital activities. My daughter cannot choose to stream My Little Pony from a data center that uses renewable power, innovative cooling, and waste heat recovery. She cannot listen to her music or call grandma using an application whose processes fundamentally start in a data center purpose-built to be sustainable with a net zero carbon footprint. In this scenario, my daughter is a passive culprit of climate change — we all are, but it

Chapter Thirty

will be this next generation that becomes the real climate champions who demand change.

It is our duty (and perhaps our biggest challenge) to arm the supply chain and ultimately the end consumer with the right information to make this choice, to empower my daughter and future generations (today and tomorrow) to be active digital climate champions instead of passive climate culprits. It is achievable if we work together.

---

1. Rozite, Vida. 2023. "Data Centres and Data Transmission Networks." The IEA. July 11, 2023. https://www.iea.org/energy-system/buildings/data-centres-and-data-transmission-networks.
2. Efoui-Hess, Maxime. 2019. "Climate crisis: The unsustainable use of online video – A practical case study for digital sobriety." The Shift Project. Jul 11, 2019. https://theshiftproject.org/en/article/unsustainable-use-online-video/.
3. Pressley, Alix. 2023. "What factors are set to drive demand for data centre transformation in Europe?" Intelligent Data Centres. May 9, 2023. https://www.intelligentdatacentres.com/2023/05/09/what-factors-are-set-to-drive-demand-for-data-centre-transformation-in-europe/#:~:text=The%20market%20in%20Europe%20is,suppliers%20of%20public%20cloud%20services.
4. Pressley, Alix. 2023. "What factors are set to drive demand for data centre transformation in Europe?" Intelligent Data Centres. May 9, 2023. https://www.intelligentdatacentres.com/2023/05/09/what-factors-are-set-to-drive-demand-for-data-centre-transformation-in-europe/#:~:text=The%20market%20in%20Europe%20is,suppliers%20of%20public%20cloud%20services.
5. Rydning, John. 2022. "Worldwide IDC Global DataSphere Forecast, 2022-2026: Enterprise Organizations Driving Most of the Data Growth." IDC. May 2022. https://www.idc.com/getdoc.jsp?containerId=US49018922.
6. 2023. "Hyperscale Data Center Capacity to Almost Triple in Next Six Years, Driven by AI." October 17, 2023. Synergy Research Group. https://www.srgresearch.com/articles/hyperscale-data-center-capacity-to-almost-triple-in-next-six-years-driven-by-ai.
7. 2023. "Worldwide Spending on AI-Centric Systems Forecast to Reach $154 Billion in 2023, According to IDC." March 7, 2023. IDC. https://www.idc.com/getdoc.jsp?containerId=prUS50454123.
8. 2023. "Investing in the rising data center economy." January 17, 2023. McKinsey & Company. https://www.mckinsey.com/industries/technology-media-and-telecommunications/our-insights/investing-in-the-rising-data-center-economy#.
9. Caton, Emma. 2023. "Europe warming twice as fast as other continents." June 26, 2023. Natural History Museum. https://www.nhm.ac.uk/discover/news/2023/june/europe-warming-twice-as-fast-as-other-continents.html.

10. 2023. "The impact of the AI Boom on the European Data Centre Market." October 2023. CRBE. https://mktgdocs.cbre.com/2299/20720f67-81c1-4d1c-b262-918199ea2dbc-539424452.pdf.
11. Merriman, Chris. "In search of the perfect data center environment." November 13, 2023. Data Center Dynamics. https://www.datacenterdynamics.com/en/marketwatch/in-search-of-the-perfect-data-center-environment/
12. Pressley, Alix. 2023. "Next-gen HPC delivers sustainability, efficiency and lower TCO for BNP Paribas." June 7, 2023. Intelligent Data Centres. https://www.intelligentdatacentres.com/2023/06/07/next-gen-hpc-delivers-sustainability-efficiency-and-lower-tco-for-bnp-paribas/.
13. atNorth. 2023. "atNorth boosts ROI and sustainable efficiencies for Shearwater GeoServices." September 7, 2023. atNorth. https://www.atnorth.com/insights/shearwater-customer-success-story.

About the Author

FREDRIK JANSSON

In his role as Chief Strategy and Marketing Communications Officer, Fredrik oversees atNorth's global strategy, marketing and communications initiatives. Fredrik joined the atNorth executive team in 2023, with nearly 20 years of experience in IT services and data centers including several executive positions at DigiPlex, STACK Infrastructure, and Tata Consultancy Services (TCS). A winner of over 50 awards for excellence, he is passionate about transformation initiatives that underpin continued rapid growth. Fredrik is widely quoted in both Nordic and international media on topics ranging from digitalization to sustainability and the data center's role in society, to corporate brand building and business transformation in a fast-paced global environment.

Fredrik holds a Masters of Science degree in Business & Economics and is globally educated through university studies in France (INSEAD), UK (London Business School), USA (Harvard Business School, Kellogg; Northwestern & University of Florida), Ireland (Trinity College Dublin) and Sweden (Uppsala University). Based in Stockholm with his wife and two children, Fredrik enjoys travelling, playing floorball and gardening in his spare time.

Part IV

BUILDING THE BUSINESS CASE: THE FINANCIAL & SOCIAL BENEFITS OF GOING GREEN

THIRTY-ONE

Reconstructing the Business Case for Data Center Sustainability

LEAD ANALYST: MARY ALLEN, INSIGHTAAS

Report Contributors: Peter Panfil, Vertiv; François Sterin, Data4; Michael Borron, Cushman & Wakefield; Peter Nisbet, Edenseven; Dean Boyle, EkkoSense

Defining the '3P' Business Case

Data center investment in the programs and technologies that improve environmental performance sway in response to market cycles, with the pendulum landing on 'more' in times of relative prosperity and 'less' when it's time for belt tightening. Green IT was born in the decades of economic expansion leading up to the year 2000; sustainability discussions were quietly shelved in favor of 'uptime' and 'reliability' in the period of economic malaise that struck in 2007 and lingered to the middle of the next decade. And in recent years, the modest growth that bookmarked the pre- and post- Covid 19 periods, coupled with increasing climate consciousness, has fostered a resurgence of interest in data center sustainability. While these patterns may only offer a rough calculus of the correlation between global economic trends and action on sustainability, they do underscore a common assumption that has served to justify varying levels of focus on sustainability in the data center world: when the economic climate allows an organization to invest appropriately, data center strategy expands to address the 'twin ecos' – ecological and economic benefits.

In this construct, the business case for sustainability is defined largely in financial terms. Aligning with conventional corporate mandates, the financial business case has inspired impressive momentum on sustainability, with innovation in the data center industry creating the efficiencies needed to balance out growth in sectoral carbon emissions associated with increased service demand.[1] Today, however, the swinging pendulum has slowed to full stop, as traditional assumptions and models prove insufficient to master our current challenge – the need to reconcile industry growth and the demands of the looming climate crisis. Exponential increases in the data generated through the advance of digitization and rising global need for social, mobile, analytics and cloud services are driving unprecedented growth in the data center sector: measured by power consumed to feed in-house servers, data center demand in the US (which accounts for approximately 40% of the global market) is forecast to grow at a rate of 10% per year from 2022 to 2030.[2] Along with investment in the sector by capital rich, non-traditional players, burgeoning demand is translating to a building boom: according to the Synergy Research Group, global spending on data center construction will achieve a CAGR of 5.4% over this same period.[3]

While mounting demand translates to significant opportunity for data center owners and investors, market pressure may also impact progress on sustainability. Today, vacancy rates for new data center sites are at an all-time low – 2.9% in the US – with development constrained by limited power availability and rising land costs, particularly in mature markets.[4] For operators looking to get to market quickly to capitalize on the emerging AI, IoT, and quantum revolutions, options are limited. With more demand than supply, operators will build where they can, with whatever energy grid is available, a response that will test plans for sustainable operation. Current market conditions could mean that widespread development of the ideal data center, built on high efficiency and clean power, will remain aspirational as power availability and time to market needs act as constraints on full blown sustainability.

But what if other dynamics also play a role, and what if other issues can drive responsible data center development? What if new, more strategic thinking can replace transactional calculations to position data center activities in a broader context with longer term outlook? What business viability risks might arise if sustainability is not addressed – or how might the calculus change if the value in addressing ecosystem and community outreach is factored into the equation? Then we support data center growth with the "triple ecos" – ecology, economy, and ecosystem – an approach that parallels classical "3 P" definitions of sustainability, even as it works to ensure the long-term viability, the sustainability of the individual data center operation.

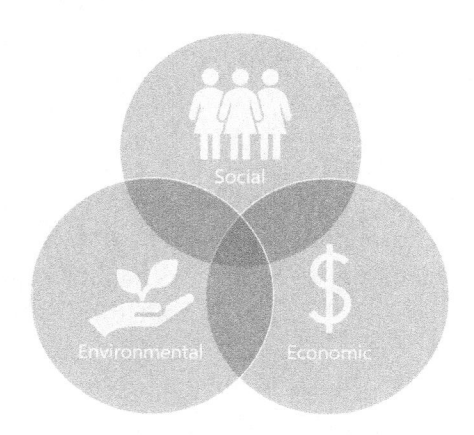

Figure 1. Triple bottom line 3 P's: people, planet, prosperity

Parsing Sustainability Inputs and Outputs: Risk or Reward?

Defined as the methods and processes organizations use to manage risks that might impact achievement of their objectives, enterprise risk management (ERM) typically involves identifying events or circumstances that present threat or opportunity, assessing their likelihood and impact, and preparing a response strategy. The goal is to proactively address risk, in order to protect or create value for stakeholders. Sustainability risk management (SRM) is a subset of ERM, a growing discipline that recognizes the influence that sustainability

Chapter Thirty-One

inputs may have on the organization's financial returns and long-term value. An effective SRM business strategy aims to align profit objectives with internal green plans and policies so that the business can grow while preserving the environment and addressing social and governance responsibilities (ESG).

Risk will vary according to industry, location, markets, regulatory regime, and the organization's objectives. In a data center context, there are several risk categories – events or circumstances that may present threat or opportunity – which can influence operational sustainability or even survivability. Categories of risk that can impact the data center, but which may be addressed through sustainability programming include resource scarcity, resilience, regulatory requirements, and corporate reputation.

Resource Scarcity

The key risk factor for the data center is energy. Historically, land and location (proximity to markets and networks) informed data center site planning decisions. As latency concerns for most applications have faded with advances in communications infrastructure, access to power has emerged as the most significant constraint on industry growth. In many jurisdictions, owners/operators are seeing local restrictions on the connection of critical infrastructure to electric grid systems, ranging from directives requiring audits on energy use and data storage to outright permit refusals, or moratoria on construction of facilities beyond certain MW limits of IT load. Many markets are looking at mandating peak load shedding for new PPAs. As countries struggle to reach Net Zero carbon targets, the ongoing electrification of other industries will only drive further competition for resources – the adoption of electric vehicles (EVs), for example, is expected to dramatically increase overall electricity consumption, as it introduces spikes in demand that can lead to blackouts in aging grid infrastructure. And in regions powered by clean energy, competition for resources is expected to intensify as data centers and other carbon-dense industries look for simple solutions to meeting environmental targets. For data center operators, ensuring access to reliable and adequate utility power looms as a business continuity threat, leading many to explore 'bring your own power' alternatives, including on-site sustainable energy generation and storage, in addition to the introduction of energy-saving systems and technologies.

Similarly, shrinking freshwater resources are urging caution on permitting, particularly in drought-stricken regions, by local authorities who must prioritize citizen needs; data center reliance on wasteful evaporative or open loop cooling techniques is shifting operator preferences for locations in watersheds that are under less stress or towards alternative tactics like greater use of free air cooling.[5] Data centers are also subject to resource risk resulting from supply chain failure – semiconductor shortages during the Covid 19 pandemic is a familiar example – or from the scarcity of raw materials, such as copper, which represents a rising issue. Copper is a critical component in networking, heat exchange, and electrical infrastructure – approximately 27 tons of copper are needed per MW of applied power in data centers[6] – however, market experts predict a supply shortfall due to electrification by the next decade.[7]

Resilience

In the data center, rule number one is 'no failure.' A data center outage may result in compromise of service level agreements with tenants, triggering delivery failure to *their* clients, setting off a cascade of financial loss and reduced trust. Increasingly, risk mitigation plans are factoring in the impact of climate change on resilience, with organizations developing adaptation strategies that extend beyond financial loss to ask, "what does it mean to live with accelerating climate change?" In the data center, this adaptation planning may encompass new siting criteria, response to increased outages due to severe weather events or supply chain disruption, new relationships with insurers, or even the need to address higher outside temperatures with additional cooling – in addition to water and power scarcity. Plans to mitigate these risks are an increasingly important factor in client retention, in the case of large customers in particular who sign multi-year contracts that call for assurance of the provider's viability in the face of climate risk.

Regulatory

Environmental regulation of data center operation varies from region to region, with jurisdictions in the Asia-Pacific region, such as Singapore, leading on ESG disclosures, and the Nordics and Europe also setting standards. In the EU, the Corporate Sustainability Reporting Directive, the EU Code of Conduct for Data Centers, the European Energy Efficiency Directive and the EN 50600 regulations require reporting on energy consumption and carbon emissions, as well as concrete energy reduction plans to drive progress on sustainability goals, such as replacement of backup diesel generators. North America lags behind, though observers expect that a financially driven SEC proposal for a climate disclosure rule to improve the quality of company reported ESG data may soon translate to reporting with more bite in the US. But like most large organizations today, data centers do not operate in isolation; they service clients across continents and may be part of large global fleets – and so are required to comply with regulation in the particular country in which they operate. According to the Uptime Institute, approximately 63% of operators globally believe the authorities in their region will require public reporting of environmental data in the next five years – even though today, just 37% collect carbon emissions data, and 39% report their water usage.[8] Fines for failure to comply can be significant: the recently passed German Energy Efficiency Act mandates that data centers report on environmental metrics, implement an energy saving system, introduce a specified share of renewable energy, engage in energy reuse, and achieve a set PUE value in operations. Maximum fines for non-compliance range from €50,000 to €100,000, depending on the violation.[9]

Chapter Thirty-One

The regulation	Who it affects	The jurisdiction	Data disclosure requirements	Start date	Penalties for noncompliance
Building emissions, Energy reporting	Owners of large commercial buildings	Various US cities & states*	Energy use &/or emissions for buildings, with some requiring reduction pathways*	Various start dates, most beginning in 2025	Fines vary by jurisdiction, most not yet finalized*
SECR	Large companies, private organizations, & LLPs	United Kingdom	Annual energy use & emissions, intensity ratio, energy efficiency measures	2018	Late filing penalties range from £150 up to £7,500
SEC	Publicly traded companies	United States	Climate risks information & GHG emissions information*	Released soon*	Released soon*
SB 253	Companies with $1B of operations in California	California	Full carbon inventory, including Scope 3*	2026	To be announced, not to exceed $500,000 per year*
CSRD	Public-interest companies with more than 500 employees	European Union	Sector-specific sustainability reporting guidelines	2025	Promulgated by each EU member state*
SB 261	Companies with $500M of operations in California	California	Climate-related financial risk & adaptation measures implemented to date	2026	Up to $50,000 per reporting year*

Figure 2. The cost of noncompliance

Reputation

Lambasted by the media as key contributor to climate change and viewed by many regional authorities as a drain on water/energy resources that generates little local employment, the data center industry faces an uphill battle in efforts to rehabilitate its reputation. Many large-scale facilities have taken up the challenge on the sustainability front, investing in environmental systems and clean energy solutions in efforts to position as climate leaders. For the hyperscale data center provider, sustainability has become a market differentiator that builds brand acceptance, employee enthusiasm, and client lists as customers work to improve their own environmental profiles. Compliance with regulatory requirements, transparency, and voluntary reporting are key tactics that can transform this risk to opportunity, which will be missed by data centers that are perceived to be wasteful of resources.

Chapter Thirty-One

Figure 3. 4 R categories of data center risk

Reconstructing the Financial Case

When neglected, these risk factors can impact the longer-term profitability and viability of the data center operation. But when sustainability initiatives aimed at mitigating risk are viewed through the lens of quarterly or annual results, questions emerge. What is involved in creating the uplift needed to adopt the technologies, processes, and training that can help the data center identify and achieve sustainability goals? How much training is needed, what are the costs, and how will the introduction of green programs affect productivity?

Depending on current state and the company's goals, answers to these questions can be complex. In cases where the existing facility is old or located in an area with high power or occupancy costs, a decision may be made to build new with state-of-the art systems, high efficiency infrastructure, and more green material components, though these strategies and technologies can be very capital intensive and take years to implement. In most instances, a useful tactic to kick start sustainable programming is to identify the 'low hanging fruit' – new approaches, technologies, or processes that deliver quick financial returns, inspiring an appetite for more work. Examples would include repurposing existing office or industrial buildings rather than constructing new data center sites, or increasing the temperature in data rooms, a tactic that requires no investment, but pays back in reduced cooling expense. Similarly, use of free air cooling or hot/cold aisle containment involves little capital outlay. In some jurisdictions, such as Quebec, Canada, power from renewable energy resources is actually cheaper than electricity from fossil-fuel generation. Each of these tactics yield savings on cost and carbon.

Since 2014, energy improvements won through low hanging fruit have stalled, with PUE hovering at approximately 1.55[10] in subsequent years. This stasis has called for more sophisticated approaches to driving improvements. A second key principle is to optimize existing assets before introducing new capital projects. For example, rescuing stranded assets from server, power, and thermal perspectives can introduce significant savings on items such as power expenditure. As these represent fixed costs that operators are resigned to spend, savings represent pure margin. Similarly, the deployment of systems and components with advanced energy efficiency capabilities can reduce losses – typically by a factor of two – producing savings that contribute to helpful total cost of ownership (TCO) calculations. With TCO, upfront investments in sustainability solutions may be amortized over time through power savings, rendering expense net neutral. At the same time, TCO methodologies allow operators to better balance progress towards multiple goals: zero carbon, zero waste, zero losses, and zero water.[11]

As high efficiency technologies reduce cooling requirements, they enable the deployment of additional compute infrastructure in existing space. For the colocation provider, this may translate to signing additional two- or three-year leases. For the owner/operator, it may mean accessing additional capacity minus the financial costs associated with new build – and the Scope 3 emissions that come with deploying new concrete, cabling, and other facilities infrastructure. Moving beyond a 'cost first mentality', this lifecycle perspective considers cost and benefits over time, as well as the interplay of different data center inputs to reduce waste, helping the operator realize the opportunity in sustainability as it evolves over generations of technology and business leadership.

Placing data center operations within a broader sustainability context introduces an additional financial calculation. While not

Chapter Thirty-One

ubiquitous, a carbon levy on GHG emissions is now applied in multiple jurisdictions, with more likely to adopt this approach going forward. In these regions, goods and services that emit more carbon in production will pay a higher tax; when carbon pricing is included in data center lifecycle costs, the operator will arrive at an environmental-inclusive 'TCO$_2$' that can inform future-facing business decisions. Carbon taxes vary from market to market, with some jurisdictions pricing carbon high enough to incent investment in sustainability measures, including the establishment of programs that specify preference for suppliers with low emissions and a verifiable environmental footprint. In the race to Net Zero by 2030, a more advanced data center provider that establishes the value in carbon savings can demonstrate more progress on sustainability goals, offering a compelling option for customers looking to deliver on their own sustainability KPIs, and creating for itself a revenue-based business case for carbon accounting.

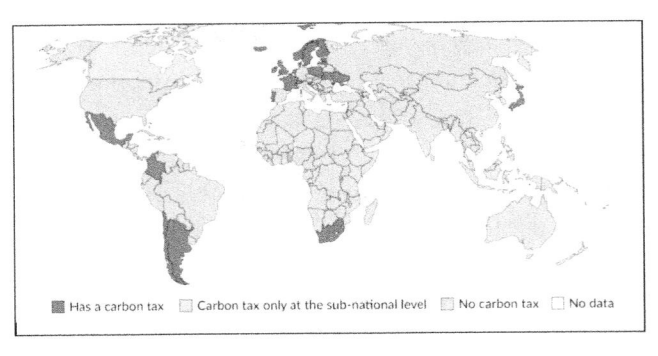

Figure 4. Which countries have a carbon tax? 2022

Building Social License

At a macro level, the data center sector is in an excellent position today. Demand for data services is at an all-time high, vacancy rates are low, non-traditional investors are entering the market to capitalize on growth potential, and technology innovation has enabled ever-expanding capability to support increasingly sophisticated applications that can solve real world problems. But is this the view held by the communities that data centers reside in? With unprecedented growth — a 100 MW facility is no longer interesting to many operators, while PUE improvements are becoming more elusive — an alternate perspective on data center value is gathering strength. In many communities, the sought-after development opportunity is now superseded by a vision of the data center as a competitor for scarce resources, including energy, land, and water, which operates in a secretive way, offering little local employment but causing negative impact on air quality and local biodiversity. This emerging analysis is affecting the welcome data centers receive from local municipalities who can withhold permitting for new build or from regional utility providers who may impose supply limits in contractual agreements. As the effects of climate change and competition for resources intensifies, this divergence is likely to grow apace.

In this context, how can the data center industry recover its image as a good, contributing corporate citizen? How can the data center create the social license that is a precondition to continued growth? The answer lies in community outreach across a variety of stakeholder groups, greater transparency and governance to build trust, and repositioning the facility as a long-term contributor, rather than enemy of social and environmental sustainability.

Empowering the Utilities

Fulfilling the energy needs of power-hungry data centers has become very challenging for many utility providers. Beyond overall consumption requirements, which can be significant in the case of larger facilities, data centers can threaten the stability of the grid. If, for example, the data center chose to remove significant load at the same time, voltages, frequencies, and heat would jump. Utilities are designed to work in steady state conditions with customer continuity; grid updates needed to address key requirements, such as managing demand fluctuation or the integration of distributed energy, are beyond the reach of many suppliers. To reduce pressure on the grid, data centers can engage in a number of activities, such as contracting long term power purchase agreements for clean energy (helps decarbonize the grid), they can improve energy efficiency, powering at least part of the campus through onsite renewable generation, or they can build partnerships with the local utility to enable grid interactivity and support grid resilience.[12]

Waste Not; Want Not

A key sustainability tactic is to reduce waste; in the data center, an economic and effective way to demonstrate commitment to sustainability and the local community is to deliver heat waste to local systems. This typically takes the form of transferring heating to adjacent office structures, but may involve the exchange of heat waste to district heating systems. In Paris, a popular approach is to heat swimming pools, while in Canada, data center provider QScale is leveraging its liquid cooling solution to maximize heat recovery and send excess heat to green houses in its rural vicinity, a priority for government that is looking to support the agricultural sector which is greening its operations. Going forward, finding opportunities for data centers to collocate with utilities and district energy providers may influence siting decisions, as the industry works to secure energy contracts with the utility: doubling the benefit of a single electron can be an attractive proposition for the sustainable data center, the municipality, and the local energy supplier.

Supply Chain Development

Heat reuse projects are not built in a day; they are built over a period of years and require that the data center, utility, integrators, and other specialist industries work together to benefit the broader community. Locating the data center within vacant commercial or industrial space and converting this for use as a district energy hub, for example, may help data centers deliver on their economic development promise as they help develop the skills, templates, and systems needed for implementation of this kind of sustainability project. But contributing to the construction of a healthy, sustainable supply chain is not limited to heat reuse. For example, there is an emerging use case for hydrogen fuel cells in data center backup power, which can replace dirty diesel backup generation, as it bolsters a nascent green industry solution. A municipality interested in green construction jobs or clean energy startups might count this type of innovation as a significant benefit that may be gained through a sustainable data center build.

Education

Knowledge sharing by the data center can work on several fronts to develop community acceptance. Collaboration on sustainable operations can raise awareness as it inspires greater action among industry peers. For example, through engagement with national industry associations and global working groups, a provider such as Data4 aims to de-risk innovation, driving progress on sustainability that can lift the profile of the entire industry in terms of environmental performance. Data4 has also created partnerships with local educational institutions to help prepare students for jobs of the future; QScale works with a local university to explore new use cases and optimal locations for heat recovery projects. Public education may involve opening up the facility to visitors and helping the public better understand the vital role that digital infrastructure plays in creating social and economic value.

Campus Design

Designed for maximum security, the typical data center has loomed fortress like, built with anonymous and impenetrable concrete structures. But it is possible to lift this veil on data center operation, which has served in the past to create suspicion. Improvements to latency and the current trend towards construction of larger facilities that can service future demand have pushed many data centers to locate in rural or suburban sites with considerable acreage. Parks can be created from excess land to welcome the public, and community amenities built onsite to support visitors, such as EV charging stations, or small transit systems to transport guests across large campuses.

These activities – working with utilities, peer groups and associations, supply chains, local innovation ecosystems and educational institutions, and structuring the data center campus to better host guests – can help to revitalize the data center image. In establishing the data center as a good corporate citizen that contributes to community health, environmental performance is a prime mover. Whether it's helping to improve grid stability, reducing demand on resources, innovating to improve efficiencies in data center or district systems, or educating to drive further understanding of strides the industry has made to reduce carbon impact, sustainability serves as the critical input that can encourage the community to engage.

Imagine

Imagine a 'Geoexchange' – a geothermal closed loop water system that acts as a utility to transfer heat across different applications. Throughout this loop sit a series of highly efficient modular data centers that operate close to Net Zero carbon, and contribute heat to other systems – a greenhouse, a swimming pool, sustainable housing, a research center with multiple campus structures, various business services, even a lobster farm – or to storage in the earth. In this distributed resource model, interactions and transactions are made in the community, close to the point of use. Based on the digitization of services, this system is reliant on the data center which provides heat and manages interactions and no longer requires social license as it is fully integrated into the community. The outside of the system is planted with vegetation, and the whole treated as a shared responsibility and shared resource. Imagine a way of living powered by the data center that aligns with sustainability principles. We have the technology and the business case – all that is missing is the will.

---

1. Over the past several decades, IT and facilities innovation has kept sectoral GHG emissions at approximately two percent of global totals.

Chapter Thirty-One

1. Eric Masanet, Arman Shehabi, Nuoa Lei, Sarah Smith and Jonathan Koomey. "Recalibrating global data center energy-use estimates." Science, vol. 367, no. 6481.
2. Srini Bangalore, Arjita Bhan, Andrea Del Miglio, Pankaj Sachdeva, Vijay Sarma, Raman Sharma, and Bhargs Srivathsan. "Investing in the rising data center economy". McKinsey & Company. January 2023. https://www.mckinsey.com/industries/technology-media-and-telecommunications/our-insights
3. Ibid.
4. Jacob Albers. Americas Data Center Update: October 2023. Cushman & Wakefield. October 2023.
5. Michael Copley. Data Centers, backbone of the digital economy, face water scarcity and climate risk. NPR. August 2022. https://www.npr.org/2022/08/30/1119938708/data-centers-backbone-of-the-digital-economy-face-water-scarcity-and-climate-ris
6. Bruno Venditti. Copper: The Critical Mineral Powering Data Centers. Visual Capitalist. November 2023. https://www.visualcapitalist.com/sp/copper-the-critical-mineral-powering-data-centers/
7. Yusuf Khan. Copper Shortage Threatens Green Transition. WSJ Sustainable Business. April 2023. https://www.wsj.com/articles/copper-shortage-threatens-green-transition-620df1e5
8. 12th Annual Global Data Center Survey. Uptime Institute. 2022. https://uptimeinstitute.com/about-ui/press-releases/2022-global-data-center-survey-reveals-strong-industry-growth
9. Dentons. How Germany's Energy Efficiency Act will impact data center operators. October 2023.
10. Uptime Global Data Center Survey.
11. In the past, a favored approach to reducing PUE was use of large, evaporative cooling systems, which consume enormous amounts of water.
12. For more on data center support for utilities and grid interactivity, see "Low Carbon Solutions: Pathways to Energy Maturity in the Data Center," in Greener Data, v. 2. JSA. April 2024.

About the Authors

Mary Allen is CCO at InsightaaS and Sustainability Lead for JSA. As journalist, analyst, and content strategist, she has covered the range of IT subjects for her own properties, and on behalf of clients. Mary created the GreenerIT and Sustainability Platform websites, capping this with a stint as sustainability columnist for Bloomberg BNA, to promote the environmental agenda within IT. She continues this passion in partnership with JSA on the Greener Data initiative.

Peter Panfil is a recognized veteran of the power industry. For over thirty years, he has held executive positions with key power systems vendors, including Liebert, AC Power, and now Vertiv, and is a frequent presenter on power and cooling issues and opportunities in the mission critical space. As VP Global Power at Vertiv, Peter now leads customer development, helping clients deploy solutions to enhance the availability, scalability, efficiency, and sustainability of their infrastructure.

François Sterin has extensive experience working in key infrastructure areas, ranging from backbone network to content distribution, data center, and energy. He has held executive roles in these critical areas for program delivery across all continents, and with major hyperscale operations including Google, OVHcloud, and France Telecom. As COO for Data4, François is now focused on helping the European operator build out a scalable and sustainable platform to support today's rapid growth of digital infrastructure.

Pete Nisbet is the Managing Partner at edenseven ltd a sustainability consultancy (part of the Cambridge Management Consulting Group), who support businesses in developing and delivering net zero strategies. Pete started his career working for SSE (a UK based Utility Company) within their operations team and since then has built a deep understanding of the Energy and Carbon sector having held senior roles in operations, commodity trading and portfolio management. Prior to joining edenseven, Pete was Managing Director for Mitie Energy (the UK's largest Facilities Management Business).

Michael Borron is a Broker and Associate Vice President within Cushman & Wakefield's Global Data Center Advisory Group. He speaks frequently about sustainability in data center site selection, and works with clients to help prepare and structure acquisitions today for a near future in which sustainability means competitive advantage.

Dean Boyle co-founded EkkoSense, a rapidly-growing global SaaS company for data center teams looking to take their operational performance to the next level. EkkoSense has a clear mission to help organizations resolve the thermal risks their data centers face from inefficient cooling strategies. As CEO he has driven the company's development to its current position as a global provider of a disruptive, artificial intelligence-powered SaaS-based data center optimization approach that minimizes data center cooling costs, helps data centers run leaner, and supports corporate ESG programs.

THIRTY-TWO

The Open Data Center: Sustainability Proves the Case for Next Generation Build

François Sterin, Data4 – Mary Allen, InsightaaS

The Practitioner's Dilemma

Recently, we welcomed a delegation of representatives from local communities around Paris to our campus. At the start of my presentation, I was met with a question I could not refuse: "Could you please sign our petition to reject a local data center project?" Attendees at the meeting were clearly divided: our local mayor is a committed supporter of data centers, but others in the room had more reservations. My reaction to the petition was also divided. As a committed environmentalist, how could I ignore the protesters' concerns? But as a data center professional with years of experience building critical infrastructure, how could I work against an industry that provides so many useful services to citizens?

This dilemma is familiar to many industry professionals who recognize both the potential climate impact of a growing data center sector, and our increasing reliance on digital platforms – for convenience, to support productivity, or to solve the world's biggest challenges, including the energy transition. But beyond personal anxiety, the petitioner's invite surfaced new questions for me. What is the source of community concern over data center deployments, and are "not in my backyard" approaches warranted? How can we do better on the sustainability front, while supporting companies' need to demonstrate business success? And how can we effectively communicate the potential for data centers to make a meaningful contribution to the health and prosperity of the communities they serve?

The reaction to this data center development is not unique, but rather part of a growing global phenomenon. In a recent example from the US, industry groups and the community in Loudoun County, Virginia, have opposed a proposed variance to environmental regulation allowing data centers to run diesel generators outside emergencies,[1] while in Germany, the new municipal plan for Frankfurt places tight restrictions on new data center builds to ease competition for land, water, and energy in what has become a rapidly growing data center hub.[2] Frankfurt's constraints on data center expansion follow moratoria imposed in Ireland, Amsterdam, and Singapore aimed at managing resource pressure on local ecosystems.

Not long ago, data centers were sought after by local communities as a vehicle for local economic development. But despite many studies showing considerable economic contribution, their modest impact on local ecosystems has translated to skepticism about the real benefit that data centers provide. As the examples above show, the view of data centers as either an inward-focused consumer of increasingly scarce resources or the source of carbon and other local pollutants – or both – is gaining momentum, and it is one that looms even more ominously in the context of sectoral growth.

At Data4, we are seeing an acceleration of demand for compute services that we have never had before, increases are in line with industry trends. The advance of new applications has led many observers to project huge growth estimates – to 38 GW (up from 13 GW today) for a growth rate of close to 300% to address AI capacity needs, according to one expert.[3] In response to this opportunity, many organizations are planning to build more and to build big – to unprecedented sizes. The Reef Group's 600 MW London data center or the 2 GW Tract project in Nevada are notable examples of the mega centers that might trigger anxiety around resource use and sustainability impact.

Today, local concerns are reflected in greater efforts to manage the industry at a state level. In the EU, for example, tighter regulation of data center operations has arrived with the publication of the European Energy Efficiency Directive (EEED), which mandates energy efficiency reporting in 2024, as a prelude to requiring action. Certain jurisdictions have taken the EEED up a notch: in its draft form, Germany's Energy Efficiency Act introduced last year would require a PUE of 1.2, 100% use of renewable energy, and reuse of 40% of heat waste by 2027, leading the head of the German Datacenter Association to label the legislation "a data center prevention act."[4] While the final Act softened many of the specific (unfeasible) requirements for data centers, it clearly outlines the terms for data center expansion going forward; facilities that operate according to strict environmental practices will be allowed, and others need not apply.

The German case signals the opening skirmish in a longer struggle that will wage between an industry in high growth mode and a society that is looking to ensure responsible development as input to broader decarbonization efforts. But how can the individual data center negotiate the gap that exists between these two imperatives? Crafting a business case that thrives on sustainability principles provides a foundation; communicating a new vision of the data center that appeals to stakeholder groups in and outside the industry will create the social license that is critical to ongoing growth – or even survival.

The Easy Bit – Proving Out the 'Hard Case' for Green Bytes

Data centers have made good progress on sustainability and the environment through the use of renewable energy and improvements in energy efficiency. The "hard" financial business case is now clear. In Europe, renewable energy is now structurally cheaper than market pricing. Power Purchase Agreements (PPAs) in France and Italy can deliver energy for less than 100 Euros/MWH while the current market rate is above 100 Euros/MWH; similarly, in Spain PPAs deliver at below 40 Euros/MWH while the market is above 60 Euros/MWH. In the context of structurally higher energy prices, every investment to improve energy efficiency is even more easy to justify. For example, costs for a new energy management system can be quickly recovered – through consumption reduction and also lower cost energy. In jurisdictions subject to carbon taxes, data centers can shrink costs further by introducing the price of carbon into capital expenses. Using a **TCO$_2$** calculation, where the total cost of ownership includes the carbon offset, carbon accounting can help justify the purchase of the most environmentally friendly version of some very usual equipment, such as switchgear or a chiller that run on GWP alternatives.

At Data4, we have taken advantage of the hard financial case in establishing sustainability goals and plans. We are currently in growth mode – our portfolio spans 34 sites with a potential capacity of 850 MW, and our plan is to build 10 new data centers a year. But we have committed to science-based targets, with the goal of being net zero by 2030, while using as little carbon offset as possible. How do we square this circle? Our Data4Good program describes our pathway to sustainable development. Data4Good consists of four "foundations" with specific objectives: reduction of our environmental footprint using a circular economy approach; social commitment to a good workplace; innovation to build sustainable technical solutions; and community engagement as a committed participant in the ecosystem.

On the environmental front, we have adopted a lifecycle approach to understand and improve the carbon, natural resource, energy and water impacts of our data centers.[5] We have reduced electricity consumption by over 20% over the past few years to achieve a PUE of 1.3 in most facilities through tactics such as the use of free air cooling and hot/cold aisle containment. We use water only to maintain humidity levels and so have reduced WUE (reaching 0.06 liters/kWh at our Marcoussis campus for example), and we reduced CUE by over 15%, through use of low-carbon HVO in our generators and GWP refrigerants in a proprietary air-cooling system. All our electrical consumption in France, Italy and Spain is approved by Guaranteed Origin Certificates, meaning our suppliers commit to feeding a kWh of renewable energy back to the grid for every kWh of electricity consumed, and we have installed solar panels on the roofs of all buildings where this was possible. Circularity strategies provide for extensive waste management, including repair, reuse of equipment, recycling and recovery of waste. For example, as part of efforts to achieve zero waste to landfill, we reuse old concrete in the construction of new data centers, helping to reduce Scope 3 emissions, which make up a significant part of our total carbon.

From 2020 to 2023, our emissions in Scopes 1, 2, and 3 have grown, but less quickly than would have been the case without these activities. A reflection of portfolio expansion, rather than inaction, these increases nevertheless call for renewed effort in order that Data4 keeps pace with net zero goals through expansion. Moving forward, we have committed to the use of AI for the optimization of energy systems, to the eco-design of new facilities with BREEAM certification, to responsible construction practices as per the Green Worksite Charter, and to the use of environmentally friendly materials (ex. low carbon concrete). We plan to locate new facilities outside hot urban centers and near sources of green energy. In addition, we have invested in forest rehabilitation in western France, and have protected a 70-hectare forest at our Marcoussis campus, a carbon sink that captures close to 46,000 tons of CO_2.

The Tough Stuff – Building Social License Through the 'Soft Case'

Buoyed by compelling financial models, Data4 is now executing an ambitious sustainability program. But what is the sound of one hand clapping? How can data centers use their achievements to build the acceptance within the broader community that is critical to growth or even ongoing operation? The next focus for Data4 is to extend strategies for outreach across a range of stakeholder groups, with activities targeted at specific pain points, with an ultimate goal of refreshing perceptions of the data center's social and environmental contributions. We are now maturing the fourth foundation of our Data4Good program – community engagement – through work with the following groups.

Industry Associations

At a national level, we are active in several industry associations. Data4 personnel hold executive positions with France Datacenter and the European Data Centre Association (EUDCA), and we helped to create SpainDC and IDA, the Spanish and Italian data center associations, as well as the Polish Data Center Association founded in 2023. We are also members of the Climate Neutral Data Center Pact. These associations have several missions – to level the playing field so all data centers can compete on an equal basis, to share industry best practices across all industry players, and to ensure that government regulations are aligned with market realities and consistent with each other. Through work in these bodies, Data4 can demonstrate conformity with state-level decarbonization goals, as well as our commitment to driving environmental innovation in peer organizations.

Supply Chain

Procurement provides us with another opportunity to drive sustainability in the industry, on a global or local basis. As a general policy, we are partial to components and materials from suppliers with the best environmental credit and give preference to Eco Vadis platinum certification. In some instances, Data4 has anticipated regulation to push decarbonization of the supply chain – for example, in its purchase of low GWP chillers in advance of the strict EU Regulation on F-GAS, which takes effect in 2025. We also work at the local level, incenting our facility management company to focus on energy efficiency, in addition to uptime.

Educational Institutions

A goal of close work on with suppliers is to create demand for sustainable products. To the same end, we are working with academic institutions to innovate new data center applications and social solutions. For example, to advance university research and digital development, Data4 has partnered with the Sorbonne Center for Artificial Intelligence to build a new AI computing workstation at the university. By providing the infrastructure needed to validate machine learning models, Data4 will support researchers across the Sorbonne's three campuses.

Beyond academic research, we have also launched the Data4 Academy, and now work with secondary schools and universities to train students looking to focus on the environment and responsible digital technology. By helping to fashion future forward careers for students, or through a collaborative program run with local associations to hire young people with no experience or qualifications, we aim to help people, and in doing so contribute to local economic development.

Utilities

Data center relationships with utilities are also changing in response to provider efforts to ensure adequate electricity supply for all customers. While energy consumption increases due to the electrification of new industries continues, grid operators are also under pressure to decarbonize, a double imperative that is putting strain on electricity suppliers. In this condition of scarcity, utilities have identified data centers as distinct and growing consumers that must be tracked, as the graph extracted from RTE, the French grid operator's planning guide (Figure 1) for 2023-2035, shows.[6]

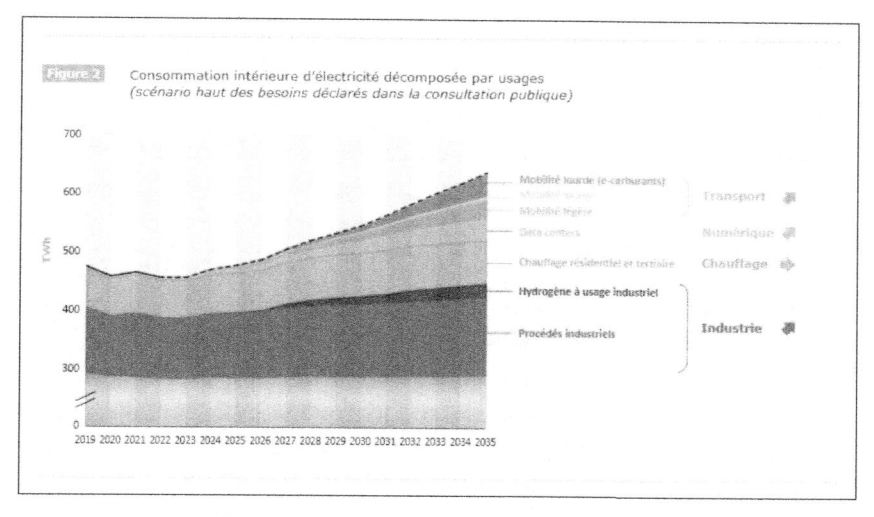

Figure 1. RTE growth forecast for electricity consumption, 2019 - 2035

At a data center level, the utilities' delivery issues have translated to different kinds of conversations. A year ago, operators could look forward to a guaranteed supply; today grid providers are asking for more flexibility in load management. For example, in response to the high voltage grid operator's request that we run our generators for hours, or even days, to address supply shortages in France during the winter of 2022-2023, we developed detailed protocols for that eventuality. And now our development team continues to innovate, looking to deploy a self-generation solution, or onsite electricity storage at scale as a response to grid challenges that might occur in the future. A key test on this front will be how to gain public acceptance for a combined cycle gas turbine, or large biomass plant!

Regional Environmental Authorities

In France, several public players (prefect, mayor, etc.) must give their approval via a Single Environmental Authorization and a building permit for all new projects. In making their decision, these players can refer to the documentation published by the Mission Régionale d'Autorité Environnementale (**MRAE**). For the Paris region, this organization has published a fact sheet describing an active cluster of data centers in the area (more than 20 projects recently built or under construction).

To explain the attraction of this region to data center operators, the authority noted that other regions (including Stockholm, Amsterdam, and Dublin) will no longer permit new builds due to environmental concerns. But the MRAE's chief concern was local pollution from generators, and the waste of heat generated from IT equipment: "A 10 MW data center can heat up around 20,000 modern apartments" was quoted several times.[7]

To work through this kind of concern, Data4 is looking to co-construct these projects with local authorities so that they fully meet local needs. That's why, in October 2023, Data4 signed a governance charter with the Paris-Saclay urban community (Etablissement public de coopération intercommunale) to formalize a win-win working relationship for regulating the development of data center structures. Data4 was chosen for this collaboration due to a unique operational characteristic: "a very clear operational commitment in terms of ecological transition and low carbon trajectory."

This commitment will play out with our new projects in Paris and Frankfurt, which will feature heat reuse on day one of operation. The PAR3 site will connect to a new district heating system in a residential area near the site, and at Frankfurt 1, a local heating company will deploy a heat plant that uses the data center's heat waste. And we also look to solutions for our existing campuses, though heat reuse is not always technically feasible, especially when the site is quite far from potential users of that heat.

Municipalities

With an economic development mandate, municipal authorities must justify new construction in terms of what it can do to support the local community. They share concerns with regional authorities over the local availability of resources, including electricity and water, and they must address local concerns over the impact of pollution from backup systems, refrigerants, noise and light pollution, and land development on biodiversity. And they have control over land use zoning through the granting of building permission. These projects must comply with various regulations, such as the "Zero Net Artificial Development" (ZAN), for example, which limits the conversion of natural areas into "concreted or roaded" areas.

To encourage better environmental performance, Data4 has embedded a Green Dashboard into its customer portal, which alerts users to the impact of running their servers on energy, carbon, water, and rare metals. Along with material on the protection of forests, the company's net zero goals, and eco-construction, this is the kind of information we share in long, patient conversations with local authorities. We have a very open policy on visits and regularly host municipal leaders and regional politicians to inform, raise awareness, educate, and build trust around the sustainability of operations, and the notion that our data center can be good community members.

The Public

Our welcome to politicians and the public is eased through the eco-design of our facilities. While many data centers present as formidable monoliths with daunting security, we have taken steps to encourage visitors (including deer!) by setting aside more green park space, creating better site access, and improving visual design. Neighbors care about the visual aspects of a facility, but with some sensitivity, this concern can be addressed. For example, the Data4 expansion in Marcoussis can be seen through the trees in winter, a visual effect that is new to the local community. To soften the impact of this new construction, we developed specific landscaping and wall coloring to preserve the local look and feel of the original view.

Chapter Thirty-Two

Many of our data center campuses are quite large – some top 200 acres – functioning more like small cities with internal service demand and delivery than as warehouses. For the larger sites, we have introduced smart programs to improve sustainability, with extra attention paid to internal mobility (such as EV charging, ebikes, and trams). The goal is to improve service delivery for onsite staff but also to provide a good experience and environment for visitors. This focus on the well-being of people is quite new in the colocation world, but an approach that we hope can help educate staff, clients, partners, politicians, and the public (including students from local schools) on the importance of data centers and the many ways they can support the local community.

To Sign or Not to Sign

Did I sign the protester's petition? After a visit to our campus where I outlined the steps we are taking to operate more responsibly, the protester countered with: "I wish the other data centers were more like you." I didn't need to sign. But we will need to continue to have active and respectful dialogue with other stakeholders, in which we describe activities that address the specific concerns of each constituency, whether this be around grid interactivity, resource conservation, carbon reduction, eco-design of facilities, or support for research and education. These kinds of initiatives highlight environmental stewardship, establishing sustainability as the basis for a new view of the data center as a contributor – not a competitor – to the community.

The key to success will be to follow talk with real action: trust and a good relationship can take years to build but can be lost in a minute. Today, the data center industry is hitting a wall – site and resource scarcity in a time of hypergrowth is butting heads with social and environmental concerns. This is precisely the time to build the sustainability credentials that will help support community acceptance of industry advancements. If the industry neglects this principle, mixing speed with a forced rush to expansion instead, there will be a higher price to pay going forward. We are now seeing this in heavier regulation and oversight of environmental performance in particular in several jurisdictions. One way or another, the data center of the future will be a sustainable one. By taking the lead on sustainability, data center operators can build with the creativity and innovation they are known for.

---

1. Larsen, Patrick. "Community, industry oppose Loudoun data center pollution allowance". VPM. April 2023. https://www.vpm.org/news/2023-04-07/loudoun-data-northern-virginia-center-diesel-generator
2. Marzouk, Zach. "Why Frankfurt is clamping down on data center sprawl". CloudPro. May 2023. https://www.itpro.com/infrastructure/data-centres/why-frankfurt-is-clamping-down-on-data-center-sprawl
3. Lima, João Marques. "Digital Bridge CEO: 'We believe the opportunity set for AI is close to 38 gigawatts'." The Tech Capital. August 2023. https://thetechcapital.com/digitalbridge-ceo-we-believe-the-opportunity-set-for-ai-is-close-to-38-gigawatts/
4. Judge, Peter. "Germany to pass Energy Efficiency Act, demanding heat reuse in data centers". DCD. July 2023. https://www.datacenterdynamics.com/en/news/germany-to-pass-energy-efficiency-act-demanding-heat-reuse-in-data-centers/
5. All facts and figures outlined in Data4 ESG Report 2022. EN_Rapport RSE DAta4 2022.pdf
6. RTE. Comprendre et piloter l'électrification d'ici 2035l.

Chapter Thirty-Two

file:///C:/Users/MARYL/AppData/Local/Microsoft/Windows/INet-Cache/Content.Outlook/SCYFYCFD/2023-06-07-synthese-comprendre-et-piloter-electrification.pdf

7. "La Ruee vers les Data Centers: Pour des implantations responsibles". MRAE Newsletter. May 2023. lettre_d_information_mrae_idf_mai_2023_no_5_data-centers.pdf (developpement-durable.gouv.fr)

About the Author

FRANÇOIS STERIN

François has extensive experience working in key infrastructure areas, including hyperscale data center, energy PPAs, network backbone, content delivery networks, and even server assembly lines. He has held executive roles in these critical areas to support program delivery across all continents, and with major hyperscale operations including Google, OVHcloud, and France Telecom. As COO for Data4, François is now focused on helping the European data center operator build out a scalable and sustainable platform to address the current rapid growth in demand for digital infrastructure.

François' broad and deep infrastructure expertise has enabled him to speak authoritatively on sustainable programming in the data center. He has elevated sustainability as a core corporate operating principle at Google, OVHcloud and now Data4 through demonstrated success in turning the energy transition to economic advantage.

About the Author

MARY ALLEN

Mary Allen is CCO at InsightaaS and Sustainability Lead for JSA. As journalist, analyst, and content strategist, she has covered the range of IT subjects for her own properties, and on behalf of clients. Mary created the GreenerIT, and Sustainability Platform websites, capping this with a stint as sustainability columnist for Bloomberg BNA, to promote the environmental agenda in IT. She continues this work in partnership with JSA on the Greener Data initiative.

THIRTY-THREE

Responsible and Sustainable Growth of Digital Infrastructure

Dean Nelson, Infrastructure Masons

When I was 11 years old, I almost electrocuted myself. That shock jump started a journey that landed me at the center of the digital infrastructure industry. Today I'm the Founder and Chairman of Infrastructure Masons (iMasons)[1], a professional association that unites more than 6,000 people who design, construct, operate and maintain the digital infrastructure that enables the digital age and the modern, digital economy. Our primary objective is to build digital infrastructure that integrates with every community in an economically, socially and ecologically responsible and sustainable way. To achieve this goal, we must ensure that our presence in every community creates jobs, improves neighborhoods, promotes equality and helps restore ecosystem balance.

None of this was even remotely on my mind when an electric shock set my career trajectory more than 40 years ago. I just wanted to rock out to Cheap Trick in my bedroom! To do that, I cut off the plug from a lamp, stripped the wires and connected them to the wires of a loose car radio I found in our garage. When I plugged this jury-rigged radio into the wall, it burst into flames! In a panic, I reached to unplug it. My hand touched both sides of the exposed wires. Electricity rushed through my body. I keeled over and, fortu-

Chapter Thirty-Three

nately, the connection broke. After I got up, stomped out the fire and carefully unplugged the radio, I grinned from ear to ear. "That was awesome," I remember thinking, and immediately wanted to know why that happened. My curiosity drove me to take electronics apart to try and understand how they work. A decade later, on my 21st birthday, I found myself in Silicon Valley starting my first tech job at Sun Microsystems with an associate degree in electronics from DeVry University. Fast forward 35 years and I've had the pleasure of driving more than $10 billion in digital infrastructure projects across four continents for Sun Microsystems, Allegro Networks, eBay, PayPal, Uber and Cato Digital. While I'm very proud of this achievement, it pales in comparison to many of my industry peers who deploy the same amount every year and, in some cases, every quarter!

In 2021, iMasons reported that the digital infrastructure industry includes 7 million data center locations around the world with a combined capacity of 105 GW and an annual electricity consumption of 594 TWh representing 2.4% of the global electricity draw[2]. Demand for electronic services is forecast to double and potentially triple the size of our industry over the next decade. While many of us in the industry have heard similar growth predictions from the birth of the internet, the cloud and even recently the edge and the metaverse, this time is different. The actual capacity demand increase in just one year is shocking. The adoption of generative AI and the pace of innovation is nothing short of awe inspiring. The hockey stick curve we've all been told about has manifested. I've never seen anything like it in the 35 years I've been in the digital infrastructure industry. It made me want to dismantle the trends and find out why. It also made me pause as I wrote this chapter for *Greener Data - Volume Two*. I believe our industry is at a crossroads. Rapid growth can lead to compromises that we cannot afford to make. This is not a one-dimensional problem, it's a three-dimensional problem. True sustainable growth must be done in a way that is **economically**, **socially** and **ecologically** responsible. Like any ecosystem, there must be a healthy balance for it to thrive. This requires a willingness to be a good neighbor in the communi-

Chapter Thirty-Three

ties where we build and a steadfast focus on decarbonization of digital infrastructure to do our part to protect the planet. We cannot afford growth at all costs.

What is Digital Infrastructure?

In the first *Greener Data* book we defined digital infrastructure as a collection of data center locations that deliver electronic services to people and machines. We then classified data centers into three categories: providers, networks and blockchain. Providers include cloud, hyperscale, colocation, enterprise, government and edge data centers that host websites and enable electronic services ranging from AI applications and data analytics to data backup and online gaming. Network data centers include a range of types including internet exchanges where internet service providers and content delivery networks exchange internet traffic as well as cell towers and base stations that transmit data between people, homes, offices and other data centers. Blockchain data centers include cryptocurrency mining and other peer-to-peer networks exchanging records of transactions. All these workloads represent the rapidly growing consumption of electronic services by people and machines.

Digital infrastructure is as important to any community as its airport, train station, waterworks, power generation, transmission lines and substations. It enables technologies that people use every day to connect, communicate, work and play. Like other utilities such as running water and electricity, digital infrastructure was a curiosity long before it became a necessity. It grew organically, out of sight, out of mind and on the back of analog technology. Early websites were hosted on single servers in office closets and bedroom corners that were reached through dial-up modems. In the late 1990s and early 2000s, the dotcom bubble fueled construction of internet exchanges. In the 2010s, the majority of businesses, governments and institutions began to shift from on-premises server rooms to leasing space in colocation data centers, building enterprise data centers, and moving their workloads to public hyperscale cloud providers. Then, boom. COVID-19 hit. The pandemic-induced lockdowns forced a shift to remote work and online school, boosted content streaming and online gaming, and spurred e-commerce for everything from food to furniture, all of which accelerated growth of digital infrastructure. Then, just as the digital infrastructure industry started to catch its breath post-pandemic, generative AI exited the research lab and turbocharged growth anew.

What shocks me today, is how quickly – over the course of my professional career – digital infrastructure moved from a nice-to-have to the enabler of the digital age. It is woven into the fabric of modern life, visible and essential. Humanity needs it and wants more. It will continue to grow faster than any time in our history. My concern is that the current pace of digital infrastructure growth and our industry's risk-adverse nature threatens to exceed our ability to build it in an economically, socially and ecologically responsible way. Let me give you a real-world example. My colleague at Cato Digital, Karim Shaikh, notes in his Greener Data chapter, "The Ghosts in the Tamarind Tree," that our industry is comfortable with a conservative business model that leaves significant data center power capacity stranded. Our company, Cato Digital, had a software solution to recoup stranded power, but the industry was not ready to embrace it even while facing global capacity constraints that limited their business growth. The primary concern was changing their current customer offerings and the perceived risk associated with it. So, we pivoted. We decided to have Cato become a customer of its own software and show the industry how to confront its fears directly. It is a live example of how we can drive positive economics – and sustainable practices – without compromising. When we lead by example, we can accelerate adoption and drive change.

Technology Adoption

From the control of fire to the creation of AI, the innovation and adoption of new technologies are markers on the storyline of human progress. What's notable today is the accelerated adoption rate[3] of new technologies. The adoption rate is the pace at which a

Chapter Thirty-Three

new technology is acquired and used by most of the public. In the late 19th and early 20th centuries, the adoption rate spanned multiple decades. Electricity took 43 years to be adopted, for example, and the automobile 34 years. Over my lifetime, I've witnessed society adopt seven world-altering technologies, from the personal computer to generative AI. Each of these new technologies had an accelerated rate of adoption compared to the last. The PC took 16 years. Generative AI was globally adopted in less than a year.

Technology	First Appearance	Adoption Rate
Electricity	1873	46 years
Telephone	1876	35 years
Automobile	1885	34 years
Radio	1897	31 years
Television	1926	26 years
Personal Computer	1975	16 years
Cell Phone	1983	13 years
Internet	1991	7 years
Social Media	2004	6 years
Smartphone	2005	5 years
Cloud Computing	2006	4 years
Generative AI	2023	< 1 year

Generative AI burst onto the scene when OpenAI's ChatGPT was released to the public on November 30, 2022. This moment, according to Shelly Palmer, Professor of Advanced Media in Residence at Syracuse University's S.I. Newhouse School of Public Communications, marks the Curation/Generation AI Boundary[4] and the birth of the Generative Era (GE). We transitioned from a time when AI was predominantly used to curate and organize preexisting content to a period characterized by AI's ability to autonomously generate content and solutions. Palmer dubbed the first full year of the Generative Era, GE 1. In the Generative Era, no content can be guaranteed original, according to Palmer. This really hit home as I saw it happening in real time with generated content becoming harder and harder to identify. He asks: What will life be like in GE 10? Exciting but scary at the same time. Generative AI, like the internet, smartphones and social media, will have fundamental impacts on society. It will be used for good and bad. We need to understand those implications and ensure proper governance so that the good outweighs the bad. Governments and corporations around the world are wrestling with these implications as the global adoption rate and impact of AI is moving faster than any technology in history.

I share this context not to debate the societal and ethical implications of AI, but to share the implications for the digital infrastructure industry.

The Impact of AI on Digital Infrastructure

Marc Ganzi, founder and CEO of digital infrastructure fund Digital Bridge, predicts that by 2028 38 GW of new capacity will be required for generative AI alone[5]. According to forecasts from the International Energy Agency, total power consumption by data centers could double by 2026 to more than 1,000 TWh[6]. Some believe these predictions are too large, others believe they are too small, but they all agree on one common theme. Our industry will continue to grow rapidly and we are not prepared for the implications of that growth. Expansion of the data center sector in the US is expected to account for more than one third of additional electricity demand through 2026 and together with heat pumps and electric vehicles account for half expected gains in total demand in Europe. Meanwhile, Africa, Latin America and India are home to 44% of the world's population yet account for just 5% of the global live data center capacity, according to DC Byte[7], a market research firm. Projects under construction, committed to be built or in the early stages of development are on pace to quintuple capacity in

Chapter Thirty-Three

those markets over the next five to ten years. It is clear that every part of the world will have significant digital infrastructure capacity growth.

AI-driven demand for digital infrastructure is also significantly impacting data center design, location and use. Some data center campuses dedicated to large language model training are being forced to locate in new regions that have access to power now rather than in established data center markets that are capacity constrained. On the other hand, most AI inferencing applications are latency sensitive and are driving metro data center expansion and a proliferation of near and far edge data centers deployed throughout cities and towns to provide instant access to digital infrastructure for people and machines. These edge data centers will enable services such as intelligent personalized chatbots and self-driving car communication networks, along with immersive content experiences such as augmented reality and gaming in and out of the metaverse.

What also became clear is that today's digital infrastructure centers of gravity – Northern Virginia and Silicon Valley in the US, Frankfurt, London, Amsterdam, Paris and Dublin in Europe, and Singapore and Hong Kong in Asia – will be replicated around the world. The need for land with power along with data privacy concerns and country-led data-sovereignty requirements will drive this localized growth on every continent. Many of these new data center builds will dwarf earlier generations. A decade ago, 10 MW was a big deal for any data center development. Today, hyperscale dedicated campuses are more than 200 MW and some are pushing into the multi-gigawatt scale. Core data center campuses delivered by most colocation providers start at 100 MW. Near edge deals range from 10 MW to 50 MW and far edge is now up to 5 MW.

Integrating Digital Infrastructure with Every Community

The increased number and size of data centers will impact every community where they are built. For decades, digital infrastructure growth was organic, largely out of sight and out of mind. The industry gained a reputation of being quiet, secretive and opaque. These traits allow our industry to acquire land, power and other resources needed to build and operate data centers without driving up costs and community resistance. Once the infrastructure is live, we prefer to remain out of the public eye. This is rooted in a desire to protect the privacy and security of the data contained inside data centers and transmitted along fiber optic cables. Yet this lack of transparency deepens community mistrust. What's more, seeking privacy through secrecy is an illusion: online maps reveal the location of nearly every data center, fiber optic cable and other piece of digital infrastructure around the world.

Meanwhile, the industry's clandestine nature precludes the authentic community engagement required to hear and address concerns that it employs few people, raises prices for land, consumes an unfair share of power and water, disturbs the peace, disrupts the view and pollutes the air. We as an industry must demonstrate we hear these concerns with steps to address them. We must show up at community meetings, listen to civic, business and government leaders and work with them to find solutions to points of contention. We must do this wherever we establish a presence, from Chicago to Cape Town and Mumbai to Montevideo. The digital infrastructure industry must demonstrate an ability to engage, compromise and adapt to the unique communities it joins.

I'm encouraged by technology platforms such as Ecosystem Intelligence[8] that are helping digital infrastructure developers rethink how to integrate data centers into the local ecosystem and help restore the landscape to its original biome. Companies that embrace this approach have turned local activists working to stop data center developments into data center champions supporting their expansion. Effective integration into local communities means a healthy balance of economic, ecological and social benefits to those who live and work there. Such strategies need to be repeatable so that digital infrastructure can seamlessly integrate with every community, from data center hubs with several gigawatts of power capacity to communities receiving their first 100-kW edge deployment. As our industry continues to grow, every community will have data centers of various sizes to participate in and benefit from the digital economy. To effectively meet the unprecedented global growth of digital infrastructure, we must become good neighbors in the communities we operate in.

Leading on Decarbonization to Protect the Planet

The timeframe of digital infrastructure's AI-driven accelerated growth coincides with commitments from our industry's – and the planet's – biggest companies to achieve net-zero carbon emissions. In today's world, rapid industrial growth and decarbonization are diametrically opposed. As I spoke with iMasons around the world, I learned that our industry's biggest companies remain committed to decarbonization, yet carbon reduction requirements are scarce in the request for proposals sent to suppliers. This is a conundrum that's put our industry's reputation on the line. We know the industry will grow to meet demand. Without a deliberate focus on decarbonization in growth decisions, our industry's carbon footprint will significantly increase and make our net-zero commitments unachievable.

Part of the problem today is that the pace of clean tech lags the demand for digital infrastructure. As a result, carbon debt will increase at least in the short term. We as an industry must track this accumulating debt and accelerate the decarbonization technologies that pay it down. This consistent carbon debt measurement will allow key decision makers to see the impact of their investments and justify solutions that simultaneously achieve economic, social and ecological goals.

In April of 2022, six months before the Curation/Generation AI Boundary, I helped launch the iMasons Climate Accord[9] (ICA), which united our industry on the decarbonization of materials, equipment and power. As we progress this initiative, it will have a compounding effect on adjacent industry efforts. For example, in 2023 the ICA governing body called for the use of less concrete where viable and to specify and deploy new methods to achieve the lowest carbon concrete possible while meeting structural, performance and cost criteria[10]. This effort requires a tight partnership with the construction industry. Concrete, steel and aluminum are responsible for 23% of global carbon emissions, while concrete alone makes up 11% of total global emissions. A tripling of the digital infrastructure industry could mean a tripling of new data centers that use these materials. The industry must implement low-carbon solutions, or it will significantly increase its carbon debt as it triples in size to meet capacity demand.

The ICA has united more than 250 companies on decarbonization of digital infrastructure. We must double down on the efforts to drive investment into solutions to track and reduce emissions. The ICA member companies represent $6 trillion in combined market cap. This is a significant amount of buying power. If we continue to lead with our wallets, we can achieve our net-zero carbon goals while our industry delivers on the unprecedented demand and growth.

Clean Energy Zones

In my role at iMasons, I have the unique opportunity to talk directly with many of our industry's most seasoned and senior executives at formal and informal gatherings around the world. The candid nature of these conversations yields a perspective that's difficult to achieve in other forums. iMasons recently aggregated and synthesized the content of these conversations into our first State of the Industry Annual Report. The report identified four critical challenges to meeting the current unprecedented demand for digital infrastructure: Access to concentrated sources of clean **power**, the ability to find, train, hire and retain **people** to build, operate and maintain digital infrastructure, a willingness to earn a positive **perception** by being a good neighbor in the communities where we build, and a steadfast focus on decarbonization of digital infrastructure to do our part to protect the **planet**.

As we worked on the report, deeper conversations about the challenges around power, people, perception and the planet surfaced a new vision for the digital infrastructure industry: clean energy

Chapter Thirty-Three

zones. These are master-planned towns or city-size areas developed around concentrated sources of clean energy to serve multiple industries, including multi-tenant data center complexes. The size of these zones and corresponding power generation will vary by each market's current capacity and growth trends. In some markets, such as Africa and Latin America, these zones could be less than 100 MW while others, such as the US, could exceed 10 GW. Complementary power-intensive industries such as battery and green hydrogen production could co-locate in these zones. Housing, schools, restaurants and retail in these zones would attract people with an opportunity to gain the skills necessary to work in and support the digital infrastructure and adjacent industries. The zones could also support next generation building materials such as carbon storing concrete that need funding and local, concentrated demand to economically scale. Similar scaling would be possible for next generation clean energy technologies including sustainable storage, renewable fuels such as hydrotreated vegetable oil (HVO) to replace diesel, small modular reactors, hydrogen fuel cells, enhanced geothermal and fusion.

Clean energy zones could enable accelerated growth of digital infrastructure across the established markets of North America and Europe and allow the emerging markets of Africa, Latin America and India to scale faster as they leapfrog many of the challenges the industry faced in the last two decades. Successful development of these zones will require coordination between the digital infrastructure industry and governments, power and water utilities, community leaders, adjacent industries and anyone else who wants to see the digital economy grow in the digital age.

While the introduction of clean energy zones in this paper is new, the concept is not. Over the last year we have seen projects emerge with similar characteristics. Amazon Web Services (AWS) purchased an entire campus on the site of a 2 GW nuclear power plant[11]. The Neom project, under construction in Saudi Arabia, is adjacent to a 3.9 GW renewable power development that is already generating more than 600 tons of green hydrogen every day[12]. These projects will have new, localized, clean data center builds that

Chapter Thirty-Three

are economically and ecologically positive while effectively establishing or expanding the local communities where they are located. The punchline here is simple. We must think differently. What got us here, will not get us there. To grow responsibly, we need to move large data centers to the power, versus moving the power to the data centers. This will enable economies of scale to deliver digital infrastructure capacity that's economically, ecologically and socially sustainable.

Shock and Awe

I was 11 years old in 1979. Little did I know my ill-guided attempt to plug a car radio into a wall socket would lead to such an amazing life journey. I have been a part of seven planet impacting technology evolutions from the wide adoption of PCs, cell phones becoming mainstream, the creation of the world wide web, the launch of social media, the wonders of smartphones, the migration to cloud computing, to today's unprecedented adoption of generative AI. One element has remained constant through all of these innovations: they require digital infrastructure to operate.

Digital infrastructure is the engine of the digital age. It is as essential as food, water and electricity. Without these utilities, the modern world would cease to function. Imagine if we lost all digital connectivity for a day, or a week, or a month? The world's 150 billion connected devices and the 100 trillion sensors behind them would stop. Chaos would ensue. The chance of a doomsday scenario at this scale is highly unlikely, yet its consideration helps illustrate the dependency of modern society on digital infrastructure. Like the steam engine and electricity, humanity depends on digital infrastructure to grow and thrive. Fulfilling the demand for digital infrastructure is not optional; how we meet it is. iMasons believes our industry's approach to addressing these expansion challenges must be deliberate. Responsible and sustainable growth that's economically, socially and ecologically in balance with communities requires collaboration with governments, utilities, development agencies, investors and civic leaders. Together we can

Chapter Thirty-Three

solve our biggest challenges and ensure a greater digital future for all.

Greener data is not just using clean energy or building more efficiently. It is aligning all elements of our combined ecosystems to ensure we are advancing people and the planet while still enabling profits through the infrastructure we deploy across the globe. Without this balance, we run the risk of causing more harm than good. Every person in the digital infrastructure industry has an opportunity to impact positive change, to challenge the proverbial status quo. I hope each of you have your own shocking moment like I did over 40 years ago - something that causes you to be curious and dig in. Find out why we make the decisions we make, what tradeoffs, apparent and unapparent, are included in those decisions and seek a better outcome.

---

1. Infrastructure Masons (iMasons). https://imasons.org
2. "Defining the Digital Infrastructure Industry". InterGlobix Magazine. February 10, 2022. https://www.interglobixmagazine.com/defining-the-digital-infrastructure-industry/
3. Iizuka, Michiko; Suzuki, Izumi; and Ito, Chiharu. Inclusive and Sustainable Industrial Development Working Paper Series. "Democratizing the adoption and use of advanced digital production technologies." 202010.13140/RG.2.2.32787.63523.
4. Palmer, Shelly. "Humanity has Reached 1GE." November 30, 2023. https://shellypalmer.com/2023/11/humanity-has-reached-1-ge/
5. Swinhoe, Dan. "Generative AI is a 38GW data center opportunity, says DigitalBridge CEO Marc Ganzi." August 9, 2023. Data Centre Dynamics.
6. IEA. "Electricity 2024." IEA. January 2024 https://www.iea.org/reports/electricity-2024, Licence: CC BY 4.0
7. DC Byte. https://www.dcbyte.com/
8. Ecosystem Intelligence. https://www.ecosystemintelligence.com/
9. iMasons Climate Accord. https://climateaccord.org/
10. "Greener Concrete for Digital Infrastructure: An Open Letter and Call to Action". iMasons Climate Accord. April 18, 2023.
11. Swinhoe, Dan. "AWS acquires Talen's nuclear data center campus in Pennsylvania." March 4, 2024. Data Centre Dynamics. https://www.datacenterdynamics.com/en/news/aws-acquires-talens-nuclear-data-center-campus-in-pennsylvania/
12. "Neom Green Hydrogen Project." ACWA Power. https://acwapower.com/en/projects/neom-green-hydrogen-project/

About the Author

DEAN NELSON

Dean Nelson is a seasoned technology executive with 32 years of experience deploying $10B of digital infrastructure projects across four continents. Dean is currently the CEO of Cato Digital, a global low cost, low carbon compute platform, the Founder and Chairman of Infrastructure Masons, a professional association of industry executives and technology professionals uniting the builders of the digital age, and the Founder and CEO of Dean Nelson Inc, a strategic advisory and consulting company serving startups, fortune 500 companies and investment firms.

Previously, Dean led Uber's Metal as a Service function supporting Uber's ridesharing business delivering over 100 million trips a week in more than 600 cities spanning 6 continents, as well as UberEats, UberFreight, UberHealth, UberForBusiness, and Autonomous vehicle and UberAir development. Prior to Uber, Dean worked at eBay Inc as the Vice President of Global Foundation Services, which served over 300 million active users enabling over $250Bn of enabled commerce volume annually. At the end of his tenure, his team successfully integrated, then split eBay and PayPal infrastructures into two independent internet companies. Prior to eBay, Dean worked at Sun Microsystems in various technical, management and executive leadership roles. Dean holds four US patents.

THIRTY-FOUR

BYOP: The Path to Utility Independence

Peter A. Panfil, Vertiv

Bring-your-own-power (BYOP) is a strategy in which data center operators deploy low- or zero-carbon distributed energy resources (DERs) on site to reduce or eliminate scope 1 and scope 2 emissions, while minimizing the friction that currently exists between operators and utilities.

As BYOP technologies evolve from their initial role as supplemental power sources to the provision of primary power to the data center, operators with on-site energy generation capabilities will have the flexibility to expand at existing sites that are power constrained, enter new markets without increasing stress on the grid, and achieve grid independence.

Changing the Relationship

Today, data center operators face the challenge of advancing their sustainability initiatives while continuing to build out the capacity required to support increased digitalization and the advancement of emerging technologies, such as artificial intelligence. They must manage this growth in an environment where grid capacity is limited and often stressed by factors such as weather, human error and aging equipment. Pressure on the grid is only expected to increase as digital transformation accelerates and global temperatures rise.[1]

This imbalance between operator needs and utility capacity doesn't just limit the ability of operators to grow capacity to meet the needs of business and society. It can also expose them to rolling blackouts and other issues when demand on the grid exceeds supply.

One result of this situation is increased friction between utilities and data center operators as operators seek capacity that utilities don't have and as utilities attempt to balance the needs of energy-intensive data centers with those of other customers.

A BYOP strategy enables a more collaborative relationship between data center operators and utilities. It can also help operators advance sustainability, lower energy costs, maintain continuity during periods of high utility demand, and pave the way to energy independence and net-zero operations.

This strategy is already gaining a foothold among large operators as key technologies in the BYOP portfolio advance to meet the current and future requirements of data center operations.

The Role of BYOP in the Evolution of Data Center Power

In the traditional data center power architecture, an uninterruptible power supply (UPS) system ensures power from the grid is of acceptable quality for use by microelectronic systems and also powers the load during short-term interruptions through its connected battery system. For outages that exceed UPS battery runtime, the load is typically transferred to a backup generator capable of providing continuous power through extended outages.

That architecture has proven effective at ensuring data center systems remain highly available as demands on those systems – and the frequency of disruptive events such as extreme temperatures, wildfires and hurricanes – have increased. But it will prove inadequate to meet the capacity, flexibility, and sustainability requirements of the future.

Emerging BYOP technologies provide operators with the ability to maintain continuity while reducing the environmental impact of their power systems, support utilities in maintaining grid stability, and remove power constraints to growth and expansion. Establishing on-site energy resources also eliminates inefficiencies that result from the transmission and distribution of electricity from central power plants to local users. As much as 5% of the electricity distributed on the grid is dissipated in transit.

One of the key drivers in the adoption of BYOP technologies in the near term is the desire by operators to reduce their reliance on backup generator systems. Using a diesel generator to support every power interruption that can't be covered by the short-term UPS battery system is an inefficient use of that resource and contributes scope 1 emissions to the data center's environmental footprint every time the generator is started.

According to the U.S. Energy Information Administration, electricity customers in the U.S. averaged just seven hours of power interruptions in 2021 from all events.[2] This suggests that most disruptions are shorter than eight hours in duration. In reality, this trend is prompting operators to consider deploying intermediate-duration backup power systems. These systems support outages that extend beyond the capabilities of the UPS battery system but are not long enough to warrant the use of a backup generator.

In the long term, operators could look to Battery Energy Storage Systems (BESS), fuel cells, or other technologies such as linear generators to further extend their ability to operate through outages without engaging diesel generators. Once established, these technologies will ultimately enable operators to establish microgrids that power data centers continuously from on-site energy resources with the utility serving as a backup power source.

How BYOP Enables Good Grid Citizenship

The addition of on-site DERs enables data center operators to become electricity generators as well as electricity consumers. This doesn't mean operators will seek to make money by selling excess electricity back to the utility or to other organizations. Their goals in adopting BYOP technologies are to use every watt they generate as efficiently as possible, reduce greenhouse gas emissions, lower energy costs, and protect themselves from grid instability. However, on-site power generation does enable them to actively support the grid community of which they are a part through frequency regulation and demand management programs that benefit all users.

Utilities must continually balance supply and demand on the grid to keep the voltage and frequency of the electricity being provided to customers within the proper range. When demand exceeds supply, voltage and frequency drops. This creates a power rebound effect that is like stretching and releasing a spring and could cause the system to become unstable. Data center operators with on-site power storage or generating capacity can participate in frequency regulation programs in which the operator provides electricity to the grid to help balance supply and demand and maintain power stability. Utilities typically provide financial incentives to customers who participate in frequency regulation programs.

With demand management, the operator uses their on-site energy storage or generating resources to reduce their consumption from the grid during periods of high demand. This benefits both the operator and the utility.

Utility costs vary by time of use with costs highest during periods of peak demand. Operators with on-site power storage or generation can monitor and predict the utility load and proactively respond to power consumption peaks by activating local BYOP energy resources to prevent peak demand charges, or they can consistently use their on-site resources to reduce their demand during times of the day when costs are highest. By reducing their demand on the grid during periods of extreme peaks, operators support the utility and other grid customers by helping to prevent the need for extreme demand management measures such as rolling blackouts. When used as primary data center power sources, DERs enable expansion at power-constrained sites or expansion into new markets where utility capacity is limited.

Chapter Thirty-Four

Key BYOP Technologies

The benefits of a BYOP strategy are compelling and various technologies and strategies are evolving to enable operators to capitalize on these opportunities.

Long-Duration Energy Storage

UPS systems have historically been deployed with just enough energy storage to bridge from the utility to the local generator and then back again. This was due in part to the size and weight of the valve-regulated lead-acid (VRLA) batteries traditionally used with UPS systems. However, with the emergence of higher-density and more compact lithium-ion batteries for UPS systems, some operators are beginning to rethink this strategy. In an effort to reduce generator starts, they are adding additional energy storage to ride through outages for longer periods without transferring to a generator. These longer-duration battery systems are typically sized to support 30 minutes to four hours of operation with transfer to the generator only being required for outages that exceed the runtime of the long-duration battery system.

Battery Energy Storage System (BESS)

A BESS uses similar core technology as long-duration battery systems, but there are key differences between the two systems. A BESS is usually connected to the critical load at the same point as the local generator and sized to support the load for one to eight hours. The BESS can be charged by electricity from the grid or on-site alternative energy power sources, including renewables. In addition, a BESS includes a power conversion system (PCS) to convert the DC power generated by the batteries into AC current, which can then be used to power on-site systems or supply electricity to the grid. This makes the BESS a highly versatile energy resource.

The batteries in a BESS must be able to handle many charge/discharge cycles at varying levels, including deep discharge, without significantly degrading their capacity or life. Lithium-ion batteries have the charging characteristics and lifecycle that make them suitable for BESS deployments and are the dominant battery technology used in current BESS packages. There are a range of emerging battery technologies that may prove suitable for BESS deployments in the future, including nickel zinc, sodium ion, and aluminum air.

Fuel Cells

Fuel cells generate power rather than storing it and, therefore, can provide intermediate- or long-duration backup power as well as potentially providing primary power to the data center. Like batteries, fuel cells are classified mainly by the electrolyte used, which in turn determines the fuel characteristics, operating temperatures, transient conditions, and ultimately, the electrical performance of the system. For data center applications, two types of fuel cells have the required characteristics: proton-exchange membrane (PEM) and solid oxide fuel cells (SOFCs).

PEM fuel cells use hydrogen as their fuel source and feature a solid polymer electrolyte that delivers high power density, enabling a smaller footprint than other fuel cells. They require only hydrogen and oxygen from the air to generate electricity and operate at relatively low temperatures (up to 80° C/176° F), which allows them to start quickly and makes them well suited for backup power applications.

SOFCs use a ceramic compound as the electrolyte. They operate at much higher temperatures (800-900° C/1,472-1,652° F) than PEM fuel cells, which eliminates the need for a precious-metal catalyst but increases startup and shutdown times. Due to their slower start times, they are better suited for continuous duty applications. They are also more flexible in their input fuel, mainly using natural gas but with some designs capable of processing pure hydrogen.

The type of fuel used by these technologies will be a determining factor in how they are used in the short and long term.

Chapter Thirty-Four

Natural gas-powered fuel cells benefit from a mature production and distribution infrastructure that makes a continuous supply of fuel available in many areas, eliminating the need to store fuel on site. Natural gas-powered fuel cells are relatively clean but do generate some greenhouse gas emissions, so may not represent a long-term solution for operators moving toward carbon-free operation.

Using hydrogen as fuel enables fuel cells to operate with zero scope 1 emissions and, when hydrogen is produced from renewable energy through the electrolysis of water, scope 2 emissions are also eliminated. Currently, most hydrogen is produced using fossil fuels through steam reforming of natural gas, partial oxidation of heavier hydrocarbons, or coal gasification. Hydrogen also lacks the robust distribution network that exists for natural gas, requiring hydrogen fuel cells to rely on fuel stored on site and limiting their use to backup power applications. Investments are being made to address the deficiencies in clean hydrogen, including $8 billion by the U.S. government, which is focused on developing hubs for clean hydrogen, production, distribution and delivery.[3]

Fuel cells are relatively slow to respond to load changes, creating transients. The UPS system's energy storage can be used to make up the difference. UPS batteries can also absorb excess power generated until the fuel cell catches up.

Renewable Energy

Renewable energy is critical to the ability of data center operators to achieve their carbon-free and zero-emissions goals. Renewables' share of the global electricity mix is growing but is only expected to approach 50% of total global power by the end of this decade.[4] That means a significant percentage of the power available from the grid will continue to be produced from carbon-based sources for the foreseeable future. Without adequate energy storage, directly powering data centers from on-site solar arrays or wind farms is impractical because of the intermittent nature of these energy sources in an industry that requires continuous power.

Chapter Thirty-Four

A BYOP strategy can enable data center operators to maximize their use of renewable energy. Battery Energy Storage Systems can be charged from on-site renewable energy sources and then use stored energy to power data center systems when renewables aren't generating power, while hydrogen fuel cells create the opportunity to transform renewable energy into clean and continuous data center power.

Grid Controller

Changing the relationship between utilities and data center operators requires the ability to receive messages from the grid and to coordinate supply and demand processes to enable DERs to respond to grid requests for frequency regulation, demand management, or loss of utility power.

This is best executed through a decentralized digital grid control system capable of automating processes to provide necessary coordination in generation, power distribution, and consumption. The controller must be able to manage DERs, the switching logic, islanding logic, and energy demand with a high degree of sophistication. For example, if a loss-of-utility message is received in advance of a rolling blackout, the grid controller must enable a synchronized disconnect from the grid and startup of DERs to ensure a "flicker-free" transition from utility to local power.

DER Management System

Today's UPS systems are evolving to add capabilities that enable the management of multiple distributed energy resources (DERs) for backup or primary power. The first step in that evolution has already begun with the introduction of grid-interactive UPS systems. This capability allows the UPS to use longer duration energy storage to enable grid services such as frequency regulation and demand management.

The UPS and battery systems also enable the use of fuel cells for backup or primary data center power by using the battery system to

Chapter Thirty-Four

absorb the transients in the fuel cell output in response to demand changes. In this instance, the fuel cell is used like a continuous-duty battery. Next-generation UPS control technology will enable more sophisticated DER management, such as automatically switching between multiple energy resources based on quality, cost and other factors.

Enabling Energy Independence and Net-Zero Operations

While long-duration batteries, fuel cells, and battery energy storage systems each deliver value independently, their real potential is unlocked when they are used in concert to enable a microgrid.

A microgrid is a self-sufficient energy system that serves a discrete geographic footprint, such as a mission-critical site, using one or more distributed energy resources that produce power either directly with fuel cells or from stored energy as with a BESS.

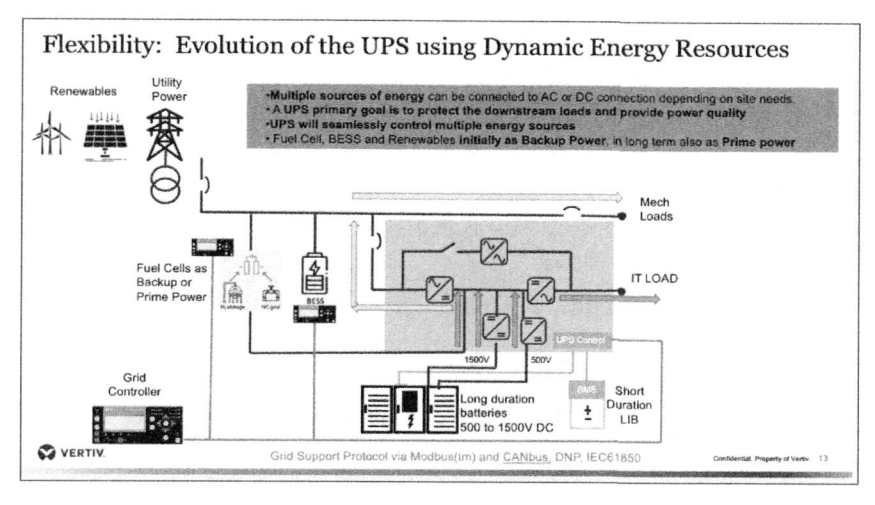

Figure 1

One scenario for how distributed energy resources can work together to create a microgrid is shown in Figure 1. In this example, a long-duration battery system supports utility outages of up to four hours, and the BESS is sized to provide backup power for up to eight hours while also supporting frequency regulation and demand management. Fuel cells are used for extended backup power and primary power. If renewable energy sources are available, they can be used to charge the BESS.

These systems are managed by the DER Management System, which also provides the traditional UPS functions of protecting downstream loads and ensuring power quality. The DER Management System works with the Grid Controller to respond to requests for frequency regulation and demand management, choosing the DER that is best equipped to meet data center or grid power requirements.

Because of their faster start times, PEM fuel cells support data center backup power requirements using hydrogen stored on site. SOFCs tap into the existing natural gas network to deliver continuous power to support some or all of the data center load. When fuel cells are supporting the data center load, the grid serves as a backup power source.

There is some concern today over the physical space required to support microgrids. PEM fuel cells in their current configuration generally have a larger footprint than a generator with a similar output and SOFCs are less dense and so require even more space per kW of energy produced. In addition, 24 or 48 hours of backup power can require multiple tube trailers of hydrogen to be stored on site.

These logistics issues are being addressed through a combination of design innovation and investments in clean energy. Solution providers are developing modular energy storage and generation packages that can be expanded vertically to enable higher outputs in smaller footprints. Simultaneously, as noted previously, investments in hydrogen infrastructure will reduce the need for on-site storage.

As progress is made on expanding the production and distribution of clean hydrogen, the use of natural gas can be phased out and this microgrid could support true net-zero operation with high availability and reduced reliance on the grid to support growth and expansion.

Chapter Thirty-Four

Managing Growth and Sustainability

BYOP technologies address the key power challenges data centers face today while enabling operators to become good grid citizens.

Packaged lithium-ion battery energy storage systems are available today that enable operators to significantly reduce their dependence on diesel generators while also supporting their utility partner in protecting grid stability and capacity. Both PEM and SOFC fuel cells have been successfully piloted in data center applications and commercial solutions are on the horizon as of this writing. As has occurred with lithium-ion batteries, the cost-per-kilowatt for these solutions is expected to decline and, when total costs are considered, they could soon be cost competitive with existing technologies while offering significant sustainability benefits.

How these technologies are applied will depend on the specific goals and pain points each critical space operator is facing. For example, operators deploying high-heat load equipment racks, such as those used to support AI, will need to maintain the continuity of the refrigerant-based cooling system when the generator bus goes down with the utility. To avoid increasing the load on the IT critical bus, the cooling system can be supported by an always-on energy source such as a BESS.

If the goal is reducing generator starts, additional energy storage or a BESS can be deployed to eliminate generator starts during short-to-medium duration outages, or hydrogen-based fuel cells can be used for backup power during longer-duration outages. A similar strategy could also be employed in support of the goal of carbon footprint reduction.

The goal of using microgrids to achieve true net-zero operation remains somewhat dependent on the development of clean hydrogen production and distribution; however, technologies such as BESS and fuel cells can be used to address a wide range of power challenges by alleviating power constraints and managing costs in a reliable and sustainable way as these capabilities are developed.

Chapter Thirty-Four

1. "The World Just Sweltered Through Its Hottest August on Record." National Oceanic and Atmospheric Administration; September 14, 2023
    https://www.noaa.gov/news/world-just-sweltered-through-its-hottest-august-on-record
2. "U.S. Electricity Customers Averaged Seven Hours of Power Interruptions in 2021." U.S. Energy Information Administration. November 14, 2022.
    https://www.eia.gov/todayinenergy/detail.php?id=54639
3. "Biden-Harris Administration Announces Regional Clean Hydrogen Hubs to Drive Clean Manufacturing and Jobs." White House news release. October 13, 2023. https://www.whitehouse.gov/briefing-room/statements-releases/2023/10/13/biden-harris-administration-announces-regional-clean-hydrogen-hubs-to-drive-clean-manufacturing-and-jobs/#:~:text=President%20Biden's%20Bipartisan%20Infrastructure%20Law,delivery%2C%20and%20end%2Duse
4. "The Energy World Is Set to Change Significantly by 2030, Based on Today's Policy Settings Alone." IEA news release. October 24, 2023.
    https://www.iea.org/news/the-energy-world-is-set-to-change-significantly-by-2030-based-on-today-s-policy-settings-alone

About the Author

PETER A. PANFIL

Peter A. Panfil is the Vice President of Global Power at Vertiv, where he leads strategic customer development for the Vertiv power business. He is skilled at solving customer challenges with the latest power and control technologies, delivering availability, scalability, and efficiency levels to meet diverse customer and sustainability needs. Approaching 30 years in the critical infrastructure space, he has held executive positions including VP Engineering and VP/GM AC Power prior to his current responsibilities. He is a frequent presenter and spokesperson for industry trade shows, conferences and media outlets serving the IT, facilities and engineering industries.

THIRTY-FIVE

Cross Pollination: People, Business & Biodiversity Working Together

Garry Connolly, Host in Ireland

Data centres are at the crossroads of two of the five "megatrends" that will shape our world over the course of this century - digitalisation and decarbonisation. Here in Ireland, that is a precarious place as the pressure to decarbonise is complicated by an ageing energy infrastructure and decision making that feels immune to recognising the economic benefits the digital infrastructure industry brings to the country. There is a growing risk that the disconnect between data centres, the communities they reside in and the economy they support could have serious consequences.

Historically, it's not uncommon for instruments of change to face pushback. Whether it was the printing press, the steam engine, or the Model T, there were naysayers and resistance. The data centre industry is not necessarily known as a beacon of community either, rather it is often seen as a world of secrecy and isolation, with facilities hidden away from public view.

The ability to engage with local communities is more important than ever before. There is a need to break away from traditional behaviours and build bridges with those around us. It's not just about hosting data; it's about being an integral part of the local fabric. Data centres are not merely running in parallel with modern society, they are here because of it.

At Host in Ireland, we believe in success through collaboration. In collaboration, we find strength and a common purpose, and that together, we can shape a future where data centres are not just isolated facilities but integral members of the communities they serve. Local councils and governments need to better understand how data centres work for the betterment of the local community, which requires building trust. Nothing builds trust more than seeing an industry doing something to improve the community. Creating opportunities to "pay it forward" can benefit everyone in the long run.

Community Building Through Biodiversity

Biodiversity is one area of common purpose where data centres can collaborate with their local communities. We can be environmentally responsible and contribute positively to the community around us. Sadly, the time has come when awareness and advocacy may not be enough. Execution and action are what is needed to protect and enhance biodiversity. There is a real opportunity to change the narrative and demonstrate that data centres can be sustainable, eco-friendly, and community-oriented.

This philosophy is what drove the creation of Host in Ireland's DCs for Bees programme[1]. It's built on a simple premise: everyone knows what a bee is and most of us are aware that our pollinators are in danger. The more you dig into it, you realise that we aren't just saving bees, but saving ourselves as 70% of our food crop is dependent on pollinators. It's becoming increasingly important to do all we can to protect and enhance bee habitats and their food sources.

The DCs for Bees programme provides a means for purpose-based community activity to encourage biodiverse habitats in our local areas. Much of this effort is driven by the desire of individuals within the data centre industry to make a difference to their local biodiversity. Whether it is the world's first data centre industry-

Chapter Thirty-Five

specific "Pollinator Plan" with 42 individual pollinator-friendly actions or "Difference Days" where anyone can get their hands dirty to make a difference or "Orchards in the Community" where families of all ages are coming together to plant fruit trees, each element of the programme is designed to empower a single person to enact change as part of a common, greater purpose.

I have been inspired to take my own individual actions. Earlier this year, I learned about the depletion of natural habitats that endangered wild solitary bees call home. Solitary bees don't live in hives like honeybees, so they need other places to lay their eggs. I went about creating 1,000 bee hotels – or "Air Bee & Bees", if you like – to provide these bees with safe and suitable nesting spots. Working with a local furniture manufacturer, I took off-cuts of wood and drilled holes in them to create safe nesting habitats for these solitary bees. We now have hundreds of bee hotels scattered across Ireland and the UK providing much needed homes for these pollinators. A simple action by one individual for a greater purpose.

The fastest growing component of the DCs for Bees programme has been "Orchards in the Community". We believe it's a true sign of success that community groups now drive demand for orchards. Nearly 300 community groups and schools - from Tidy Towns, Community Gardens, residents associations, men's sheds, biodiversity groups, agro forests, beekeepers, sports and health clubs, and more - have gotten involved with or benefitted from the programme.

Some have planted trees to rejuvenate existing orchards. Others are rewilding land to repair damaged ecosystems and restore landscapes. Schools are receiving orchards to become part of the life science curriculum focusing on fruit and insects. Charities are also reaping the benefits with orchard donations to beautify the landscape and enhance the experience for their beneficiaries.

One of the communities involved with the project, Abbeyleix, was recently recognised as the winner of the SuperValu TidyTowns competition for 2023. The Abbeyleix Orchard Project is part of an effort by the town to create an attractive and functional landscape that delivers in terms of recreation, habitat, food and climate[2]. Orchards from the DCs for Bees programme have been planted throughout the town. These orchards play an important role in the community, providing a focal point and gathering space where people and nature can successfully work together. Abbeyleix has embodied the spirit of community we hoped for when creating the programme.

Managing for Unintended Consequences

From the start, we let science be our north star. We knew as the programme grew that focusing on orchards was the right decision for the right time. Socially, orchards not only promote biodiversity but also serve as communal spaces, enhancing social connections, as demonstrated by Abbeyleix. They offer urban green spaces, enriching the environment and fostering community engagement.

Scientifically, we wanted to ensure we were mitigating any unintended consequences of our actions. From the beginning, we made the conscious choice to work alongside the National Biodiversity Data Centre and the All-Ireland Pollinator Plan. These organisations are leading the way in reversing the trend of the reduction of bees in Ireland through research-based, ethical and indigenous methods. This collaboration ensures the actions we took were as impactful as possible.

As part of this collaboration, we have been able to help jump-start the creation of pollination corridors throughout Ireland. Because the orchards distributed as part of the programme are all the same type and species of fruit tree and planted in multiple locations during one growing season, the Irish National Biodiversity Centre is able – for the first time – to track concurrent pollination success. The 'like-for-like' count will give an accurate picture of the levels of pollination across the country.

Each person/organisation/community group who plants an Orchard is asked to go out and record the number of apples, plums or pears growing on the trees each year and upload this count onto the National Biodiversity Data Centre website. This Pollination Service can only be conducted when the same species of trees are planted during the same dormant window in various locations

Chapter Thirty-Five

around the country.

A Catalyst for Change

DCs for Bees has been an excellent example of how social, environmental, and economic dimensions can harmonise to support a shared cause. It has become a catalyst for how digital infrastructure companies think about biodiversity and sustainability within their organisations.

It's not a greenwashing exercise, but rather a change that opens the door to new opportunities. Conversations have been created with policymakers at a time when they are needed most. Infrastructure and construction projects are actively looking for ways to incorporate nature-positive designs into their developments. The reallocation of land around data centres is being repurposed for a longer-term approach to sustainability with roof space for gardens and wall space for living walls/vertical gardens. Acres of land are being opened up for biodiversity purposes and to be shared with the local community.

Data centre operators are seizing opportunities both in Ireland and abroad. CyrusOne is devising custom landscaping and biodiversity plans for new developments, along with exploring ways to retrofit existing campuses. In Dublin, this includes introducing features such as pollinator-friendly wetlands, native wildflower meadows, green walls with climbing plants, berms featuring native woodlands, the preservation and planting of new hedgerows, and the establishment of heritage orchards. This not only provides vital stops for pollinators like bees but also transforms the perimeters of their campuses into community-friendly spaces for everyone to enjoy.

Keppel Data Centers in Ireland have enhanced their facility landscapes to be more welcoming to pollinators, such as by planting hawthorn shrubs around the perimeter and sowing over 800 bluebell bulbs, both of which serve as excellent pollen sources for bees. Equinix is following suit by incorporating pollinator-friendly designs into their campuses, including planting orchards, pollinator-friendly plants, and installing bee hotels.

One of the founding principles of the DCs for Bees programme has been to not only take action ourselves, but to inspire others to do the same in their local communities. By providing a blueprint and a single sense of purpose, we know we can have a much bigger impact than Ireland and the data centre industry alone.

The programme saw its first international expansion with a "Difference Day" in Northern Virginia in 2022. Working in conjunction with JK Community Farm, 7x24 Exchange, and Loudoun County Economic Development, more than 140 volunteers came together to plant 37 raised beds. These beds are being used for pollinator-friendly crops which will help improve the health of the bee population and increase JK Community Farm's food donation yields by over 20,000 pounds annually. Each raised bed can be utilised for a minimum of 10 years. As each bed is expected to generate enough food for 1,000 meals each year for families facing food insecurity in Northern Virginia, that equates to 10,000 meals over the life cycle of the bed.

The Business Case for Biodiversity

Corporate social responsibility has often been thought of as merely a benefit for improved reputation or employee and customer loyalty, but it can be so much more. A focus on biodiversity is a sign of a forward-thinking company. By considering the long-term impacts of their operations on the environment, businesses can ensure their sustainability and resilience in a changing world.

An increasing number of companies are realising their fates are intricately tied to the health of the planet and are integrating biodiversity conservation into their core operations. In fact, adopting good sustainability practices can tie closely to financial performance. The concept of "ESG Alpha" is that good and transparent sustainable practices can help a company achieve higher returns compared to the market average[3].

The business case for biodiversity, therefore, extends beyond altruism to encompass a strategic and competitive advantage. Ernst & Young has outlined several considerations on why biodiversity is important to businesses. One consideration is that investors may begin diverting capital away from businesses that directly and indirectly cause adverse biodiversity impacts and into those that are "nature-positive."[4] Much as we see regulations coming into play on climate change, the same could happen for biodiversity. There is a motivation for businesses and industries to get ahead of the curve and self manage their biodiversity impact before governments mandate that they do so.

Consumers are also willing to support companies that are publicly stating their biodiversity plans and reject those that do not. In Bain & Company's biodiversity playbook for businesses, researchers highlight how consumers are rewarding businesses who invest in biodiversity efforts. One European dairy business appealed to customers with biodiversity-oriented messaging and saw engagement rise by 20%.[5]

Economic Benefit of Community & Biodiversity

It's not just individual businesses that can see a benefit, but our global economy as a whole. The World Bank reported in 2021 that global economies depend on healthy natural ecosystems. Over half of global GDP is generated by industries dependent on ecosystem services.[6] The World Economic Forum believes there is economic growth and resiliency to be had from ensuring biodiversity as there is a 9-to-1 return on investment. For every dollar spent on biodiversity, there is $9 worth of economic benefits.[7]

On the flip side, there is also real harm that can potentially happen if we let natural ecosystems collapse. Nature loss, including those from pollinators, could cause a drop in global GDP of 2.3% – in the amount of $2.7 trillion – by 2030 if this happens. Not to mention the horrific impact on food security if these ecosystems disappear.

Community engagement has an economic benefit as well. According to the International Association for Public Participation, public participation promotes sustainable decisions by recognising and communicating the needs and interests of all participants, including decision makers.[8] This plays a pivotal role in enhancing the economic well-being of a community. The shared sense of responsibility between local businesses, individuals and government representatives creates opportunities to collaborate on economic growth initiatives.

Ultimately, when a community is engaged, it can harness its collective potential - something we've seen time and time again with the Orchards programme. A community is a concept that can have different meanings depending on the context. However, one that has resonated within Host in Ireland since its inception is the idea of a group of people who share something in common, such as a location, an identity, an interest, or a goal. We have always found a common purpose to work with each other without boundaries or concerns about balance sheets. DCs for Bees exemplifies this even further.

Every drop of water creates a ripple effect. Each one of us has the power to create long-term change. When it comes to biodiversity, the time to take action is now. The digital infrastructure community is going to have to work harder than ever to align with global sustainability and biodiversity targets. It's for all our benefit to make the world a more habitable and sustainable place. We have the technology and the tools at hand to make a difference with our infrastructure. We need to take that same energy and demonstrate our commitment to our local communities by restoring habitats, planting flowers, growing orchards and so much more. When all is said and done, let's get more done than said!

---

1. Host in Ireland. 2019. "DCs for Bees" https://www.hostinireland.com/dc-s-for-bees
2. Abbeyleix. 2023. "Abbeyleix Orchard Project" https://storymaps.arcgis.com/stories/e28db31db1e64d3aaa0d2a7316bf64e6
3. Howitt, Richard. Bold, Frank. 2021. "Sustainability is an Investment not a Cost." ESG Investor. November 19, 2021. https://www.esginvestor.net/sustainability-is-an-investment-not-a-cost/

4. Gazzo, Alexis. 2022. "Why biodiversity may be more important to your business than you realize." EY.com. April 25, 2022. https://www.ey.com/en_uk/assurance/why-biodiversity-may-be-more-important-to-your-business-than-you-realize
5. Davis-Peccoud, Jenny. Murray, Euan. Seemann, Axel. Morrison, Askin. 2023. "The Nature and Biodiversity Playbook for Business." Bain & Company. July 26, 2023. https://www.bain.com/insights/the-nature-and-biodiversity-playbook-for-business/
6. The World Bank. 2021. "The Economic Case for Nature." The World Bank website. July 1, 2021. https://www.worldbank.org/en/news/infographic/2021/07/01/the-economic-case-for-nature
7. Quinney, Marie. 2020. "5 reasons why biodiversity matters – to human health, the economy and your wellbeing." The World Economic Forum website. May 22, 2020. https://www.weforum.org/agenda/2020/05/5-reasons-why-biodiversity-matters-human-health-economies-business-wellbeing-coronavirus-covid19-animals-nature-ecosystems/
8. International Association of Public Participation. 2023. "IAP2 Core Values." https://www.iap2.org/page/corevalues

About the Author

GARRY CONNOLLY

Garry Connolly is the Founder of Host in Ireland, a strategic global initiative created to increase awareness of the benefits of hosting digital assets in Ireland and Irish companies delivering international data centre projects. A self-proclaimed "stubborn digital optimist," Garry is a much sought-after keynote speaker, panellist and moderator at global industry events.

THIRTY-SIX

Embracing Net Zero Economics as the Path to Sustainability

David Craig, Iceotope

Big problems require bold ideas. Climate is changing and one of the most pressing issues we face as a society is how we are going to address that change. Make no mistake, this will determine the future of our planet. Weather patterns around the world are becoming more extreme with record-breaking temperatures and an ever-growing number of fires, floods and more powerful hurricanes than we have ever had before. Urgent action is needed now.

Sustainability requires a new way of thinking. We are at a unique point in history. Much like a skeptic eyeing an oncoming storm, we have long seen disruptive forces on the horizon. Artificial intelligence, bigger and hotter chips, and the inevitable march of technology – these aren't unknowns. They are inevitabilities. Our IT infrastructure needs to be up to the challenge in the most sustainable way possible.

Yet, we seem to respond to these mega waves of change with an incrementalist approach. In the data center industry, sustainability discussions often become a siloed conversation on energy efficiency, and while important, it's an incomplete narrative. Real change demands a holistic approach, encompassing embodied carbon, IT components, and renewable energy. Shifting the mentality towards responsible resource use, sustainable practices, and systemic change – from design to end-of-life disposal – is key. A comprehensive strategy can lead to greater sustainability gains and provide companies with a competitive advantage that is critical to helping them reach net zero commitments.

The Positive Economics of Net Zero

The perception of sustainability as a financial burden is a lingering challenge for businesses. This is a short-term mindset that tends to overlook the long-term benefits and returns associated with sustainable practices. Part of the challenge comes from the fact that the current total cost of ownership (TCO) models are too narrowly focused on one or two data streams supplying the models. More holistic, well-rounded TCO tools are needed to articulate the benefits of sustainability overall because it is not just a checkbox on an eco-conscious consumer's list. There are fundamental business benefits of good sustainability.

For an emerging generation of consumers – both professional and personal – sustainability is a litmus test for businesses in an era where ethical considerations weigh heavily on purchasing decisions. According to a World Economic Forum report,[1] 66% of survey respondents, and 75% of millennial respondents, said they consider sustainability when making a purchase. Businesses are paying attention and using sustainability as a criterion for vendor selection. Financial service organizations, for example, are leading this effort by incorporating sustainability metrics and targets in their RFPs that go out to bid. Carbon will be a fundamental piece of data to win new business.

Sustainability can catapult businesses into a future of growth or condemn them to a struggle for survival. Companies adopting strong sustainability policies and practices will perform better financially over the long term than those that don't. This is in part due to the idea that those who prioritize sustainability are often better positioned to adapt to changing market conditions, and to attract top talent, build stronger relationships with customers and stakeholders, and manage risks more effectively.

A Gartner study from 2019[2] shows what differentiates winning companies in times of change: "First, progressive business leaders prepare to navigate turns even before the turns are clearly in view. Second, their mindset and actions before, during and after the turns separate their organization from the pack and determine its long-term destiny." Those that invest when change is happening are the companies that rocket and accelerate out of the downturn. Sustainability, when wielded strategically, becomes a catalyst for simplifying supply chains, reducing inventory, and, above all, enhancing the balance sheet.

Environmental, Social and Governance (ESG) policies are starting to be seen as a key driver of corporate performance. The NYU Stern Center of Sustainable Business conducted an analysis[3] of 1,000 studies on ESG and financial performance and found that sustainability initiatives at corporations "drive better financial performance due to mediating factors such as improved risk management and more innovation. Studies [also] indicate that managing for a low carbon future improves financial performance." Better ESG performance was found to correlate with higher annual returns by as much as 3.8%, with a potential compound effect of 20% to 45% over a decade.

Every step we take on this matter is a step in the right direction. Maintaining a collective commitment to sustainability requires a concerted effort across industries. Thousands of companies implementing ESG best practices, tracking carbon emissions, and using less energy will make a difference. Collaborative initiatives, innovative technologies, and transparent reporting mechanisms further solidify this path toward a greener future. The challenge then becomes staying focused on the bigger goals and not getting trapped in the minutiae of incrementalism.

Chapter Thirty-Six

The Cost of Incrementalism

Human nature at its very core is resistant to change. Our brains are hardwired to protect us when something triggers a fear response. As individuals, we see it as fight or flight. As societies, we show fear in the resistance to cultural change. When it comes to sustainability, we can't let fear of bold ideas and new approaches get in the way of progress.

The longevity of sustainability decisions being made right now is akin to a lifestyle change for the data center industry. The right technology solution isn't good for one or two generations, it is a 15- and 20-year life cycle. Decisions and investments need to be made with a long-term perspective. Incrementalism might buy us another 18 months, but it won't get us 20 years.

When it comes to data centers, the dance between power and cooling dictates the rhythm of operations. Take for example a colocation data center that has a 7MW data hall housing 800 racks and plenty of power availability. All it takes is one client with 200 AI graphics processing units (GPUs) to tap out the cooling capacity of the data hall. That is 600 racks left stranded that the operator can't sell because there is no more capacity to cool the data center. This illustrates a predicament that often unfolds when data centers, configured for the traditional ebb and flow of energy consumption, find themselves unprepared for the voracious appetite of emerging technologies. This isn't just about empty racks, but lost revenue and wasted resources because the data center cooling cannot meet the demand.

With record-breaking summer temperatures around the world in recent years, the amount of energy required to cool a data center has increased. For traditional air-cooled data centers, this rise in ambient temperature poses a challenge beyond energy usage. Cooling towers and other evaporative cooling techniques for heat rejection are popular with larger data centers because of their high efficiency and large cooling capacity. However, they use evaporation which consumes vast amounts of water, a particular challenge in regions facing regular drought conditions. Public pressure is quickly mounting on data center owners to reduce their water usage. In 2022, Thames Water[4] announced they were going to launch a review of the impact of data centers on water supplies in and around London for this very reason. The last thing the data center industry wants or needs is public perception to turn against them for consuming too many natural resources.

The costs of incrementalism are real and broad. The embedded cost of carbon considers the entire production process of a built asset. There are monetary costs when it comes to green levies being imposed by local or national governments. Not to mention the opportunity costs to consider. It takes two years to build a data center today, but if that could be abbreviated into six months, is that better for the industry? Or consider the cost of failure – if the true cost of downtime is millions of dollars an hour, is it not worth exploring new technologies?

New Technologies for a New Way of Doing Business

Technology offers us a path forward to address current climate challenges. ESG objectives are driving data center businesses to meet the demands of a low-carbon economy. However, there are challenges when it comes to embracing the needed change. Many of the "low hanging fruits" of technology are new ways of doing business. They entail moving away from a well-known technological solution to ones that have greater perceived risk.

Luckily for the data center industry, there are new technologies that are having a transformative impact and are no longer just more sustainable alternatives to the status quo. Precision Liquid Cooling is one such technology. Servers today are designed to be air cooled. However, at a time of denser compute and data gravity, traditional air-cooling technologies are reaching their limits. Precision Liquid Cooling significantly reduces energy and water consumption as well as the cost of data center design, build and operations – making a liquid-cooled data center simpler and more efficient than any alternative.

If we return to our point about stranded capacity, one signifi-

Chapter Thirty-Six

cant revelation lies in the excessive server provisioning that has become the norm. The gradual investment in additional servers – albeit for well-intended reasons – can create a blind spot in the substantial operational costs that have been invested, not to mention their inefficiencies. The perceived expense of liquid cooling capex becomes a small investment when compared to the hidden costs of running servers at only 30% capacity and three times the number necessary. The carbon output, financial drain, and resource consumption embedded in this traditional approach reveal a dire need for reevaluation.

There are also less obvious impacts on the industry. Take the fact that there has been a seismic shift towards flexible working, accelerated by the COVID-19 pandemic. This has not only reshaped our work habits but also triggered profound consequences for commercial properties and, unexpectedly, sustainability. With so much commercial real estate sitting empty or underused, there is a brownfield opportunity for data center space. With liquid cooling technologies enabling enterprise-level data center density in even the harshest or previously unsuitable environments, new spaces can be repurposed for housing data. This is good for businesses, but also has positive implications for property investors.

The impact on business models is profound. Beyond immediate efficiency gains, the adoption of liquid cooling disrupts the conventional ways data centers are built, challenging established norms in supply chains, security, and overall simplicity. This disruption is not just a challenge but an opportunity to forge new alliances and redefine operational structures. Data center operators, integrators, and businesses alike must adapt to the evolving landscape or risk being left behind.

To make this possible, one key thing must occur: we must break the siloed mentality between IT and business decision makers. Sustainability demands a broader perspective that focuses on the longevity of decisions. These are not just technical decisions as the impact on the business is significant. The investment cost of a data center is substantial. Sometimes what happens is that the costs can become so baked in, we don't fully understand how onerous they

Chapter Thirty-Six

have become. Best practices and "the way we've always done things" can overshadow opportunities for efficiency and new technology approaches. Current TCO models don't reflect these new approaches and impede the industry's ability to fully understand the business benefits of sustainability.

Are We Ready?

In facing the pressing climate crisis, bold ideas are indispensable. Embracing sustainability necessitates a revolutionary shift in mindset that puts aside old habits of incrementalism. The question then becomes are we ready to embrace these changes? Are we prepared to take on these transformative changes?

Sustainability isn't a singular problem we can engineer our way out of. It is a broader tapestry encompassing energy efficiency, carbon, IT infrastructure, and renewable energy sources. Though change may seem daunting, adopting sustainable practices and investing in new technologies offers benefits beyond carbon reduction; it fosters client attraction and retention strategies for data centers. This requires a broader conversation internally between all the stakeholders of the business to fully incorporate and maximize its benefits.

Adopting sustainable policies shouldn't merely be a checkbox. It's a strategic move towards a future of growth. For companies daring to innovate and reimagine business practices, there is a reward. The competitive advantage is there to be had, if they are willing to embrace it. The economic impact of sustainability isn't a distant reverberation; it sets the rhythm of progress. Those integrating it as a core mission, aligning every operational facet, aren't merely weathering the storm – they're thriving within it.

The best corporations don't just want to be seen as doing the right thing, but to be genuinely *doing* the right thing when it comes to sustainability. Let's give them a path forward to make that possible. It's no longer about optics, but rather our competitive ability to survive and keep our planet healthy. Make no mistake, these aren't just long-term goals we are talking about either. There are economic

Chapter Thirty-Six

benefits to be had today in making these changes. There are technologies to implement today that can play a significant role in this. Those who will become the heroes of this story are those who demonstrate bold leadership and embrace the changes that need to come.

---

1. McKinsey & Company. 2020. "The State of Fashion 2020." https://www.mckinsey.com/~/media/mckinsey/industries/retail/our%20insights/the%20state%20of%20fashion%202020%20navigating%20uncertainty/the-state-of-fashion-2020-final.pdf
2. Wiles, Jackie. 2019. "Act Now to Fund Innovation and Growth." Gartner. May 6, 2019. https://www.gartner.com/smarterwithgartner/act-now-to-fund-innovation-and-growth.
3. Tensie Whelan, Ulrich Atz, Tracy Van Holt and Casey Clark, "ESG and Financial Performance: Uncovering the Relationship by Aggregating Evidence from 1,000 Plus Studies Published between 2015 - 2020." NYU Stern Center for Sustainable Business. https://www.stern.nyu.edu/sites/default/files/assets/documents/NYU-RAM_ESG-Paper_2021 Rev_0.pdf.
4. "Thames Water reviews data centres' water use as London hosepipe ban looms." Financial Times. https://www.ft.com/content/8d8bf26f-5df2-4ff6-91d0-369500ed1a9c?accessToken=zwAAAYLKgAJokdONi_JvXfJP9tOR0DaVAO0anA.MEQCIH6bb-aejZpXadbdm3fUKI98Cvum4wN5klboVZWVeEFZAiBl4Yr4cDTtJ-lt9fpEM5yl0Ediz5L9JRT35KxfKeBuqg&sharetype=gift&token=9ce26678-bb38-4498-a4a2-e7d6bead3132

About the Author

DAVID CRAIG

David Craig is CEO of Iceotope. Having worked his way up through Unisys and IBM in global procurement roles, he moved on to lead the commercial integration of Prudential Assurance and Scottish Amicable. From the merger, he moved next to turn around a leading British refrigeration company and to start a consultancy, which he sold three years later to Amey.

He was then invited to join a late 1990s tech boom disaster, which subsequently became Scotland's third largest software company. Craig has done a few turnarounds since, but now primarily leads Iceotope and a life science business.

THIRTY-SEVEN

How to 'Paint' a Successful Sustainable Business Case

Pete Nisbet, Edenseven

It is hugely important to build a strong business case: done correctly you can move forward, but done poorly and you end up wasting your time, the business' money, and risk damaging your reputation with your superiors. Within the world of sustainability, it can also create yet another delay in the forever-closing gap between you and your net-zero targets.

So, what should you do? In this chapter, I will outline some thoughts on what makes an effective business case, some of the internal processes that an organization needs to implement in the process, and – importantly – how to emphasize its strong environmental benefits without shifting the focus too far from keeping the business profitable. However, to do this we might need to start by looking at things slightly differently.

Having been on both sides of the table throughout my career – delivering the 'case' for a business case, and being on the receiving end – what gets it over the line? In my experience, it is the obvious factors, i.e. clear facts, numbers, data, etc., but there are also the often overlooked – but equally significant – aspects, such as building up the engagement, education of the key stakeholders involved, and making sure to use the right language throughout.

Chapter Thirty-Seven

It has become clear to me that without winning '**hearts and minds**', some of the best business cases will never be agreed upon or delivered. This boils down to the fact that if stakeholders are unclear about what they are attaching their name to, the easiest response for them is to simply say 'No'. 'No' inevitably leads to a loss of momentum, and a lack of momentum is the biggest issue that the business world currently faces regarding the challenge of climate change.

A consistent issue is businesses struggling to recognize the importance of projects or programs focused on carbon reduction and prioritizing them against the normal "business as usual" (BAU) list that they have to deal with on a daily basis. This isn't to say that all businesses striving to reduce their emissions should just be waved through, but what it does mean is that it may be to the benefit of the individuals who are responsible for developing these programs to focus more on the personas that they are selling to, and what is really important to them.

As a Managing Partner at edenseven, a consulting company that prides itself on data-driven sustainability strategies, we are constantly advising organizations on building and producing net zero strategies and deployment plans to achieve their ambitions. As a part of this process, we have sat in multiple meetings over the last few years in which Heads of Departments or Directors of Functions cannot get a 'signoff' from the key stakeholders to whom they are pitching. *Why is this? Simply put, it comes down to storytelling. To put it another way: 'painting the right picture'.*

When you live and breathe sustainability on a daily basis, it becomes easy to believe that everyone else is on the same page as you. Most of the world's population cares for the planet – that is for certain – but sometimes there are other forces at play, especially when it comes to running a business. These can be as large and looming as ongoing financial security, retention of contracts, investments into existing products and services, and more. So – believe it or not – decarbonization might end up lower down on the list of priorities!

So, how do you create a business case for net zero without

framing it as something that could distract and potentially damage the long-term financial stability of an organization? Let's break down the key elements a bit more.

Researching Your Position

A business case isn't created from a 'light bulb' moment. No senior team that is worth their position is going to show up one day and commit to the development and deployment of a net zero strategy that will be a part of the business, from conception to fruition, without clear facts and figures to supplement it.

To decipher these statistics, you need to build a picture of the current market, how it is evolving, and what is coming up on the horizon. This means that a business case needs to evaluate three key areas:

- **Customers**: Put bluntly, without customers there is no future. If you do not meet their needs, they will simply go elsewhere. So it is imperative to understand what they are thinking in regards to sustainability, and what their priorities are. With a large-scale trend like climate change, it is always better to engage with customers early on, rather than finding out that it is missing from your contracts and services by experiencing a lack of retention further down the line.
- **Suppliers**: On average, between 70 - 90% of a business' emissions come from its supply base. This means that, for a senior team to commit to a target or program of work, they will need to assess whether the biggest area of greenhouse gas emissions in their portfolio will become a hindrance to achieving it. The key factor in any organization's journey to net zero is collaboration, and using this to create a clear view of the current supply base is key.
- **Regulation**: This is the sticky part of a change program, when you have to ask whether there is

anything about the business that must change. It may begin by reporting requirements such as TCFD, CSRD or ISSB, but within each of these they will also need to show evidence of clear benchmarking and plans to make reductions. Unlike **Customers** and **Suppliers**, **Regulation** often comes with a deadline and a penalty if it is not met. No senior team wants to be seen as non-compliant, as this can create seriously damaging headlines for a business.

Understanding Your Finances

Businesses run on profit; if you aren't profitable in the long term, then you are not going to exist. This means that a business case needs to show a clear return on investment, proving that it will either generate new revenue, retain contracts, or reduce costs over its term.

This ought to be a very logical point to make; however, my associates at edenseven and I have witnessed too many failed business cases linked to sustainability. These cases focused solely on the environmental benefits without outlining its financial structure. It is important to remember that there will always be someone who is responsible for the budget - and that person will or should be in the room.

This is how you can ensure this:

- **Know your numbers**: Firstly, it is important to be clear. Avoid confusing your audience and be ready to defend your numbers; not having them available is never a sufficient excuse. Uncertainty or lack of clarity will likely result in being caught unprepared. When that happens, it could take you months to resell what could have been initially secured with just a couple more hours of preparation.
- **Know your business**: A keen knowledge of the business in question is essential: really understand them

Chapter Thirty-Seven

as an organization, and make sure you know what makes them tick. For example, if they have a big focus on the retention of existing clients and your business offers a directly positive impact on this area, then *make this a point*; don't waste time focusing on something that you know is not specifically going to hit a business goal.

- Take into account the **Total Cost of Ownership (TCO)**: One of the biggest challenges when 'going green' is the perception that it comes with excessive costs. One of the reasons for this is that many business cases do not take into account the TCO and the returns that it will bring in the long term. When competing against short-term returns for BAU, you need to make sure, yet again, that you are *painting the right picture*.
- **Level the playing field (aka - Carbon Pricing)**: How do you win against BAU programmes when they are equipped with clear and quantifiable numbers? We have already talked about the importance of stating returns on investments, but in some cases, no matter how hard you try, emissions reduction cases might actually mean that your electricity usage is going to *increase* as you offset fossil fuels. The easiest way to level the playing field in this situation is to create a "cost of carbon". This will move the carbon cases up the priority list and drop the negative ones down. How you choose to carry this out can vary from organization to organization, but it is important to maintain consistency in how this is approached (i.e. across departments, regions, etc.), especially where budgets are managed as one.

Educating Your Team

By 'education', I don't mean making individuals believe in climate change. This is about ensuring the senior team understands the reasons why the decarbonization of their operations and supply chain is positive for business. This applies across two fronts: **envi-**

ronmental (i.e. doing the right thing) as well as **financial** (making sure to protect the long-term health of a business).

It is immediately clear within any strategy or transformation program that is deployed across businesses of any size that, if there is no sign-off from the senior team, then the chances of success are low, if not non-existent. *So, how do you get the senior team to properly engage and commit to something?*

In some instances, you encounter a team of individuals personally committed to reducing carbon emissions and doing the right thing as 'global citizens'. As suggested above, while this sentiment is commendable, regrettably, it is often not the case. People certainly care, but in the short term there are a million-and-one factors to worry about. So, if a 2030 or 2040 target is agreed, it needs to come with a mechanism to make this commitment a reality - and now! Put simply, it must be a cold, hard objective, and one which has a financial impact on the individuals as well as the business.

Is this a bad thing? No! Performance bonuses have been a feature of business for centuries. Clear objectives that resonate with everyone, not just one individual, and are governed in a way in which 'just about' doesn't equate to success, ensure a focused mindset and establish clear, quantifiable targets.

Keeping Your Business Engaged

Once you have the senior team on board, there is still the need to bring the rest of the business with you. The good news is that half of the battle is already won if there is true leadership, but if this is not demonstrated or consistently reinforced then it will be obvious for everyone to see. This priority may seem disparate from the building of a business case, but it is a critical element given that the ideas and innovation rarely come from the senior team itself. As we know, there is not one single silver bullet to reconcile this: it is going to be a multi-layered process to achieve net zero, and will need many business cases to be developed and presented in tandem.

- **Communication:** Merely announcing your target once will not work. You need to bang the drum consistently to create awareness and make sure that net zero objectives become embedded into the culture of the business. If this isn't done, then employees, customers, and suppliers will see through you in an instant. It is important to create a comms plan and deliver it effectively.
- **Commitment**: To generate innovation for business case development, you will need to make it easy for people to present ideas and ultimately be listened to. If you don't give employees the freedom to think and be heard, then you may as well hand it over to the board to generate the ideas – which would be a big mistake.

Learning the Language

There is a common misconception that every senior stakeholder knows everything; that they know their job inside-out, as well as everyone else's. I'm sorry to break this myth, but that isn't the case at all. Why? There have been hundreds of books written on leadership that make the point that the best leaders are those who surround themselves with people who are more skilled and technically proficient than themselves. There is also the simple point that they do not have the capacity to absorb all of this information about everything.

What this means is that when you are building a business case, you need to write it and present it in a way that the audience will understand.

You can't expect them to understand the language and jargon that you use on a daily basis. The world of sustainability has thousands of abbreviations (TCFD, CSRB, etc.), and sometimes – we have to

Chapter Thirty-Seven

admit – we like to let people know how clever we are, don't we! Well, if this is your purpose in life, you might struggle to progress any business case at all.

Remember: the easiest thing is to say 'No' when something is too confusing and not clear. Keep it simple and lose the jargon. *Paint the right picture in a way that everyone understands, and don't leave the senior stakeholders scratching their heads about what you are proposing and where the value is.*

So, What Have We Learnt?

There is a graveyard of failed business cases throughout time, and piles of paper continue to stack up for those that are linked to emissions reduction. To prevent the inevitable from happening, there is a need to look at business case writing and presenting in a different way.

This is not to say that the traditional elements of a business case should be ignored. In a world where cost pressures are on the rise for most businesses across most sectors, the cold hard facts have never been more important. The bottom line is that senior decision makers need facts and figures, but 'painting the picture' about the wider benefits will improve your success in not just one pitch, but will provide a framework to execute multiple business cases, which in turn will ultimately accelerate emissions reduction.

Within these numbers, you should also try to **think differently**. Consider implementing a carbon pricing component into all of your company's business cases to 'level the playing field'. This will make your business ask the question on emissions every time there is a request for expenditure. It doesn't need to be so punitive that it brings the business to a standstill; rather, it gradually applies pressure on non-emission-reducing business cases, becoming ingrained within your culture before you know it.

Also consider creating a forward view or horizon scan to ensure the reader is aware of what is happening right now with the customers, suppliers and regulations, as well as how the market is

Chapter Thirty-Seven

evolving. This will mean there will be more focus on the **TCO** of your business case and its longer-term benefits.

You need to **educate your stakeholders** – in a motivating way, by explaining how this fits into the long-term strategy of your business case, and how this will help evolve the business itself for the better. This might take time, and it may need to be done at a slower pace than is ideal, but putting in the groundwork early means that stakeholders will remain engaged. Once there's a unified mindset with clear communications, it will allow the wider teams to have the freedom to be innovative. *Empowering a workforce to think differently will allow the momentum to start to build, and this will create a new wave of innovative thinking.*

Final Thoughts

I have purposely left one of the most important parts of building a business case to the end. The easiest thing to say is 'No', because saying 'Yes' means that you've made a commitment to something, and ultimately it has your name against it. Saying 'No' may well mean that the business case just doesn't stack up, but if you make sure that you know your numbers, know your business, engage with the stakeholders on the wider view, then you have a good chance. However, you may still fail if you get the language wrong.

There is an aversion to **simplifying the messaging in the world of sustainability** and it is easy to get caught in a mindset that everyone understands the abbreviations so embedded in our industry, and that these same people have an infinite amount of time to absorb and learn what is being said. **News Flash:** This is simply not the case. For a business case to succeed, you need to lose the jargon and make it crystal clear what you are pitching, and how it is going to benefit the business moving forward both financially and environmentally.

Ultimately, creating a strong business case is a process. Creating one which has potentially unquantifiable elements such as carbon emissions can also seem impossible. But, there is always a way to create a structure and add value to these component parts. You

Chapter Thirty-Seven

don't have to rip the traditional structure up, but for business cases that are focused on achieving net zero, there is definitely a need to think differently, or momentum will be slowed, and targets will be missed.

Let's not allow this to happen, as the opportunities for business are huge. So, get **painting that picture**!

About the Author

PETE NISBET

Pete is the Managing Partner at edenseven a sustainability consulting business which is part of the Cambridge Management Consulting group of businesses. Pete started his career over 25 years ago working for SSE (UK based Utility business) holding operational and trading roles where he built a detailed understanding of the global energy and carbon markets. Pete then progressed into senior positions within consulting and services businesses where he led award winning teams to design and deliver net zero strategies for a wide range of organisations within the public and private sectors.

Pete firmly believes that a data led sustainability strategy, can deliver significant environmental and financial result for businesses in the short and long term.

THIRTY-EIGHT

Every Watt Counts - How Incremental Changes Can Deliver Major Sustainability Gains

Samuel Rabinowitz, LANTANA LED

Introduction - A Funny Thing Happened on the Way to the Opera

Mark Twain wrote, "The two most important days in your life are the day you are born and the day you find out why."

In my experience, there tends to be more than a single "why" but instead multiple purposes in life that our exploits, adventures, and pursuits of passions uncover.

For me, the arts are my first love and what I always thought I would pursue as part of my career. I grew up in New York City in Greenwich Village, right downtown in the beating heart of New York. I was a complete drama nerd as a child and grew up going to the Metropolitan Opera and Broadway shows, learning Shakespeare, and singing and performing. After earning a business degree along with a master's of classical voice from the Manhattan School of Music, I decided to move west with a plan to pursue both business and music. This led me to discover a new passion — technology — and ultimately to find my place in the lighting industry.

Little did I know that my move from New York to San Francisco would lead me to trade in the big lights and hustle and bustle of

Chapter Thirty-Eight

New York City for the thrill of turning on LED lights in data centers.

Imagine moving to a new city all by yourself, and starting from scratch with nothing but a dream and a small singing gig. Eventually, I found my way to a company called Project Frog, Inc., a pioneer in industrialized construction that sought to enhance the built environment through innovations in lighting, air, sound and energy. This is when my focus on sustainability started — and when I discovered the true "why" for my move to the Golden Gate City.

Seeing an opportunity to expand innovation beyond Project Frog, I took on the challenge of developing and managing the lighting division. After significant and rapid growth, LANTANA LED was born and now operates as an independent company where I oversee business strategy and direction for the company, building a strong culture, leading the executive team as CEO, and ensuring the sustainability of our products for data center and commercial deployments (while also keeping my hand in the arts through performing at various opera and theater companies around town).

In terms of sustainability, I've learned a lot over the last eight years about how small changes can make a big difference. That's an important lesson - especially as the data center industry faces a reckoning when it comes to its environmental footprint. It's time for all of us who can make an impact in facility design to "face the music" (if you will). Unless operators and product suppliers prioritize sustainability gains, we won't move the needle in any meaningful way toward net-zero facilities.

How Micro, Product-Level Efficiencies Can Turn into Macro, Programmatic Leaps Forward

The kind of incremental changes product manufacturers can make to improve sustainability might seem small, but collectively they can result in major gains. To use a music analogy, it's like voices joining together in a chorus, layering with each other to create a monumental harmony. That's how I think about macro and micro changes — one voice alone sounds small, but combined with others, greatness can be achieved.

Imagine if instead of relying on a single manufacturer to produce eco-friendly products, we could encourage 10 or 15 manufacturers to make energy-efficient adjustments to their products. This would create a cumulative effect and considerably improve the overall energy efficiency of a data center.

And that's just one data center. But now if you're building 10 data centers, or 20 data centers, energy savings can quickly be measured in megawatts at a time. And that, to me, is where micro-level products have a macro-level effect.

If every manufacturer focuses on making their products more efficient, even by a small percentage like 10%, and they manage to achieve this goal, then the overall efficiency of an entire building or a set of data centers can improve significantly. This means that customers building such facilities can benefit from a substantial increase in overall efficiency, which can translate into cost savings and other advantages.

This is a crucial aspect and what I see going on in data centers right now. It's so exciting, and one of the things that thrills me about being in this industry.

The Lighting Industry's Often-Overlooked Role in Data Center Sustainability

The IT infrastructure industry is an oft-cited culprit of carbon emissions in discussions on global warming. Why? The truth is data centers and data transmission networks consume vast supplies of energy – about 2% of global energy,[1] according to industry research. Another concerning statistic? According to the U.S. Department of Energy, data centers are one of the most energy-intensive building types, consuming 10 to 50 times the energy per floor space of a typical commercial office building.[2]

While the IT infrastructure industry is critical in providing the building blocks of our future society and economy, the industry recognizes the need for increased energy efficiency and is looking at various sources.

As a result, major efforts are underway and have resulted in a flurry of new ideas and approaches to improve data center energy efficiency, such as better airflow management, hot aisle/cold aisle arrangements, variable-speed fans for equipment cooling, and consolidating lightly used servers to name a few. But more still needs to be done if the data center industry is to rein in its considerable energy usage. This underscores the relevance and timeliness of LED lighting in today's data center.

Although it may be an afterthought for many, lighting can have a material impact on a data center build program.[3] Lighting alone accounts for 3-5% of a data center's energy consumption every year. In an individual facility at scale or a scaled data center operations program, this is significant, making efficient lighting a key consideration for a facility's overall energy consumption. Furthermore, lighting in data centers has implications for safety, security, temperature stabilization, maintenance and productivity.

How LED Lighting Brings Sustainability, Efficiency and Cost Savings Gains to Data Centers

Data Center lighting design goes beyond simply illuminating the space. Distributed low-voltage power and LED lighting are rapidly gaining popularity in data centers thanks to their risk mitigation strategies and energy and waste efficiencies. Let's dive deeper into the benefits of LED lighting for data centers and why it's the prevailing choice for energy consumption-conscious data centers.

Energy Conservation | LED lights are far more energy efficient than traditional lighting. Studies have shown that using energy-efficient technologies such as LED lighting can reduce data center lighting energy usage by up to 70%, which is good news for a data center's overall power usage effectiveness (PUE).

LED lighting is also known to produce significantly less heat than alternative forms of lighting, which is ideal for temperature-sensitive server rooms. Because cooling represents a significant energy draw for data centers, the ability to deploy lighting systems that don't contribute to hotter server rooms helps operators conserve energy from cooling and reduce associated cooling costs over time.

Energy-efficient LED lighting is a top choice for a variety of other industries and commercial settings and is championed by the U.S. Department of Energy as a highly energy-efficient lighting technology that has the potential to fundamentally change the future of lighting in the United States. The department projects widespread use in the near future, estimating that by 2035, a majority of lighting installations will use LED technology, resulting in up to 569 TWh of energy savings, or roughly the output of more than 92 1,000 MW power plants.[4]

Cost | Quality LED light bulbs last longer, are more durable, and offer comparable or better light quality than other types of lighting at a lower operating cost. In some cases, data centers can reduce the number of fixtures while still maintaining the same illumination levels, as we found in a recent exercise with a colocation data center.[5] Distributed low-voltage power also eliminates the need for costly power distribution units and associated infrastructure, thereby reducing capital expenditures.

LED lighting also offers other benefits, including reduced maintenance time and enhanced safety.

Maintenance | Maintenance is another area where distributed low voltage power and LED lighting provide advantages due to LED lighting's longer lifespan than traditional lighting. According to the U.S. Department of Energy, a quality LED bulb can last three to five times longer than a compact fluorescent lamp (CFL) and 30 times longer than an incandescent bulb.[6] Furthermore, distributed low-voltage power reduces the number of cables required, making it easier to manage and maintain the system.

This, in turn, reduces the risk of downtime and improves system efficiency.

This is particularly important as labor shortages continue to affect new data center builds and ongoing data center site maintenance.

According to a recent study,[7] the construction industry faces a shortage of more than half a million workers (546,000) in 2023. This issue is confounded by an aging workforce and fewer workers entering trade careers. The result is more time-consuming data center projects at a time when the demand for new data centers is soaring.

This is a big deal for companies tasked with building massive data center campuses of a million square feet, requiring anywhere from 300 to 500 electricians on-site daily.

At LANTANA LED, we're contributing to the labor solution by making lighting installation easier. We thought, "Why use a highly skilled electrician to install a light fixture when a low-voltage technician, who costs 25% less, can install that fixture?" Not only does this save on hourly labor cost, but it also reduces installation time. According to an independent study by Inglett & Stubbs, a premier electrical contractor experienced in digital infrastructure, installing low voltage LED lighting vs. line voltage lighting in a 40,000-square-foot hyperscale data center saved approximately 1.38 installation hours per fixture, resulting in a total labor time savings of 375 hours.[8]

Safety | LED lighting along with distributed low-voltage power systems and power over ethernet (PoE) offer many safety benefits. LED lights produce less heat making them cooler and reducing the risk of combustion or burns. They are also constructed from break-resistant materials and do not contain any harmful chemicals. Additionally, the distributed low voltage power (DLVP) and PoE lighting of LED technology allows for remote control, enabling workers to maintain and operate the lights from a safe distance, reducing the likelihood of injury from electrical shocks and falls.

As data centers heed the call to take their power consumption more seriously, LED lighting provides an important resource for sustainability gains in previously overlooked areas within their infrastructure. Put simply, LEDs have a significantly longer lifespan than traditional lighting, offer enhanced safety features, and deliver comparable or better light quality than other types of lighting at a lower operating cost.

Necessity is the Mother of Invention: How Data Center LED Lighting Got Off the Ground

LANTANA LED is not your typical lighting company. It grew out of its progenitor's aspiration to provide a better occupant experience through optimal lighting for the prefabricated buildings it designs, manufactures and delivers to various industries. We scoured the market for LED lighting that met our design aesthetic and functional requirements but were unable to find anything that met our standards.

Consequently, Project Frog developed its first LED lighting fixture internally about 12 years ago. This was the advent of broad-scale commercial application of LED technology in lighting. A team composed of architects, engineers, and product experts, including Ted Colburn (the genius behind the original product) developed a remote DC-power six-foot fixture. Originally it was just for internal use in our own buildings. But we recognized the need and decided to put it on the market and launched LANTANA LED.

At the time that we launched the product, our LED fixture was, in fact, the most efficient LED commercial fixture in the world. It had the highest efficiency rating for light output worldwide and it remained at the top for many months. We have kept that drive for innovation and energy efficiency at the core of our DNA.

While LANTANA LED started with one original product, over the years we've expanded to offer a wide spectrum of commercial LED lighting products, delivering entire data center packages, as well as continuing to work in education, government, and general commercial.

Chapter Thirty-Eight

How Sustainability Needs to Penetrate Every Aspect of Product Design

We've continued our sustainability path based on our initial product development. It's good for the customer because it means they use less energy and lower their power costs. It's also good for the planet because lower energy usage translates into lower carbon emissions. We're firm believers in the circularity concept — that is reducing waste as much as possible, including factoring reuse into the product design. When a user is done with a product, it should go back into the supply chain, not the landfill. (Our recycling practices are discussed below).

We always want to be cognizant of making our products more energy efficient. It's something that all data center product providers need to keep in mind at every stage of product development. Sustainability is thinking about all the possibilities for eco-friendly practices — whether it be in manufacturing, delivery, or operations — at every single level we must look through a lens of, "How can I make this more efficient?"

It's a journey that we must take with our customers. Customers need to choose partners that place a premium on sustainability in product design. Fortunately, I have never seen a more dedicated focus on using energy-efficient products, in terms of manufacturing practices, than in the digital infrastructure industry.

As product developers, who want to ensure sustainability is baked into our product design, we can ask ourselves questions like:

- *How can I use fewer resources to deliver the same function?*
- *What are the new manufacturing processes that we can implement to result in less waste?*
- *How can we use recycled materials?*

For example, at LANTANA LED, we use recycled aluminum, which makes 100% of our linear fixtures' extruded spine.

How can I recycle my entire product at the end of its life? | We have developed a reuse/recycle program that allows us to take back our fixtures and either rehab them, refurbish them, and resell them, or break them down into components that can be melted down and put back into the production line, such as for aluminum or acrylic extrusions.

How can I use the most efficient components? | For us, that means the LED chips we use in product design. If we use the most energy-efficient chips on the market, balancing that with cost of course, we can ensure that our products are the most energy-efficient out there. We also must ensure that the heat dissipation is adequate for elevated ambient operating temperatures.

How can I source parts and other resources locally? | Part of that locality includes thinking through delivery methods for products to ensure we're not hiring a ship then a plane and then a truck all to deliver one fixture. Instead, locally sourced resources for production help to cut down on transportation emissions and other environmental effects.

How to Choose the Right LED Lighting for Your Data Center

As we've stated previously, LED lighting provides numerous labor, cost, safety, and other benefits. But what criteria should you consider when selecting LED lighting for your data center? Here are six important areas to keep in mind:

Efficiency | Studies have shown that using energy-efficient LED lighting is a win-win for your facility and the environment since it reduces data center lighting energy usage, which translates into lower energy costs and a reduced carbon footprint.

When examining an LED's energy efficiency, operators should

look for lighting with a high lumen output per watt, note the fixture's lifespan and consider the light's heat emission, which can impact cooling requirements for their center.

Budget | Quality LED lighting may have higher upfront costs than traditional lighting, but the long-term savings in energy consumption and maintenance make it the better choice. Simply put, quality LED light bulbs last longer, are more durable, and offer comparable or better light quality than other types of lighting at a lower operating cost.

Safety | LED lighting is safer in a variety of ways than incandescent or fluorescent lighting, including being cooler (reducing the risk of combustion or burnt fingers) and is free from harmful chemicals making them environmentally friendly and safer to handle during installation and disposal.

In choosing a lighting solution for your data center, remember that placement and power types pose different safety hazards. For example, distributed low-voltage LEDs and PoE (Power over Ethernet) lighting enable remote control, allowing workers to control the lights from a safe distance away from hot aisles and sensitive equipment. Maintenance personnel can service lights without the risk of falls and are less likely to experience electrical shocks than LED fixtures using line voltage.

Luminance | Lumens measure the amount of light emitted by a fixture, so the higher the lumens, the brighter the light will be. All lighting uses lumens to quantify how much light they produce. However, the difference is that LED lights can produce the same lighting intensity (i.e., number of lumens) as other lighting types, but at a lower wattage — so the data center uses less energy to achieve the same lighting quality.

For data centers, experts recommend choosing fixtures that meet

50 foot-candles at the 3-foot horizontal plane. Fixtures with high-lumen outputs that provide a greater spread of light can reduce the total fixtures needed while still meeting the illumination requirement. This results in decreased fixture costs and additional savings in installation and maintenance.

Color Temperature and Rendering | Two critical parameters that significantly impact your environment's visual comfort and aesthetic appeal are the Color Rendering Index (CRI) and the Correlated Color Temperature (CCT). CRI, a scale from 0 to 100, quantifies the light source's ability to faithfully reveal objects' true colors compared to an ideal or natural light source. A high CRI value, typically above 80 for most LED lights, ensures vibrant and authentic color representation. On the other hand, CCT, measured in Kelvin (K), indicates the color appearance of the light itself, ranging from warm (lower Kelvin values like 2700K-3000K, producing a yellowish-white light) to cool (higher Kelvin values like 5000K-6500K, emitting a bluer white light). Beyond aesthetics, a CCT of at least 4000K with a CRI of 97 carries biological benefits. It closely mimics the effects of natural daylight, which can help regulate circadian rhythms, improve mood, enhance alertness, and increase productivity.

Dynamic and tunable options allow owners to adjust the CCT and CRI of individual fixtures after installation. Not only can adjusting your LED lights to a higher color temperature during work hours boost productivity, but studies have shown that cooler, bluer light also improves cognitive performance. Adjusting the color temperature is especially helpful for preventing eye strain from visually demanding tasks like reading or working on a computer.

Longevity | LED lighting offers a much longer lifespan than traditional lighting, which equates to fewer lighting refreshes over time offering significant cost savings. LED lights not only last longer but also maintain a consistent level of brightness throughout their

Chapter Thirty-Eight

lifespan. This contrasts with traditional lighting solutions that gradually dim over time until they eventually burn out.

When comparing lighting solutions for data centers, operators and engineers need to know that light fixtures can fail in high-heat environments. Choosing fixtures that are UL-Certified for Elevated Ambient Operating Temperatures and offer long lifespans are critical considerations for data center lighting to ensure continuous operation and prevent constant, costly replacements.

The Future of Data Center Lighting - How New Technologies Will Drive Even More Energy Efficiency

The future is bright (pun definitely intended) for lighting innovations that will drive even more energy efficiency in the data center industry going forward. Along with the growing use of LED lighting — which has the potential to revolutionize the data center industry's approach to illumination — several other energy-saving avenues are emerging, such as lights-out data centers and AI-driven lighting controls.

In a lights-out data center, automation and remote management technologies allow the facility to operate without the need for constant physical oversight. This includes the ability to operate with minimal or no lighting, which further reduces energy consumption. Modern LED systems can be easily integrated with these intelligent lighting controls, enabling data center operators to dynamically adjust lighting levels based on real-time needs.

Artificial intelligence, meanwhile, is emerging as a key player in enhancing data center energy efficiency in many ways, including lighting. AI-driven lighting controls enable real-time monitoring and adaptive adjustments based on various factors such as occupancy, ambient light levels, and even employee preferences. With occupancy sensors powered by AI, lighting can be dimmed or turned off automatically in a section of the facility that is unoccupied, saving energy without sacrificing safety or operational efficiency. This level of granular control is difficult to achieve with traditional lighting systems but becomes feasible through the integration of AI.

Chapter Thirty-Eight

Another technological advancement on the horizon is nanotechnology, which holds the potential to create ultra-efficient light sources with minimal energy waste. While still in development, the research includes exploring nanocrystal use in LED lighting, which would make it even more efficient and longer-lived.

Closing

We are at a pivotal moment of exponential technological growth, where we can do things that we never imagined even five years ago.

How Did We Get Here?

It's not because people sat back and said, good enough. It's because people asked, "How can I do this even better?" And I think the answer is sustainability. There is no "good enough." We should always be pushing the bounds of technology so that we can make all of our lives, and all of our environments, better.

Sustainability is no longer just an option—it's an imperative. At LANTANA LED, we're committed to creating energy-efficient lighting solutions that help data centers reduce their carbon footprint and operate more sustainably. But we can't do it alone. Every company providing products to the data center industry has a vital role to play.

Whether it's innovating in cooling technologies or developing more efficient infrastructure, each advancement contributes to a more sustainable future for the industry. Because when we all work towards a common goal of sustainability, the impact is not just significant—it's transformative.

---

1. International Energy Agency (IEA). "Data Centers and Data Transmission Networks." https://www.iea.org/energy-system/buildings/data-centres-and-data-transmission-networks

2. U.S. Department of Energy, Office of Energy Efficiency and Renewable Energy. https://www.energy.gov/eere/buildings/data-centers-and-servers
3. EYP Mission Critical Facilities. May 26, 2021. "Sustainability in Data Center Lighting Design." Angelica Hermanto, https://www.eypmcfinc.com/post/data-center-lighting
4. U.S. Department of Energy, https://www.energy.gov/energysaver/led-lighting
5. A Case Study on Achieving Illumination Goals with Fewer LED Fixtures, https://info.lantanaled.com/hubfs/2024%20Product%20Brochures/Case%20Study%20Shedding%20Light%20on%20Efficiency.pdf
6. U.S. Department of Energy, Office of Energy Saver, https://www.energy.gov/energysaver/led-lighting#:~:text=In%20comparison%2C%20incandescent%20bulbs%20release,longer%20than%20an%20incandescent%20bulb.
7. Associated Builders and Contractors, "Construction Workforce Shortage Tops Half a Million in 2023, Says ABC," February 3, 2023, https://www.abc.org/News-Media/News-Releases/construction-workforce-shortage-tops-half-a-million-in-2023-says-abc
8. Installation Analysis of Line Voltage vs Low Voltage LED Lighting, an independent study by Inglett & Stubbs, https://info.lantanaled.com/hubfs/2023%20LANTANA%20Spec%20Sheets/New/Cost%20Analysis%20(5).pdf

About the Author

SAMUEL RABINOWITZ

Samuel Rabinowitz is the esteemed CEO of LANTANA LED, an innovative provider of sustainable commercial LED lighting solutions. Sam holds distinguished professional certifications including, DCIS (Data Center Infrastructure Specialist), DCIE (Data Center Infrastructure Expert), and DCES (Data Center Engineering Specialist) showcasing his expertise in data center infrastructure and energy management, which directly contributes to LANTANA LED's success and reliability.

Before leading LANTANA LED, Sam honed his skills in leadership roles at Project Frog, including Finance, Corporate Strategy, optimizing Supply Chain, and other core functions.

Sam holds a bachelor's degree in Political Science from Haverford College and a master's degree in Classical Voice from Manhattan School of Music, making him a skilled leader with a unique combination of analytical and creative skills.

Sam is a committed cyclist and passionate about music. He regularly sings with opera and musical theater companies in the Bay Area and is an active member of the American Guild of Musical Artists (AGMA).

Sam is not only a dynamic CEO but also a vibrant contributor to his community. His leadership at LANTANA LED continues to illuminate the path to sustainable and efficient commercial lighting solutions, while his passion for music enriches the cultural fabric of the Bay Area.

THIRTY-NINE

The Interconnected Domains of Finance, Sustainability and Innovation

Scott Willis, DartPoints

In an era driven by the relentless pursuit of technological progress, data center facilities stand as the silent guardians of our digital world. They are the unsung heroes, ensuring the smooth operation of our digital lives while simultaneously raising concerns due to their environmental impact. It's a paradoxical challenge: as data centers become increasingly essential for resource management and enhancing security, they also contribute significantly to our planet's energy consumption. Experts, with a tone of alarm, predict that by 2025, these facilities will consume a staggering 20% of the world's power supply.

The looming environmental crisis has prompted a paradigm shift in the tech industry. An increasing number of organizations are turning their gaze toward the future, embracing eco-friendly data center solutions. What's noteworthy about this shift is that it signifies more than just a fleeting trend; it represents a profound and lasting transformation, one that resonates deeply with our shared responsibility to safeguard the environment.

But why is this shift towards greener data centers so crucial, and how does it translate into tangible benefits, both financially and socially? Below, we will delve into these questions, uncovering the compelling reasons behind the urgency to act sooner rather than later.

Green data centers, as we shall explore, are not merely a symbol of environmental stewardship. They are the bedrock of cutting-edge technology, poised to revolutionize the way we perceive and interact with our digital infrastructure. The integration of state-of-the-art IT infrastructure within these environmentally conscious havens guarantees not only higher reliability but also significantly improved uptime. These are not just statistics; they are the lifeline of your company, positioning you as a leader in technological innovation.

As we venture into the realm of green data centers, we'll explore the interconnected domains of finance, sustainability, and innovation. Examining trends and real examples from DartPoints we will illustrate the transformative benefits of sustainable initiatives in their data centers. This highlights how embracing the green revolution enhances not only financial performance but also contributes to a healthier, more sustainable world.

Financial Benefits

Sustainability and Capital Investments

Data centers, known for their substantial capital requirements, have historically turned to credit, loans, equity, and debt as primary sources of funding. However, the digital infrastructure sector is increasingly prioritizing sustainability. Many companies are now pledging to reduce their environmental impact and participating in eco-friendly initiatives.

The appeal of sustainable financing options like Green Bonds and Sustainability Linked Loans (SLLs) lies in their ability to attract a more diverse range of investors. This not only broadens the availability of funds but also lowers the cost of capital. These financing options come with stipulations that enforce accountability, requiring companies to allocate capital to environmental projects that align with their sustainability objectives. Failure to meet these commitments results in financial penalties. Investor interest, customer demand, and employee retention are key

Chapter Thirty-Nine

driving forces behind the adoption of sustainable financing practices.

Sustainable financing sources range from traditional funds to specialized ESG-focused investors. It must be noted that this approach comes with its set of challenges, including ESG audits, compliance requirements, and rigorous reporting. To facilitate this transition, the International Capital Market Association (ICMA) has released guidelines for sustainable financing, encompassing principles for Green Bonds, Sustainability-Linked Bonds, and Sustainability Bonds. In essence, the shift towards sustainable financing within data centers signifies a growing commitment to eco-conscious practices and a greener future for the industry.

Government Incentives for Green Initiatives

Much like the process of raising capital, dealing with environmental regulations and incentives involves a mix of advantages and challenges. As global internet usage continues to expand, environmental regulators are increasingly focusing their attention on data centers. These facilities currently account for 1-2% of the world's electricity consumption, and projections indicate this figure could escalate to 13% in the next decade. To put this into perspective, data centers presently consume as much energy as 33 nuclear power plants, with a significant portion of this energy being wasted due to inefficient air-cooling systems.

Governments frequently employ a range of incentives designed to encourage sustainability and eco-conscious practices. Several programs and schemes around the world cater directly to data centers that adopt eco-friendly practices. These incentives not only benefit data centers but also contribute to broader environmental and economic objectives. Given the potential financial advantages that data centers can accrue from exploring these incentives, it is wise to delve deeper into the possibilities.

Subsidies are available at both state and national levels in various countries, and some cities and counties also offer them. Additionally, utilities and other organizations provide grants to

Chapter Thirty-Nine

support environmentally friendly businesses. Here are just a few examples:

- *US Federal Tax Incentives*: Offers deductions for the incorporation of energy-efficient systems in business infrastructures, encouraging a shift towards greener technology.
- *BCA-IMDA Green Mark Scheme* (Singapore): Recognizes and rewards companies for reducing environmental impacts, fostering a sustainable business ecosystem in Singapore.
- *CSDDD (EU)*: The Corporate Sustainability Due Diligence Directive (CSDDD) is part of the European Green Deal – a set of policy initiatives by the European Commission with the overarching aim of making the European Union's climate, energy, transport, and taxation policies fit for reducing net greenhouse gas emissions by at least 55% by 2030.

At DartPoints, we actively engage in various energy provider programs that offer incentives for investing in energy-saving initiatives. This not only aligns with our commitment to green initiatives but also allows us to earn credits or reimbursement for a significant portion of our investments. We have successfully implemented this approach not only in Greenville, South Carolina, but also in other markets.

Operational Efficiencies

Green data centers are at the forefront of enhancing operational efficiency while also embracing sustainability and cost savings. Energy efficiency lies at the core of their operations. To this end, data centers employ a range of innovative strategies. Virtualization, for instance, optimizes server usage by consolidating multiple virtual servers on a single physical server, leading to a significant reduction in energy consumption. Moreover, advanced cooling techniques,

Chapter Thirty-Nine

including hot/cold aisle containment and free cooling, are employed to maintain optimal temperatures within data centers while simultaneously minimizing energy usage.

A crucial aspect of energy efficiency in green data centers is the use of energy-efficient hardware. This encompasses servers, storage devices, and networking equipment designed to consume less power without compromising their performance capabilities. Furthermore, many green data centers are powered by renewable energy sources such as solar and wind, not only reducing operational costs but also making substantial strides in lowering the carbon footprint associated with data center operations.

Continuous monitoring and management systems play a critical role by providing real-time data on energy consumption and efficiency. With this data, intelligent systems, many utilizing artificial intelligence, can make dynamic adjustments in cooling systems and power distribution, ensuring the data center operates at peak efficiency. DartPoints has discovered that through the deployment of precise temperature management, they can effectively direct cooling precisely where and when it's required, thereby minimizing unnecessary energy consumption. This efficient regulation not only cuts costs but also supports environmental sustainability. Through the integration of advanced automated controls and thorough monitoring systems across its data centers, DartPoints achieves peak efficiency in power consumption and cooling, thus reducing its environmental impact. The objective is to achieve an ideal balance between operational excellence and energy conservation.

In addition to optimizing energy use, green data centers leverage modular designs and flexible infrastructure to further enhance operational efficiency. These design principles are built around the idea of adaptability, which is crucial in the rapidly evolving digital landscape. The ability to scale up or down efficiently and without disruption is a significant advantage. This adaptability also reduces downtime, as maintenance and upgrades can be executed on individual modules, guaranteeing that the data center continues to function smoothly.

Chapter Thirty-Nine

Data Center Innovation for Sustainability

In the era of rapidly advancing technology, the quest for more sustainable and environmentally responsible data centers has gained significant momentum. As the world's reliance on digital infrastructure continues to grow, the environmental impact of data centers has become a pressing concern. To address this challenge, data centers are increasingly turning to an array of cutting-edge technologies to revolutionize their operations, driving them towards greener, more sustainable practices. By harnessing the potential of emerging innovations, data centers can not only bolster their sustainability efforts but also dramatically improve energy efficiency and minimize their ecological footprint. In this dynamic landscape, the fusion of technology and environmental stewardship is poised to reshape the future of data centers, enabling them to be at the forefront of the global shift towards a cleaner, more sustainable digital ecosystem. Within this section, we explore three key areas that are revolutionizing the landscape of data centers: Artificial Intelligence, heat recycling, immersion cooling, and flexible infrastructure and modular design.

Artificial Intelligence/Machine Learning in Data Centers

In the dynamic realm of data centers, the advent of artificial intelligence and machine learning (AI/ML) has ushered in a transformative era. It's no longer a matter of choice, but a compelling necessity, driven by the pressing need to align with environmental, social, and governance (ESG) standards. These mandates have elevated sustainability and social responsibility to the forefront of data center objectives in the foreseeable future.

A pivotal element of this transformation revolves around the application of AI and ML algorithms in cooling optimization. Tech giants such as Google have set a remarkable precedent by using these algorithms to target cooling precisely where it's needed most. They adapt to workload fluctuations and varying power demands, yielding impressive results. Early adopters have reported substantial reductions in power usage effectiveness, thus enhancing energy efficiency and overall sustainability. Furthermore, the seamless integration of AI algorithms with Data Center Infrastructure Management (DCIM) software heralds a new era in energy optimization. This synergy enables real-time monitoring, predictive analytics, and fine-tuning of data center operations, delivering superior energy efficiency and resource utilization. This not only reduces operational expenses but also aligns with broader environmental sustainability goals.

The integration of AI and ML-driven automation is reshaping modern data management, bolstering energy efficiency, reducing carbon emissions, and diminishing reliance on human intervention. This mitigates risks associated with delayed updates, human errors, and security breaches while expediting tasks and providing valuable insights into server configurations to meet the real-time demands of AI applications. Proactive AI predictive maintenance further enhances reliability and sustainability.

As DartPoints and other data centers venture into software-based management and machine learning, they streamline operations, enhance cost-efficiency, and increase adaptability. This transformative shift prepares them to confront the challenges of a digitally transformed business landscape, where AI and automation contribute to sustainability and competitiveness, while meeting environmental and operational efficiency requirements. In implementing these measures, DartPoints asserts that data centers not only enhance efficiency but also position themselves for a more sustainable and competitive future. This future is shaped by ongoing technological innovation, continuously reshaping the landscape of modern data management.

Circular Economy and Data Center Heat Reuse

The conventional view of data centers' heat as an environmental concern has shifted, with it now being recognized as a valuable resource that can bring benefits to communities and the environment. To align with sustainability goals, data centers are undergoing a transformative change, embracing a circular economy model that emphasizes reducing waste and reusing resources. Historically, data centers consumed significant energy to regulate their temperatures, resulting in excess heat. This new perspective positions data centers as leaders in sustainability, redirecting their heat output to support the environment and local communities through innovative and eco-friendly methods. Examples of these approaches include heating nearby buildings and homes, contributing to greenhouse farming, maintaining pleasant water temperatures in swimming pools and fish farms, and assisting in the eco-friendly production of wood pellets. This creative heat repurposing not only reduces environmental impact but also enhances the well-being of local areas, highlighting the promising collaboration between technology and community welfare in the pursuit of a greener future.

Recycling waste heat from data centers holds the potential to reduce their carbon footprint, aligning with global climate change mitigation efforts. Beyond reducing environmental impact and saving money, waste heat utilization enables data centers to enhance energy efficiency and contribute to a circular economy. Key benefits of harnessing waste heat include substantial reductions in energy consumption, cost savings through decreased reliance on traditional cooling methods, and even the generation of additional revenue streams by selling or repurposing waste heat for heating nearby buildings, water systems, and various industrial processes. This approach helps data centers achieve higher energy efficiency ratings, aligning with stringent energy standards.

In parallel, the development of new urban district heating and cooling schemes is now ramping up at the same time as several cutting-edge technologies are driving this shift, such as heat recovery systems that capture waste heat and redirect it for various purposes, including heating water or buildings. Thermoelectric generators (TEGs) convert waste heat into electricity, further reducing dependence on external energy sources. Collaborative efforts with district heating networks allow data centers to distribute waste heat to local communities, reducing the need for traditional heating systems.

Chapter Thirty-Nine

Liquid immersion cooling technologies capture excess heat, which can then be used for space heating or industrial processes.

The transformation of waste heat from data centers is not just a matter of environmental responsibility; it is also a pathway to economic savings, revenue generation, and long-term sustainability, ultimately creating a win-win situation for data center operators and the communities they serve.

Immersion Cooling

To address the growing concerns about the environmental impact, cost, and performance limitations associated with traditional mechanical air cooling in data centers, several innovative and sustainable cooling techniques have been developed. One of the most promising advancements in this field is immersion cooling, which includes full-immersion and direct-to-chip/cold-plate cooling methods. These approaches involve submerging servers and hardware components in specialized dielectric fluids, eliminating the need for energy-intensive mechanical cooling systems like fans and refrigeration. This shift to liquid cooling offers a range of benefits that can lead to significant improvements in data center sustainability and efficiency.

Traditional forced air-cooling methods have limitations, such as inefficiency in heat removal, typically capping out at about 25 kilowatts per rack. In contrast, liquid cooling offers a more efficient means of transferring heat away from electrical components. This increased efficiency results in reduced energy consumption and enhanced processing capacity, ultimately leading to a greener and more high-performing data center infrastructure. Moreover, liquid cooling can also lead to reduced space requirements and downtime, contributing to overall cost savings.

At DartPoints, we've embraced sustainable technology through our investment in Liquid Edge—a direct-to-chip liquid cooling system. Utilizing advanced Two-Phase Liquid Immersion Cooling technology, Liquid Edge not only optimizes efficiency in a compact 360 square foot space but also significantly minimizes environmental impact. With the capacity to deliver up to 1.2 MW of compute power and an impressive Power Usage Effectiveness (PUE) as low as 1.028, Liquid Edge establishes new standards in energy efficiency. Its operation, surpassing traditional air-cooling methods by an astonishing 4,000 times, represents a substantial stride toward eco-friendly computing. Additionally, the remarkable 70% reduction in water usage underscores DartPoints' steadfast commitment to preserving vital resources.

As DartPoints and similar data centers continue to evolve toward next-generation energy-efficient designs, collaboration among various stakeholders, including data center managers, engineers, and environmental experts, will be essential. The integration of sustainable cooling techniques like immersion and direct-to-chip liquid cooling presents an opportunity to significantly reduce carbon emissions, lower water usage, and enhance the overall performance of data centers. These advancements not only align with environmental sustainability goals but also offer cost savings and increased processing capacity, making them a critical component of the data center infrastructure of the future.

Flexible Infrastructure and Modular Design

In addition to optimizing energy use, green data centers leverage modular designs and flexible infrastructure to further enhance operational efficiency. These design principles are built around the idea of adaptability, which is crucial in the rapidly evolving digital landscape.

The ability to scale up or down efficiently and without disruption is a significant advantage. This adaptability also reduces downtime, as maintenance and upgrades can be executed on individual modules, guaranteeing that the data center continues to function smoothly.

Furthermore, flexible infrastructure allows businesses to customize their data center setup to match their unique requirements. This tailoring ensures that resources are allocated efficiently, maximizing energy efficiency and overall operational performance.

By incorporating these strategies and technologies, green data centers not only contribute to environmental goals but also position businesses for a competitive edge in the digital world. Their reliable and cost-effective IT services are the product of these sustainable practices, making green data centers an ideal choice for businesses looking to balance performance, cost, and environmental responsibility.

Closing

The adoption of sustainable and green data center practices is being propelled by a powerful convergence of regulatory mandates and the changing preferences of customers. In this evolving landscape, integrating these practices into your business operations is more than just a compliance matter; it represents a strategic approach to future-proofing your enterprise in anticipation of new government regulations. While the initial investments in sustainable infrastructure might not provide immediate, tangible returns, they are an instrumental means of positioning your business for long-term success as increasingly stringent environmental standards become the norm.

Furthermore, sustainability is not merely a box to check off on the regulatory compliance list; it can also offer a distinct competitive advantage. More and more companies are incorporating sustainability and green initiatives as pivotal criteria in their Request for Proposals (RFP). To secure contracts and clients in this evolving landscape, it may be necessary to showcase the long-term benefits of these practices and perform a comprehensive risk analysis. This involves carefully balancing the current economic conditions with the potential future rewards of going green. Waiting for a more favorable economic climate before making the transition may, in fact, leave your business trailing far behind the curve as the demand for sustainable practices intensifies in the marketplace. Therefore, adopting sustainable and green data center practices is not just a compliance necessity but a strategic maneuver that has the potential to secure your business's future and offer a competitive edge in a progressively eco-conscious world.

---

1. Vardhman, R. 2023. "15 Crucial Data Center Statistics to Know in 2023." Techjury: July 27, 2023, https://techjury.net/blog/data-center-statistics/.
2. Thomas, A. 2022. "How AI and automation make data centers greener and more sustainable." EY: December 1, 2022, https://www.ey.com/en_in/technology/how-ai-and-automation-make-data-centers-greener-and-more-sustainable
3. Edwards, J. 2023. "Data Center Cooling Techniques Target Sustainability: Multiple cooling approaches promise more powerful and energy-efficient data centers." Information Week: March 23, 2023, https://www.informationweek.com/sustainability/data-center-cooling-technologies-target-sustainability

About the Author

SCOTT WILLIS

Scott Willis serves as DartPoints' President and Chief Executive Officer and also serves as a member of the Board of Directors. Mr. Willis is a recognized global technology leader in the communications industry with a demonstrated track record of building successful businesses for both large and small organizations on a significant scale. He has extensive leadership experience transforming organizations, setting strategic direction, overseeing complex operations, and confecting corporate alliances while delivering growth and profitability to the business.

Scott has the right balance of strategic leadership, vision, enthusiasm, and operational and technical expertise for building sustainable customer relationships. Mr. Willis brings over 30 years of experience in the technology industry with a history of proven success. Scott has served in executive leadership roles at respected technology companies, including Ericsson, Nokia, BellSouth, and Sprint.

Mr. Willis holds a B.B.A. in Finance from the University of Oklahoma and an M.B.A. from Wake Forest University Babcock Graduate School of Management. He also holds continuing executive education certificates from Stanford University Graduate School of Business and Columbia University Graduate School of Business.

FORTY

Using Green Micro Data Centers to Solve UN SDG 6 and 7

R. Scott Salandy-Defour, Liquidstar

What if green data centers could be used to address the United Nations Sustainable Development Goals (UN SDGs) #6 for clean water and #7 for clean energy on the African continent?

This may sound ambitious, but it's not just a pipe dream.

Challenges and Opportunities in Africa's Digital and Environmental Landscape

In Africa, there's a pressing need for basic utilities and infrastructure: over 600 million people lack electricity[1], 418 million don't have access to basic drinking water[2], and nearly 871 million are without broadband[3].

As we move deeper into the digital age, data centers are also increasingly considered vital infrastructure. However, Africa is at a crossroads. With the rise of artificial intelligence (AI) and Large Language Models in the context of a widening digital divide, there's a real danger that Africa might miss out on this digital revolution. Africa's data could end up being mined and processed overseas, then sold back at a premium, much like its natural resources were in the past. The potential for African nations to lose control, or more specifically, first rights over their "digital oil" is a scenario of utmost concern.

On the energy front, Boston Consulting Group's Vivian Lee has reported that in the US alone, data center electricity consumption is expected to increase from 2.5% or 126 TWh to a potential maximum of 7.5% or 390 TWh of total usage[4]. For reference, the entire electricity demand across all of Africa is currently only 700 TWh[5].

Home to 17% of the world's population, Africa faces a significant digital infrastructure gap. The continent accounts for 13% of the world's mobile connections and 5% of broadband connections, yet hosts only a mere 1% of the world's data centers[6]. This is in stark contrast to North America, which accounts for 7.5% of the world's population and 36% of the world's data centers[7].

Demand for data centers in Africa is expected to exceed supply by 300% according to Moritz Breickmann as customer expectations rise and new data sovereignty laws come into effect. A rapid increase in capacity to 1,200MW by 2030 is needed to support the growth potential of the continent's digital economy[8]. According to McKinsey the market for data centers globally is going to increase rapidly as the global spend on construction of data centers is expected to reach almost $50 billion annually[9]. Additionally as edge computing becomes more prevalent the addressable market will grow from $176 billion in 2022 (an increase of 14.8 percent from 2021) to $274 billion in 2025[10]. Making modular micro data centers that can fit into constrained areas in densely populated urban environments more important.

Meanwhile, as climate change is exacerbating conditions worldwide, Africa is bearing the brunt of global warming more than anywhere else, despite contributing the least to carbon emissions. Africans, on average, contribute 1 ton of CO_2 per year compared to North Americans, who contribute 10 tons[11]. The continent is currently experiencing some of its worst droughts. The World Meteorological Organization has noted that Africa's warming rate is slightly higher than the global average[12]. The International Monetary Fund (IMF) predicts that, in the next 15-20 years, Africa's most vulnerable states will face four times as many extremely hot days as other states in areas where water access is already scarce[13].

At first glance, global warming, lack of electricity, lack of internet, lack of water, and lack of data centers may seem separate issues, but they are closely related. Without consistent access to key infrastructure, building data centers becomes even more challenging, especially in an environment ripe with construction delays and foreign currency risks. Also, global warming can have a significant impact on operations: Google and Oracle, for example, both faced downtime during a heatwave in Europe in 2021[14].

On the African continent, as the earth gets warmer, the population increases, and the data universe grows more than 10 times from 2020 to 2030 to reach 660 zettabytes—equivalent to 610 iPhones (128GB) per person[15] it will become even more difficult for the continent to keep up. While the demand for data centers is rising, the resources required to operate them will become increasingly constrained.

Green Data Centers: Liquidstar's Sustainable Waypoints in Africa

Liquidstar's micro data centers, or Waypoints, can help ensure a more equitable and green future for digital Africa while helping the continent take advantage of this massive market opportunity. Waypoints are renewable-powered edge AI micro data centers. These aren't just any data centers; they're designed to empower local communities with not only data processing capabilities but also essential services like electricity, water, and internet access.

Chapter Forty

And here's a cool twist (pun intended): the Waypoints' cooling system uses an innovative thermal management system that harnesses water from the atmosphere to cool the data center. This method is particularly relevant in regions facing water scarcity, as it doesn't rely on the consumption of local water sources.

Powered by a combination of solar energy and biogas from human waste, the Waypoints use low Earth orbit (LEO) satellite internet to connect a distributed network of Waypoints, each with one 12.5 kW high-density server rack, that replicates a small data center (75 Waypoints equal one small data center). Using an energy balance algorithm, any excess electricity is sold to locals via rentable batteries, and any excess water used to cool the micro data center is sold to locals, with any remainder used for thermal storage or recycled back into the micro data center rack for cooling.

From a community standpoint, individuals pay to rent the batteries, pay for water or ice, and pay for the internet, all for less than they would normally pay for these services from other providers.

Chapter Forty

Evolution of Liquidstar's Waypoint: Pioneering Sustainable Technology in Emerging Markets

The Genesis of Liquidstar

Liquidstar was founded in 2018, originally in response to the devastating aftermath of Hurricane Maria in Puerto Rico. The company's inception stemmed from the realization that nearly 3,000 deaths occurred post-storm[16], primarily due to the lack of access to electricity and clean water. While companies like Tesla installed large batteries and solar panels, it was evident that despite these efforts, the existing grid had been completely destroyed. This highlighted a critical insight: while generating power can be straightforward, constructing, operating, and maintaining a distribution infrastructure presents significant challenges in terms of complexity and cost. Moreover, in areas lacking electricity access, the reliance on diesel generators became apparent. These generators not only contributed to pollution but also required intricate supply chain logistics to maintain fuel supplies.

So we developed the idea of building a solar generator and distributing rental batteries from the generator or Waypoint. The original concept was that when the generator isn't being used or if there was excess energy it could power a cluster of GPUs to perform proof of work Ethereum blockchain mining, train AI models, or act as a render farm. Then when there was a disaster, we could provide batteries for rent, water and internet in disaster zones and use excess energy for the micro data center. This was key because free solar or electricity doesn't work if there is no revenue incentive to maintain installed capacity.

We quickly learned that basing a business on sporadic disasters was challenging, specifically, how do you operate a data center if a specific unit has to go completely offline for months. We shifted our focus to UN SDGs 6 and 7, aiming to create a Decentralized Autonomous Utility that would offer access to electricity, water, and internet, with excess energy powering micro data centers. This solution was designed to address flaws that we had observed in the economics of large-scale electrification in emerging markets and small solar systems. Moreover, the payment systems in these markets were inadequate.

Our early efforts focused on solving these issues through decentralization and the use of self-sustaining data centers funded by their own tokens. However, recognizing the need to collaborate with larger entities and the complexities within the blockchain industry, we shifted towards a more centralized approach.

Ethereum's transition to proof-of-stake also led us to revise our business model and diversify the computational services provided by the Waypoint. Coincidentally, the rise in demand for AI training by OpenAI and Starlink's global coverage announcement allowed us to enhance our micro data center's capabilities and initiate our first large-scale real-world test.

Pioneering Prototype in Jamaica

Our first prototype in Jamaica aimed to test the micro data center concept. We installed a 32.5 kWp grid-connected system at a rural school with 70 kWh of batteries. This project provided an opportunity to collaborate with local communities for installation and to identify potential need for engineering improvements.

Chapter Forty

This primarily solar-powered micro data center utilized three bonded Starlinks and offered Wi-Fi access to the school and local community. For this, we used immersion cooling. To test the center's capabilities, we hosted educational videos and ran a locally hosted Large Language Model (LLM) in the Waypoint. We also fine-tuned our energy balance algorithm, which redirected excess electricity to the school, saving them thousands of dollars in energy costs.

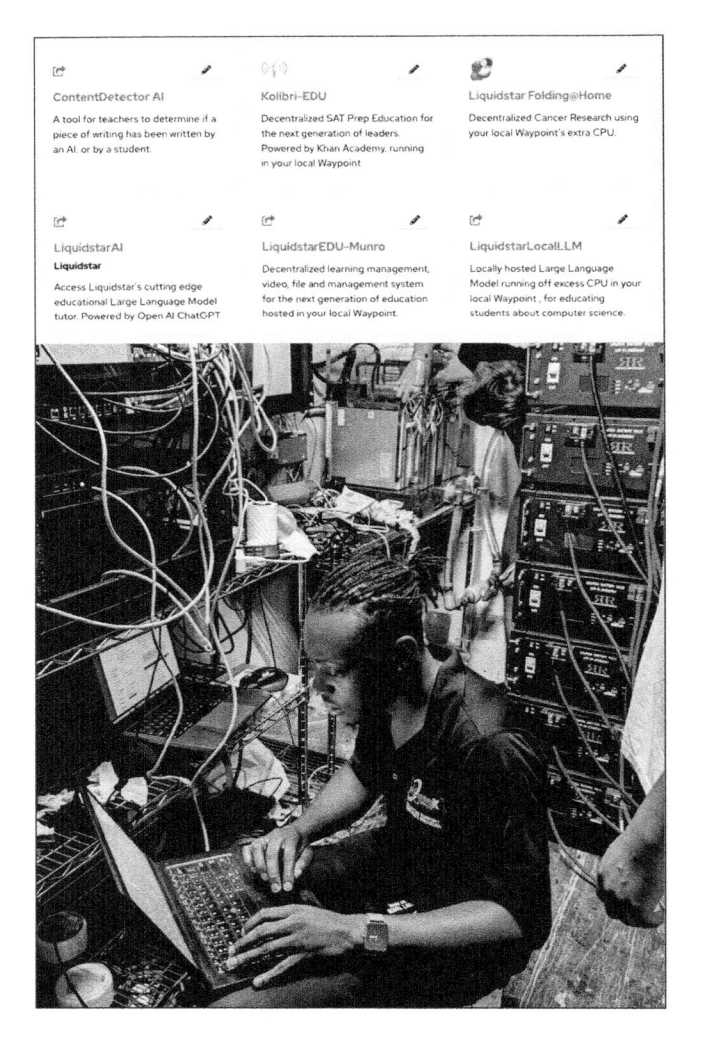

ContentDetector AI
A tool for teachers to determine if a piece of writing has been written by an AI, or by a student.

Kolibri-EDU
Decentralized SAT Prep Education for the next generation of leaders. Powered by Khan Academy, running in your local Waypoint.

Liquidstar Folding@Home
Decentralized Cancer Research using your local Waypoint's extra CPU.

LiquidstarAI
Liquidstar
Access Liquidstar's cutting edge educational Large Language Model tutor. Powered by Open AI ChatGPT

LiquidstarEDU-Munro
Decentralized learning management, video, file and management system for the next generation of education hosted in your local Waypoint.

LiquidstarLocalLLM
Locally hosted Large Language Model running off excess CPU in your local Waypoint, for educating students about computer science.

Chapter Forty

In terms of learning, we encountered challenges in supply chain and logistics that are endemic to emerging markets - often, if something breaks, it's not in stock locally - and working with local contractors, whose experience and working styles can differ can be problematic as some of the latest hardware is not available in the country. Despite these challenges, ultimately this prototype was a success, running for six months straight with minimal interaction from us with the only issue encountered fixable remotely with local staff. Unfortunately, and unluckily, that Waypoint was struck by lightning!

Indonesia Prototype: Testing a Micro Data Center with Accessible Infrastructure for Locals

Our next deployment was in Sumba, Indonesia. This unit was entirely off-grid and tested the Waypoint's use of water cooling, atmospheric water generation, and battery rentals with surplus electricity. Learning from our experience in Jamaica, this unit was properly grounded. We also tested data center interconnection between this Waypoint and the Jamaican one before the latter was struck by lightning. This system has 16.650 kWp of solar and 60 kWh of battery storage and 20 250 Wh rental batteries. This waypoint uses water from an atmospheric water generator to cool the micro data center and provide drinking water to the community.

A significant finding here was the rapid adoption of internet

Chapter Forty

services. Local data usage skyrocketed from 6 GB in the first month to 1.8 TB by the fifth month. The immediate demand and subsequent waitlist for rental batteries and water highlighted the community's needs. To address conflicts over resource allocation, we distributed a portion of the micro data center's revenue to locals via Stellar USDC and Moneygram, improving financial inclusion in the market.

Djibouti Pilot: Integrating Learnings

After this, we conducted our first pilot in Djibouti. This pilot combined the features, capabilities, and learnings from our tests in Jamaica and Indonesia to focus on the micro data center and energy balance algorithm. Unlike previous deployments, end users were required to pay for the excess electricity, water, and internet resources they consumed.

In terms of power electronics, the current setup utilized two Fronius inverters and one Victron inverter, along with a backup quad-fuel diesel generator. This current iteration of the Waypoint has 12 kWp

Chapter Forty

of solar and is connected to an existing 4 kWp array. It supports 80 rentable 250 Wh batteries, two rentable 2.4 kWh batteries, and two rentable electric bikes. Additionally, people can purchase water from an Atmospheric Water Generator and access the internet.

To our surprise, 100% of the batteries were rented within hours of operation. However, we paid close attention to how dust and temperature impacted solar panel productivity. In Djibouti, many dusty days with temperatures above 110 degrees Fahrenheit led to a significant decrease in solar production. Additionally, the lack of weather radar stations in an emerging market like this meant sudden storms could impact energy production unpredictably.

Today, we use custom software to monitor and operate the charging station and micro data center remotely. The micro data center currently performs proof of work and proof of stake blockchain mining and validation as a proof of concept. We are also using excess CPU for the Folding@home distributed computing platform and for storing company files.

This platform will eventually enable us to offer other services to locals, like educational services, virtual medicine, and financial inclusion. We can monitor carbon credits generated by our system using a solar data logger, creating a potential carbon credit that reflects the number of people impacted and how it was used. A percentage of the revenue from the charging station is going to be given back to locals via Stellar USDC, collectible in local currency only at Moneygram or distributed to their phones by a local mobile money provider.

In this pilot, we are also testing the integration of our heat pump, AWG (wire gauge) and cooling system for the micro data center. We have been able to double our water production by collecting condensate from the heat pump and reducing cooling energy consumption by 10%.

Chapter Forty

Redefining Data Center Strategies for Emerging Markets: The Liquidstar Opportunity

Africa's Pioneering Green Data Center and the Need for a Balanced Approach

Africa's groundbreaking green data center in Kenya, powered by geothermal energy and anticipated to consume up to 70 MW upon completion[17], marks a significant step forward. However, at Liquidstar, we believe a balanced approach incorporating large, medium, small, and micro data centers is essential, particularly in developing regions where models from the developed world may not be applicable. The global supply chain and logistics challenges related to large data centers underscore this need.

Overcoming Energy Constraints and Construction Delays

According to real estate services firm CBRE, power availability issues can extend construction timelines of large data centers by two to six years. These delays are compounded if new substations, transformers, or upgraded transmission lines are required. Even backup diesel generators can take up to 90 weeks to procure[18].

To address these challenges, companies like Schneider Electric, JLL, and Lumen are turning to modular data centers, which offer faster deployment times. Our experience in Africa suggests that if established firms face these challenges, they are likely more pronounced in emerging markets.

Based on our first-hand experience with these challenges in emerging markets, we understand that green solar-powered modular micro data centers can eliminate a lot of these delays. Power generation, cooling and internet connectivity are all built into the unit so engineering or construction quality becomes less risky. Even if initial labor costs might be higher, the system is more scalable over time, a fact that reduces costs.

Addressing the Multifaceted Challenges in Emerging Markets

Emerging markets, particularly Africa, face immense challenges, ranging from extreme temperatures to often unreliable core infrastructure for resources including electricity, water, and internet. Financially, large infrastructure projects are exceedingly challenging. McKinsey reports that in Africa, 80% of projects falter at the feasibility and planning stage, with another 50% failing between feasibility and financial close[19].

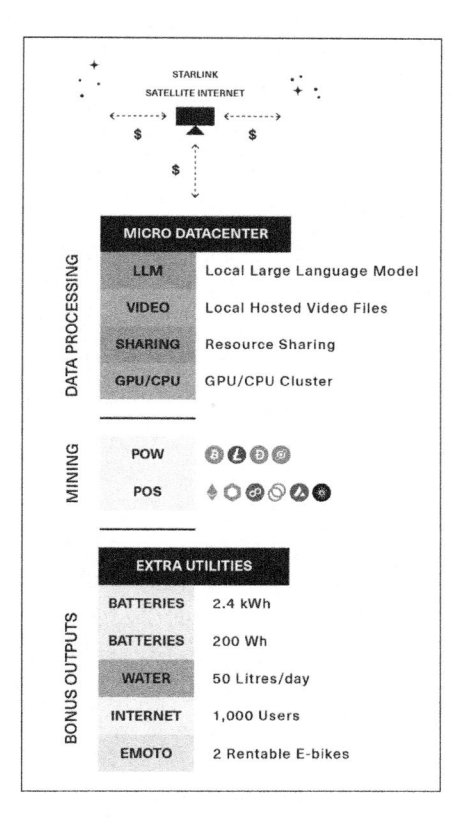

```
                    STARLINK
                SATELLITE INTERNET
              <------>  ▼  <------>
                   $         $
                      ↑
                      $

              ┌─────────────────────────┐
              │    MICRO DATACENTER     │
DATA          │  LLM    Local Large Language Model
PROCESSING    │  VIDEO  Local Hosted Video Files
              │  SHARING Resource Sharing
              │  GPU/CPU GPU/CPU Cluster

MINING        │  POW   ● ● ● ●
              │  POS   ● ● ● ● ● ●

              │    EXTRA UTILITIES
BONUS         │  BATTERIES  2.4 kWh
OUTPUTS       │  BATTERIES  200 Wh
              │  WATER      50 Litres/day
              │  INTERNET   1,000 Users
              │  EMOTO      2 Rentable E-bikes
```

Political risks and licensing delays further complicate projects that pass financial close. In our view, small modular infrastructure projects offer reduced risk through geographic and political diversification and allow for scaling up services as demand is proven.

Green data centers, particularly Waypoints, can serve as a nonpartisan tool for local politicians, showcasing the country's innovation while enhancing the lives of rural residents. Improving the lives of individuals in rural areas within these markets is crucial, as many

Chapter Forty

of these people are significantly affected by climate change. Additionally, many capital cities in emerging markets cannot afford further migration from these rural areas.

For example, in one pilot location we've identified for Liquidstar in Kenya, the Waypoint would be located on the campus of a school and provide electricity, water, and internet to the school. But it could also support the surrounding community, increasing electricity and water access for the smallholder farmers located nearby, while it attracts and connects youth to farming and data center services (each Waypoint offers the potential to generate between 3-5 local jobs). An added benefit is that with access to the internet, farmers would have the opportunity to leverage the latest IoT devices to improve crop yields, thus further contributing to the local economic impact and growth. Rather than pure ICT play, in these deployments, Waypoints and micro data centers support education, farming, employment and ICT initiatives, building support and stakeholder adoption within local and federal governments.

Electrification Challenges and the Role of Waypoints

The electrification of previously off-grid areas in emerging markets presents a "chicken and egg" problem. Many projects suffer from energy takeoff issues because people without electrical devices have a low demand for electricity, leading to the assets' unprofitability, and their fall into disrepair. At the same time, many individuals in these communities may have inconsistent incomes, which exacerbates the issue.

Liquidstar's Waypoints offer a solution by targeting areas with cheap or free land, providing all necessary data center infrastructure, and moving into operation within three hours of delivery. The flexibility of Waypoints, coupled with LEO satellite technology, allows for the efficient use of Africa's abundant solar energy, converting it into digital data. Even if data centers are only used for crypto mining, they represent a customer that is always hungry for electricity and processing power, eliminating energy takeoff issues for off-grid rural installations, as they significantly

Chapter Forty

reduce the cost per kWh for normal data center operations. This is a true win-win.

The ability to relocate infrastructure in response to changing conditions is another significant advantage. This flexibility allows for the optimal placement of Waypoints and the ability to move to more profitable and safer areas when necessary.

What's Next for Liquidstar and Green Micro Data Centers

Driving Down Costs through Custom Engineering

At Liquidstar, our focus is on reducing the cost of each Waypoint through custom engineering. Achieving an estimated 70% reduction in deployment costs, when compared to integrating off the shelf components, while enhancing solar capacity is pivotal for our success. By collaborating closely with contractors we have uncovered several cost-reduction strategies, including integrating the cooling system more effectively, minimizing the number of Direct Current to Alternating Current conversions, reducing our reliance on inverters, and implementing an advanced thermal management and storage system.

Most importantly as we reduce the costs we will be able to increase system efficiency (conversion of sunlight to productive uses) by 30%.

Innovative Features in the Next Waypoint Iteration

The forthcoming Waypoint iteration is designed to charge 40 kWh of rentable batteries, produce up to 300 liters of water per day, and power a 12.5 kW high-density rack. A notable feature will be its ability to capture waste heat for multiple effect distillation, broadening the types of water that can be purified. The total energy consumption of this system is projected to be a maximum of 500 kWh per day. To support this, the system will be equipped with 100-150 kWp of solar power and 200-300 kWh of battery storage.

On the software side we plan to make our Waypoint Management Dashboard more robust and begin to explore additional

Chapter Forty

features. One area we are considering is turning the Waypoints into Decentralized Physical Infrastructure Networks or DePIN and using blockchain based payment rails. By creating an asset backed token representing the total compute/storage available in the network, total electricity, total water, and total available bandwidth, we will be able to better and more transparently manage the supply and demand of all of these resources for end users.

Financial Targets and Industry Trends

Reaching our price target of $150,000 per unit is ambitious but grounded in the observed decline in the costs of solar generation and battery storage. The module price will fall from $0.22 per Watt-peak of generation capacity, in summer 2023, to $0.097/Wp in 2030.[20] The US National Renewable Energy Lab forecasts that the cost of battery energy storage systems could fall by 16-47% by 2030.[21]

Exploring Micro Carbon Capture

As we progress, Liquidstar intends to explore micro carbon capture. This initiative aims to utilize the waste heat from the Waypoint to aid in the carbon capture process, potentially enabling us to capitalize on carbon credit sales. This innovative approach not only advances our technological capabilities but also contributes to our environmental sustainability goals.

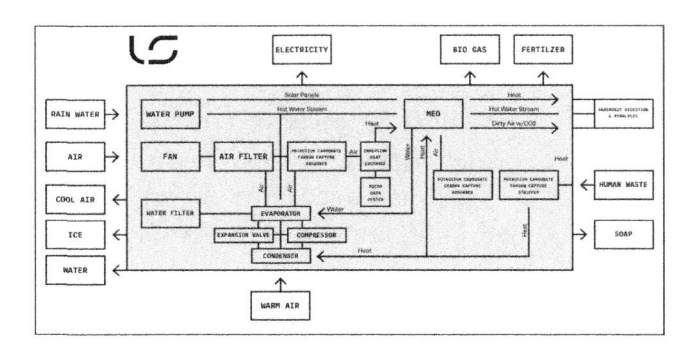

Chapter Forty

Future Outlook and Impact on Local Communities

Looking ahead, the most exciting prospect for using Waypoints is to provide hyper-localized services. Connecting individuals to locally hosted LLMs and generative AI could revolutionize education and healthcare in these communities. The internet connection also enables access to virtual tutors or doctors.

Our vision at Liquidstar is to turn sunlight into digital data, making AI accessible to everyone. We aim to deploy 100 Waypoints in the next two years and eventually 100,000, potentially transforming into the world's largest infrastructure company and significantly contributing to UN SDGs 6 and 7, thus transforming countless lives globally.

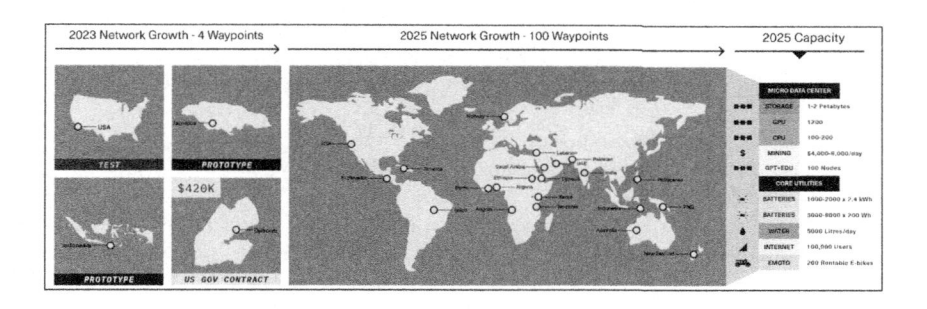

1. Magome, M. *"'What can we do?': Millions in African countries need power"*. AP News. March 25, 2023. https://apnews.com/article/electricity-africa-just-energy-transition-d20d1ba86e90c3b9c81f0fc76979acfc
2. Sall, M. "Africa to drastically accelerate progress on water, sanitation and hygiene – report". UNICEF. 2022, March 22, 2022. https://www.unicef.org/senegal/en/press-releases/africa-drastically-accelerate-progress-water-sanitation-and-hygiene-report
3. Munga, J. "To Close Africa's Digital Divide, Policy Must Address the Usage Gap. Carnegie Endowment for International Peace". April 26, 2022. https://carnegieendowment.org/2022/04/26/to-close-africa-s-digital-divide-policy-must-address-usage-gap-pub-86959
4. Boston Consulting Group, LeFleur, R., Goel, K., & Khoury, B. . The Impact of GenAI on Electricity: How GenAI is Fueling the Data Center Boom in the U.S. LinkedIn. September 13, 2023. https://www.linkedin.com/pulse/impact-genai-electricity-how-fueling-data-center-boom-vivian-lee/

5. International Energy Agency. . Africa Energy Outlook 2019 – Analysis - IEA. International Energy Agency. November 1, 2019. https://www.iea.org/reports/africa-energy-outlook-2019
6. Abendanon, M. "Data center growth in Africa creates new opportunities". NTT. October 6, 2022. https://services.global.ntt/insights/blog/data-center-growth-in-africa-creates-new-opportunities
7. Daigle, B. "Data Centers Around the World: A Quick Look. International Trade Commission." May 2021. https://www.usitc.gov/publications/332/executive_briefings/ebot_data_centers_around_the_world.pdf
8. Breickmann, M. "Africa's data centre growth opportunity | News+. IJGlobal." March 6, 2023. https://www.ijglobal.com/articles/170785/africas-data-centre-growth-opportunity
9. McKinsey, Bangalore, S., Srivathsan, B., Bhan, A., Del Miglio, A., Sachdeva, P., Sarma, V., & Sharma, R. "Why invest in the data center economy." McKinsey. January 17, 2023. https://www.mckinsey.com/industries/technology-media-and-telecommunications/our-insights/investing-in-the-rising-data-center-economy
10. McKinsey, Bangalore, S., Srivathsan, B., Bhan, A., Del Miglio, A., Sachdeva, P., Sarma, V., & Sharma, R. "Why invest in the data center economy." McKinsey. January 17, 2023. https://www.mckinsey.com/industries/technology-media-and-telecommunications/our-insights/investing-in-the-rising-data-center-economy
11. Tiseo, I. "Global CO_2 emissions per capita by region 2022." Statista. January 4, 2024. https://www.statista.com/statistics/497616/worldwide-co2-emissions-per-capita-by-region/
12. Farge, E. . Africa endures more severe warming than elsewhere, posing risk of conflict. Reuters. September 4, 2023. https://www.reuters.com/world/africa/africa-endures-more-severe-warming-than-elsewhere-posing-risk-conflict-2023-09-04/
13. Azour, J., & Selassie, A. A. "Africa's Fragile States Are Greatest Climate Change Casualties. International Monetary Fund". August 30, 2023. https://www.imf.org/en/Blogs/Articles/2023/08/30/africas-fragile-states-are-greatest-climate-change-casualties#
14. McKinsey, Bangalore, S., Srivathsan, B., Bhan, A., Del Miglio, A., Sachdeva, P., Sarma, V., & Sharma, R. "Why invest in the data center economy". McKinsey. January 17, 2023. https://www.mckinsey.com/industries/technology-media-and-telecommunications/our-insights/investing-in-the-rising-data-center-economy
15. UBS Editorial Team. "How the data universe could grow more than 10 times from 2020 to 2030". UBS. July 28, 2023. https://www.ubs.com/us/en/wealth-management/insights/market-news/article.1596329.html
16. Hernández, A. R., Schmidt, S., & Achenbach, J. "Study: Hurricane Maria and its aftermath caused a spike in Puerto Rico deaths, with nearly 3000 more than normal". Washington Post. August 28, 2018. https://www.washingtonpost.com/national/study-hurricane-maria-and-its-aftermath-caused-a-spike-in-puerto-rico-deaths-with-nearly-3000-more-than-normal/2018/08/28/57d6d2d6-aa43-11e8-b1da-ff7faa680710_story.html

17. Mbego, S. Fully Green Data Centre Unveiled In Kenya. CIO Africa. September 1, 2023. https://cioafrica.co/africa-first-green-data-centre-launched-in-kenya/
18. Dolven, G., Lynch, P., & Ruttner, J. "High Demand, Power Availability Delays Lead to Record Data Center Construction". CBRE. September 14, 2023. https://www.cbre.com/insights/briefs/high-demand-power-availability-delays-lead-to-record-data-center-construction
19. Lakmeeharan, K., Manji, Q., Nyairo, R., & Pöltner, H. (2020, March 6). Solving Africa's infrastructure paradox. McKinsey. March 6, 2020. https://www.mckinsey.com/capabilities/operations/our-insights/solving-africas-infrastructure-paradox
20. Murray, C. (2023, June 20). "BESS costs could fall 47% by 2030, says NREL." Energy-Storage.News. June 20, 2023. https://www.energy-storage.news/li-ion-bess-costs-could-fall-47-by-2030-nrel-says-in-long-term-forecast-update/
21. Dahlmeier, U. "Empirical approach shows PV is getting cheaper than all the forecasters expect." PV Magazine. December 5, 2023. https://www.pv-magazine.com/2023/12/05/empirical-approach-shows-pv-is-getting-cheaper-than-all-the-forecasters-expect/

About the Author

R. SCOTT SALANDY-DEFOUR

Prior to Liquidstar, R. Scott was a former management consultant with 8 years of experience at Booz Allen Hamilton and PA Consulting. Scott has conducted emerging technology consulting services for a variety of US utilities, helping them analyze and assess pilots that leverage the latest cutting-edge technologies. Specifically, Scott has worked with utilities to help them analyze how IoT, wearable devices, and big data can improve operations. Outside of the utility space he has done emerging technology assessments for the UN, healthcare, and retail.

About JSA Publishing

JSA Publishing is a division of Jaymie Scotto & Associates (JSA). For more information on brand identity, PR, marketing, publishing and events for the digital infrastructure industry, please visit JSA.net.

For more information on the Greener Data movement, including other educational resources and a company directory, please visit GreenerData.net.

Printed in Great Britain
by Amazon